78349

HM
291
.S58873
1984

Social stigma : the psychology of marked relationships / Edward E. Jones ... [et al.] ; with a special contribution by Rita de S. French. -- New York : W.H. Freeman, c1984.
x, 347 p. : ill. ; 24 cm.
Bibliography: p. [320]-337.
Includes index.
ISBN 0-7167-1591-0

1. Stigma (Social psychology)
2. Interpersonal relations. I. Jones, Edward Ellsworth, 1926-

01 MAY 85 10230869 CMMMxc 83-25352

• SOCIAL STIGMA •

A Series of Books in Psychology

SOCIAL STIGMA

THE PSYCHOLOGY OF MARKED RELATIONSHIPS

Edward E. Jones

Princeton University

Amerigo Farina

University of Connecticut

Albert H. Hastorf

Stanford University

Hazel Markus

University of Michigan

Dale T. Miller

Simon Fraser University

Robert A. Scott

Center for Advanced Study in the Behavioral Sciences

With a special contribution by Rita de S. French

Stanford University

W. H. Freeman and Company

New York

Library of Congress Cataloging in Publication Data
Main entry under title:

Social stigma.

Includes bibliographies and index.
1. Stigma (Social psychology) 2. Interpersonal relations. I. Jones, Edward Ellsworth, 1926-

HM291.S58873 1984 302.3′4 83-25352
ISBN 0-7167-1591-0
ISBN 0-7167-1592-9 (pbk.)

Printed in the United States of America

1 2 3 4 5 6 7 8 9 0 MP 2 1 0 8 9 8 7 6 5 4

• CONTENTS •

• PREFACE •

THE PRESENT VOLUME attempts to provide a social psychological analysis of the stigmatizing process and of related problems that may characterize relationships between those who are "deviant" and those who are "normal." Each of the authors has written other chapters and has been involved in other collaborative enterprises, but it is fair to say that none of us has been involved with a topic any more engrossing or challenging than that of stigma. It is engrossing, at least in part, because each of us is deviant in some respect in someone's eyes and can readily imagine (if we have not actually felt) the sting of stigma and discredit.

The present volume is decidedly not a book of readings or even a set of edited chapters. It is a genuine group product that has emerged out of many, many hours of discussion and that generally represents an evolved consensus. Naturally, differential responsibilities were allocated, and personal emphases remain, but the mutual influence and collaborative editorial consultation occurred at a level that is unusually high for a book with so many authors.

But let me begin at the beginning. In 1960, the American Psychological Association sponsored a three day series of meetings in Miami Beach devoted to the psychology of the physically handicapped. To a large extent, the assembled research psychologists were not experts or authorities on the topics to be discussed. This was basically true of a subgroup concerned with the social psychology of the handicapped, consisting of Albert Hastorf, Harold Kelley, John Thibaut, and myself. True, Hastorf had done several studies on responses to physical disability, and I had done two experiments focusing on the perception and evaluation of emotionally disturbed persons. But none of us had any of the rich real-world experience of William Usdane, a resource person who knew the practical problems handicapped persons have to face, and who tried to anchor our flights of theoretical fancy in the reality of his experience with rehabilitation efforts. Harold Kelley prepared a lucid summary of our anything-but-lucid brainstorming, and this was subsequently published under all of our names as part of the American Psychological Association's Miami Conference Report.

Almost two decades later, a conversation between Hastorf and Gardner Lindzey (Director of the Center for Advanced Study in the Behavioral Sciences) set the stage for what was to be irreverently labeled the "stigma group," assembled as Fellows of the 1980-81 Center "class." This group, which I was to help assemble and lead, turned out to be a very fortunate blend of disciplinary background, personal experience, and research perspective. In addition, it quickly became apparent that we liked each other and were comfortable in each other's presence—an essential condition for the inevitable self-disclosures that accompany discussions of stigma! The "stigma group" as a whole met once or twice a week to improvise on what was typically a very sketchy agenda. We also, of course, shared frequent dyadic conversations that were often very productive. During the course of the Center year we gradually convinced ourselves that our discussions should somehow be formalized and made available to others. Thus the decision to write a book was made. After considerable debate, a table of contents was agreed upon and primary responsibilities for the various chapters were determined.

In addition to Albert Hastorf and myself, the group at the Center consisted of:

Amerigo Farina. Professor of Psychology at the University of Connecticut and the author of numerous essays and experimental reports on reactions to those labeled as mentally ill or emotionally disturbed. His primary responsibility was to review and conceptualize the dimensions of variation within the stigma family. The result appears as Chapter 2.

Hazel Markus. Associate Professor of Psychology at the University of Michigan, whose research and theories of self-schemata proved highly useful in the analysis of stigmatizing reactions. This becomes apparent in Chapter 4 on "Stigma and the Self-Concept" for which she was primarily responsible.

Dale Miller. Professor of Psychology at Simon Fraser University, whose background of research on attributional processes and subjective feelings of justice was highly relevant in our discussions. Miller was primarily responsible for placing the phenomena of stigma in the broader context of stereotypy and behavioral expectancy research, concerns that are highlighted in Chapter 5.

Robert Scott. Then Professor of Sociology at Princeton University, now Associate Director of the Center for Advanced Study in the Behavioral Sciences, Professor Scott was unable to spend the full year at the Center, but his periodic visits and correspondence were invaluable in alerting us to the important sociological literature on deviance and labeling. His own command of the literature is apparent in Chapter 3, which places the phenomena of stigma in a broader social system context.

After the group members had dispersed to their home universities it became apparent that Hastorf's newly acquired administrative duties precluded his full attention to the planned chapter on "long-term relationships." We were fortunate to be able to recruit Dr. Rita de Sales French to write this chapter. She joined the group at a follow-up Princeton conference (see below) and managed the difficult task of fitting her analysis into the overall plan of the book. Because of these special circumstances, Dr. French is listed separately as the author of Chapter 8. We are grateful for her contribution.

The authors, individually and collectively, have many people and many institutions to thank. First and foremost, we should like to express our collective gratitude to the Center for Advanced Study in the Behavioral Sciences, and to Gardner Lindzey, its Director. Without the opportunity to spend a year in intense discussion under the facilitative circumstances of Center life, this book would never have been conceived. We would like to think that the present volume is prototypic of what the Center hopes to accomplish when it brings together special project groups for a year of planning, discussion, and writing.

Our work at the Center was facilitated by a grant from the National Institute of Mental Health (5T32 MH14581-5) and by a grant from the John D. and Catherine T. McArthur Foundation. We are also grateful to Princeton University for making it possible, through its Herbert S. Langfeld Fund, to assemble the group in Princeton (January, 1982) for a conference and for discussions of progress on the various book chapters. The Foundation for Child Development provided much appreciated travel funds for our final gathering at the Center in August of 1982. General support from each of our universities is also deeply appreciated. Amerigo Farina would like to give his special thanks to the graduate school of the University of Connecticut for making excellent facilities available for writing.

National Science Foundation research grants to Edward E. Jones (BNS802-3307), Hazel Markus (BNS800-5749), and Dale Miller (BNS762-2943), as well as National Institute of Mental Health grants to Albert Hastorf and Robert Kleck (29446) and to Hazel Markus (MH 29753) also facilitated the completion of the present project. Robert Scott's contributions were facilitated by support from The American Philosophical Society and the Princeton University Committee on Research in the Humanities and Social Sciences.

We also owe a collective debt to the inventors of word processing computers, and dedicated local experts who used them to render our chapter drafts more intelligible. These experts are: Betty Csiki (University of Connecticut), Joan Parker (Stanford University), Lois Reid (Simon Fraser University), Elaine Bacsik and Arlene Kronewitter (Princeton University) and the very effective secretaries at the Center for Advanced Study in the Behavioral Sciences. It would be difficult to catalog the numerous ways in which Mary Ann Opperman kept the present project moving toward completion. We are especially grateful for her skill and good humor during the complex task of negotiating permissions.

The comments of many readers of individual chapters were very helpful. Constructive critics in our debt include: Susan Beletsis, Jenny Crocker, Perrin French, Caroline A. Jones, Irwin Katz, Anna Power, Edwin M. Schur, David Spiegel, Gita Wilder, Peggy Thoits, and Antonia Zeiss.

Finally, we are especially grateful for the insights provided by Nick Zirpolo, Bert Brodie, Dennis Clark, John Preston, and Joseph Villareau. They have helped us to appreciate the remarkable human potential for adapting to physically disabling traumas. We very much appreciate the time they spent with us.

Edward E. Jones

Princeton, NJ 08544
November 10, 1983

• CHAPTER ONE •

The Terrain—
Focus of Concern and
Some Preliminary Distinctions

THIS IS A BOOK ABOUT SOCIAL RELATIONSHIPS that involve at least one person who is vulnerable to being labeled as deviant and, thus, being stigmatized. Such relationships are neither rare nor esoteric. We have each participated in them, either as the "deviant" or as the "normal" partner. Such relationships are often characterized by disruptive emotional, cognitive, and behavioral processes. The complexity of these processes and the variety of their outcomes challenge social psychological analysis. In an effort to highlight both the complexity and the ubiquity of stigma, we begin with a somewhat haphazard tour through recent copies of some daily newspapers.

> *January 27, 1982.* An AP report describes an impasse between a crippled man and his Catholic diocese. Although the man and his former nurse are very much in love, the church refuses to marry them because of his impotence and, therefore, his inability to "consummate the marriage."
>
> *September 30, 1982.* UPI reports that majorette Peggy Ward will be barred from Friday's football game. The reason? Miss Ward is 1½ pounds overweight. She is 5 foot 4 and 127½ pounds. This weight exceeds the guidelines established by the band director. The school superintendent supports the band director, but Miss Ward is fighting back by fasting to make the limit in time for the game. But, the event has been psychologically costly for the majorette. "The pressure and intense publicity surrounding the controversy apparently became too much at one point for Miss Ward, who telephoned her mother . . . in tears and asked to be taken home from school."
>
> *September 3, 1982.* Evan Kemp, Jr., who has had a neuromuscular disease for 34 years, writes to the *New York Times* complaining about the Jerry Lewis Muscular Dystrophy Association Telethon. "With its emphasis on 'poster children' and 'Jerry's kids,' the Telethon focuses primarily on children. . . . By celebrating dis-

abled children and ignoring disabled adults, it seems to proclaim that the only acceptable status for disabled people is their early childhood. The handicapped child is appealing and huggable—the adolescent or mature adult is a cripple to be avoided. . . . Even the Association's research emphasis has . . . unfortunate implications. The Telethon's critical stress on the need to find cures supports the damaging and common prejudice that handicapped people are 'sick.' As sick people, it follows that we should allow others to take care of all of our needs until a cure is found."

September 27, 1981. The *New York Times* reports that New York University's medical school must accept for readmission a qualified student who has a history of serious psychiatric problems. The Civil Rights Office of the Department of Health, Education, and Welfare issued a finding in 1979 that the student was a handicapped person and that New York University had discriminated against her by refusing to readmit her.

November 26, 1981. A UPI report in the *Hartford Courant* is headlined "Teenager Describes How It Feels to Be Retarded." The article describes how the teacher of a trainable, mentally retarded 17 year old transcribed his thoughts in a brief book. An excerpt: "Sometimes it makes me want to cry inside because I am retarded. I am retarded, but sometimes other people may forget about me being retarded. I can't stand it if someone teases me, it makes me feel weird inside. I can't stand it! Nobody likes that. But when they realize that they are hurting my feelings sometimes they come over and apologize to me."

Eileen Oginty writes in the *Chicago Tribune* about Susan Nussbaum, a paraplegic who has become an activist for the rights of disabled people. Miss Nussbaum reflects on her thoughts after a freak auto accident left her spinal cord irreparably damaged: "Suddenly I was one of those people my mother used to tell me not to stare at on the street. I thought if I didn't die in the hospital, I would kill myself when I got out."

December 28, 1980. In the *San Francisco Chronicle,* columnist Bob Greene discusses the widespread tendency to label Mark David Chapman (John Lennon's murderer) an "ex-mental patient." He quotes extensively from an interview with Kathryn McIntyre, who herself was hospitalized three times with severe depressive episodes. "Right after the shooting, doormen and policemen were quoted as saying that the murderer was a 'wacko' and a 'screwball.'

No one thinks twice about using those kinds of words. But do you think the news media would broadcast a quote from someone describing a murderer as 'nigger?' It would never happen. . . . The offshoot is troubling. If you have a sore throat, you think nothing of going to a doctor and asking for treatment. But if you have mental or emotional problems, you might hesitate before asking for psychiatric care; you know instinctively that you will be branded for the rest of your life as an 'ex-mental patient.'" As if to confirm this, David Obel in the August 4, 1981, edition of the *New York Times* notes that "thousands of men and women all over the United States are paying for psychotherapy out of their own pockets instead of applying for the mental health insurance coverage provided by their employers. [They feel that they] dare not risk disclosure of their emotional problems in the workplace."

November 1, 1981. Ron Harris discusses in the *Los Angeles Times* the trials of Ricardo Appling, a black executive who moved into an affluent white neighborhood on the edge of Beverly Hills. Appling was twice picked up by sheriff's deputies, who suspected he was burglarizing what was actually his own home and was often stopped and questioned by police about his reasons for being in the neighborhood. One day while the family was away at the zoo, the inside of his home was virtually destroyed by vandals. The words "nigger" and "black niggas" were spray-painted on appliances, walls, and curtains. Television sets were smashed or thrown in the pool, expensive antiques were destroyed, and the keys were ripped out of the piano.

Portions of a letter published in the New York Times, June 5, 1980:

"To the Editor:

Anyone visiting the much-vaunted Picasso exhibit at the Museum of Modern Art is in for an unpleasant surprise: He will find that it is, apparently, a show for the handicapped. . . . The main entrance to the museum . . . is to be used *only* by people in wheelchairs. . . . Only persons in wheelchairs are permitted to use the elevator. And, most absurdly, there is an exit from the building proper to the garden cafe for the "physically disabled" only. A guard stands by to prevent anyone else from using it, lest perhaps one of us throw someone in a wheelchair off the ramp. . . . This discomfiture imposed on the vast majority for the dubious benefit. . . . of a tiny minority is being duplicated all over the country. It is one of the most astonishing phenomena, and greatest scandals, of the current American scene that this absurdity is receiving virtually no press coverage. . . . It would be nice if no one were crippled or blind, and one should make every provision for the convenience of those less fortunate. But it is insane to gear everything to those in wheelchairs. People so confined simply cannot lead the life of someone not handicapped, and it is stupid to pretend they can".

This letter brought a number of subsequent responses, including one that concluded with the remark that "I simply thought that it was wonderful that MOMA realized that an inability to walk is not equal to an inability to see, and thus should not preclude admission to an art exhibit. MOMA's fine effort in providing a means for such art lovers to experience this once-in-a-lifetime show at minimum, if any, inconvenience to others should therefore receive accolades."

November 7, 1981. Manira Wilson, *Hartford Courant* staff writer, talks with Kenneth Jernigan, president of the National Federation of the Blind. Jernigan acknowledges that he cannot drive a car or see the sunset, but also notes that 50 percent of the population can't have babies. "Suppose a man moped around and took to crying, 'I can't have a baby'? They would lock him up . . . I don't wake up in the morning and think 'I'm blind. How terrible it is.' I don't think about it much at all." Jernigan added that a short person usually does not think about his stature until he cannot reach something on a high shelf.

A UPI report from Pittsburgh reports that the job of a blind math teacher is in serious jeopardy because of the difficulty she is having with disciplinary problems in her classes. Her students pelted her with paper balls, tied her shoes together, and stole money from her purse. She has also spent hours removing chewing gum wads from her long black hair. The article notes that she has been suspended with pay, pending a hearing.

As the forgoing anecdotes suggest, the phenomena of social stigma are all around us. We cannot escape frequent contact with those who deviate noticeably from norms of appearance or behavior, and these contacts raise fascinating questions for social psychology—questions that are both theoretically and practically important. It is the dramatic essence of the stigmatizing process that a label marking the deviant status is applied, and this marking process typically has devastating consequences for emotions, thought, and behavior. Many words have been applied to the resulting status of the deviant person. He or she is flawed, blemished, discredited, spoiled, or stigmatized. In the classic case, the mark or sign of deviance initiates a drastic inference process that engulfs impressions of the deviant target person and sets up barriers to interaction and intimacy. Thus, a "normal" person may feel repelled by and try to avoid the physically disabled, former mental patients, severe stammerers, or members of particular ethnic out-groups. There are many departures from this prototype of hostile rejection, however, and we shall try to encompass in this book some of the diversity of reactions to signs of deviance. We shall also try to avoid being locked into the perspective of normal insiders looking at deviant outsiders. It is generally understood that the stigmatizing process is relational. That is, a condition labeled as discrediting or deviant by one person may be viewed as a benign and charming eccentricity by another. We may look upon an armless mother (as portrayed on the television show "60 Minutes" on May 24, 1981) as a grotesquerie or see her coping as an incredible triumph of the human spirit. What is deviant in one culture or one subgroup may be the norm in another.

There are, of course, certain conditions that lend themselves readily to widespread stigmatization in any culture. It is perhaps natural for students of stigma to focus on the problems of the blind, the retarded, the crippled, the former mental patient, the ex-convict, and certain ethnic groups. Nevertheless, some of the fascination with the topic, and whatever insight we may have, undoubtedly springs from our own experiences (temporary and benign as they may be) as targets of discrediting labels.

Each of us can probably remember many instances in which we felt at least momentarily stigmatized by our deviant status. Perhaps we have or can remember having acne, along with the feeling that others must be disgusted by our appearance. Perhaps we have a slight speech impediment or an occasional stammer. Or we have experienced the "shame" of having an alcoholic mother or a retarded brother. Some of us may recall instances where we were caught cheating or lying, where it seemed, at least for a while, that our basic integrity was at stake. Perhaps we come from the "wrong side of the tracks" or a city, country, or region that is deprecated in many jokes. Perhaps we remember acquiring nicknames that hurt—"tubby," "four-eyes," "baldy," or "tanglefoot." On occasion we have undoubtedly expressed an opinion that turned out to be at odds with the clear consensus of a group we were anxious to impress, an opinion whose expression seemed to invite derision or scathing disbelief. To these fairly benign examples may be added such potentially stigmatizing labels as being black, old, female, alcoholic, mentally ill, crippled, epileptic, ugly, obese, cancerous, and retarded.

The average "normal" person, in other words, has had at least some experience dealing with a condition that is generally acknowledged to be potentially embarrassing, discrediting, or stigmatizing. In using such examples to argue for the pervasiveness of stigma, we do not mean to suggest that acne is the discrediting equivalent of mental illness, or that one's identity is as surely spoiled by premature baldness as by cerebral palsy. In Chapter 2 we will make important distinctions between various potential stigmatizing conditions and emphasize the effects of variations along several underlying dimensions. In this introductory chapter, however, we do want to speak in generalities about what such conditions have in common, and we shall take a little license in stressing the similarities rather than the differences.

THE GENERAL DOMAIN OF OUR CONCERN

We intend to focus in this book on a particular category of social relationships—those in which one participant has a condition that is at least potentially discrediting. We shall be concerned with the cognitive and affective underpinnings of such relationships and with the behavioral problems they entail. We shall also be concerned with the course and development of such relationships over time.

Some Terminological Distinctions

Social psychologists have traditionally been interested in the processes and consequences of cognitive categorization, particularly categories involving other persons. It has become a widely shared belief that category labels make a difference, because once a label is applied, further information processing is guided by its connotations. It is a major premise of this volume that words are not only important in organizing experience, but that they also shape affect, or emotions, and behavior. It is understood that names can indeed hurt as much as sticks and stones. It is not surprising, therefore, that the authors have agonized at length over an appropriate vocabulary for encompassing the tangled processes involved in the acts of labeling that have discrediting consequences for the target person. We have discussed, even argued at length about, the differences between stigma and stereotype, prejudice and discredit. The result is a consensus along the following lines.

Our central interest is in interactions between a so-called normal person and the bearer of a "mark" that defines him or her as deviant, flawed, limited, spoiled, or generally undesirable. The mark may or may not be physical: It may be embedded in behavior, biography, ancestry, or group

Figure 1.

membership. It may also be possible to conceal it. The mark is potentially discrediting and commonly becomes so when it is linked through attributional processes to causal dispositions, and these dispositions are seen as deviant. Furthermore, the discredit becomes more consequential when the deviant dispositions are judged to be persistent and central and, therefore, part of the marked person's identity.

At various times we have found ourselves referring to this normal-deviant dyad as observer and victim, the able-bodied and the disabled, the stigmatizer and the stigmatized, and the labeler and the labeled. None of these appellations is satisfactory over the entire range of possibilities we wish to discuss. The "observer" is usually also an actor, and the "victim" may or may not be victimized. The "disabled" may be quite able. The word "stigma" carries a melodramatic tone when applied to some of the situations we shall deal with. Finally, consistent references to "labeler" and "labeled" invoke a perspective that we do not entirely accept (reasons for which will be presented at several points in the chapters that follow).

Our solution to the vocabulary problem is a partial one, and one that is not entirely satisfactory. We wish both to avoid neologistic jargon and terms burdened with highly affective or evaluative significance. Guided by such considerations, we have chosen the word *mark* as a generic designation covering the range of condition indicators that may give rise to the stigmatizing process. The mark may be a pair of obviously paralyzed legs or unseeing eyes. It may be deviant comportment suggesting drug abuse or alcoholism. It may be information (true or false) that the bearer is gay, under psychiatric care, or dying of cancer. *Mark* is thus our generic term for perceived or inferred conditions of deviation from a prototype or norm that *might* initiate the stigmatizing process. The term has some advantage over similar terms in that it is more neutral and flexible in its applicability. While the word *mark* is perhaps misleading in its apparent reference to physical signs of deviance, it does lend itself to prefixes and suffixes that facilitate communication. The bearer of a discrediting mark shall herein be called a *markable* person. The person perceiving or inferring the mark shall be called a *marker*. The target of a marking act shall be called a *marked* person. Thus, a marker may or may not convert a markable into a marked person.

The marked person may or may not be *stigmatized*. To mark a person implies that the deviant condition has been noticed and recognized as a problem in the interaction or the relationship. To stigmatize a person generally carries a further implication that the mark has been linked by an attributional process to dispositions that discredit the bearer, i.e., that "spoil" his identity. To use a vivid example, Joan meets John who has recently received electroshock treatment for a severe depressive episode. Initially, since Joan is unaware of this bit of John's history, we can only describe him as *markable*. At the same time, John knows he can be marked, since he is aware that knowledge of his history of mental illness may have a significant impact on Joan's acceptance of him and, therefore, on the nature of their interaction. His own behavior may be clearly affected by his markability—especially if he is uncertain as to whether or not Joan knows his history and if he is uncertain about what her response would be to such knowledge.

If and when Joan finds out about John's mental illness *and* recognizes that this information has important implications for their relationship, she becomes a *marker* and John moves from markable to *marked*. If in marking John, Joan reorganizes her knowledge of him and then perceives his subsequent behavior as support for an impression of pervasive danger and unpredictability, then the marking process has edged into the more devastating realm of stigma.

Although such a stigmatizing impression is typically accompanied by negative emotions, these feelings are often mixed with the positive emotions of sympathy and nurturance, thus creating a state of ambivalence in the marker. The stigmatizing process thus links the mark to a central aspect of the marked person's identity or dispositional makeup, and complex emotions are typically aroused. The depressive might be marked but not stigmatized if the marker truly believed either in the transience of depressive conditions or in the permanent efficacy of electroshock. In such cases, the knowledge of psychiatric treatment would probably not engulf Joan's impression of John and would not become the most important single thing about his personality—the aspect in terms of which all other aspects must be understood.

Thus, we shall try in the chapters to come to restrict our discussion of stigma to cases where substantial negative affect is involved, often mixed with positive feelings, and the target is significantly discredited through an attributional reorganization process. Through this process the target may be seen as genetically flawed, fatally unglued, morally degenerate, or overwhelmed by physical incapacity or the bitterness resulting from it. In each case the person cannot be dealt with except on terms that consider his deviant mark as an integral part of his identity. Impression engulfment is thus the essence of stigma.

Having made this commitment to a rather formal terminology involving marks, markers, and markables, we nevertheless do not intend to commit heavy-handed pedantry just for the sake of slavish consistency. Thus, when it seems appropriate, we shall speak of the disabled or the physically limited, of observers and victims, of normals and deviants, and of particular conditions that are often the grist for stigma. We wish gently to coax the reader into the domain of markers and markables when it is important to be precise or to avoid begging the question; we do not expect the reader to discard the existing terminology when such precision is unnecessary or when other terms are more precise for the subset of phenomena under discussion.

Stigma and Stereotype

Stigmatizing reactions can vary greatly in the degree to which they are perceived as justifiable, either by the marked person or the marker. At one end of a continuum, negative affect (discomfort, revulsion, hostility) is seen as less than completely justified by the marker. There is, therefore, conflict and ambivalence, guilt and inhibition. At the other end of the continuum, negative affect is seen as totally justified, supported by a belief system often designated as a *stereotype* because of its rigidity and unresponsiveness to ameliorating information. The nature and consequences of stereotype formation will be discussed at length in Chapter 5, but here we will consider the relationship between stigma and stereotype.

Abby Rules on the "Virgin" Label

From *"Dear Abby," Trenton Times,* January 10, 1983

Dear Abby:

I have this problem and really don't know whom to ask, so I'm turning to you.

I used to be what you would call a lesbian, but that is all in the past. I have never had a love affair with a male but I have had a few affairs with females.

I have met this guy whom I really love, and we plan on getting married. He thinks he is marrying a virgin. I told him I was one and I think I am, but now I wonder. Am I?

"Questions in St. Paul"

Dear Questions:

Technically you are a virgin. . . . (A few lesbian experiences during one's adolescence does not necessarily a lesbian make.)

We assume that there is always a strong tendency for stigmatizing reactions to move in the direction of stereotypes that rationalize or explain the negative affect that is involved. This is true whether we are talking about the stereotypes associated with racial prejudice or serving to rationalize one's avoidance of the physically handicapped. In both cases, we would argue, stereotypes gain their impetus because of the intolerability of unexplained and unjustified negative affect. At the very least, such affect predisposes the individual to perceive and emphasize negative characteristics and attributions to explain one's discomfort or hostility. This is not to say, of course, that all stereotypes are invented *ad hoc* to serve individual purposes. Most stereotypes are shaped in important ways by social influences. Indeed, as Chapters 4 and 5 explain in detail, social consensus is important at every stage of stigmatizing and stereotyping processes. Consensus helps define the latitude of accepted deviance in appearance and behavior (as we note in Chapter 3), and often does this by noting specifically the states or conditions to be marked. Consensus is also important in determining the contents of those belief systems associated with stigmatizing reactions, and in determining the behavioral fate of stigmatizing evaluations. Certainly, our stereotypes about mental illness are determined in important ways by social signals that make salient the moments of bizarre behavior, the incompetence, or the unpredictability of "nuts," "wackos," or "crazies." It is also difficult to avoid the negative stereotyping of retarded persons, since the label "stupid" makes such frequent appearances in conversation. It is, perhaps, the favored put-down term of children of all ages.

Thus, stigmatizing reactions may or may not involve elaborate stereotypes, but the marking process is likely to drift toward stereotype formation over time in the service of affect justification. Potential markers who interact frequently with marked persons are likely to have developed elaborate stereotypes about the marked condition. Those stereotypes will be based partly on accurate information and partly on the need to explain otherwise unjustifiable affect. We should emphasize, however, that despite this natural drift, a hallmark of the stigma domain is the frequency of doubt, conflict, and unresolved ambivalence. We will be especially interested in those cases in which hostility, prejudice, and discrimination are not fully "explained" by clearly developed stereotypes.

SOCIAL INTERACTION: A GENERAL CHARACTERIZATION

As the subtitle of this book suggests, our primary focus will be on social interaction and the role that stigmatizing conditions play in interpersonal relationships. Thus, we are not primarily interested in the adjustment problems of the marked person, or in teaching potential markers how to think about the disabled. Rather, our concern is with "marked relations," with the diverse assortment of interactions that occur between markable and unmarked persons. Therefore, it is important to establish a conceptual framework for considering the complexities of social interaction. The following framework is a very general one, but we hope it also serves in subsequent discussions to highlight the special characteristics of marked relationships.

As we will note many times throughout the book, interactions take many forms and serve many purposes. As a crude first approximation, we may distinguish between the following: (1) casual encounters (on buses, in the classroom, in supermarkets), (2) role-based interactions, including those specifically based on the mark (doctor-patient) and those independent of it (teacher-student); and (3) close relations (husband-wife, parent-child, close friends).

As social psychologists are beginning to realize (e.g., Kelley 1979; and our own Chapter 8), these three interaction types have many dimensions, but it is possible, we believe, to list a limited number of general concepts in terms that enable us to discuss interactions of diverse types: *expectancies* (both cognitive and affective) about the other person; the *self-concept*; interaction *plans* and *goals*; *stimulus cues* (appearance, context, and behavior); *perceptions*; and *attributions*. These concepts will prove useful when we examine the functional interrelationships between cognitive, affective, and behavioral processes. Our analysis begins with the initial stages of social contact, proposes a set of important controlling variables, and then considers the shifts in emphasis among those proposed variables as the interaction is transformed into a more lasting and more intimate relationship.

The term *interaction* is generally used in social psychology to capture the interdependent actions of two or more persons. We may think of any conversation as a prototype: one person speaks, the other follows with a contingent remark, the first responds to the second, and so on. Most analyses of interaction tend to emphasize or focus on overt behavior itself, perhaps because of its special status as observable and consequential. But underlying or surrounding the overt behavior is a host of cognitive and affective variables that also need to be identified and understood. Furthermore, a special and intriguing feature of social interactions is their ongoing, sequential quality. Thus, as conversations and other interactions move through time, the variables governing the interactions themselves may take different values and weights. This is part of what happens as casual interactions become transformed into close relations. But even within the most casual of interactions, sequence effects may be of crucial importance. This will be apparent in the following hypothetical account of the initiation of a relationship between a marked and an unmarked actor.

Jean anticipates her freshman year in college with an eagerness tempered by a few anxious qualms. She is informed during the summer following her high school graduation that her roommate will be a girl named Ruth, that Ruth is from St. Louis, and that Ruth is handicapped—she has lost a leg in an operation to prevent the spread of cancer. These minimal facts are all that Jean knows about Ruth. Ruth is simultaneously informed about Jean, told that she comes from Chicago, and probably makes the assumption that Jean is without any significant mark of deviance or disability. Upon receipt of this information by both freshmen, processes are set in motion that may have important consequences for the future relationship between Jean and Ruth. Jean has never really known a severely handicapped person. She approaches the first day of school, and her first meeting with

Ruth, with a set of expectancies (perhaps in the form of rather uncertain hypotheses) about what it is going to be like to interact with Ruth. If pressed to articulate these expectancies, she might say, "Well, I suppose it's going to be kind of grim. I mean, how can I ever share what she has been through? She's probably either very bitter and morose, or maybe incredibly noble and brave about the whole thing, in which case, I'll feel like a frivolous drip. In any event, I am going to try to be helpful and sympathetic without being exploited or made to feel guilty. I want to see myself as the kind of person who can handle such a relationship and get the other person to know me and to like me."

Ruth, on the other hand, expects Jean to be disappointed at the roommate assignment and, at the very least, uneasy in the impending relationship. Most of the girls Ruth has known, of course, were "normal," so she has a large background of experience with girls like Jean, but her experience since the amputation, of normals responding to disabled persons like herself, has been much more limited. She suspects that most people are disgusted by missing limbs, but she also guesses they are usually ashamed of being disgusted and want to conceal their disgust. She expects Jean to be very friendly and polite, all the while wishing that she had been assigned a "normal" roommate like herself. Ruth is fairly resigned to what will probably turn out to be a superficial relationship, but she intends to do what she can to be especially considerate and to convey her interests and talents and sense of humor in such a way as to put her disability in the background where she thinks it belongs.

We can identify three classes of variables in this hypothetical case that are present at the initiation of the relationship. Both Jean and Ruth have *expectancies* derived in some complex way from past social experiences, accounts in the press, TV dramatizations, and perhaps associated attempts to fantasize what it must be like to be deviant. Jean and Ruth expect each other to have certain attitudes, behavioral dispositions, quirks, and resistances. In some cases such expectancies might be designated stereotypes, but Jean and Ruth seem instead to have hunches or hypotheses about what to expect. Their expectancies are no more than vague probabilistic inferences that recognize a wide range of actual interaction possibilities. These expectancies seem to lack the elaborate structure and built-in rigidity of most stereotypes.

Both Jean and Ruth also have vague but potentially important interaction *goals*. Jean wants to get Ruth to "know me and like me," to succeed in handling the relationship and making it a good one from Ruth's point of view. Ruth wants to come across as somebody who just happens to be an amputee, but who is really a person with many other assets and interests who can make a valuable contribution to a relationship. In addition to these goals, we can also discern behavioral *plans*, vague though they may be at the outset. Thus, Jean is going to try to be "helpful and sympathetic." Ruth intends to be especially considerate and to reveal the riches of her personality. Whereas the expectancies refer to someone else's probable characteristics and behavior, goals and plans are intimately related to considerations about the *self*. We can detect in Jean the ambition to prove to herself that she is the kind of person who can create a positive relationship with an amputee. In any event, her self-concept will probably be affected in important ways by how well she succeeds in achieving her goal. Similarly, Ruth's self-concept is involved in shaping her goals and plans, and it will be affected by the fate of the relationship.

Getting away from the particulars of Jean and Ruth, we propose that all interactions are launched by actors who bring expectancies about each other and a self-concept that helps to define preliminary interaction goals and behavioral plans. Of course, the expectancies, goals, and plans may be exceedingly vague or they may be highly articulated. The expectancy category is typically a mixture of cognitive and affective hypotheses. Thus, we expect certain things to happen and we expect to feel a certain way about them. Both cognitive and affective expectancies in marked relationships are heavily influenced by social definitions of deviance and social prescriptions for dealing with deviant persons. (The social functions of deviance labeling are highlighted in Chapter 3.) The affective expectancies involved in marked relationships are likely to be very complex and confused. (The role of affect, and especially affective ambivalence, is discussed in Chapter 7.)

The goals and plans are likely to be implicit, and not a part of calculated awareness. We may "plan" our interactive behavior only in the sense that we choose certain gestures and lines of discourse rather than others. We may not be consciously aware of the choices we have made, but the choices usually have some element of strategic significance within the interaction (a fact that will receive more elaborate attention in Chapter 6).

The goals and plans of the two actors may mesh, may be congruent, or they may clash, so that the attainment of person *A*'s goals guarantees that *B* cannot attain his. To change our example to illustrate this point, Jean might have the goal of minimal contact with her disabled roommate, whereas Ruth's goal may be the same as portrayed—to build a rich and rewarding friendship. A relationship initiated with such incompatible goals or incongruent plans would seem ill-fated.

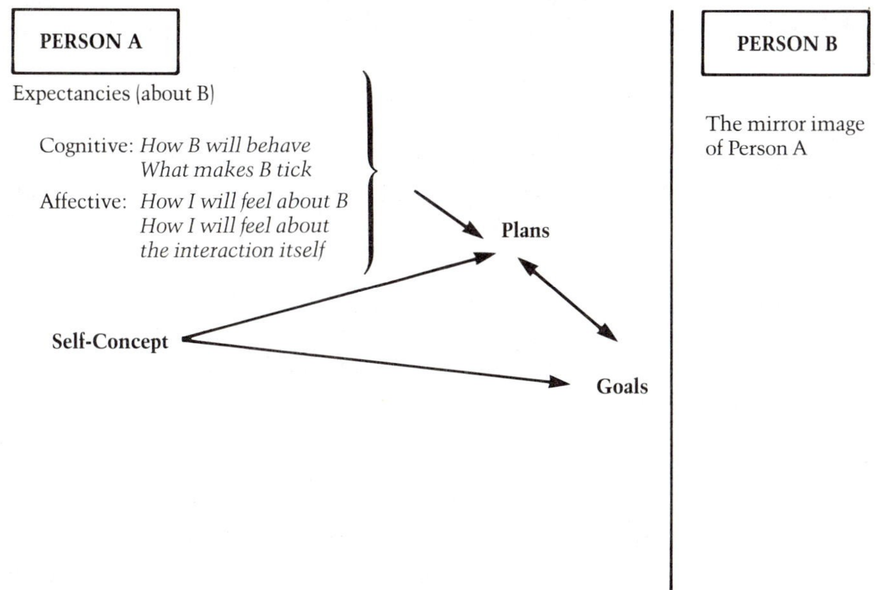

Figure 2. Preinteraction Stages

The preinteraction stage is summarized in Figure 2. The double arrows connecting goals and plans are intended to suggest that the two may not be very clearly separated in this preinteractional phase. The goals of each actor are directly linked to the actor's self-concept, but the plans are conditioned by the actor's expectancies—his impressions of his partner. These conditional plans in turn have some impact on interaction goals.

Now let us imagine that *A* and *B*, or Jean and Ruth, actually meet. Immediately several new variables are introduced which may or may not lead to revisions in the preinteractional expectancies, goals, and plans. Initially, there are *appearance* and situational *context* cues, followed quickly by overt interactive *behavior*. Each of these sources of data or information can either confirm or disconfirm expectancies, make goals more or less attainable, and dictate certain behavioral plans rather than others. Jean may have expected Ruth to be drab and unattractive, only to find her stunningly beautiful. Jean may have expected Ruth to be morose and yet find her perennially cheerful. Ruth may have expected Jean to be repelled and yet find her casually accepting. It will be noted later that appearance cues are important mediating factors in the response to deviant marks. The same may be even more obviously said about the mediating importance of the marked person's self-presentational behavior.

It is crucial to note here that the *perception* of the other person and the interpretation (*attribution*) of his or her behavior may be conditioned in important ways by the initial expectancies, goals, and plans. There is an abundant social psychological literature emphasizing the biasing effects of expectancies or hypotheses on the processing of relevant information. Basically, the data show that confirmatory information triumphs over disconfirmatory information, all other things being equal. Thus, we are selectively attuned to evidence that seems to confirm our expectancies or hypotheses; also, we retain it better than evidence that is disconfirming.

Attributions, or the causal meaning we assign to behavior, may be influenced even more than perceptions by the expectancies we have when we enter an interaction. We may perceive the cheerful commentary of a disabled veteran accurately enough, but we may also attribute this to defensive denial, if we have the strong hypothesis that all amputees are unhappy. We may expect, then, that a biasing process will operate generally to favor the confirmation of expectancies. This need not mean, however, that expectancies do not change. The changes that do occur may be changes in the marker's hypotheses about the particular marked person or even about others in the same marked category. Ruth may be impressed by Jean's casual acceptance and conclude that although most people are uptight about grotesque physical disfigurements, Jean does not seem to be one of them. Or Jean may see that Ruth is unfailingly cheerful and discard her notion that all disabled people are bitter and morose. (The conditions under which expectancies change will be discussed more fully in Chapter 5.)

Confirmation pressures may operate even more strongly when strong affect is involved in the initial expectancy. The need to rationalize or justify this affect may lead to extreme distortions of perception and attribution in the processing of information. In short, bias in the processing of information about another person is likely to reflect a mixture of cognitive and motivational determinants. We may be biased, in other words, both because of the miscarriage of habits of thinking, and because of certain needs to justify our emotions or to support motivated behavior.

The initial behavioral stages of interaction are diagrammed for actor *A* in Figure 3, which is intended to show that expectancies may or may not be modified, and often receive a confirming boost from biased perceptual and attributional processes. The addition of the prime symbol in the diagram indicates the possibility of some change. A specific plan explicitly linked to an interaction goal (which may or may not have changed) as an alternative way to achieve the goal has been ruled out by features of the situational context and by various implications of *B*'s appearance and

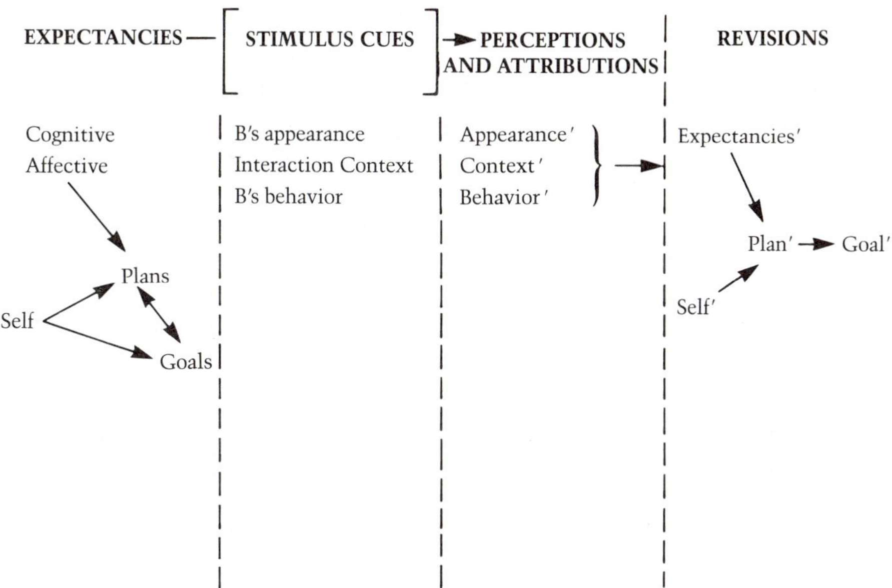

Figure 3. Initial Stages of Interaction: Actor *A*'s Perspective

behavior. The self, at this stage, is still portrayed as one of the determinants of plans and goals. The prime symbol after the self is to suggest that even the self may change, if only momentarily, as a function of feedback from *B*'s behavior in the particular context. (The changing role of the self-concept as both an agent and a target of change is discussed in Chapter 4.)

Further along in the interactive behavioral sequence, each actor's behavior has even more important ramifications for his or her own cognitive and affective processes. As *A* and *B* interact in the unfolding of their respective behavioral plans, an array of complex feedback processes—often involving vicious or beneficent circles—is typically set in motion. Thus, if Jean begins to act out a plan of aloofness in order to attain the goal of minimizing intimate contact with her new roommate, this could in turn cause Ruth to withdraw, which would confirm for Jean her suspicion that Ruth feels basically self-sufficient or at least not comfortable with normal friends. (This kind of expectancy-behavior-expectancy confirmation link will be analyzed at length in Chapter 5.)

Expectancies may produce behaviors from either partner in a marked relationship that can lead to irrevocable consequences. It may happen that a marker's early misreading of a situation may produce revealing faux pas that have their own momentum. Once the marker reveals perhaps through

... cues of awkwardness or aversion, that he is upset by the mark or views the marked person as helpless or discredited, that conveyed impression may resist attempts at corrective updating. Thus, even though the marker committing the faux pas may actually change what he expects, he may be unable to extricate himself from the implications of the earlier faux pas.

Affective changes can also result from self-relevant actions within the relationship. The expectancy, as we have noted, often carries an affective component. Visual contact with the markable person may augment or refine that affect. It is now widely accepted in social psychology (cf. Leventhal 1980) that our own behavior can generate, augment, or alter our emotional state. Not only does affect lead to behavior, behavior can shape affect. As behavior unfolds in a marked relationship, our responses may add new sources of emotion, especially if the behavior has implications for the self-concept. Thus, negative affect may be generated as a consequence of guilt about early behavioral "errors" or what the marker views as his or her inability to convey appropriate compassion. In such cases, affect is generated by cognitive dissonance between one's behavior and how one wishes to see oneself.

To indicate some of these possibilities, we introduce the behavioral component with its implicational possibilities in Figure 4. This diagram is intended to indicate the impact of behavior on subsequent cognitive and affective processes, some of them mediated by salient features of the self-concept. The suggestion that *A*'s expectancies change over time, in response to incoming behavioral information from *B*, is simply a conceptual way of alluding to the acquaintance process, or the growth and change of *A*'s impression as he or she gets to know more about *B*. The self-concept also changes, perhaps in more subtle ways, as *A* monitors his or her own behavior and the reactions of *B*, and puts together the combined implications for the self of each interaction episode.

In summary, the present interaction framework describes a set of distinctive internal processes (affective and cognitive expectancies, self-concept, plans, goals, perceptions, attributions), external cues (appearance, situational context, behavior in the context), and the overt behavior itself. As interactions proceed through time, cues shape internal processes which in turn shape behavior, which in turn shapes again the internal processes. Figure 5 is a schematic attempt to summarize the preceding diagrams in order to capture the interplay between cognition, affect and behavior in marked relations over time. The differences between marked and other relations, to the extent that there are any, are not defined by the presence

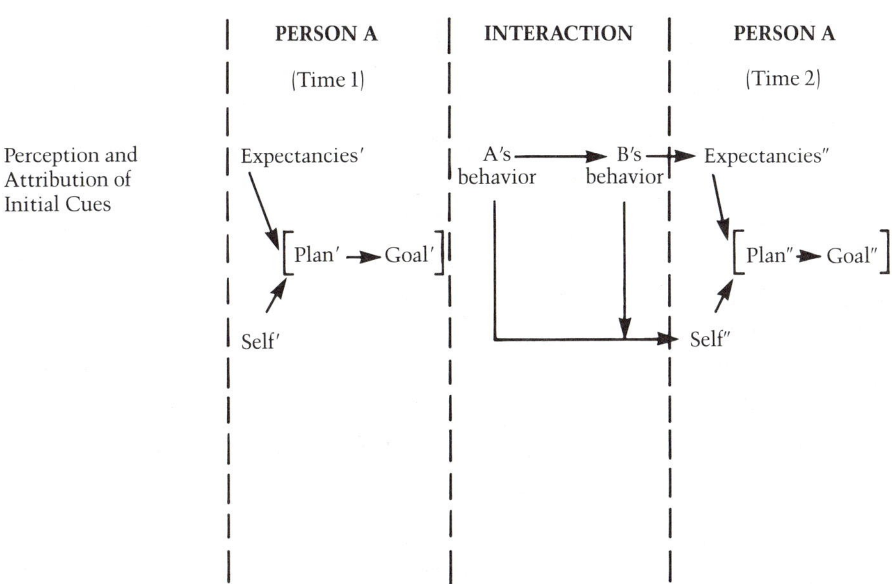

Figure 4. Intermediate Stages: The Impact of *A* and *B*'s Behavior on *A*'s Cognitions

or absence of these categories, but by their particular contents and, perhaps, in the interactions between them.

As complicated as this picture is, it could be even further complicated by the recognition that under the expectancy term, we should include cognitive representations of the other person's plans, goals, expectancies, and attributions (cf. Asch 1952). *A* not only has his own plans and goals, but he has some perception of what *B* probably wants to get out of the relationship, and he may reflect on *B*'s impression of himself and the dispositions *B* attributes to him. In the early stages of a relationship, we may be dealing with stereotypes about stereotypes. Jean may expect Ruth to expect her to be aloof and hostile or to feel extreme discomfort in the relationship. This may or may not be actually the case, of course, so a relationship may involve various levels of misunderstanding, especially at the outset.

A final question remains concerning the changes in the framework variables as we move from relatively short-term interactions to close, intimate, stable relationships. The same variables may be sufficient for prediction and explanation, but their relative weight or importance may shift. For example, each partner's expectancies are presumably more stable and less affected by new behavioral information. We shall now consider the

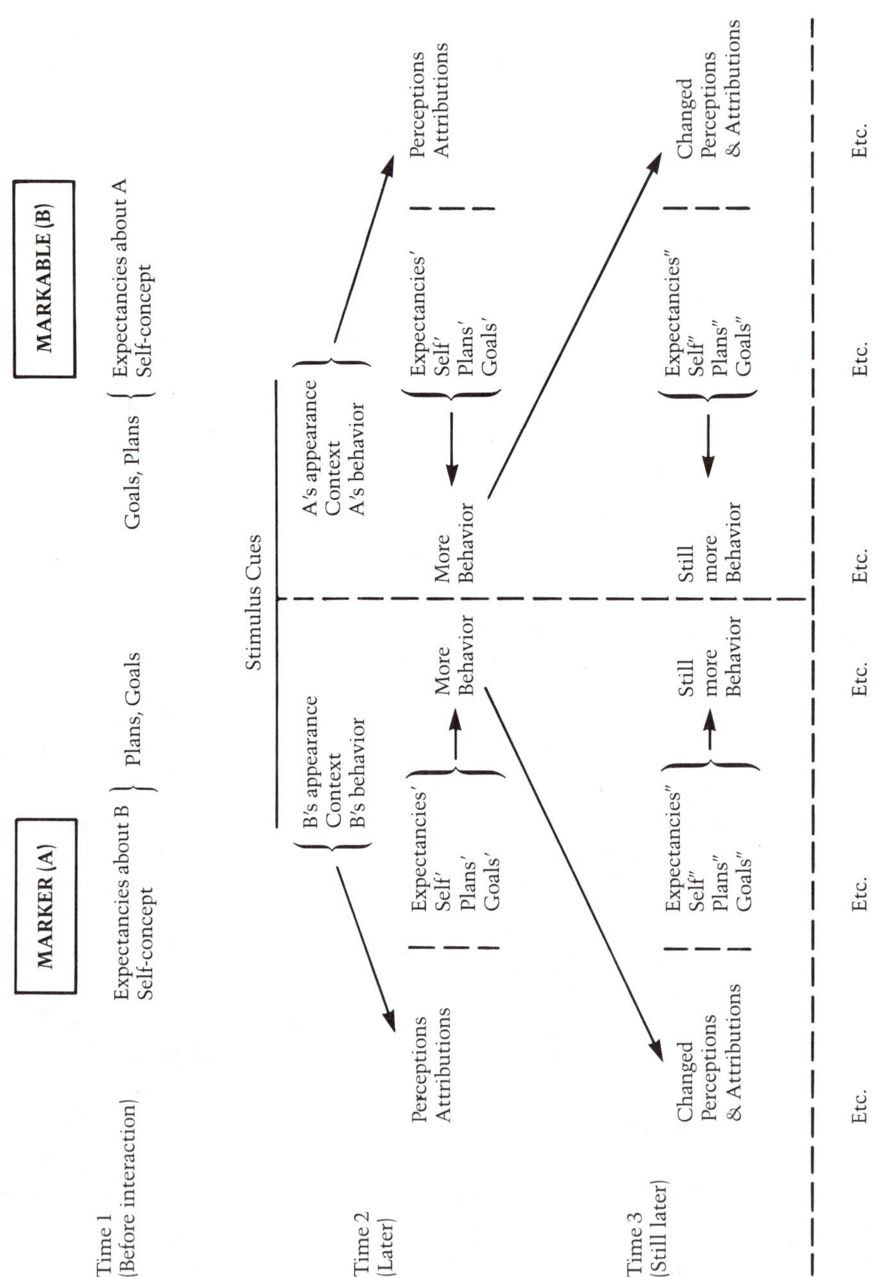

Figure 5. Expectancy-Behavior Sequences over Time

characterization of close relationships and reexamine the status of the variables we have introduced.

Let us approach this characterization by returning to Jean and Ruth at the end of their sophomore year. They have roomed together for two years and have become close friends. Each now has complex and differentiated expectancies about the other. Whereas initially these expectancies were largely category-based, they are now largely target-based (cf. Jones and McGillis 1976). Jean has had many opportunities to observe Ruth respond to different settings. From these experiences she has formed a clear impression of her particular dispositions and those expectancies that persist about a female amputee are likely to be submerged in, or modified by, her individuated impression of Ruth. One suspects that, in such long-term relationships, specific goals and plans become less important. This is so because interactions between Jean and Ruth are either automatic rituals (who showers first in the morning, how and when to help each other) or planless "bull sessions" in which the only goal may be consummatory self-expression or intimate self-disclosure. In a similar fashion, one might suspect that appearance cues have diminished in importance. Certainly, we would expect Jean to be less repelled or upset by Ruth's stump. But beyond that, it is probably the case that attractiveness in long-term relations is carried more by attractive actions than by an appealing physical appearance. Most of us have had the experience of getting to know and like people whom we initially judged to be physically unattractive, only to wonder later why we ever thought so. The reverse experience also happens, though probably with less frequency, if only because unattractive behavior is more likely to promote avoidance than the revision of one's impression about physical appearance.

Much information typically is transmitted via the interactions that comprise a long-term relationship. Each partner develops elaborate attributional understandings that place individual remarks in meaningful contexts. Thus, Ruth may learn to distinguish between what Jean says she wants and her actual goals. To use Kelley's (1979) framework, each person grows to understand how the other values different kinds of outcomes, and, especially, to understand the other's "interpersonal dispositions." These are dispositions that involve transformations of interdependence as the relationship progresses. Especially important are transformations that indicate to *A* that *B* is taking *A*'s outcomes into account. Thus, *B* may take great satisfaction from *A*'s triumphs or show great consideration for *A*'s activity preferences. The more numerous and more varied the contexts of interaction forming the history of the relationship, the more likely it is that *B* will find opportunities to make it clear that he is acting out of regard for *A*'s outcomes in addition to his own. The most interesting "transformations," therefore, are those in which individualistic goals give way to goals that maximize joint outcomes, or, to put it somewhat differently, egoism gives way to altruism. In a very real sense, the operative self-concept is itself transformed by the relationship. Kelley's analysis is a very general one, but it provides a useful framework for considering the role of stigma in close relationship discussed in Chapter 8.

PLAN OF THE BOOK

As stated in the Preface, we view the stigmatizing process as a prototypical phenomenon for social psychological analysis. Goffman (1963) argues that the normal and the deviant are not persons but perspectives. With marked relationships these two perspectives intersect and generate dramatic affective, cognitive, and behavioral consequences. Social psychological theories are particularly adapted to explain the interplay between cognitions and interactive behavior, and it is our hope that a judicious selection of contemporary theoretical notions will shed new light on the nature of the stigmatizing process. But the application of theoretical insights to an important social problem is only one of our goals in writing this book. Equally important is information in the other direction: We hope to learn from the phenomena of stigma some lessons that illuminate basic cognitive and behavioral processes. It is our conviction that marked relationships throw into relief many important features of cognitive bias and the role of affect, of expectancy persistence and change, of the transformation of relationships over time, and of the accommodation of beliefs to behavior. We hope to highlight potential contributions to our general understanding as well as convey what the special perspective of social psychology has to bring to our understanding of stigma.

In Chapter 2 we shall take a commonsense view of the ways in which various stigmatizing conditions may differ from each other. What important dimensions of variation have been identified in the literature? With what differential reactions have these dimensions been associated? How do common sense and theoretical reasoning about the importance of personal responsibility fit with the actual data on reactions to accidental versus self-generated marks?

Chapter 3 will attempt to place the phenomena of stigma in a broader context of social rules and the labeling of deviance. When and why are the labels of deviance applied, or when and why are marks attended to? What functions for society are served by the marking process? How has the symbolic interactionist tradition typically handled the stigmatizing process? Chapter 4 focuses especially on the role of the self as an active, ongoing process. The impact of a mark or stigma on the self-concept will be examined in detail, along with the implications for the self-concept of adopting various coping strategies. The social comparison process—its role in self-formation and in the definition of deviance—will be considered.

In Chapter 5 the social psychology of stereotypes will be considered, with particular reference to their likely fate in ongoing interactions. We will discuss the conditions under which stereotypes and expectancies are likely to generate their own confirmation and those under which they are likely to be disconfirmed. In particular, we will focus on the disconfirmation of false beliefs as a consequence of social interactions in the marked relationship.

Chapter 6 discusses the strategic options available to marked persons and markers in achieving social gratifications in marked relations. Problems associated with concealing the mark are discussed, along with the tactics for reducing its salience. When the mark is clearly known and clearly salient, there are still a number of self-presentational techniques that may augment the marked person's power and, therefore, increase his comfort and security in the relationship.

In Chapter 7 the role of affect will take center stage. We will examine the potential sources of anxiety, disgust, hostility, and sympathy during the course of marked relationships. Especially in conditions of disability or ethnic membership, negative affect is often inhibited by social norms. This may be one source of the ambivalence often noted in describing reactions to deviant people. Other theories of ambivalence will be reviewed, along with a careful consideration of affect indicators and differential levels of response.

In Chapter 8 we will take a close look at recurrent social interactions, especially intimate relations involving family members and close friends. The chapter will try to identify the conditions favoring adaptation versus exacerbation over time.

Finally, Chapter 9 will attempt to summarize the main propositions and conclusions of the book and address certain possibilities of "destigmatization."

• CHAPTER TWO •

The Dimensions of Stigma

CHAPTER 1 focused on the similarities between stigmatizing conditions and what they have in common. In this chapter, we are concerned with the important variations among them, and we will examine the seemingly most critical dimensions or elements underlying the total array of all possible marks. In selecting these key dimensions, we were guided by how much they influence the role of a mark in interpersonal interactions. Three specific criteria were employed in arriving at the six dimensions we will use.

1. Available research indicates the dimensions are important in understanding the effect of marks in interpersonal interactions.
2. The dimensions are especially relevant for aspects of the stigmatizing process emphasized in this book. These include the emergence of a condition as a socially degrading mark, the development of a self-concept by the stigmatized, and self-presentation strategies.
3. The dimensions, for theoretical reasons, should appear promising in guiding future research.

The six dimensions or factors selected are the following.

1. *Concealability.* Is the condition hidden or obvious? To what extent is its visibility controllable?
2. *Course.* What pattern of change over time is usually shown by the condition? What is its ultimate outcome?
3. *Disruptiveness.* Does it block or hamper interaction and communication?
4. *Aesthetic qualities.* To what extent does the mark make the possessor repellent, ugly, or upsetting?
5. *Origin.* Under what circumstances did the condition originate? Was anyone responsible for it and what was he or she trying to do?
6. *Peril.* What kind of danger is posed by the mark and how imminent and serious is it?

We will first review in some detail the most relevant literature concerned with the identification of the crucial variables or dimensions of stigma. This literature, which played a role in the selection of the six dimensions listed above, will make it possible to compare our list with those suggested by others. After that, for each dimension, we will examine, where possible, research findings and consider how each influences the role of degrading afflictions in interpersonal relationships. We will then briefly look at some additional variables or conditions that also affect the interpersonal role of a mark, albeit in a seemingly less crucial way than do our six emphasized dimensions.

PRIOR EFFORT TO IDENTIFY THE CRUCIAL VARIABLES

We are hardly the first to be concerned with the important components of stigma. At least eleven empirically grounded discussions have been published, dating back to 1957 (Freeman 1961; Jensema and Shears 1972; Jones, Gottfried, and Owens 1966; MacDonald and Hall 1969; Northcraft 1981; Orcutt 1976; Schwartz 1957; Shears and Jensema 1969; Siller et al. 1968; Tringo 1979; Vann 1970). As an example of what these efforts are like, we can briefly review the study by Shears and Jensema (1969). Students and psychiatric technicians were given a list of 10 quite diverse stigmatized conditions, including blindness, amputation, and mental illness. For each condition, the subjects were asked to complete a social distance scale, ranging from "would marry" to "would live in the same country." Relatively clear groupings of more and less acceptable conditions were found. For instance, mentally ill and retarded individuals were least acceptable. The authors concluded that six important dimensions determined the social reactions to the afflictions: (1) visibility of the condition, (2) interference in the communication process, (3) social stigma associated with the disability, (4) reversibility prognosis, (5) extent of incapacity, and (6) difficulties the condition imposes on daily living routine.

The Shears and Jensema study is illustrative of how many investigators have approached the problem, but, in fact, the research overall is very heterogeneous. In some studies, the focus has been on a single stigmatizing condition, such as obesity or mental disorder. Others have tried to find significant variables using groupings of stigmas, such as sensory losses (blindness, deafness) or internal disorders (heart condition, diabetes). Still others have approached the problem using dozens of stigmatizing conditions, seemingly attempting to be exhaustive. The procedures relied upon to arrive at the significant variables have also been diverse. Some workers have employed rational and intuitive methods, while others have relied entirely on inductive statistical procedures. When a rational approach has been used, the investigators have sometimes attempted to reason out what the main dimensions are. They have then assessed the social attitudes toward stigmatizing conditions they judged to exemplify their dimensions to varying degrees, and ultimately compared their empirical results to their rational expectations. On the other hand, others first measured attitudes and feelings toward blemishing afflictions and were then guided by the results in trying to discover the crucial dimensions. When more formal statistical methods have been relied upon, factor analysis was used in several instances. In these instances the researchers still need to reason out what the nature of the factors is and generally they choose names to describe them. However, other statistical techniques have been used, such as asking subjects to group blemishes into categories based on similarity and then submitting the judgments to a hierarchical clustering analysis.

The subjects of these studies have also been quite diverse. As is the case for research on many topics, college undergraduates, and, to a lesser extent, high school and graduate students, are the most frequently used subjects. Rehabilitation workers, people selected from the community, and relatives of the stigmatized individual, such as the spouse, are also employed.

In none of the 11 studies being considered here did the afflicted themselves serve as subjects. However, there are less pertinent studies where the stigmatized were the subjects. Also, these investigations vary with regard to the social roles in which the marked individual would or would not be acceptable. Subjects were asked to express their attitudes toward and beliefs about mental patients, paraplegics, stutterers, and lepers, considering the afflicted persons in the roles of parents, friends, marriage partners, and coworkers. They may also have been asked how they would feel about being afflicted with that condition themselves.

In view of all this diversity of approaches, there is a surprising degree of consistency in the dimensions of stigma held to be crucial by the investigators. For example, the concealability of the mark is almost always reported as one of the important dimensions. The number of dimensions found to be important in these eleven studies ranges from one, a general rejection factor, to eleven. The median number reported is four. We will now try to provide more exact information about the extent of agreement concerning the important components of stigma, and, especially, we will try to indicate the degree to which the dimensions used in this book are the same or similar to those identified by others. To do this, we have simply examined the dimensions reported in these studies and for each dimension we have decided whether it is or is not the same as one of our six.

Admittedly, this process entails some degree of arbitrariness, but most of the decisions were quite objective. For example, in Freeman's study (1961) of attitudes toward one stigmatizing condition, mental disorders, the following four factors were identified: the etiology of mental disorders, the possibility of recovery from mental disorders, the patient's responsibility for acquiring a mental disorder, and attitudes toward mental hospitals. As will be seen by examining the detailed descriptions of our dimensions in this chapter, three of the dimensions identified by Freeman are like our own. Etiology as well as responsibility are like our origin, whereas recovery is like our course. Attitude toward mental hospitals is unlike any of the factors we use and this seems to reflect the fact that Freeman is concerned with a single stigma—mental disorder. In comparing the factors used by us to those identified by others we found that of the total of fifty factors identified by the eleven studies being examined, thirty-six, or 72 percent, were the same as one of our six dimensions. The remaining fourteen were mainly of two types. One type consisted of factors found in studies limited to one or a few blemishes, such as the factor "attitudes toward mental hospitals" or a factor found by Vann (1970), who was concerned only with obesity, which he labeled "fat man stereotype." The second type consisted of factors more pertinent to long-term relationships between the marked and markers, such as "capacity for normal life" identified by Jensema and Shears (1972). And, as was indicated, while we will consider long-term relationships, our major concern is with initial or early encounters between the "normal" and the stigmatized. Thus, it appears that there is some general consensus that the six dimensions of stigma that we are using are the important ones in determining how marks in general influence interpersonal relationships.

CONCEALABILITY

Concealability is a dimension that focuses on those characteristics of marks that make some irrevocably obvious to all involved in a relationship, while others remain completely undetected to some participants, generally the potential markers. We can better understand this dimension by considering some specific degrading conditions. Having been a psychiatric patient, being mildly retarded, and being a paraplegic are conditions along this dimension ordered from concealable to increasingly nonconcealable. This property of any given mark is not usually totally fixed and unchangeable. Actually, in the usual case, any blemish can be made more or less obvious, depending on what the afflicted individual says or does, on the characteristics of those in interaction with the victim, and on the circumstances of the interaction. President Franklin Delano Roosevelt, whose legs were paralyzed by polio, as most Americans knew, managed to present a public image of a reasonably able-bodied man. An important technique he used was arranging to be seen publicly and to be photographed only when his handicap would not be evident (e.g., while sitting down). One of the authors (A.F.) of this book had a student who successfully concealed for a year the fact that he had a grossly deformed and unusable right hand. Only after being informed about this by other students was the author aware that the student always kept the affected hand in his pocket.

The Stigma of Psychotherapy

From Sobel, D., "Thousands with Mental Health Insurance Choose to Pay Own Bill," *New York Times,* August 4, 1981.

Thousands of men and women all over the United States are paying for psychotherapy out of their own pockets instead of applying for the mental health insurance coverage provided by their employers. Their reason, according to psychiatrists and psychologists treating them, is that they dare not risk disclosure of their emotional problems in the work place. . . .

"I can remember cringing," one [psychiatric patient] said, "when I realized that if I took the job I had sought, I would have to turn in my medical bills to the personnel manager, to be forwarded to the insurance company. Instead, I took another job without this requirement."

Another patient, a twenty-year-old college student, said: "I have been thinking about using my psychiatric benefits to pay for my treatment. I'd rather pay cash, although I don't have much money and this is a sacrifice. I have taken a computer course and know that anyone with a terminal can get my record simply by punching in the right code. . . . I must consider my future. I have the ambition to one day go into politics."

[In testimony before the House Ways and Means Subcommittee on Health, Dr. Marcia K. Goin, head of the American Psychiatric Association's Confidentiality Committee testified:] "When medical information gets around . . . it can lead to social embarrassment, strained or broken ties with family, friends and co-workers, career and economic damage of insurance benefits or refusal of admission to graduate school." . . . Dr. Goin

> **cited the case of a man who was using his health insurance for psychotherapy to treat alcoholism. His employer found out about it through his company records, called him into his office and lectured him sternly. The employee was so devastated by this experience, Dr. Goin said, that he began drinking again, even though he had not used alcohol for several years.**

Clearly, concealability is a critically important dimension of stigma. At one extreme, markable persons can be in a position where no one knows about the problem, or, at the other extreme, they must always be "on stage," contending with the social effects of their affliction. The importance of concealability in influencing how a mark will affect social interactions is indicated by a number of articles. Gussow and Tracy's report (1968) on stigmatizing conditions considers the requirements to produce the hypothetically ultimate blemish for eliciting negative social reaction. The first criterion listed is that it be externally manifest. Obviously, visibility plays a central role in producing a negative social reception. Consequently, we find that stigmatized individuals who can conceal their affliction will do just that. Kleck (1968) found that epileptics, whose seizures were controllable by drugs and hence could be hidden, revealed their condition to very few people, even concealing it from some persons who were important in their lives. Freeman and Kassebaum (1956) discovered the same pattern of behavior among a group of male illiterates. The subjects were enormously ashamed to be illiterate, and they seemed to do all they could to disguise their inadequacy. Many wore glasses with heavy horn-rimmed frames and windowpane lenses ("bop glasses") to appear studious, and they pretended to understand symbols that actually they could not manage. No wonder, then, that so many investigators interested in stigma have, like us, concluded that the concealability of degrading conditions is a factor of basic importance.

Many of the more bothersome consequences of blemishes can be avoided by the marked individuals when their condition can be hidden. At least for initial and early encounters, the reception accorded such persons can be quite normal and ordinary. Hence, their social life might be reasonably satisfactory, despite their potentially disruptive and degrading problem, if the problem remains unrecognized by society. Research supports this commonsense expectation. A relevant study by Roden, Shapiro, and Lennox (1977) investigated the social, educational, and occupational history of a group of epileptics whose condition was not complicated by revealing symptoms, such as the neurological handicaps often associated with epilepsy. Although afflicted by seizures, they appeared to have been normally successful in all areas of functioning, and they had performed significantly better than epileptics who had detectable associated symptoms. In contrast, a study by Felice (1977) shows what happens when someone is openly marked even though the marked person suffers from no organic or functional problems and his or her problem is entirely limited to being socially stigmatized. Her exceptional group of subjects were lower caste college students in India, at institutions also attended by upper caste members. By some means not revealed by the author the untouchables, the lowest caste members, were easily recognized as such by the upper caste members. She examined social and friendship choices and found that while the untouchables desired social interaction and wanted to establish friendships with members of the upper castes, they were strongly rejected.

However, we must not conclude that if a mark can be successfully concealed by the marked person it will have no effect on interpersonal relationships. Aside from the more obvious effects of hiding it (such as keeping an affected hand in one's pocket), guilt and shame may be engendered, particularly if the mark involved is an abhorrent and unacceptable personal experience, such as having been sodomized or having engaged in such grossly psychotic behavior as smearing feces. These feelings may be debilitating and preclude appropriate social behavior. The marked person may also fear discovery, which may seem highly probable if a long-term relationship with another individual is contemplated, as in marriage. Moreover, the deceptive act of misrepresenting one's self may have an adverse impact on the secretly blemished individual. These considerations, especially fear of discovery and anticipation of the catastrophic social consequences that might ensue, make us believe that the social interaction of a marked person will be affected even when others are entirely ignorant of the stigmatizing condition.

Thus far, attention has been focused on how marks may be unrecognized by the "normal," and we have considered the markable person's ability to conceal them to some degree from others. There may, however, also be circumstances in which one person is marked by another without realizing that he is the victim of the stigmatizing process. The marker may look upon the other with disdain and derision, or possibly with guilt and concern over his ungenerous feelings, while concealing these feelings from the stigmatized. There are many examples of such relationships. One is the case in which an individual exudes an offensive odor and he is not aware that he is doing so. Although this has been made hackneyed by deodorant advertisements, it does occur, and it has been systematically examined in an experiment to which we will return (Levine and McBurney 1977). In this instance, the marker's behavior might be very strongly influenced, and even though the marked person is unaware of his condition, he might detect unexpected patterns in the marker's behavior, misattribute them, and therefore respond in inappropriate ways.

Another example is that of one person behaving toward another in a fashion he believes to be appropriate and witty, while the other views the behavior as gauche and disgusting and indicating that the other is a member of an unacceptable group. The first person might talk about defecation, for example, a humorous topic in his circle of friends. In the second person's social group, perhaps, the topic is considered in extremely bad taste. Here, too, the blemish is concealed from the stigmatized, and it is the marker who controls its visibility. However, we believe that frequently the markable person is well aware that he or she possesses characteristics that *some* others regard with stigmatizing disdain. What at times may not be clear to the markable individual is whether a specific other is such a person or not. This type of situation may very well be highly anxiety provoking, leading the markable to look constantly for evidence of denigration. This state of uncertainty may conceivably be more upsetting and disrupting to the markable than being overtly and recognizably stigmatized, as suggested by some research, which will be described at the end of this section.

The Impact of a Mark's Visibility on an Initial Interaction

It is apparent from the foregoing discussion that the impact of a mark on an initial or early interpersonal interaction will be quite different depending on whether it is or is not visible or known to one or both parties concerned. This has been the conclusion reached by a number of investigators on the basis of their research results (Centers and Centers 1963; Richardson 1969). Several studies provide information about the specific effects of a visible mark on the behavior of the afflicted individual who is initially meeting another person. We will review these studies and then consider the plight of the "normal" marker in interaction with a stigmatized other.

Should We Make People Work to Decide Whether Someone is Retarded?

From Pines, M., "Down's Syndrome Masked by Surgery," *New York Times*, August 31, 1982.

No matter how well they act, no matter how much they have learned or how close they come to having normal intelligence, children with Down's Syndrome

> **always stand out in a crowd because of their recognizable features, which label them "retarded."**
>
> **Now, a leading Israeli psychologist . . . advocates a series of relatively minor plastic surgery operations that can make these children less conspicuously different and "more socially acceptable."**
>
> **[The parents of the first child to undergo the operation] were so pleased with the operation that they began a national campaign to urge other doctors to do such surgery. Because of the operation, they said, their daughter had been freed from the stigma of Down's Syndrome, had been treated normally by other children and adults and had made enormous strides in social development. . . .**
>
> **One young man who used to spend his time clowning as a defense against stigma, rapidly improved his behavior after seeing his new appearance.**

In some of this research, subjects were told that the person they were about to meet believed that they, the subjects, had suffered a mental disorder, whereas a control group of subjects believed the other was aware of no such information about them. In some studies, subjects were not truly stigmatized (Farina, Allen, and Saul 1968), but in others the subjects had actually been in a mental hospital (Farina et al. 1971). A comparable study was done with physically disabled subjects. The salience of their mark was manipulated by either having them interact with an unmarked other or with someone who was also disabled and with whom we can suppose they felt less stigmatized (Comer and Piliavin 1972). The results of the studies were quite consistent. When the blemish was known or salient, the marked individual behaved less competently—he was more tense and uncomfortable and acted in such a way as to alienate the other individual.

For the unmarked person, initial or early interactions may not be so uniformly disagreeable. To some people under some conditions, it may even be pleasant to observe that the other has a notable shortcoming. Comparison between self and another under such conditions can make the unmarked individual feel fortunate and perhaps euphoric. However, both common sense and systematic studies indicate that meeting a stigmatized person is usually stressful and engenders disagreeable feelings. Studies that have measured the behaviors manifested by unmarked people initially encountering a stigmatized person show the "normals" are tense, cautious, and find the experience unpleasant (Davis 1961; Farina & Ring 1965; Kleck 1968a; Langer et al. 1976).

Another question is pertinent to the issue of concealability. When someone who is stigmatized knows others are aware of the stigma, what does he do? This is a very broad question, it raises complex issues, and it could properly be broached in the context of several of the other dimensions of stigma. Furthermore, it will be considered in Chapter 6 in another context. Here we only wish to point out what is a common pattern of behavior, given the conditions described. The marked person attempts to disavow or minimize the blemish and tries to persuade others that the unfavorable characteristics generally associated with its presence are not true. This strategy was eloquently described by several of the handicapped individuals who were interviewed in preparation for writing this book. A blind undergraduate student reported doing whatever he could to convince people he had just met that his thought processes were quite ordinary and like those of other people. Systematic studies show this pattern of actual self presentation to be common among people stigmatized in a variety of ways (Farina, Allen, and Saul 1968; Farina, Thaw, and Boudreau 1979; Thaw 1971). For example, people who believe others think them stupid may talk at length and pretentiously, evidently to show that they are thoughtful and intelligent. And those who think they are considered nervous and maladjusted often make great efforts to do well on a task requiring relaxed concentration because good performance would indicate good mental health.

For long-term and close relationships, the concealability of a mark typically plays a quite different role than it does in initial and short-term interactions. Of course, in either type of relationship the less salient and disruptive the blemish, the less the difficulty posed for the social interaction. However, unlike an initial encounter, it does not seem possible to conceal a mark from those who are in close and repeated contact with the afflicted person. Family members and old friends will almost invariably become aware of the condition. Nevertheless, those whose mark is concealable still appear to have a great advantage over those afflicted with a problem that cannot be hidden. First of all, the former can choose the proper time to disclose the problem's existence, and so, unlike the blind student referred to earlier, they will have an opportunity to demonstrate their worth and humanity before the mark makes that process more difficult or impossible. And, what is of great importance, the former can more successfully hide their marks from the rest of society, thus removing one source of awkwardness or embarrassment that would otherwise confront spouses or family members. Ex-mental patients and ex-prisoners will typically display no obvious cues regarding their former status, and, to most others, they will be ordinary people. For some, the visible mark can be effectively removed, as in the case of a former narcotics addict who has developed needle tracks—

linear pigmented streaks on the skin over the veins used for injections. Surgical removal of the mark is possible and it is thus not recognized by employers, the police, addicts, and other cognoscenti (Shuster and Lewin 1968).

In the case of the mentally retarded, even if they are able to manage their affairs, the social stigma of retardation is so severe that they must hide their mental status or else normal life in society would be impossible (Edgerton 1967). Therefore, "most school-identified retarded children disappear into society as adults" (Gottlieb 1975, p. 101). Statistics reported by Richardson (1975) support the above assertion. To wit, the prevalence rate for *severe* mental retardation, which cannot be hidden, remains constant before and after the school years. However, the prevalence rate for *mild* mental retardation decreases 50 percent after the school years. Those individuals live among us, perhaps awkwardly and fearfully, but successfully hiding a strongly stigmatized condition. When the degrading affliction cannot be hidden, the marked person may still be able to improve his life in society by reducing the mark's saliency. This process is illustrated by Richardson (1969), who reports that preadolescent children who had an arm amputated were unwilling to use a prosthetic arm. They found its usage exceedingly bothersome and annoying. When they reached adolescence, however, and social and heterosexual relationships became more important, they asked for prosthetic arms. Evidently, their experience convinced them that lessening the conspicuousness of their affliction would improve their social relationships.

Another issue becomes important when we turn to long-term relationships. The similarity among stigmatizing conditions decreases as marked and marker become familiar, and, concomitantly, the differences among these afflictions become increasingly dominant. Therefore, marked relationships that have endured over a long period of time are less apt to be characterized by uncertainty, discomfort, and turmoil than such relationships in early encounters. Rather, it is the effect on practical, day-to-day functioning of the mark or shortcomings associated with the mark that take on critical importance. Thus, neither the paraplegic nor the coworker with whom he shares an office are likely, after a while, to be concerned about the response of the other to the affliction, nor whether it should or should not be talked about. Instead, such issues as space in the office for the wheelchair and problems created by the disability within their social life, such as the crippled person's inability to get to the marker's apartment, are likely to be prominent. Hence, for long-term relationships, the particular nature of the mark is of critical importance. Some marks permit the afflicted individual, and those about him whose lives are interdependent with his own, to lead a reasonably normal life. Others do not. A recovered former mental patient can live quite normally with others, while a quadriplegic faces a severely limited life and those about him may have to devote a significant portion of their own time to his care.

These more mechanical consequences of stigmatizing conditions are of less interest to us than their more direct interpersonal impact. However, consideration of their role in day-to-day existence is pertinent at this point since the degree to which they interfere with normal living seems, to some degree, to be correlated with visibility. The more evident and nonconcealable the affliction, the more it seems to interfere with such normal life functions as moving, working, and caring for oneself. Obvious and striking conditions like amputations, paralyses, and blindness are also ones that have the most restricting effect on the usual normal functions. On the other hand, if the blemish cannot be seen, the possessor can generally function quite normally. If this correlate of visibility exists, as it seems to, it means that hidden marks in comparison to visible ones make social life easier for the afflicted, both because others are not adversely affected by their appearance and because they need not help them or make special efforts because of their condition. Hence, we would expect that, in general, individuals who have concealed marks would be better adjusted than people whose blemish is apparent. Some research supports this expectation. Goldberg's study (1974*a*) is especially convincing because he compared the adjustment of children with scars from facial burns to that of children with congenital heart disease, a much more life-threatening condition. He found the children with heart disease were better adjusted. In another publication (Goldberg 1974*b*, p. 75), he concludes that a "visible physical disability with slight functional limitations may have a more profound effect upon vocational and educational adjustment than an invisible physical disability with moderate functional limitations."

While concealment would usually seem better for all participants in a relationship involving a mark, that may not always be the case. Conceivably, there are conditions and circumstances that can make concealment a detriment. One problem raised by a hidden mark is that of disclosure or revelation that does not arise with a visible blemish. Someone who seems outwardly quite normal but is later found to have leprosy may not only appear blighted by a heinous condition, but may also appear deceitful and dangerous. This will be discussed in more detail in Chapter 7. A visible problem may sometimes be more manageable and permit easier adaptation for all concerned than an unseen but present entity. A mental disorder in remission may continue to be feared just because the visible signs of a "relapse" may be very ambiguous. Several researchers in the area have concluded that visible blemishes may sometimes be preferable to invisible ones. Thus, Shears and Jensema (1969, pp. 94–95) state, "Visibility of a disability could actually assist in reducing awkwardness since the need to explain deviant behavior would be reduced and the perceiver would know from a distance what the encounter would require." English (1971) believes the visibly impaired may be preferred by employers over the functionally limited since the behavior of the former may seem more predictable.

The possibility that an immediately evident blemish is sometimes beneficial to the afflicted is not intuitively obvious, and data supporting it do not now exist. However, an exploratory study recently examined a related possibility and the results are similarly counterintuitive (Farina and Burns 1982). Stigmatized individuals who believed others were aware of their blemish were less adversely affected, in that they were less tense and less self-conscious, than those who were unsure about whether their condition was or was not known.

COURSE OF THE MARK

This dimension focuses on those features of marks that determine the pattern followed by socially degrading conditions over time. Some of these conditions, particularly bodily blemishes, spontaneously become less stigmatizing and sometimes actually disappear over a period of time. For example, someone can have acne or visible burn scars that heal and are less defacing with the passage of time. Other conditions, such as being a dwarf or being blind, are relatively immutable and the passage of time does not greatly alter them. Still others will become more debilitating and socially alienating, as is the case with some brain diseases, old age, and leprosy.

Unquestionably, the course followed by marks significantly influences their role in interpersonal relationships. A number of researchers and theorists concerned with stigma have come to just this conclusion. Gussow and Tracy (1968) are among these. Earlier we referred to their list of characteristics required to produce the hypothetically ultimate condition in causing social rejection. Of the eight criteria they give, three are concerned with the condition's course over time. The three criteria are that the condition (1) be progressively crippling and deforming, (2) be nonfatal and chronic, running an unusually long course, and (3) appear to be incurable. In fact, empirical investigations have indeed found course to be important. Schwartz (1957) studied the perceptions, beliefs, and attitudes about mental patients held by the wives of the patients. She found that whether the wives believed the mental disorder was or was not *alterable* made an important difference in their attitudes and outlook. A somewhat similar study was done by Freeman (1961) with subjects who were relatives of mental patients. Belief that people can recover from mental illness was associated with favorable attitudes toward the afflicted relative. Shears and Jensema (1969) found that the acceptability of people with one of ten stigmatizing conditions was, in part, determined by whether or not the condition was reparable. Irreparable conditions caused victims to be less acceptable.

Naturally, the course followed by a mark will not necessarily affect all aspects of interpersonal interactions in which the mark is involved. Thus, Levitt and Kornhaber (1977) measured the response of people to a female confederate who was made to appear either permanently or temporarily physically handicapped. She asked people walking on a New York City street for money either while using Canadian crutches, which made her appear to be permanently crippled, or while wearing a plaster cast on her leg, and so seeming to be only temporarily incapacitated. She was given more money in each of these handicapped situations in comparison to a control normal condition. But the permanence of her handicap, although clearly recognized by the subjects, made no difference in how she was treated.

The course dimension of marks is actually quite complex, and a number of factors that are important influences on the role it plays must be considered. First, course is, to some degree, bound to other dimensions of stigma, especially to concealability and origin. If a mark is entirely hidden, as, for example, having been in a mental hospital, the issue of what course it will follow may not emerge for the marker and it may be of little moment to the markable. On the other hand, for an obvious condition, such as an inability to walk, course becomes exceedingly important to both marker and markable. Whether or not the afflicted will ever walk again will have an impact on both persons, and it may be an important factor in determining their relationship. In fact, visibility of the mark is closely related to both the pattern it will follow over time and to the techniques that are available to alter that pattern.

Origin is also tied to course since certain origins predetermine a mark's pattern over time. Some genetically caused conditions follow an inflexible course that cannot be changed—for example, shortness of stature, some types of mental retardation, and some physical deformations. Being personally responsible for causing one's own blemish will also often determine what happens, such as how the marked person will be treated by others.

Immoral and illegal acts are degrading because the perpetrator is presumed to be accountable for them. To the extent that someone or something else can be blamed for an evil act, for example, undue influence by another party or a chance occurrence, to that degree the perpetrator is correspondingly less stigmatized. Therefore, even though we would like to consider the role of each dimension individually and separately from the others for the sake of clarity and simplicity, they are in fact often intertwined, and the role they play is consequently very complex.

Altering the Course

The most crucial matter regarding the course of marks is changing the pattern they follow. To begin, a fundamental distinction must be made between *actual changes* in the course in contrast to *beliefs* held by the parties involved about the pattern the mark will follow in the time to come. Let us first consider actual changes, and here we will refer primarily to visible physical blemishes. Clearly, a definite alteration in the appearance of a mark can have wide-ranging social consequences that may be favorable or unfavorable. A face-lift that makes someone look younger, shedding a large amount of excess weight, or replacing a missing front tooth can all lead to a better social reception both from people acquainted with the marked individual before the change and from new acquaintances. Aside from the effects of this improved social reception, such beneficial changes can also lead directly to increased self-esteem for the marked individual. The blemished person, looking better to himself, is also likely to feel better about himself.

Above and beyond actual changes wrought in the mark, the beliefs held by marker and markable about the future course of the condition may be of very great importance. No one, including marker and markable, really knows exactly what pattern a socially degrading condition will display. Beliefs about changes vary from person to person, some beliefs being wildly inaccurate, and these beliefs unquestionably affect the role that marks play in interpersonal relationships. If a marker is of the general opinion that obese people typically remain fat, he will probably treat a fat person more negatively than someone who thinks that losing great amounts of excess weight is common. The fat woman who is confident she will soon be of normal weight will likely have greater self-assurance and be less pessimistic about her future than a comparable person who expects to remain fat indefinitely. While such general opinions will have their sway, beliefs about course are also liable to be influenced by the specific features of a particular marked relationship. For example, the afflicted person may appear resolute and competent to the observer, who may therefore come to believe the other person can eliminate the blemish or reduce its salience. Obviously, such a belief can be of the greatest importance concerning how the afflicted individual is treated.

For these reasons, we believe it is important to make a distinction between actual changes and beliefs about changes in the course of a mark. We also believe studies can be designed to allow the measurement of the independent contribution to social interactions of these two sources of variance. However, in the typical interpersonal relationship involving stigma, the state of the mark at that time, beliefs about what changes occurred in the past, and expectations about likely future course changes all exert a complex and interactive influence. An overwhelming affliction like quadriplegia may so dominate the relationship that beliefs about past and future changes may exert only a minor influence. In most cases, however, the course of the mark is a highly relevant feature affecting the marked relationship.

In what follows, we will consider changes initiated both by the blemished individual and by others. We will then review the techniques for altering the course of different types of marks. In so doing, we will be concerned both with actual modifications in the course of the mark as well as with beliefs and changes in beliefs about its future course. Finally, we will consider the techniques available for modifying the progression of degrading conditions and the social significance of employing these techniques.

Course Changes by the Markable

In very few instances, the pattern followed by a blemishing condition will be totally unalterable. Typically, the bearer of the blemish has the greatest stake in instituting ameliorating changes, and it seems likely that most often the course changes are initiated by the afflicted. The greatest pressure for change upon the marked individual is probably exerted by nonconcealable and prominent defacing characteristics of the body. The burgeoning use of surgical procedures provides dramatic evidence of the need people feel to remove or reduce these abominations. Whole medical specialties have evolved because of people's crucial needs to be rid of these blemishes. Plastic or aesthetic surgery is now commonplace, and it has even developed subspecialties. Most of these costly procedures do not improve physical health or behavioral functioning. Indeed, not only does the marked person undergo an operation that routinely kills a certain proportion of those receiving it, but permanent physical debilities may be sequelae. There are face lifts, "nose jobs", and techniques for enlarging the breasts; and, reminiscent of days of stripping blubber aboard wooden whaling ships, there are procedures for stripping fat from obese people. There are even radical alterations of stomach and intestines to induce weight loss when will power is not equal to the task. Dentistry also has specialists whose function is primarily to make people's appearance more socially acceptable, and we can gauge the importance of appearance by the fact that people endure years of inconvenience and pain from orthodontic devices installed in their mouth. When total elimination of the visible mark is impossible, medical techniques may, nevertheless, be available to reduce its salience. For example, prosthetic devices can replace missing members and grant a close approximation of normal appearance.

Certain other blemishes can be changed by the possessor without the aid of specialists. Some fat people do succeed in permanently losing enough weight to shed the stigma of obesity. However, in some instances, removal of the stigma does not gain the formerly marked person full social acceptance, if his history is known. Gussow and Tracy (1968) report that lepers who have been cured or physically appear quite normal are allowed a very limited role in society. They are only accepted as "career patients," spokesmen for people afflicted with leprosy. Perhaps such social reactions help to explain why formerly overweight people may persist in viewing themselves as fat when they are no longer fat. Perhaps through some means that remains to be understood, all stigmas leave a permanent social blot and a psychic scar on those who formerly possessed them. (A fuller treatment of this and similar issues can be found in Chapter 4.)

Not only will the stigmatized person feel pressure to change the course of the mark as a result of his own and other people's negative reaction to its presence, but society will typically expect that actions to remove the mark be instituted. Whether the mark is visible or invisible, if its existence is known, efforts to remove it are usually expected and sometimes they are demanded. Someone with a growth on the face, or a man known to expose himself to children, is likely to be pressured by others to avail himself of the appropriate remedies, such as medical treatment in the former case and psychiatric help in the latter. Concurrence with social demands brings approval and better acceptance, whereas failure to comply can elicit severe sanctions that might result in the removal of the offending individual from society.

Because this section is concerned with course changes by the markable, we must consider one more issue; that is, the conditions that seem to be stigmatizing but whose course is entirely unknown to the possessor. There appear to be many such blemishes that plague human beings. For example, bulimia, binges of eating enormous amounts of food followed by vomiting, is often initially very puzzling to the victim. Similarly, the survivors of the Hiroshima atomic explosion noted the internal changes and the external developments of radiation sickness, but generally had no idea of what was happening to them. Under some such circumstances the victim can do little that is specific toward altering the course of the mark and find himself in an anxiety-provoking situation. When the cause and subsequent course of the blemish are not understood, the victim will often seek reassurance and information from knowledgeable people. Thus, someone with a strange skin eruption will probably see a physician as quickly as possible and the alien blemishes may be removed or explained in a manner that makes them less mysterious and frightening. However, there are some people who acquire conditions that they find too degrading or threatening to talk about with others, such as venereal diseases and, most recently, Auto-Immune Deficiency Syndrome (A.I.D.S.). Even more likely to be kept secret are moral blemishes, such as bulimia, and especially those that can bring punishment, such as pyromania. Therefore, there may be many people who are markable for a variety of reasons, whose condition is known to a few others, who are unaware of what pattern their affliction will follow, and who are unable to take effective action to alter its course.

Course Changes by Others

Not all efforts to change the course of a mark are initiated by the afflicted individual. A variety of other people, including family members and those designated by society for these special functions, such as the police, may begin the process. Indeed, in the case of marks afflicting children, the family may be mainly or solely responsible for course shifts. Distorted limbs, cleft palates, and birthmarks may all be normalized before the child is fully aware of the social significance of such blights. In the case of adults, we are all prey to certain degrading states that we fail to recognize as problems. Either in ignorance of the severity of the condition or of relevant solutions, we may fail to initiate course changes. Certain serious mental disorders are characterized by a belief on the part of the victim that he is perfectly normal, and his behavior, no matter how bizarre it seems to others, is quite reasonable under the prevailing extraordinary circumstances. For example, psychotic men sometimes assault a complete stranger, falsely believing the innocent and bewildered stranger is about to attack them. In this state they are unlikely to seek therapeutic help on their own. Alcoholics often are poor judges of how excessive and uncontrollable their drinking has become. The first steps to alter this socially unacceptable behavior may be taken by a concerned relative, a policeman who must monitor the behavior of people in public places, or a supervisor who has the responsibility for making his workers productive.

How and by whom course-changing actions are initiated will almost certainly affect both markers and markables. We noted earlier that actions initiated by the afflicted will probably meet with social approval. In cases where others initiate course-changing processes, the stigmatized person may be blamed for his failure to act and encounter disapproval. Obviously, this social reaction will not occur in every instance where someone makes no effort to change the course of his mark. A baby is not expected to seek treatment for a cleft palate, but for a stigmatized adult to be taken in hand by others, who attempt to remove his blemish, generally implies that the adult is helpless and incompetent, which adds degradation to that already generated by the mark. (An interesting exception is the seeking of psychiatric help, which may itself be stigmatizing because it emphasizes the nature and severity of the disability.)

Altering the Course of Visible and Invisible Marks

How much a mark's usual course can be altered by appropriate intervention is obviously a function of each specific condition. Furthermore, the nature of the method that can most effectively be used is also largely determined by the particular blemish. However, the methods that are effective with visible stigmas have certain common elements, and they differ from procedures that can change the course of concealable stigmas. On the other hand, efforts to change the course of concealable stigmas face certain problems in common.

In the case of visible marks, we have already considered some of the more common and effective techniques for altering their course (e.g., surgical procedures, diets). The changes they produce are usually clear and objectively measurable. We all can see and pretty well agree about the extent to which someone's nose or teeth are crooked, and we can note how people respond to a blemished person after intervention in comparison to the way he was treated before. We encounter quite a different situation, however, when we examine procedures to make change in the course of nonvisible marks. Consider individuals stigmatized because of their inappropriate, immoral, or illegal behavior. Such behaviors include cowardice, commission of crimes, drug and alcohol abuse, and deviant sexual acts. There is no procedure that can make it immediately evident that, for example, someone who was in prison has wiped away the fact that he was a thief in the same way that a formerly obese person can show to himself and others that he is not fat. Perhaps most individuals in this group merely try to hide their problem and make no effort to change its usual course. However, a strong need may arise to repair one's self for social image and then effective techniques of change will be sought. A desire for self-respect may require that the transgression's contemporary negative significance be somehow reduced or neutralized. This may call for making reparations, expiation, or suffering, depending on the blemish, the individual, and the circumstances. The marked one can confess, give personal possessions to some suitable cause, or devote his life to saintly goals. We do not know how often this kind of effort to change a mark's course is actually made, but certainly it is a common literary theme, and it is widely believed that sinners do sometimes have a change of heart and thereafter become the most moral and incorruptible among us.

A similar need to gain social acceptance may prompt other forms of reparative behavior. This may be particularly likely in the case of individuals who are well known to the public, such as politicians or major league sports figures. Their transgressions often become national news and they obviously cannot conceal their past. Therefore, we see well-known ball players convicted of a crime giving time and money to help ghetto children and former governors or presidential aides active in campaigns against alcohol or drugs, apparently trying to convince society that even good people can be victimized by such dangerous snares. One difficulty in successfuly completing these public reparations is that the conversion may be viewed as a self-serving and insincere strategy. The public figure courts the danger that he will not only continue to be burdened with stigma but that he will be branded as a hypocrite as well.

Only a very limited amount of research bears on the issue of removing stains caused by immoral or reprehensible behavior. That information suggests certain blemishes may be effectively removed by readily available strategies, while others are difficult or impossible to counteract. Trice and Roman (1970) examined alcoholism and the role of Alcoholics Anonymous in gaining social forgiveness and acceptance for the former addict. They point out several reasons why AA is so successful, perhaps to an extent that is unique. The cause of alcoholism, drinking, is very clear, and hence its cure, abstinence, is quite unambiguous. Moreover, it is easy to see when abstinence is not being practiced since the backslider cannot conceal for long his or her resumption of drinking. Also, AA operates in accordance with the basic American values that a sinner can repent, repudiate his disreputable past, and make a "comeback." On the other hand, it is more difficult for the public to ascertain if someone believed to have been a mental patient or a thief is now really "normal," because the variables controlling those conditions are unclear. A study by Schwartz and Skolnick (1962) indicates some of the problems encountered by people bearing this type of moral stain. The study suggests that those accused of a crime continue to be regarded suspiciously even when evidence is provided that shows that the accused is innocent. Specifically, employers responded negatively to an applicant accused of assault even when he had been tried and acquitted. Even when the employers also saw a letter from the trial judge testifying to the applicant's innocence, the applicant was still viewed negatively in comparison to a control condition.

If we now take a very broad overview of the techniques available for altering the course of marks, we can discern a noteworthy difference between those that are suitable for visible marks and those effective for nonvisible degrading states. *Actual changes* are crucial in altering the interpersonal consequences of visible blemishes. If a given individual is very unattractive physically, there is rather little that can be done to change her social reception or to make her feel more self-confident, except by improving her appearance. Proclamations to the general public that unattractive people are just as good as anyone else will probably only succeed in making people feel guilty for not liking homely persons. This is not to say that efforts to bring about changes in the degree of stigma attached to a visible condition are wholly ineffective. They probably have some of the desired impact, especially with certain marks. The "Black is beautiful" slogan appears to demonstrate this belief, but for most observable degrading states, removal or reduction of the mark is essential in order to produce a significant change in the stigmatizing process.

Next, consider marks that are not visible, in which case observable changes are not possible. For these marks, beliefs take on paramount importance in determining their interpersonal consequences. If a former mental patient or an ex-convict is to be socially accepted by those aware of his blight, they will probably need to believe that whatever was responsible for the past problem no longer prevails. The mental disorder must be viewed as cured or the criminal tendencies as curbed. Social acceptance is possible if the culprit is seen as having paid his debt to society and as having learned his lesson. Since beliefs are so important for these kinds of blights, it becomes understandable that groups like mental health associations, interested in bettering the lot of some of these disgraced persons, should mount such large-scale and persistent efforts to change public beliefs. If marker and markable can be convinced that mental disorder is like any other disease and that it can be cured as effectively, then the afflicted individual is fully rid of his mark.

The Interpersonal Implications of Change Techniques Employed

Finally, we should take note of the fact that the remedies employed for changing a mark's course may themselves influence interpersonal relationships above and beyond whatever changes in the mark they bring about. The very fact that a particular remedial technique is utilized discloses information about the nature of the mark and the markable. Effective remedies for a mark promise its reduction or removal, whereas useless techniques suggest it will remain unchanged. Therefore, someone with cancer would likely be regarded one way if he was about to undergo surgical removal of a tumor and quite differently if he was relying on a cure that was believed to be wholly ineffective. Most people would be more positively disposed toward an individual who has undergone successful surgery, because they can plausibly believe he may soon be rid of the life-threatening problem. Another element is involved, however, that will elicit a negative response. Marked individuals using ineffective remedial techniques, such as laetrile, will probably appear irrational and foolish.

We believe an inference that is the opposite of the preceding one, i.e., that ineffective remedial techniques tend to elicit negative social reactions, can also be drawn. That is, when a negative social reaction to the use of certain techniques exists, it probably means that the technique is viewed as ineffective in removing the stigma. An article by Bar-Levav (1976) is particularly relevant to this argument. The author points out that Representative Gerald R. Ford was asked a noteworthy question during the Senate hearing on his nomination to be vice-president of the United States. He was asked if he had ever needed or received psychiatric treatment, which the candidate emphatically denied. Bar-Levav points out that the question was "an accusation which threatened the very confirmation of his nomination" (p. 473). In other words, if he had received such treatment, his mental health would be questionable, and he might have been judged unfit for high office. Would this have happened if psychiatric treatment were considered to be routinely effective in making someone totally mentally healthy? We think not. Learning that someone has used ineffective techniques to alter the course of a blemish reveals that he possessed a degrading condition and that it is probably still there.

DISRUPTIVENESS

The third dimension, disruptiveness, is somewhat different from the others. It is not as conceptually clear, it may be less independent of the other five, and it is not as demonstrably fruitful in clarifying the role of stigma in interpersonal interactions. In contrast to concealability and peril, for example, disruptiveness has to be viewed as more tentative and its usefulness is more in doubt.

By disruptiveness we mean that property of a mark that hinders, strains, and adds to the difficulty of interpersonal relationships. Of course, this capacity is a hallmark of stigma and is inherent in various dimensions of blemishing conditions. The more visible, dangerous, and aesthetically displeasing the mark, the more destructive of smooth interpersonal interactions it will be. Most people who find themselves seated on an airplane next to someone with an obvious and disfiguring skin disease would find it very difficult to maintain their aplomb while conversing with the afflicted passenger.

Adding to the problem of providing a clear and precise description of disruptiveness is the relative lack of attention given to the subject by other students of stigma. However, some pertinent research does exist. Siller, Ferguson, Vann, and Holland (1968), using factor-analytic procedures, identified a variable that they called "interaction strain." Vann (1970) used the same technique and found a factor that he called "antipathy and interaction strain." These variables seem very similar to our dimension of disruptiveness, and, consistent with our thinking, the preceding studies suggest the presence of a noteworthy component of stigmas, the effect of which is to some extent independent of the other five dimensions recognized by us.

More specifically, what do the various disruptive features have in common? Examples of marks that we believe have this property are stuttering, mental disorders, and eye disturbances, such as strabismus, which interfere with normal eye contact. In fact, any condition that makes appropriate interpersonal interaction patterns uncertain and unpredictable, that stridently calls attention to itself and away from other characteristics of the other person, and that blocks or distorts the communications process, has the capacity to be disruptive. Attitudes, which play an important role in many aspects of stigmatizing conditions, appear to be of little importance with regard to disruptiveness. Thus, someone who holds Jews in high regard and attributes desirable characteristics and intentions to them would be unlikely to behave toward them in a stigmatizing manner. In contrast, some marks seem to disrupt interpersonal interactions by a more basic process, and changing the attitudes of the interacting individuals would not help matters. For example, changing someone's attitude toward stutterers to a more favorable one would not make stuttering any less disruptive for that person. We should also note that serious disruptions of interpersonal interactions may occur in the absence of any obvious blemish. We need only imagine two strangers who do not speak the same language sitting down with each other to have dinner.

Although marks are not the only cause of disruptiveness, some marks seem capable of being disruptive to a high degree. A mental disorder is a good example of such a condition. It appears to be a common experience for professionals in training to find themselves flustered, upset, and confused when they initially enter a psychiatric ward. Even relatives on their first meeting with a family member after his hospitalization for a psychiatric disorder may experience similar bewilderment and awkwardness. Perhaps the main ingredient responsible for such emotional upheavals is that mental patients are viewed as highly unpredictable by the general public (Farina 1981). Therefore, people who are not familiar with mental patients probably do not expect customary comportment, and their fear that any wild, wholly unforeseen behavior is possible may preclude a normal interaction on their part. In talking about public attitudes toward mental patients, Rabkin makes the following noteworthy statement: "Unpredictable behavior, seen as frightening and disruptive, typically invites rejection and avoidance" (Rabkin 1980, p. 21)

Perhaps the most relevant studies bearing on the disruptiveness of mental disorders are those showing that the more apparent the mental disorder, the more disruptive it is. This pattern is uniformly shown in each of eight studies (Brown, Wooldridge, and Van Bruggen 1973; Doherty 1971; Kellam, Durell, and Shader 1966; Phillips 1964; Pollack et al. 1976; Rabiner et al. 1971; Schwartz, Myers, and Astrachan 1974; Yamamoto and Dizney 1967). It is important to observe that this increased disruptiveness does *not* seem to be due simply to the increase in the severity of mental disorders. At least two of the eight studies show that disruptiveness is related to the degree to which the mental patient's behavior is unpredictable and deviates from what is expected, and it is not, for example, a function of the degree of psychopathology as indicated by diagnosis (Phillips 1964; Yamamoto and Dizney 1967). Concerning the rejection mental patients experience, Phillips states, "Rejection appears to be based on how visibly the behavior deviates from customary role-expectations, rather than pathology of the behavior from a mental hygiene point of view." And, in deciding when patients should be released from the hospital, we should consider "a patient's tendency to be disrupting to others" (pp. 686–687).

Perhaps a key behavior responsible for the disruptiveness of mental disorders is nervous behavior. Tension and nervousness are very common in all kinds of mental problems, and a series of studies was done to learn the role of tension in the social relationships of mental patients. In the first of these, a confederate in the role of a job applicant was interviewed by workers already on the job whose task it was to assess how good a worker the applicant would be if hired (Farina, Felner, and Boudreau 1973). The applicant was described as a former mental patient to some workers and as an ordinary applicant to others. Under each of the two conditions the applicant behaved in a tense and nervous way with half the workers, while with the other half he was calm and relaxed. The confederate was clearly and strongly rejected when nervous, whether in the role of mental patient or not. The study was replicated four more times with different workers of both sexes, a total of five different confederates of both sexes were employed, and the studies were done in a variety of work settings (Farina and Hagelauer, 1975; Farina, Murray, and Groh 1978). The results of the five studies were virtually identical. Whether male or female, ex-mental patient, or average person, a nervous and tense individual was disliked and unequivocally rejected by the workers. The consistency and strength of these findings are noteworthy, and we believe they are in keeping with most people's intuitions. We are very uncomfortable in the presence of tense people and the question is "why?". It seems unlikely that we have acquired negative attitudes about such individuals because of a history of punishing interactions with such people. The process seems primitive and unmediated. Is nervousness a cue to mental disorder, and, specifically, does it signify unpredictability? Much remains to be learned, but one conclusion seems justified. Nervousness disrupts interpersonal interaction.

Another condition that disrupts the smooth flow of interpersonal relationships is stuttering. We have all had the experience of painfully waiting while a stuttering companion struggles to say words we have already inferred and wished we could complete for him or her. The experience must be even more painful for the stutterer than the listener. A pertinent article appeared in the May 24, 1981, edition of the *San Francisco Sunday Examiner and Chronicle*. The article described how Lester Hayes, an outstanding professional football player, had been plagued with the problem of stuttering most of his life and, as a result, "had suffered the tortures of the damned." While much research has been done on some aspects of stuttering, not very much is known to explain why we are so conscious of stuttering and so sharply pained by it. Consistent with our views, Shears and Jensema's (1969) experiments led them to conclude that stuttering is disruptive because it interferes with interpersonal communication. They also concluded that being deaf and having a harelip are similarly interfering and hence are also disruptive. A study by Emerick (1960) supports our belief that attitudes do not play the same role in disruptive conditions that they do in other aspects of stigma, such as being degraded for racial or ethnic membership. He found that the more favorable the attitudes of people toward stuttering, the more salient and noticeable they found stuttering to be.

Finally, a study by Langer, Fiske, Taylor, and Chanowitz (1976) suggests that visible marks may, under certain conditions, disrupt interpersonal relationships by placing the nonstigmatized member in a conflictful and uncomfortable state. The authors believe that visibly stigmatized people are novel stimuli, and the marker both wants to stare at them and yet adhere to the social norm of not staring, particularly at one who may be hypersensitive to stares. To reduce this disruptive conflict, "normals" avoid marked others. The authors did find support for their theory in several experiments. When people thought they were unobserved, they stared more at a novel than a more usual person, whereas when they were being watched that did not happen. Also, when given prior opportunity to look unobtrusively at a marked individual, the individual was subsequently avoided less than when no familiarization was allowed.

If this theorizing is correct, it would have some interesting implications, mostly of a practical nature. Those who are to meet and work with blemished people would interact more smoothly if, prior to the meeting, they could unobtrusively observe those with that particular blemish. Those with a given mark, such as paraplegia, would be given a generally better social reception if portraits of people afflicted with paraplegia were widely posted. If the process described by Langer et al. is, as we believe, an instance of the more general process of disruptiveness caused by such factors as conflict and communication blockage, the implications are broader and more theoretically interesting. This process might be partly responsible for hostility between members of different social classes and dislike for foreigners because communication with them would be difficult. Here, too, experiments could easily be done to test this supposition.

AESTHETICS

The concept of aesthetics refers to what is beautiful or pleasing to the senses. Though scholars have long discussed the nature and determinants of aesthetic appeal, we are a long way from understanding why one object is beautiful and another plain or actually ugly. In certain domains, however, aesthetic judgments are in striking agreement, and the physical attractiveness of human beings is one such domain. Bodily proportions can be more or less pleasing. Disfigurements, such as a missing limb, a twisted body, a club foot, or distorted facial features can dramatically affect how attractive someone is to others. Some people seem ugly to most observers and because of that they are strongly stigmatized. Aesthetics is, therefore, an important dimension of marks.

Many researchers concerned with stigma have, like us, concluded that the aesthetic dimension is an important one. Siller, Ferguson, Vann, and Holland (1968) and Vann (1970) used similar procedures to identify the presence of an aesthetic factor in interpersonal relationships involving stigma. The former researchers labeled the factor "proximate offensiveness," while the latter called it "rejection of intimacy," but both factors refer to a response of rejection, revulsion, and disgust to people marked by certain conditions. Several kinds of degrading conditions have been identified as repelling for aesthetic reasons. Centers and Centers (1963) believe that the amputee children they studied were rejected by other children for aesthetic reasons—a lack of "wholeness." This view is supported by English (1971), who argues that a number of studies suggest "that an 'aesthetic' factor strongly influences social and personal preference of non-disabled persons for the disabled" (p. 11). Tringo (1970) believes an aesthetic factor is responsible for the social rejection of people with marks not involving missing members. Specifically, he believes that dwarfs and hunchbacks are rejected because of "an aesthetic factor" (p. 304).

A hallmark of the aesthetic dimension's role in stigmatization is that it engenders a primitive, affective response (which is discussed more fully in Chapter 7). We have a "gut reaction" to certain marks, which is in sharp contrast to the cognitive, attributional stigmatizing processes elicited by other conditions. As an example of the latter type of reaction we can consider how people are likely to respond to an ex-prisoner. The former prisoner can be physically attractive and personally charming and will not be rejected on those grounds. But what we know of his criminal history initiates a complex mixture of affective and cognitive processes. If the crime committed is not heinous, there can be a calm, rational selection of the proper behavior to display toward the lawbreaker. On the other hand, if we meet someone whose face has been horribly burned, the affective reaction is immediate, and cognitive processes typically play a secondary ameliorative role. We may believe we should act toward the person with the appalling face as we would act toward anyone else, but our uncontrollable revulsion betrays our feelings. Nevertheless, the impulse to recoil from the negative aesthetic impact may be tempered by cognitive constraints in the shaping of overt behavior, even if the intense affect of revulsion is impossible to conceal.

The primitive and basic nature of affective reactions to disfigurements or physical deviance is suggested by their appearance early in life. Richardson (1969) has reviewed research showing that children as young as four months apparently display this immediate response. Specifically, subjects were shown three-dimensional models of human faces that were either normal or were distorted in shape. The children smiled less when shown the abnormal faces. It does not seem probable that the different reactions observed are a result of arbitrary cultural standards of beauty acquired by the infants. Familiarity, however, may play an important role since most of the faces the child has seen are not distorted. While it may be possible to argue about the origins of the response and the importance of learning, it is not arguable that this reaction is negative and powerful. There are numerous words and phrases in our language to describe affective reactions to physical deviance, and they apply regardless of whether the target is another person or oneself. They include disgusting, nauseating, offensive, sickening, repelling, revolting, "gross," makes you shudder, loathsome, and turns your stomach. An illustrative item from Vann's (1970) aesthetic factor concerns reactions toward fat people: "They're disgusting to see naked." Chapter 4 contains the thoughts of a fat woman responding with revulsion to the sight of her own thigh. It is instructive to consider part of that woman's response here: "It was enormous, it was gross, it was like a diseased limb, the kind you see in pictures of jungle natives" (Millman 1980, p. 180).

Some insight into how powerful the effect of some deformities can be is provided by an incident reported by Dr. Robert Chase (1981). A team of American plastic surgeons opened a clinic for the treatment of cleft palates in a Mexican city. One boy was brought by his mother with a brown bag entirely covering his head in order to avoid shocking others with his appearance. The power of this factor seems largely responsible for the burgeoning amount of plastic or aesthetic surgery, a development that may make truly deviant physical appearance even more of a rarity than it is now. One of the authors (A.F.) remembers his childhood years in Italy in the 1930s, where he saw many hunchbacks and people with goiters and other deformities. Today they seem to have practically disappeared from the country.

Bald Female Sheds Wig

From Simmons, C. "Actress Overcame Serious Difficulty—She Is Completely Bald,": *Chicago Tribune*, September 4, 1981.

> **"When I [singer-actress Jean Pace] was four, my hair just came out in clumps. There was no illness. Nothing. My parents took me to all kinds of specialists . . . everybody had hair, but me. I felt like I was cursed. I felt like I was the black sheep . . . I used to cry every day in school. Kids used to chase me and try to pull my wig off so they could call me 'baldy' and. . . . stuff like that. . . . "**
>
> **Once, when she was in junior high school in Los Angeles, a girl accidently bumped into her and knocked off [her] wig. . . . Pace was determined that would never happen again. She put a strip of tape around her head and fastened the wig with hairpins.**
>
> **"I used to sleep in my wig and everything," Pace recalls. "The wig was it. I slept, ate, dressed and bathed in it. . . . "**
>
> **One hot, summer day she looked in the mirror and decided to take off the wig. "I said, 'I've got a nice face. Why don't I just go without hair?' I told my mother; and she said, 'Oh, you wouldn't do that.' And I said, 'Yes, I would.'"**
>
> **"People think it's a downfall not to have hair when it is not a downfall, it's an advantage. You can do both things: You can go with or without (hair)."**

Although research on affective response to severe physical disfigurement and deformity is sparse, there is a rapidly expanding literature on the importance of physical attractiveness in social life. It is neither possible nor desirable to review all this research; instead, we will consider some of the most relevant findings. To begin, people generally respond to others as though they agreed with the statement that "physical beauty is a sign of interior beauty, a spiritual and moral beauty" (Schiller 1882). In an unthinking equation, it is apparent people believe that what is beautiful is good and what is ugly is bad. There is also a striking degree of consensual agreement about who is ugly and just how ugly any given individual is. This agreement is surprising, we believe, because it runs counter to assumptions more compatible with the democratic tenets that everyone deserves a chance and that if one person does not find us attractive, someone else will. Unfortunately, the facts indicate that if one person does not find us beautiful, no one else will either. Physical attractiveness can be reliably rated very quickly, literally in a matter of seconds (Walster et al. 1966). Apparently, we merely need to glance at a person to determine just how attractive he or she is and how good-looking he or she will be considered by others. As evidence of the high reliability of such judgments, two coefficients reported for two independent judges rating two samples of subjects in one study were .93 and .94 (Farina et al. 1977). Of course, such high consensus findings do not speak to the possibility of cosmetic remedy or the role of adaptation through acquaintance. The huge beautification industry suggests that large numbers of people believe that personal appearance can be improved. Many studies using the same confederate as attractive for one condition and unattractive for another do suggest that beauty is an easily alterable quality. However, these studies seem routinely to make an attractive confederate ugly for the second condition by starting with an attractive assistant and equipping her with sloppy clothes, wigs, facial scars, or glasses (e.g., Davis and Farina 1970). In real life, to the extent that everybody is already trying to look as attractive as possible, there are surely limits to what beautification can accomplish. Moreover, the longer-term studies of the influence of beauty indicate, as we shall see, that if we are ugly we will typically bear this burden all of our lives.

Research has shown that someone's degree of attractiveness influences his and, especially, her interpersonal relationships in very important ways. Many studies have unequivocally demonstrated that how others *perceive* us is determined by our beauty or lack of it. As the other side of Schiller's coin would suggest, uglier people are assigned all kinds of undesirable qualities. They are expected to do evil things, and their misdeeds are judged as more wicked than if the same thing was done by a better looking wrongdoer (Dion 1972; Dion, Berscheid, and Walster 1972; Miller, Gillen, and Schenker 1974). People are inclined not to think about unattractive people after they have met them, and they are more likely to forget them than more attractive acquaintances (Kleck and Rubenstein 1975). Also, the adequacy of adjustment of unattractive people is viewed as less good than that of better looking individuals (Cash et al. 1977). We would expect from such exploratory studies that unattractive people would be treated differently and more negatively than those who are attractive, and that is indeed what happens. For example, a study of incarcerated female delinquents found that the uglier they were, the less likely they were to be taken on trips to town (Cavior, Hayes, and Cavior 1974). Work done by attractive people is accepted as better than identical work done by unattractive persons (Landy and Sigall 1974). Moreover, people will actually work harder for someone who is good looking than someone who is not (Sigall, Page, and Brown 1971). And even something lost or forgotten is less likely to be returned if the owner is unappealing (Sroufe et al. 1977).

Obviously, such different experiences are going to have a different effect on unattractive people from that on beautiful people. Some research suggests that people's view of the world and of themselves is colored by their own appearance. Thus, Kirkpatrick and Cotton (1961) report that the less attractive people are, the less happy they are in their marriages. Berscheid, Walster, and Bohrnstedt (1973) found that for both sexes the less attractive people judged themselves to be, the lower their self-esteem. The face seems to be the crucial body part, and these investigators state that those "who are satisfied with their faces are more self confident" (p. 123). What is starkly clear is that the behavior of people is influenced by the degree of their attractiveness, presumably as a result of the way others treat them. The very important thing to note is that these behavioral effects go well beyond the momentary, specific response of an unattractive person reacting to a slight or mistreatment by another individual. The noteworthy behavioral effects are insidious and seem to result from chronic repetitions of such experiences. The end result can be a permanent molding of the personality, at times in a drastically unfavorable way.

Consistent with our reasoning, research shows that the interpersonal impact of physical appearance is not limited to the early phase of a relationship, as might be supposed. Conceivably, upon making the acquaintance of a given person, such qualities as humor, warmth, social competence, and intelligence might come to the fore, and appearance, initially the only thing known about that person, might become correspondingly less important. Hence, after a period of interaction, it could happen that attractiveness is no longer a factor and ugly and good-looking people are treated comparably by their friends and acquaintances. However, while such factors as social skills probably do become more important as relationships develop, looks continue to be influential. Mathes (1975) had people meet for five different periods and measured the impact of attractiveness over these sessions. It was found that the interpersonal influence of the attractiveness remained strong and undiminished over the course of the meetings. McGarry and West (1975) studied the interactions between residents of a center for the mentally retarded and the staff caring for them. The period of acquaintance extended for years in many cases. Nevertheless, it was found that the physical attractiveness of the residents predicted how well they were treated by the staff. A very similar study by Dailey, Allen, Chinsky, and Veit (1974) substantiates the findings reported by McGarry and West. Dailey et al. observed that the more attractive residents had more frequent and more pleasant interactions with the aides. The implication of these findings is that homely people are not only treated poorly by new acquaintances, they may also receive unfavorable treatment from long-term acquaintances. If future research substantiates this possibility, it would mean that the bad treatment is both frequent and, because it also comes from people who have become important to the homely individual, it is also more painful and disturbing.

Such treatment would make life difficult and unpleasant for an ugly person, and we might reasonably expect that the adjustment to be made by such unlucky people would, on the average, be less adequate than that of good-looking individuals. In fact, a number of studies indicate that is exactly what happens. Hobfoll and Penner (1978) presented interviews of attractive and unattractive people to therapists in training and had the therapists rate the self-concept of the interviewee. The attractive interviewees were rated as having more favorable self-concepts than the unattractive ones, even when the raters only heard the interview and were not influenced by appearance.

Evidently, the impact of social reaction to one's appearance is already clear by the ages ten to twelve. Lerner and Lerner (1977) examined the relationship between physical attractiveness and several measures of adjustment for fourth grade and sixth grade children. Homely children were found to have poor peer relationships and to be judged as poorly adjusted by their teachers. The most dramatic reports of the effect of looks on behavior, however, are two sets of studies of mental patients. The second (Napoleon, Chassin, and Young 1980) is an independently conducted replication of the first (Farina et al. 1977). These investigations tested the supposition that since it is difficult for unattractive people to achieve a satisfactory social adjustment, more of them should be mentally disordered than otherwise comparable attractive individuals. Both investigations found hospitalized mental patients to be less attractive than control subjects, and it did not appear that hospitalization was responsible for the homeliness. Photographs taken prior to the onset of mental disorder revealed that those who later developed psychiatric problems were already unattractive. O'Grady's study (in press) lends further support to our belief that homely people are more likely than others to have difficulty in adjustment. Unattractive college students believed it was more likely that they would develop a mental disorder during their lifetimes than their more attractive peers.

A provocative implication of these studies is that if we could intervene early in life and improve people's looks, we could either reduce their chances of becoming mentally disordered or make it more likely that, once stricken, they could return to community living. A study by Kurtzberg, Safar, and Cavior (1968) reports data consistent with this implication. Prisoners about to be released from incarceration were treated with cosmetic and reconstructive plastic surgery to make them more attractive. It was found that those nonaddict male offenders who received surgery had lower readmission rates than comparable offenders who had no surgery.

Despite the compelling evidence for the positive effects of physical attractiveness on personality and social relationships, it remains to be said that beauty, rather than ugliness, is sometimes a handicap, at least in the case of beautiful women in search of a career. A study of hiring practices reported that whereas attractive men were consistently favored over unattractive ones, attractive women were more often rejected for managerial jobs than similarly qualified unattractive women (*New York Times*, June 22, 1980).

In conclusion, while there are some exceptions, ugly or physically deviant people are clearly disadvantaged both by the immediate negative affect they elicit and by the longer term cumulative consequences of coping with the avoidant and rejecting behavior of others. Since they are functionally intact and our culture dictates that punishment should be directed at behavior, not appearance, the stigmatization they encounter seems particularly hard to endure. True, the aesthetic preferences of societies do change somewhat, as may be gauged by viewing movies or photos of 1940s-era Miss Americas. These women, considered the most beautiful in the world at that time, seem overweight and not strikingly beautiful today. Therefore, unattractive people can perhaps hope to be in vogue in the future. But standards of personal beauty seem to change slowly and very little. Consider how beautiful we now judge the people sculpted by the Greeks and Romans to be. While these statues may influence our tastes to some degree, surely they indicate the remarkable constancy in aesthetic preferences over the span of two and one-half millenia.

ORIGIN

The term *origin* rather clearly delineates the dimension of degrading conditions we will now examine. This dimension refers to how the mark came to be, and it in turn breaks down into numerous subdimensions: congenital in comparison to noncongenital causes; when the mark originated during the course of life; the rapidity or slowness of its onset; and the afflicted individual's own role in engendering his or her mark. As we will see, differences in the way the marks originated can greatly affect how others view and treat the afflicted individual, as well as how the victim feels and behaves.

The effect of the marked person's responsibility for creating his or her own mark seems especially important, and more work has been done on this than on other facets of origin. Many researchers and theoreticians concerned with stigma hold that the afflicted person's role in producing the mark is an important influence in the stigmatizing process. There is also general agreement that a marked individual is treated better when he or she is judged not to be responsible for the condition. This view is stated by Freidson (1966, page 76): "When the individual is believed to be responsible for his deviance, some form of punishment is likely to be involved in the way others respond to it. When he is believed not to be responsible, permissive treatment or instruction is used in his management." A similar view is held by Vann (1976), who asserts that being held responsible for a discrediting condition results in being more disdained and in being more severely punished. Comparable beliefs have also been expressed by Northcraft (1981), Orcutt (1976), and Siller, Chipman, Ferguson, and Vann (1967).

The Impact of Responsibility on the Marker

As will become apparent, the issue of responsibility is complex. Nevertheless, there is experimental support for the widely expressed belief that a victim's responsibility for his or her own mark can lead to negative treatment by the marker. Three studies were done explicitly to test this hypothesis. Farina, Holland, and Ring (1966) employed a confederate in the role of a naive person who, in one condition, presented himself as having suffered from a mental disorder. They varied the confederate's responsibility for his disorder by having him report either a pathogenic and unhappy childhood or a fortunate and happy childrearing history. The subjects, as expected, described the confederate as less responsible personally for his mental disorder when he had experienced an unhappy upbringing. The crucial part of the experiment required that the subject convey a message to the confederate by administering an electric shock to him, the strength and duration of which could be varied by the subject. It was found that when the victim was *not* held responsible for his mental disorder, he was given less painful shocks than when he was.

What may or may not be a less grave socially degrading condition, namely, the emanation of an offensive body odor, was studied by Levine and McBurney (1977). Responsibility was varied by describing the odor as due to insufficient bathing or to an incurable metabolic imbalance for which the person was not responsible. There, too, it was found that the individual with the body odor was evaluated more favorably when he or she was not responsible for it.

Perhaps the best study of this issue was conducted by Vann (1976), who chose for his experiment a very severely stigmatized mark—obesity. His subjects, male students, met a 5 feet, 10 inch male confederate who weighed

265 pounds and who was presented to them as another subject. The procedure required the confederate to talk about himself, and he revealed to half the subjects that he had a gland disorder, Frolich's syndrome, and could in no way control his fatness. To the others, he described himself as someone who was quite healthy, but who was fat because of an excessive fondness for eating. Using a procedure very similar to that employed by Farina et al. (1966), the subjects were then required to shock the confederate. The results were consistent with those of the other two studies reviewed. "Given the opportunity, observers react more antagonistically. . . . toward an obese confederate if he is held responsible for the disfavored status than if he is held to be an innocent victim" (Vann 1976, p. 116). In addition to these behavioral findings, when the obese person was viewed as responsible for being overweight, he was less favorably evaluated.

These three very pertinent studies tell us that when a marked individual is known to be responsible for the degrading affliction possessed, he or she is more likely to be treated negatively and to be viewed unfavorably. However, responsibility cannot normally be known with certainty. To be sure, blemished individuals are probably held responsible for some conditions (e.g., crime, alcoholism, obesity) more than for others (e.g., being ugly, being very short), but observers will generally have little accurate information pertaining to personal responsibility. Nevertheless, they are still concerned with the issue and are likely to form relevant beliefs. It seems we all feel the need to know what role a blemished acquaintance had in producing the mark. What is important to note is that these beliefs can evidently affect an ensuing interpersonal relationship. Data prompting this conclusion come from several studies focusing on mental disorders. Freeman (1961) interviewed relatives living in the households where 649 formerly hospitalized psychiatric patients were living. He found that the more the relatives believed the patient was to blame for the onset of the psychiatric problem, the less probable they considered it that the patient would eventually recover. In a similar but more intensive study, Schwartz (1957) interviewed the wives of twenty men hospitalized for mental disorders in an attempt to understand the wives' beliefs about the disorders and their feelings about the husbands. If the husband's problems were viewed as due to his own decision, interests, and values, the wife was very hostile and derogatory toward him. On the other hand, when the cause of the disorder was believed to be a sickness, the wife was likely to excuse the disorder and accept the husband. One wife holding this belief is quoted as saying "he can't help it" (p. 284). While these results are consistent with the hypothesis that personal responsibility for a blemish leads to negative evaluation, we need to be mindful that the studies cited are correlational. Thus, it may be that it is a negative view of the afflicted that causes him to be held responsible for his problem.

Apparently, responsibility may be attributed to the victim of a misfortune for transparently self-serving reasons, particularly if the misfortune is egregious. At times we are confronted with highly upsetting sights, such as children starving or poor people begging, searching garbage cans for food, and living in sickness and squalor. These sights will make most of us feel very guilty, and we may be able to reduce our guilt by providing help. However, we often find it difficult or impossible to provide help, so other mechanisms come into play. One of these (Lerner 1970) is to conclude that, since it is a just world, the sufferers must deserve their fate, having brought their misfortune upon themselves through laziness or sin. This belief may not only wipe away both the guilt and the disagreeable prospect of having to give time and money, but it provides a comforting illustration of how evil will get its just desserts. The example we selected, poverty, is in fact a good illustration of blaming the victim as a self-protective process. There is a long history of assigning more responsibility to the very poor for their poverty than they probably deserve. Handlin (1963) traces this explanation to an ancient European doctrine that itself serves the purpose of absolving those exposed to the suffering of others from feeling bad or from intervening. Namely, one's role in this world is assigned by God and it is immutable. In America, however, this explanation required change. "Men were not born, but rose or descended, to their ranks. That one met with fortune and another with disaster could not have been fortuitous; merit and deficiency had to be part of a larger design" (p. 37). And as Kerbo (1975) has asserted, "thus poverty has traditionally been explained by referring to the characteristics of the poor themselves" (p. 73). We should note that it is self-protective for the rich to hold the poor responsible for their own poverty, but the degree of responsibility certainly remains to be demonstrated. What is not in doubt is that the belief is widely and strongly held. Summarizing relevant research, Kerbo (1975) states that, "Most people in the United States attribute poverty to a general lack of morals and effort on the part of the poor" (p. 173).

While poverty is a mark that has frequently led to blaming the victim, the assumption that misfortune in general must somehow have been deserved appears to be ubiquitous. Particularly pertinent in this context is the work of Lerner and his colleagues, who derive the observed derogation of victims of misfortune from "the just world hypothesis" (Lerner 1970). According to this view, everybody believes the world is a place where people generally get what they deserve and deserve what they get. To believe that our own good deeds and hard work may come to naught and, indeed, that we can encounter a calamity for totally fortuitous reasons, is simply too threatening to most of us. And yet we see people whose lives have been shattered and who seem like us in every way. Are these paraplegics, blind people, and sufferers from cancer really innocent victims, and are we, therefore, candidates for suffering the same fate? The just world hypothesis posits that in these circumstances we are likely to reject that possibility as intolerable and to conclude that those stricken individuals are really wicked, or at least foolish, and deserve their fate. Considerable experimental evidence in support of the hypothesis has been gathered (Lerner 1970). Perhaps callous or cruel responses to marked individuals gain impetus from this disposition to interpret the mark as evidence that the victim is being justly repaid for some mistake, indiscretion, or evil act—even though there is no specific evidence to support such a conclusion.

Responsibility's Effect on the Markable

Let us now consider the effect of responsibility from the perspective of those who bear the affliction. We would expect that self-blame for a personal blemish would make marked individuals feel worse and more fearful of being stigmatized than if they viewed themselves as not responsible for their problem. That is, it would seem that the effect of responsibility on the victim would be similar to its effect on the observer, although we would also expect some resistance to severe self-derogation. Indeed, some evidence supports this expectation of self-derogation when the victim accepts responsibility for his plight. Kerbo (1975), in his study of belief about responsibility and stigma, found that those who blamed the "poor for poverty are more likely to feel stigmatized by receiving welfare" (p. 179). He also found that welfare recipients who believed that God was responsible for their poverty felt less stigma than those who rejected that explanation. Presumably, the more a divine force is considered responsible for the misfortune, the less the welfare recipient need blame himself. The implication that religion may play an important exculpatory role in the lives of marked individuals is also present in results reported by Cameron, Titus, Kostin, and Kostin (1973). They compared normal and handicapped subjects on a number of variables, including satisfaction with life and whether they had ever contemplated suicide. The two groups were found to be remarkably similar. However, the handicapped were considerably more religious. It may be that, for the handicapped, religion serves the purpose of lifting the burden of personal responsibility for their afflictions.

Sometimes responsibility for a mark has negative consequences beyond those attributable to the presence of the mark itself, since it discloses characteristics of the bearer that are themselves abhorrent. For example, the causes of certain conditions (e.g., syphilis) are associated with reprehensible comportment and a squalid lifestyle. Referring back to that intriguing list of components making up the ultimately degrading affliction, we should here note that one component is that it "be associated with low standards of living" (Gussow and Tracy 1968, p. 318). And Siller, Chipman, Ferguson, and Vann (1967, p. 82) report that moral disapproval of such conditions as acne is due to their association with uncleanliness.

While the role of personal responsibility, a crucial component of a mark's origin, seems rather simple, further consideration makes it clear that it is actually extremely complex. We cannot examine here all the complexities in detail, but we will at least allude to some of them. First, as Brickman (1982) has pointed out, we must distinguish between responsibility for *causing* a blemish and responsibility for *maintaining* it. For example, we may not be blamed for creating the ugly wart we have on our nose but we may very well be blamed for not having it removed. The impact of these two types of responsibilities, on both the marked and the marker, may be different. To the observer, the presence of a remediable blemish may signify that the marked person is lazy, careless, stupid, or that he is a member of a group or class where such aberrations are acceptable.

Also, the factor of personal responsibility may operate in a particularly complicated fashion in mental disorders. Research indicates that when mental disorders are considered to be diseases, the victim tends not to be held responsible. If such problems are attributed to bad habits or incompetence, the disordered individual is more likely to be blamed. However, when they are viewed as "ill," or view themselves that way, the affected are also thought to have much less control over their fate than when they are judged responsible. And people with psychiatric problems who feel they are not in control do little to improve their mental state. Instead, they rely on drugs and therapists for help and feel there is little they can do to help themselves. Similarly, if the victim is considered sick and not able to control his or her state, observers will feel there is little these marked people can do to help themselves, they are not considered good prospects as employees, and they are blamed more for becoming involved in an accident (Farina et al. 1978; Farina and Fisher 1982; Fisher and Farina 1979). One conclusion prompted by these studies of mental disorders is that not being responsible for the problem is sometimes a handicap rather than a benefit to the victim. Not being responsible can mean the mark's course is viewed as less likely to be altered in a favorable direction, and, thus, the marked person is apt to be treated negatively. A full discussion of the consequence of altering the course of marks is found in the section on "Course" in this chapter.

Another indication of the unexpected ways in which responsibility functions in the field of mental health is given by the results of a study by Fletcher (1969). He found that the consequences of attributed responsibility for a mental problem were quite different for a man whose psychiatric symptoms were those of aggression, as compared to someone who became withdrawn. For the aggressive case, attribution of *high* responsibility meant the more deviant the case, the more likely was the respondent to favor psychiatric referral. However, for the withdrawn case, it was the perception of *low* responsibility that led to greater probability of referral as deviance was perceived to increase. Another relevant study is the one by Farina, Holland, and Ring (1966), aspects of which have already been discussed. As was indicated, subjects learned that another subject, who was actually a confederate, had been in a mental hospital and had either had a happy or a pathogenic childhood. As expected, he was held less responsible for his mental problems in the latter than in the former condition and, consistent with other findings, he was treated more favorably. However, when he was viewed as less responsible, he was also regarded as less likable and more contemptible than when he was blamed more for his problems.

A further complication is that some marks are clearly consequences or side effects of noble and admired characteristics. Therefore, personal responsibility may have positive connotations for the Hussar with the black patch over his eye or the war veteran whose leg has been amputated.

Finally, the significance of responsibility for a mark is affected by the *intent* of the responsible party. One who is paralyzed as a result of an accident caused by his own careless driving is, in a sense, responsible for his condition. However, he would probably be much less stigmatized than someone paralyzed by jumping off a bridge in a suicide attempt. In the latter case, the harm was more clearly avoidable and whatever sympathies we feel for the paraplegic may be tinged by the awareness that he brought on his own paralysis while trying to end his life. The act of attempted suicide will perhaps be more salient than the resulting paraplegia, and the victim may appear incomprehensible and alien.

There are other aspects of origin that have received much less attention than personal responsibility but that, nevertheless, seem important, and because these have been relatively neglected, their role in interpersonal relationships is presently somewhat uncertain. Whether a deformity or a handicap is genetically determined or has an environmental origin probably affects both the stricken person and the normal with whom he or she is interacting. It would appear that those with congenital marks are more distant and alien to an observer. Most of us find it difficult to imagine becoming like a dwarf or hunchback, but we can, perhaps too readily, identify with someone who has cancer.

In addition to the difficulty people may encounter in finding sympathy for a genetically blemished person, research suggests that "congenital disabilities are believed to inevitably lead to warped personality development" (Siller, Chipman, Ferguson, and Vann, 1967, p. iv). It appears, then, that to the general public, someone with a congenital deformity may be viewed as a monster both mentally and physically. It is informative, in this context, to consider the novel *The Hunchback of Notre Dame*. The abhorrence such unfortunate people evoke can be gauged by the fact that parents of deformed newborn infants frequently choose to let them die and the physicians involved routinely concur. Understandably, this practice is seldom discussed publicly, but it was formally investigated in the state of Connecticut as a result of newspaper revelations. On September 10, 1981, the *Hartford Courant* described a report to the General Assembly by Thayer Baldwin, Jr., chief of the Bureau of Health System Regulation. The article stated that Baldwin "did not find a single physician who would go to great lengths to oppose a parental decision to decline treatment" for babies with congenital defects. Pertinently, he contrasted this with the fact that "in many cases . . . doctors have gone to court to override parental objections to medical treatment for children without permanent congenital handicaps. Baldwin said he views such disparity in attitude as 'a problem of discrimination against the handicapped.'" As to how congenital origin affects the victims themselves, there is no information on this at all as far as we know. We would guess that it probably has less influence on them than it does on the public. They probably think of themselves as human beings with the same values and rights as others despite their genetic handicap.

Rapidity of Onset of the Mark

The final aspect of origin we will consider here is the rapidity of onset of the problem. Certain marks have a practically instantaneous development, such as paraplegia following an automobile accident. It is not uncommon for an able-bodied person, suddenly and without any preparation, to become a cripple confined to a wheelchair. Other problems develop insidiously, such as certain paralytic diseases that ultimately lead to complete loss of movement. Do these different rates of acquisition make any difference? We think they certainly do. To return once more to the hypothetical condition that causes ultimate social degradation, one of its listed characteristics is that it "have an insidious onset" (Gussow and Tracy 1968, p. 318). However, insidiousness will probably make the problem appear more debasing to the normal observer than to the victim of the condition. At any rate, it is surely important to consider separately the effect of this variable on marked and marker. For the victim it may be more endurable to have some horrible affliction manifest itself gradually, thus permitting adaptation, rather than to suddenly be confronted with the condition in a full-blown form. Supporting this is the reaction of people to being told they have leprosy (Gussow and Tracy 1968). While leprosy is unquestionably an insidious disease, the *diagnosis* can be totally unexpected, and patients are often overwhelmed at suddenly learning that they are lepers and face all the cataclysmic consequences traditionally implied by the disease. On the other hand, there are some data indicating the normal is more accepting if the stricken individual's problem is of recent rather than of more remote origin, even if the problem is judged permanent in each case (Schwartz 1957). Perhaps a rapid onset makes at least some blemishes more tolerable to the observer and more difficult to bear for the victim. The research reviewed suggests this.

The possibility of rapid onset may have relevance for an astonishing discrepancy that often exists between the beliefs of observers and handicapped individuals. Normals think the mood and life experiences of stricken individuals must be highly negative and unsatisfying, whereas the victims themselves are often happy and find life to be rewarding (Cameron et al. 1973; Hunt 1966).

It may be that those of us who suffer such a horrible misfortune as permanent paralysis initially react with despair and gloom (Kelley et al. 1960). Given time, however, human beings are so resilient that satisfactions are found in the new life they lead, and they soon find themselves as happy as before the tragedy. If we consider it, neither the happy nor unhappy experiences we all have had have changed our level of happiness permanently, but an observer meeting a hopelessly crippled individual cannot give full weight to adaptation and can only imagine his or her own response at meeting such a fate. The imagined response, understandably, is one of being overwhelmed and shattered. When the victims of recent disasters are seen, they will be generally deeply affected, perhaps depressed and inconsolable. Observers can easily comprehend their feelings and be sympathetic and supportive. But what about meeting someone whose misfortune happened long ago and who seems quite content and well-adjusted? To most people that will be a surprising, even shocking reaction. Assuming they do not attribute the victim's psychological state to deception, they may see something special, different, and occult in someone who reacts to disaster in such an unimaginable manner. It may be, as Hunt (1966) has eloquently argued, that such people challenge our whole view of the world. If fundamental things, such as an inability to walk or see, are irrelevant to happiness, then what about our goals and values, such as the rewards expected of an education or having a family and children? Are these all delusions and snares? Being confronted with such satisfied hopelessly crippled people suggests that we do not understand life and that happiness is much less well-understood and under our control than we would like it to be. Perhaps this process is one cause of stigmatization.

PERIL

The last dimension, peril, focuses on the dangers posed by stigmatized individuals. This dimension is most often relevant when considering mental patients, people who have committed violent crimes, and those whose diseases are believed to be contagious. Yet few of the efforts specifically intended to identify the major components of stigmatizing conditions have focused upon danger as an important element. Strangely, the two studies that have found peril to be a factor have attended to only one kind of threat posed by marked people, i.e., the anxiety they evoke about our own vulnerability (Siller et al. 1968; Vann 1970). For example, in the Vann study, one item that emphasizes the peril factor is, "Seeing someone who is obese makes me worry about becoming obese myself" (p. 695). But there are many other ways by which marked people threaten those about them, and the fact that they remind us of our own frailty does not even seem to be the most obvious or significant danger.

Though investigators explicitly looking for the elements of stigmatizing conditions have paid scant attention to peril, other researchers and theoreticians have clearly recognized the great importance of this factor. Henry Steadman (1980), a researcher and administrator with the New York State Department of Mental Hygiene, believes the essence of stigma is fear. Lehmann, Joy, Kreisman, and Simmens (1976) conclude, on the basis of their own research and a review of the literature, that "the element of threat is more likely to lead to rejection than other aspects of deviance" (p. 332). Investigations of a variety of blemishes have shown that the more dangerous the possessor is thought to be, the more rejected he or she is. For instance, the more dangerous homosexuals are judged to be, the more they are stigmatized (Bobys and Laner, 1979). With mental disorders, the danger-rejection association seems to be particularly close. Morrison (1980) states, following a review of the literature, that "one of the major factors behind the public's . . . rejection of the mental patient is that of dangerousness" (p. 702).

Some of the great variety of dangers posed by marked people are more obvious than others. Actual physical threat to life and limb, such as from a "furious" mental patient (the term used to describe dangerous patients in colonial America), is extremely salient to people. The present lay terminology for such an individual is "madman" or "raving maniac". But even the most feeble and helpless of socially degraded human beings also threaten others, even when they can in no sense do any physical harm to anyone. The emaciated and dying cancer patient may make us starkly and disagreeably aware that a similar fate can befall us. The paraplegic blocked by stairs or the disoriented and confused blind person places upon us the burden of intervention and rescue. In fact, marked persons always seem to pose some form of threat, and it may be that danger, in its many forms, is the most fundamental characteristic of stigmatizing interactions.

The Stigma of Cancer

From Moran, M., "Players: A Fresh Start for Dan Lloyd," *New York Times,* February 24, 1983.

Dan Lloyd [a former linebacker with the New York Giants football team] was 26 when he learned he had lymphocytic lymphoma, a cancer of the lymph nodes. . . . Lloyd . . . spent much of last year disputing opinions that the chemotherapy had made his bones more brittle and the muscle tissue more soft, increasing the chance of injury. Then after Lloyd reluctantly retired from the Giants, he said he discovered that the whispers within Giant Stadium had spread to football offices everywhere.

"All of a sudden, I am a slow healer," Lloyd said "They were telling general managers that kind of stuff: 'He's a slow healer.' That's what made me mad."

[When Lloyd went to see John McVay, the former Giants coach who is now administrative vice-president of the Forty Niners, he said] "I didn't even get to

> **shake hands with him . . . that's when the medical thing really hit me. I think they were really scared off by the medical information."**

Let us begin with the danger of physical and/or verbal attack posed by some marked persons since this peril is so salient. In particular, mentally disordered individuals are perceived as posing this kind of threat. Before the era of the mental hospital, which began about 1850, a major distinction was made between those mentally afflicted who were "furious" and those who were not (Deutsch 1965). The two groups were treated very differently. Little distinction was made between "furious" madmen and murderers and other criminals, whereas the remaining mental patients were either ignored or treated as paupers. Even now the hospital staffs in direct contact with mental patients have both formal and informal appellations, the main purpose of which is to indicate how dangerous any given patient is. Thus, we have such formal designations as criminally insane, combative, and assaultive. And, as far as the public is concerned, mental patients are indeed dangerous creatures. Nunnally found in 1961 that, in comparison to concepts like "average man," mental patients were regarded by the general public as very much more dangerous and unpredictable (pp. 46, 270–272). In a more recent community survey (1975), this belief apparently persists: Only 17 percent of the respondents agreed that "mental patients are not dangerous" (Rabkin 1980, p. 21).

The probable causes responsible for this image of psychiatric patients held by both mental health workers and people in the community are very complex. The mass media are blamed by several investigators concerned with this issue. Scheff (1963) asserts that newspapers are determined to find a history of mental disorder in the background of people who commit sensational crimes, and they emphasize this history in their reporting. Examples of such occurrences are readily found. An article by Bob Greene appeared in the *San Francisco Chronicle* on December 28, 1980, complaining about this practice, which he held to be pandemic. The article was printed shortly after singer and musician John Lennon was killed, and Mark David Chapman was accused of the murder. Green states that the "phrase 'Ex-Mental Patient' has appeared in headlines all over the world to describe Chapman." Gerbner (1980) is in agreement with this judgment, and, furthermore, he demonstrates by systematic investigations of television programs that TV portrays mental patients as highly dangerous. His studies lead him to conclude that "the vast majority of mentally ill characters on

TV . . . are not only dangerous, but also are touched with a sense of evil" (p. 47). We should not conclude, however, as these investigators seem to be urging, that all mental patients are innocent victims of bad publicity. There are good reasons for believing that some present and former mental patients really are dangerous. Thus, the mass media may not be entirely arbitrary and capricious in their practices, and the public may not be foolishly credulous about this matter. For example, Steadman (1980) showed in one study that for violent crimes former mental patients had arrest rates three times as great as members of the general population. Moreover, it does not appear that the general public views all mental patients as threatening and indiscriminately rejects them. Rather, some are considered a threat, and it is those patients or former patients judged to be dangerous who are unacceptable and who are ostracized (Linsky 1970; Tudor, Tudor, and Gove 1977).

Any person with a condition that is associated with a high probability of physical violence will very probably be stigmatized, but even the capacity to be unpredictable, erratic, or irrational can be highly threatening when possessed by persons who are in, or may gain, positions of high social power. Since the more power someone has, the more harm that person can do, it seems likely that society will be very reluctant to assign mentally questionable people to positions of power and that candidates for important jobs will be carefully screened to be certain they are balanced and reliable. It does not make a great deal of difference to the public if a ditch digger or a garbage collector runs amok. Because they lack power over others not in the immediate vicinity, they can only do a limited amount of damage. On the other hand, a doctor or an airplane pilot is in a position to do more serious and more general harm to others, and a political or military leader can cause worldwide disaster, as demonstrated by Hitler. We think the fear of the amplified effects of irrationality linked with power probably explains why Senator Thomas Eagleton was forced to resign as a vice-presidential candidate in the 1972 election, after it was disclosed that he had received psychiatric treatment, and there was very little resultant protest. We also think that Bar-Levav (1976) is correct in his analysis of the proceedings of the Senate committee hearings on Gerald R. Ford's nomination to be vice-president of the United States. As already noted, Ford was asked if he had ever needed or received psychiatric treatment and the candidate emphatically denied this. That was an accusation that, if true, would probably have disqualified him to hold that high office.

Another important and obvious kind of peril inherent in certain marks is the danger of physical contamination. The plagues that at one time periodically swept the world strikingly illustrate the extreme danger that some infectious conditions can generate. They also illustrate accompanying reactions of social rejection and hostility. It has been estimated that of the 100 million inhabitants of Europe, 25 million died of the "Black Death" plague that raged throughout the continent in the fourteenth century. A memorable novelistic account of how plague victims were treated by society is given by Manzoni (1962), perhaps Italy's most celebrated writer. He describes a plague that broke out in Milan in the seventeenth century. A nobleman, Don Rodrigo, discovers he has it, and he instructs a servant, Griso, to fetch him a doctor. Griso, who had cautiously been keeping his distance, returns instead with two *monatti*, removers of the infected, who wore red uniforms and bells on their legs, thus alerting the population to the danger of contamination. Seeing them, Don Rodrigo reaches under his pillow for a pistol but the *monatti* overpower him. He is then carried off to the *lazzaretto*, where quarantined people allegedly receive treatment, but where in actuality they are left to die.

There are many other conditions that elicit the fear of contamination or contagion. These include not only those that are occasionally contagious, such as tuberculosis, but also conditions like cancer and physical disability that pose no actual threat of transmission from afflicted to observer. Gellman (1969) asserts that parents "are reluctant to permit a close relationship between nonhandicapped and disabled children. Unconscious beliefs that disability is contagious lead to segregation of the handicapped" (p. 4). Leprosy is surely the most striking of the afflictions prompting fears of contagion. From biblical times to the present, this disease seems to have evoked unbridled horror in people, and it has galvanized society to protect itself and to take action against the carriers of the scourge. Some arresting facts about societal reaction to this disease were revealed in a program televised by San Francisco's KQED on April 19, 1981, which documented Kalaupapa, a leper colony in Hawaii. Until 1969 inhabitants of Hawaii who developed leprosy were taken, forcibly if required, to that colony. In earlier years, a bounty was paid to anyone who identified a leper, and by 1900 there were over 1,000 people in the colony. There were still 125 people living there in 1981. Even little children were inspected for signs of the disease, and if these were found, they were simply plucked out of their environment and taken to Kalaupapa. An inhabitant of the colony, Bernard Punikaiea, was interviewed on the program and spoke as follows: "I was taken away at the age of six—incarcerated is the correct word—I had committed no crime, yet I was ill. And my illness was perceived to be a threat to the community, so I was tossed away, you know. They fed me, they clothed me, they took away my humanity. They took away my dignity." In the United States,

Gussow and Tracy (1968) report that state laws pertaining to lepers are varied and differentially enforced. However, "aliens are usually constrained to seek treatment at Carville [a leprosorium] or face the possibility of deportation" (p. 318).

Learning that one has leprosy is a cataclysmic experience. First, there is the expectation that one's body will disintegrate, a "fantasy of the worst that can happen to one's body—*a fantasy of total maximal illness*" (Gussow and Tracy 1968, p. 319). Moreover, instead of sympathy and nurturance from society, the sick anticipate being banished for life. "Psychologically, leprosy patients typically exhibit a sense of total rejection by society and initially even by themselves" (p. 321). The only role they seem to be allowed in the normal world is that of "career patient," speakers to society at large on behalf of all leprosy patients. Richard Marks, an inhabitant of Kalaupapa, succinctly describes the situation: "Leprosy was—about the most feared disease [because] . . . banishment was part of getting sick." Not only were patients deprived of virtually all the comforts they knew at about the same time they realized they had a dreaded disease, but the conditions under which they were forced to survive were sometimes horrible. "They would charter a ship to bring them in from Honolulu. . . . There were times when the patients were just dumped over the sides of those ships. They had to swim to shore. . . . Temporary shelter was put up. . . . But the wind just destroyed 'em all. There was nothing to stop the wind. Conditions were just so bad, and, of course, there never was a regular supply of food . . . or building materials . . . or anything else for that matter. . . . A doctor wouldn't come within twenty feet of a patient."

To be sure, changing conditions in the United States and Western society as a whole have reduced the *practical* importance of this aspect of peril, i.e., the threat of infection. We no longer have plagues and hardly anyone has ever met a leper. But in other countries, such as India, the danger is still present and important. And in our own country, the threat of being contaminated or of contaminating others may exist in a more virulent fashion than the real peril posed would justify. That is what Gellman (1959) is saying when he asserts that handicapped chidren are segregated because of fear of contamination. An experiment by Tringo (1970) indicates that this kind of peril continues to play a crucial role in the social rejection of marked people who realistically pose the threat of contagion. He presented twenty-one different handicaps or sicknesses to subjects and asked them to indicate the acceptability of people possessing those conditions. He found that people with tuberculosis were less acceptable than amputees, the blind, cancer patients, and paraplegics. He concludes that "tuberculosis has a contagious connotation that may be a factor in its low placement on the social distance scale" (p. 304).

The most convincing evidence that people are unrealistically fearful of physical contamination from blemished individuals is provided by Wheeler, Farina, and Stern (1981). They report that one-third or more of their college student subjects indicated agreement with the following items, which refer to mental patients. "I would not go swimming in a pool used by a group of mental patients," and "I would wash my hands after touching a mental patient." The same proportion indicated disagreement with the following items. "Drinking from a water fountain in a mental hospital would not bother me." And "I would let ex-mental patients work in restaurants."

Another and fairly obvious kind of danger that marked people present is the danger of social rejection because of association with the blemished person. Individuals who would be "clean" and normally acceptable to others when alone can, by association, acquire some of the socially degrading characteristics of a marked person. Goffman (1963) has recognized and labeled this phenomenon "courtesy stigma" (p. 30). We would like to distinguish several forms that this peril of association with the degraded can take, since each type seems to have different consequences for both marked and marker. In all cases, however, this peril can exist in addition to, or in the absence of, the possibility that he or she will infect or harm us.

First, there is the mere fact of association with stigmatized individuals. Even if no permanent relationship is indicated, by being with a stigmatized person, the associated "normal" is still likely to be degraded. Posner (1976) says that "in our society it is not only the deviant who is stigmatized but also those who are associated or acquainted with the deviant. . . . Even an innocuous or casual walk down the street with a stigmatized other tends to stigmatize a person who accompanies such an individual" (p. 27). Why social degradation is transmitted in this way is strange and not at all easy to understand. Is it that someone who accompanies a cripple or a blind person is suspected of hiding a similar problem, thus explaining why the two are acquainted? Could it be that the "normal" of the pair is assumed to be so lacking in friends that he or she must gravitate toward marginal individuals? Whatever the mechanisms, this phenomenon is surely a significant handicap for the newly marked person who would like to return to the community and live among old friends. The old friends will be well aware of the social consequences of interacting with the afflicted individual. Although they may continue the relationship through loyalty, they are likely to seek an avenue of escape from the uncomfortable dilemma and adopt strategies of gradual disengagement. Of course, the marked person is also conscious of the burden he or she imposes on others by socializing with them. A desire not to hurt others may lead the afflicted individual to terminate old relationships. Another mechanism that perhaps operates to produce the same end result is when the newly crippled or blind person may believe that others naturally resent the burden he or she imposes and may suspect former friends of maintaining a relationship out of pity. Under such conditions, pride might lead the marked individuals to take the initiative in severing the relationship. Anecdotal reports suggest that in many instances the person who becomes marked is the one who ends longstanding interpersonal relationships.

It's For Your Own Good

From "People in the News," *Hartford Courant,* March 19, 1982.

Charles J. Sabatier, Jr., 36, is the Assistant Director of the Massachusetts Office of Handicapped Affairs and is paralyzed from the waist down. He got on a Delta Airlines plane at Boston's Logan International Airport Wednesday en route to Miami to address the U.S. Conference of Mayors and a flight attendant tried to get him a blanket. Sabatier said he didn't want one, but she said he had to have one and before you know it he was arrested by State Police for disorderly conduct. A Delta spokesman says the blanket is a safety measure so paraplegics can be saved quickly if there is an emergency. Sabatier says the whole blanket idea discriminates against the handicapped. "Having to sit on a blanket dehumanizes me, stigmatizes me, not to mention the embarrassment it causes me."

Then there are longer-term or permanent types of association with marked people that seem capable of imparting a deeper and more enduring stain. One's occupation, in particular, can transmit the social degradation of those with whom one works. We should distinguish social rejection caused by the actual work one does from rejection due to association with blemished individuals, even though both processes may operate to sully someone's social status, and we may, in practice, be unable to tell how much each is contributing. Pimps and prostitutes are probably degraded because of what they do, and their low status is not a result of association with stigmatized others. Even a hangman seems not to be rejected primarily because his work brings him into contact with criminals. Although society can so dislike a hangman that he is threatened with attack by the public if recognized on the street (Goffman 1963), we believe this happens mainly because he snuffs out the life of convicts and not because of mere association with them as a consequence of his work. On the other hand, the loss of esteem from which some mental health professionals suffer appears due in part to their association with mental patients. Unlike the work of a surgeon, the public knows little about what psychiatrists and psychologists actually do. What is known is that such people work closely with mental patients, and they are held in significantly lower regard than comparable professionals of the same social class (e.g., doctor, nurse) who are not associated with mental patients (Nunnally 1961). Rejection because of long-term or permanent association can evidently be very strong. Posner (1976) relates one instance of such rejection involving the morgue attendant at a hospital, John, whose work entailed the management of corpses. People avoided him and he seemed quite apologetic about his job. "For example, John always cleaned himself and changed into a tie and shirt before lunch, even though other members of the medical staff did not do so" (p. 31).

Surely the most severe peril posed to a "normal" individual is when he or she has a genetic association to a stigmatized person, especially if the mark itself has a genetic origin. We can leave an acquaintance and even a friend who is cursed with a degrading blemish. A job is harder to give up, and it may entail considerable sacrifice, but that, too, can be done. But to free ourselves of a genetic association means the marked person must be disowned and abandoned. Since he or she may be a parent, a sibling, or a child, that is an extreme step to take—and even that may not help, after all. If the blood relationship to the afflicted is known, the person seeking dissociation may still be regarded as tainted, and, furthermore, he or she may be looked down upon for the callous self-serving abandonment of unfortunate relatives. Generally, therefore, the "normal" member of such a genetic association must endure this misfortune.

Birenbaum (1970) has provided us with some detailed information about this process among mothers of mentally retarded children. The birth of the defective child greatly changes and restricts the activities of the entire family since it can no longer fully adhere to conventional cultural roles. Social visits with neighbors are less frequent and the range of people invited to their home is curtailed. Embarrassment and uncertainty about informing friends is typical, and an initial appearance in the neighborhood with the child can be traumatic. In sum, Birenbaum states that "the acquisition of a courtesy stigma, becoming the mother of a mentally retarded child, is accompanied by an alteration of the mother's relation to the community" (p. 205). In the Kalaupapa documentary, Alice Kamaka, a seventy-five-year-old Chinese woman, who was brought to the colony at the age of eight, was interviewed. She said: "My family, it was worrying about it. You know, how Chinese was scared of leprosy. Ooo, one in a family—is disgraced the family" (p. 22–23).

A similar severe besmirchment of relatives is found by Sack, Seidler, and Thomas (1976) in their study of families of imprisoned people. The imprisonment is "a family crisis, in which social stigma plays a considerable role." Moreover, Sack et al. report that not only is social stigma transmitted to relatives, but some children of imprisoned parents acquire the mark itself, i.e., criminal behavior. A group of those children began manifesting antisocial behavior shortly after their parent's incarceration. The authors suggest that "one way to hold onto a lost parent, now defined as bad and in need of punishment, is to take on some of the parent's characteristics, even if antisocial" (p. 625).

Although much thought has been devoted to the issue of peril and social contamination, systematic research is just beginning. The most pertinent study is by Weyand (1983), who examined the effect of a close, genetic association to an afflicted individual. Her subjects, male college students, heard, via a tape recording, the experimenter interview one of several male confederates who were described as people scheduled to attend the university the following semester. The subjects were asked to send a tape-recorded message to the interviewee warning him of possible problems they would face on the campus and they were also asked to evaluate the interviewee. In one condition, the subjects learned that the interviewee's father had suffered a mental disorder, whereas control subjects received no such information. The behavior toward the interviewee with the afflicted father and the way he was evaluated was the same as that shown toward afflicted individuals themselves (e.g., Farina, Murray, and Groh 1978).

It remains to be noted, of course, that association with the stigmatized does not always lead to social degradation or even to fears of it. For one thing, those whose contact with crippled and deformed others is limited to clearly defined roles, such as rehabilitation and custodial care, are not likely to suffer from stigma as a result of social contamination. Also, there are many situations and conditions in which association with marked individuals is considered quite appropriate and without consequences for the status of the associated unmarked individual. (As noted above, however, mental health professionals may be victimized by "courtesy stigma".)

In addition to the kinds of threats we have considered, it seems that marks are dangerous in several other ways, but little information about these remaining perils exists, and we will give them only brief consideration. As indicated at the beginning of this section, one likely consequence of meeting people afflicted with certain kinds of blemishes is that we become starkly aware of our own frailty. Both Vann (1970) and Siller, Ferguson, Vann, and Holland (1968) found this to be a component of people's reactions to those stigmatized in a variety of ways. The marked person is a "stimulus which activates anxiety about one's own vulnerability" (Siller et al. 1968, p. 652). Obviously, we will be more threatened by an affliction we are likely to incur, such as cancer, than by one which is unlikely to affect us, such as becoming a dwarf or a Siamese twin. Even the latter conditions, however, indicate how dangerous the world is and how vulnerable and frail human beings are.

There may also be the danger of a different sort of contamination from people who are stigmatized because they lead Sybaritic, self-indulgent lives. There are many such people—prostitutes, gamblers, drug addicts, and indolent pursuers of *la dolce vita*. Those with such life styles may be attractive companions for a few who find it exciting to live at the edge of depravity, but for the majority, such profligates threaten moral contamination. Freud's concept of "reaction formation" may account for some of the fervor behind the condemnation of those who flaunt conventional morality, with the most tempted showing the most vehement hostility toward those who appear to be enjoying forbidden fruit.

Finally, there is at least one more kind of danger to be faced when certain stigmatized people are encountered. Some have been brutalized by misfortune—they are paralyzed, handicapped, stricken by diseases—and, therefore, they have a moral right to receive help from others who have been luckier. A blind person or someone in a wheelchair who can't manage a curb or enter a building places a strong obligation on those nearby for help. A deformed individual may be, at least appear to be, shunned by others and in need of a friendly conversation. Hence, marked individuals pose a mild danger in that they obligate us to provide this help. This obligation becomes a serious threat when association with the afflicted is not a once-only matter but a continuing one—as when the victim is a neighbor or a coworker. In such cases, an initial commitment to help may imply future obligations. After all, can we help a crippled coworker into a building and then not help him with the elevator, getting him to the desk, and so on? And can we give a hand today but refuse to help the next day? There is a tar-baby prospect that once we are engaged in soothing the plagues of a sufferer, there is no easy way to extricate oneself from continuing duty. This may explain why people will be reluctant to help a permanently marked individual, but will help someone with a temporary handicap, such as a broken leg.

ADDITIONAL VARIABLES OR CONDITIONS

The six dimensions we have selected as important do not constitute the only possible set that could be used. Although we have argued that those six are central and particularly useful dimensions, there are other factors and conditions that influence the role marks play in interpersonal interactions.

The *kind* of mark involved in the interaction will typically make an important difference. For example, the research by MacDonald and Hall (1969) indicates that sensory disorders, such as blindness and deafness, generally will have a less drastic and severe effect on interpersonal relationships than emotional disorders, such as those involving irrational fears. Also, the *nature of the interaction* in which the normal and marked individual are engaged is important in determining the impact of the stigma on the relationship. In an initial or short-term relationship, it may indeed be easier to interact with a blind person than someone who is emotionally upset. On the other hand, living with someone who is blind may entail many more problems than living with an anxious and nervous person, given that the nervous individual is not constantly in turmoil but gets upset only when certain special circumstances prevail. In contrast, under some conditions at least, many blind individuals are in perpetual need of help. Next there are differences in the various *areas of functioning* in which the marked person is engaged, such as the vocational, the parental, and the marital spheres. It appears, for example, that many afflictions, such as heart conditions, deafness, and facial disfigurements will have more of a negative influence in the vocational than in other areas of functioning (MacDonald and Hall 1969).

In addition to these variables, there are also the *individual characteristics* of the marked person that will interact with the blemish to produce a specific effect upon the relationship. Consider meeting for the first time a man whose mark is that he has been in a mental hospital. How we feel and behave in his presence will very likely be affected by whether he is more than six feet tall, in his twenties, and of powerful physique, or is sixty-five and weighs 130 pounds. His clothing and the attractiveness of his face may also make a difference. Although these variables have not been studied very much, and it is difficult to conceptualize them for systematic experimentation, there is more than conjecture to indicate they are indeed important. Farina, Thaw, Felner, and Hust (1976) presented each of four confederates as either mentally retarded or mentally disordered, to independent groups of subjects. The effect of the mark on the interaction was significantly influenced by the personal characteristics of the confederates. For example, relative to the normal condition, one confederate was treated better in the mentally retarded condition (i.e., shocked a shorter time) whereas another confederate was treated less well (i.e., shocked a longer time). Just what the determining personal characteristics were, whether stature, comportment, tone of voice, or some other factor, remains a mystery.

Aside from aspects of the mark and of the markable, variables from other sources also play a role in relationships in which stigma is involved. The *characteristics of the other member* in the interaction, the "normal" or marker, will certainly influence the behavioral interchange, as a number of studies indicate. The role and prior experience of the marker is one such determining factor. People who come into contact with those who are stigmatized by a particular condition, such as a mental disorder, appear to view those affected with that problem more favorably as a result of the contact (Wright and Klein, 1965). This suggests a number of potentially important things about the stigmatized, such as that, relative to normals, they can interact more satisfactorily with those with whom they have had contact, and who are consequently less affected by the mark. They would include friends and family members. It also seems probable that a person's occupation, which will entail certain qualifications, characteristics, and attitudes, can influence reactions to markable people positively or negatively. Thus, stewardesses, whose job qualifications emphasize physical attractiveness, were found to be significantly more negative and rejecting of physically disabled persons than were typists (English and Oberle 1971). Also, anxious persons and those who are intolerant of ambiguity (i.e., who find an uncertain and unsettled state of affairs very disagreeable) appear to be exceptionally rejecting and inhospitable toward marked individuals (Yuker, Block, and Campbell 1960; English 1971). This rejection may occur because interacting with the stigmatized will typically enhance ambiguity and anxiety, uncomfortable feelings ordinarily present in such persons in greater measure than usual.

Finally, the *situational circumstances* under which the interaction takes place will affect a mark's role in interpersonal behavior. Obviously, conditions can vary in a number of ways: the degree of physical or psychological threat posed, whether other people are present, and whether the setting is familiar and, therefore, facilitates well-established response patterns. The role of these numerous and probably potent situational factors is amply illustrated by research, which has varied the clarity for the marker that he is behaving in an unusual fashion because of the other's affliction. Thus, Dutton (1976) showed that black patrons without a tie were more likely to be admitted to Canadian restaurants requiring ties than were comparable white patrons. However, when tieless black patrons tried to enter shortly after whites had been denied admission for wearing no tie, the blacks were also likely to be refused entrance. Several studies have shown (Farina 1982) that subjects will deliver a more painful shock to a former mental patient than to a control when the circumstances are such that they are relatively unaware of what they are doing. When they are more conscious of their behavior and they are better able to monitor it, the amount of pain inflicted upon ex-mental patients and control does not differ.

The process illustrated by these studies extends well beyond the situational variables that are of concern here. We are persuaded that this process is very important in understanding stigma, and it will be discussed in a later section of this book. However, the circumstances under which marked and marker meet can influence this process, and the interaction can thus be affected. Hence, we will here give a brief overview of this process, focusing on how it is subject to situational influences. Stigmatized individuals arouse diverse and often contradictory motives in most of us. We may feel guilty and in need of making amends toward some marked individuals (e.g., blacks) because we know that those like them have been treated unjustly. Or we may experience a sense of abhorrence and disdain that precludes our caring about whether they are unfairly treated or not (a probable response to known child molesters). However, all of us have typically been exposed since childhood to the moral principle that people should all be treated equitably and fairly. Marks that indicate racial membership, loss of physical abilities, and past disease should be disregarded. To the extent that the situation allows us to monitor the evenhandedness of our behavior, we may try to treat the marked person like anyone else. But when circumstances make it difficult to ascertain if we are or are not being just, the marked person may be treated quite differently. Sometimes he will be treated better and sometimes he will be treated worse than a nonstigmatized person. It is important to discover the conditions determining whether an extremely favorable or an unfavorable reaction will occur.

In our consideration of stigma, we will concentrate on a limited number of crucial variables rather than attempt an exhaustive treatment of all variables that may possibly play a role in stigmatization. Therefore, the focus of this book will be on the six central dimensions of concealability, course, disruptiveness, aesthetics, origin, and peril. However, the foregoing additional factors will not be disregarded.

• CHAPTER THREE •

Social Determinants of Reactions to Stigma by Others

THE PURPOSE OF THIS BOOK is to understand interpersonal encounters and relationships that involve people who have been marked and those who are regarded as normal. To achieve this purpose, we shall analyze the immediate contexts in which these encounters occur and the beliefs, experiences, expectancies, and feelings brought to them by the individuals who interact.

The purpose of this chapter is to place the analysis of the marking process and marked relationships into a larger social context. Our aim is to examine those features of the social matrix within which marking occurs that shape the reactions of the discrete individuals who are interacting. Although potential markers—the "normal" members in marked relationships—have their own unique affective, cognitive, and behavioral reactions to deviant others, they are also members of corporate social bodies, i.e., groups, communities, and societies, and their reactions to stigmas are profoundly influenced by that fact. It is the group that sets the standards its members use to evaluate one another, as well as providing the contexts in which these evaluations are made and expressed. Therefore, a full understanding of marked relationships requires attention to the role of social-systems dynamics in the marking process.

The primary literature that considers these dynamics is, of course, sociological. This rich and provocative literature has much to tell us about the social conditions under which audiences of markers may or may not be inclined to stigmatize individuals. It has less to say about how these social conditions are translated into individual reactions. Although the primary emphasis of this chapter will be to articulate the sociological perspective, some attempt will also be made to speculate about how pressures at the social-system level may be transformed into individual response tendencies.

If there are differences between sociology and social psychology with respect to the referents of research, the basic view about stigma that is taken in both literatures is, by and large, the same. That is, stigma is seen in both as an emergent property, as a product of definitional processes arising out of social interaction, and not as an attribute that people automatically have when they acquire a trait or quality that may be discrediting.

Stigmatization is seen as a process in which particular social meanings come to be attached to categories of behavior and to individuals. This is the view developed by Goffman (1963) in his essay on stigma and is central to Schur's analysis of the labeling perspective (1979).

Sociological theory and research on stigma address two issues that are germane to understanding the role of social and cultural factors in the marking process. The first is related to peril, which, as we have seen in Chapter 2, is a significant component of stigmatized reactions. The first part of this chapter will discuss what sociologists have to say about the social bases of the feelings of peril and threat that stigma can arouse in markers. The second issue is related to the issue of variations in audiences' sensitivities to stigma and their tolerance for it. Throughout this book we show that people's awareness of qualities and attributes that stigmatize others, as well as people's tolerance for those they mark, vary greatly. The second part of this chapter discusses some of the social and cultural factors hypothesized to be associated with variations in perceptions and reactions to stigma.

In evaluating our discussion, the reader may find it helpful to be aware of the types of stigma that sociologists have written about and on which we will be drawing. Most of the essays cited in this chapter pertain to stigmas based upon what Goffman has termed bodily abominations and character blemishes (Goffman 1963). This does not mean, of course, that our remarks are irrelevant to tribal stigmas, but only that our ideas have emerged from theory and research based on stigmas of other kinds.

THE PERIL OF STIGMA

In Chapter 2 peril was identified as a significant component of stigma. Members of groups indicate by their response that stigmatizing marks are threatening to them. Many people have pointed out that the nonstigmatized may act toward the marked individual as though they feel exposed to danger through association with them, and that marked people may arouse in so-called normal persons a prescient sense of danger (Goffman 1963; Schur 1979; Hunt 1966; Scott 1972). Why should this be the case? Why are stigmas threatening and what exactly do they threaten?

Neighborly Understanding

Sutherland, N.S., *Breakdown*. New York: Stein and Day, 1976, p. 35.

[The author, an eminent psychologist, spends most of the book describing his own mental breakdown. At

> **one point, however, he describes the result of a brief visit by a fellow patient to a Sunday church service near her home.] She returned to her home with a woman who lives opposite her. The neighbor said: "I suppose you will be moving away from here when you come out of the place." When the patient expressed puzzlement, she said: "Well, it would be much better for everyone on the street if you did—it would be embarrassing to have you still around."**

One answer to these questions is that group members feel imperiled by stigmatized people because some marks pose a direct and immediate threat to the physical well-being of others. Chapter 2 explained the sense in which such judgments are correct and the sense in which they are not. We noted that feelings of peril based on real or probable physical danger are justified in some cases, such as feelings aroused by those who commit violent crimes, but are not justified for other types of stigma, such as severe physical impairments or facial disfigurement. The fact that we feel imperiled when in the company of people possessing qualities such as these indicates that the source of the threat we experience is not exclusively, or even principally, physical. It is primarily symbolic. The carriers of stigmatizing marks symbolize something perceived as threatening to our individual and collective sense of well-being. In order to understand what this entails, we must consider what makes up this sense of well-being. Phenomenological social scientists have shed important light on this topic through their work on collectively shared conceptions of reality.

Phenomenological sociologists, such as Berger and Luckmann (1966), use the term "social order" to refer to the systems of shared meanings that members of a group, community, or society know and experience as their reality. They point out that through systems of shared meanings, objects, persons, and events are identified, arranged, and categorized to impart to group members a firm sense of "the way things are." They emphasize the idea that each group's experience of reality tends to become an all-embracing frame of reference. This totality is called a "symbolic universe" to denote the idea that within each group's set of shared meanings, every kind of human experience can be rendered meaningful and interpretable. That is, within each shared system of meanings, everything has its place, in the sense that everything that group members are aware of they are able to "make sense" out of. It is, then, their experience of reality.

One reason why systems of shared meanings develop is because they enable us to achieve stability in our relationship to the world. Human beings differ from other animals in that our relationship to the environment is not given in our basic genetic or hereditary makeup. We have the capacity to adopt our basic biological equipment to a wide, continually changing range of activities and experiences. Berger and Luckmann call this our "world-openness" (p. 45). Because of it, we are highly adaptable, yet we lack the innate mechanism that could provide us with stability in our relationship to our environment. As Berger and Luckmann state, "if the human organism had to rely upon its own resources alone for existence, that existence would probably be chaotic" (p. 49). Therefore, the reason why human beings need a symbolic frame of reference for ordering social reality is because we are basically unstable in our relationship to the natural order.

Although systems of shared meanings are univeral features of all corporate social units, the content of each group's symbolic universe is unique. The discipline of anthropology is a celebration of this fact. Countless studies of human cultures throughout the world show that each group's system of shared meanings entails a particular and special delimitation from a vast range of possible ways of classifying and interpreting the world, and of imbuing it with meaning. The phenomological social scientist would go on to say that the closure achieved by the special symbolic universe of a society encapsulates its members. It wraps them within a kind of protective cocoon of orderliness and meaning that then shields them from unencumbered exposure to natural order (Hebb 1955).

The ideas that natural order is complex, awesome, mysterious, and terrifying to human beings, and that direct exposure to it would immobilize us, is a main theme in the writings of many phenomenological social scientists. The work of Ernest Becker (1973) exemplifies this approach. Becker writes that in creating man, "nature seems to have thrown caution to the winds. . . . She created an animal who has no defense against full perception of the external world, an animal completely open to experience" (p. 50). Unlike other animals, who live in the moment, man expands his inner self to include his own personal past. His curiosity and knowledge extend to past centuries and his fears of the future. "He lives," Becker writes, "not only in a territory, nor even on an entire planet, but in a galaxy, in a universe, and in dimensions beyond visible universes" (p. 51). This, and the certain knowledge of his own death, gives man an experiential burden that Becker calls "appalling" (p. 51).

Like Berger and Luckmann, Becker believes that a full understanding of our condition would drive us insane. We live in a world so filled with beauty, mystery, and terror that if we ever were to see it as it truly is, we would be paralyzed to act. To live in the world openly is to invite unbearable anxiety.

How, then, do we cope with this "appalling" burden. Becker believes that the fear is so haunting to us that it is the well-spring of much of our activity. In fact, he sees human culture and human character as creations that grow out of this fear. In order to deal with our burden, we invent and create the limitations of perceptions and the equanimity that are necessary for us to live. We do this collectively in the form of culture, and individually in the form of human personality. Human character and human culture allow us to achieve a kind of blind obliviousness through social games, psychological tricks, and personal and collective perceptions that are, Becker notes, "so far removed from the reality of our situation as to be forms of madness . . . agreed madness, shared madness, disguised and dignified madness, but madness all the same" (p. 27). He continues:

> Man cuts out for himself a manageable world: He throws himself into action uncritically, unthinkingly. He accepts the cultural programming that turns his nose where he is supposed to look; he doesn't bite the world off in one piece as a giant would, but in small manageable pieces, as a beaver does. He uses all kinds of techniques, which we call the "character defenses": he learns not to expose himself, not to stand out; he learns to embed himself in other-power, both of concrete persons and of things and cultural communities. The result is that he soon comes to exist in the imagined infallibility of the world around him (p. 23).

Thus, social order and human character traits work to support a grand illusion. We are literally driven away from reality and self-knowledge, and toward those things that support the lie of our character and the lie of our culture. As Kierkegaard thought, our character and our society are dual structures built to avoid perception of the "terror, perdition and nihilation that dwells next to every man" (as quoted in Becker, p. 70). It was in fact, this insight that led him to realize that the real task of modern psychiatry is to help persons to discover the structure that can best shield them from reality, to discover what he called "the most legitimate and effective foolishness" (as quoted in Becker, p. 270).

Courtesy Stigma

(From "Suspect's Family Lives as Outcasts," *San Francisco Chronicle*, May 15, 1981, a United Press item)

Ankara, Turkey. The mother of Mehmet Ali Agca, the terrorist accused of attempting to kill Pope John Paul

> **II, said her family has been outcast by those around them because of her son's crime. Muzayyen Agca, 50, and another of her sons, Adnan, 20, "are sorry for him [Mehmet] and we are amazed at what he has done."**

The social order is a public order, and because it is public, it is resistant to change. Douglas (1966) explains: "It [social order] has authority, since each is induced to assent because of the assent of others. But its public character makes its categories more rigid . . . a private person may revise his pattern of assumptions or not. It is a private matter. But cultural categories are public matters. They cannot so easily be subject to revision" (pp. 38–39). For this reason, the symbolic universe "hardens" and "thickens" in the process, assuming the appearance of an objective reality that is fixed and firm. In this way, it acquires the quality of being real. Its public character means that it confronts people as something "out there," independent of them and imbued with the power to prod them into acting and thinking in prescribed ways. We experience it as external and coercive, a stable, fixed, firm, and hard entity as real as the physical world. And yet, as we have seen, social order actually entails the creation of an illusion of order.

Within this view of human existence, everyday life is seen as consisting largely of ordering activities. The means by which human beings order experience are socially constructed and socially transmitted. They are the product of a socially created interpretation of the world. The phenomena of stigma must be understood within this activity and must be seen as a product of it. When seen in this light, we gain an important insight into why stigma is imperiling and what stigmas imperil, for the peril of stigma derives from its implications for the typifications we use to order and interpret the world.

The system of meanings that we share consists of typifications or recipes of the world that enable us to order and interpret it. These typifications are "taken for granted," in the sense that we experience no doubt about them until we encounter circumstances that call them into question. They are, in effect, invisible parts of routine everyday life. Our collectively shared views of the world can only be taken for granted as long as they are not challenged. When we are faced with challenges to the typifications that order our world, we are made aware simultaneously of the precariousness of what we otherwise experience as reality. Such challenges confront us with "marginal situations." These are what stigmas entail. Berger and Luckmann (1966) explain that stigma and deviance "constitute a 'night side' that keeps lurking ominously on the periphery of everyday consciousness.

Just because the 'night side' has its own reality, often enough of a sinister kind, it is a constant threat to the taken-for-granted, matter-of-fact, 'sane' reality of life in society. The thought keeps suggesting itself that, perhaps, the bright reality of everyday life is but an illusion, to be swallowed up at any moment by the bounding nightmare of the other, the night-side reality" (p. 91).

There is an additional point about marginal situations that must be understood if we are to appreciate fully what is involved in our affective reactions to stigma. Our reactions to marginal situations of all kinds are powerfully conditioned by the experience of death. Death is the marginal situation par excellence. It is the ultimate disruption of the way we order our lives. Thus, fear of death is the foundation of all threats to the normal ordering of experience. Schutz (1971) terms it the "fundamental anxiety" (p. 228). In this role, anxiety about death makes marginal situations of all kinds troubling. In death we see most clearly how it is that marginal situations cause people to call into question how people order their experience.

We are now in a position to understand better why stigmatized conditions are perilous and what they imperil. They cause disorientation to our typical ways of ordering the world. They call into question the validity of our system of shared meaning and the typifications they entail. The fear and anxiety, the powerful affect aroused in us by people who are maimed, deformed, disfigured, irrational, ill, demented, or mentally handicapped, in part arise from the fact that such conditions stand as stark reminders of the very things we devote so much of our individual and collective energies to shutting out, ignoring, and avoiding.

Doctor's Discretion

From Cohen, L., "Probe Finds Doctors Let Babies Die," *Hartford Courant*, September 10, 1981.

Doctors will do little, if anything, to save the lives of severely ill newborn babies with serious deformities if parents ask that the children be allowed to die, a state inquiry has concluded. Thayer Baldwin, Jr., Chief of the Bureau of Health System Regulation, . . . said he did not find a single physician who would go to great lengths to oppose a parental decision to decline treatment for babies with such problems as severe mental retardation or spinal bifida, a congenital birth defect that can cause paralysis and physical deformities. Baldwin said doctors occasionally withdraw from

a case if they disagree with the parental request, but said he could find no case of a doctor taking strong action to save a baby, such as requesting court protection.

This idea is expressed brilliantly in an essay on stigma by Paul Hunt (1966), a sufferer of muscular dystrophy. Hunt has spent all of his adult life in institutions among people like himself, who suffer from severe, often progressive physical disabilities. He has written about what he believes that he, as someone who is young and chronically disabled, symbolizes to society at large. He states that for the able-bodied, normal world, he is a symbol of many of the things they fear most, "tragedy, loss, dark and the unknown. Involuntarily we walk—or more often sit—in the valley of the shadow of death. Contact with us throws up in people's faces the fact of sickness and death in the world" (pp. 155–156). He continues: "No one likes to think of such things, which in themselves are an affront to all our aspirations and hopes. A deformed and paralyzed body attacks everyone's sense of well-being and invincibility. People do not want to acknowledge what disability affirms . . . . that life is tragic and we shall all soon be dead" (p. 156).

This insight leads Hunt to see an irony in our reactions to those disabled people who achieve contentment in life. When confronted with someone who is not only coping with tragic circumstances, but is positively contented with life, the able-bodied are strongly inclined to deny the reality of the adaptation. He writes: "The disabled person is simply making the best of a bad job, putting a good face on it . . . when it becomes obvious that there is also a genuine happiness, another defensive attitude is taken up. The 'unfortunate' person is assumed to have exceptional courage" (p. 148).

Such reactions, Hunt suggests, appear to be required by normal individuals to safeguard a particular set of values, where someone's sense of security depends on this being maintained. He writes that the normal person "almost wants the disabled person to suffer, as a confirmation that the values denied him are still worthy and important and good. If he shows no obvious signs of suffering, then he must challenge people whose own worth seems to them to be bound up with their more fortunate position in life" (p. 148).

Hunt's essay points up another facet of the threat that stigma can entail that clarifies further the complicated reactions we have to those we stigmatize. Central to Goffman's analysis of stigma (1963) is the idea that so-called normal people view stigmas as signs of moral defect. To be stigmatized is to be morally denigrated and tainted. Although this reaction may be justified in some cases (e.g., child molesting), it is puzzling why it should also occur in other cases, such as physical deformities, leprosy, sensory deficits, even mental disorders. As we have already noted in Chapter 2, recent work by experimental social psychologists on the "just world hypothesis" (Lerner and Miller, 1978) enables us to understand this puzzling attribution. People who are born deformed or who become maimed by disease or accident during their lives, those who inexplicably go insane or encounter misfortunes that leave them marked with abominations of the body or characterological blemishes can confront us with a direct challenge to our conception of the world as a just place. This conception is important because it enables the individual to confront the physical and social environment as if they were stable and orderly, thus, supporting a commitment to long range goals. In the face of such a challenge, we can abandon the idea that the world is just and that life is fair, or we can attribute qualities to the victim which make his or her misfortune seem deserved. Because the belief in a just world is so important to other facets of our life, we may be tempted instead to believe that the person is evil or immoral, and, therefore, deserving of his or her fate. This attribution enables us to preserve our view of the world as just and still account for the individual's unhappy plight.

We do not wish to imply that the only reason why attributions of immorality are made to the stigmatized is because of our belief in a just world. Another important reason has to do with the process by which systems of shared meanings, once developed, are given legitimacy. According to Berger and Luckmann (1966), each new generation is confronted with established patterns developed by past generations as "things" that are external and coercive. The generation that derived the patterns that our generation has learned, understands the functional utility of the patterns they invited because they have had a direct experience with the conditions or problems that required its creation in the first place. To the extent that the pattern that is described actually solves the problem, subsequent generations will have no knowledge of the original problem, and this fact may prompt those who learn it to wonder why they must abide by it. To deal with this, each generation tends to imbue established patterns with moral legitimacy, claiming in effect that its particular way of doing things is not only the way things are to be done in its domain, but also the right way to do them. Thus, systems of shared meanings are heavily imbued with moral legitimacy. Consequently, anything that threatens this system of meanings is vulnerable to an attribution of immorality. Stigma, as matter out of place in a system of shared meanings, is therefore likely to be imbued with such an attribution.

We return to our original questions: Why do people feel imperiled by stigma and what do stigmas imperil? One answer to these questions is that certain stigmatizing conditions can entail threats to our physical well-being. More important, however, are the threats that stigmatizing marks entail for our psychological and social well-being. These threats grow out of universal human needs to envelop ourselves in the protective wrapping of culture and character traits in order to be shielded from unencumbered exposure to natural order. People who are deformed, disabled, irrational, disfigured, or deviant in other ways create marginal situations that call into question our most taken-for-granted understanding of the world. They can remind us that our secure experience of everyday reality is illusory. Stigmas, therefore, confront us with some of the most perplexing and troubling questions about meaning and human existence.

SOCIAL DEFINITIONS AND AUDIENCE REACTIONS

The reactions of audiences of observers to individuals who possess qualities and traits that are stigmatizing are central to the experience of being a marked person. In this section we discuss sociological research and writing about the social determinants of people's sensitivities toward the presence of stigma in their midst, and of people's tolerance for those whom they have marked.

To begin with, it is important to appreciate the fact that people's reactions to traits and qualities that can mark a person are not automatic. They are problematic. Sociological studies of rule-violating behavior in our society provide strong support for this assertion. For example, studies of such diverse forms of deviant behavior as mental illness, crime, deafness, blindness, obesity, speech impediments, juvenile delinquency, alcoholism, and drug abuse show that because a person engages in the behavior in question or possesses the relevant trait or attribute is no guarantee that he or she will be labeled as deviant or be stigmatized because of it. In fact, paradoxically, the evidence suggests that a vast majority of instances of rule violations that occur are ignored, normalized, disregarded, or are in other ways not attended to, so that most persons exhibiting the behavior or possessing the relevant trait are perceived and dealt with as ordinary people would be treated. Results of sociological studies of mental illness illustrate this point.

In a summary of such studies, Horwitz (1982) cites the results of epidemiological surveys in which community members were asked whether they have experienced various thoughts, feelings, and behaviors that psychiatrists consider symptomatic of mental disorders. These studies typically show that in the United States, about 20 percent of the general population can be diagnosed as "severely" psychiatrically impaired, and that an additional 50 percent have symptoms that psychiatrists would diagnose to be indicative of "mild or moderate" instances of mental illness. From these studies, Horwitz calculates that there are fourteen unlabeled cases in the community that would be labeled as mental illness by a psychiatrist for every case that is actually labeled by the public.

In other research, ordinary community members were asked to make judgments about hypothetical case studies of people portrayed as showing signs and symptoms of different types of mental disorders, such as paranoid schizophrenia, simple schizophrenia, alcoholism, classical anxiety neurosis, character disorders, and phobias. Subjects were asked to read accounts of people whose behavior accords with each type of disorder and to state if they regard the person as mentally ill. These studies show that most lay people do regard the paranoid schizophrenic as mentally ill, but that only two-thirds of them rate the simple schizophrenic in this way. Similarly, only half regard the alcoholic as mentally ill, and far less than half regard the person with an anxiety neurosis, a character disorder, or a phobia as mentally ill.

There Goes The Neighborhood

From Geist, W. E., "Housing a Home: Neighbors Balk at Residence for Retarded," *New York Times*, February 2, 1982.

As part of a nationwide trend, the state of New Jersey is moving 4,000 mentally retarded people out of institutions into residential neighborhoods. Group homes for mentally handicapped people are established as discreetly as possible, with neighbors not notified till after the purchase of a home is final. This is followed by carefully orchestrated informational meetings with video-tape presentations, audiences full of sympathizers and plenty of complimentary coffee. . . . Despite their best efforts, organizers say, they find bringing a group house for the mentally retarded into a quiet, suburban neighborhood about as inconspicuous as bringing in a 747 with the wheels up.

> **[In one representative community there was considerable resistance to the purchase of a house to be used for mentally retarded children.] "This will destroy the character of the neighborhood," said Isabel Palmer, who lives across the street.**
>
> **"It is highhanded," said her husband, Jack. "They did not listen to our objections. They do not care what we think."**
>
> **"It may be good for the retarded people," said another neighbor, "but they should not put it in a nice neighborhood like this."**
>
> **"This is big brother coming in," another said. "We have our life savings tied up in our home, and we rely on zoning to protect our investment. If this were any other business or even a boarding house, they couldn't locate here."**
>
> **Vincent O'Neill told of his 33-year-old son, who lives in such a home. "It has been the answer to our prayers. We worried that when we passed on, he would lie on the floor of an institution with no one concerned. Now he lives five minutes from us in a home, a real home, and we can drop in to see him."**
>
> **Nina Deutz, a neighbor who supports the home, said she had seen New Providence residents fight such things as the coming of a McDonalds' restaurant and a local diner. "Those people are eating hamburgers now and drinking coffee at the diner," she said. "This, too, will blow over."**
>
> **"Something like this," said another neighbor who supports the coming of the group home, "makes people ask themselves questions about themselves that they would rather go through life not asking, let alone having to answer."**

These data indicate that although all groups in our society have labels for people who act in mentally aberrant ways, the actual application of these labels to particular individuals is problematic. Only a few of the behaviors that eventually will be labeled as mental illness are initially seen to be clear signs of a psychiatric disturbance. Instead, symptoms of mental disorders are usually vague, ambiguous, and open to different interpretations. The recognition of mental disorders is not a simple process, then, but one that becomes crystallized only after a complex series of interpretations have been made.

Thus, the possession of a trait or quality that may be stigmatizing is no guarantee that the possessor will be marked because of it. It is because of this fact that the distinction explained in Chapter 1 between the marked and the markable is made. This distinction raises a number of important questions. Under what conditions are members of a group most likely to mark others and why? Among all those who might be marked, who is most likely to be the target of audience disapprobation and why? Sociological studies of deviant behavior supply some answers to these questions.

Commonality of the Marking Condition

First, different groups use different standards in judging the actions of their members. These standards, often implicit, derive in part from the prevalence of the phenomenon that is being judged and the extent of participation and involvement in it by members of the group as a whole. Wilkins (1965) points out that, in general, the more common a phenomenon is within a group, the greater the amount of deviation from a hypothetical standard a particular case of deviancy will have to be in order for it to prompt a noticeable reaction from group members. For example, even mildly aberrant behavior by a previously institutionalized mental patient in a community that has had little exposure to such persons can prompt stern public reactions (Cumming and Cumming 1957), whereas in communities with a great deal of exposure to such people, such as Geel in Belgium (Roosens 1979), even extreme behavior will go unnoticed, with public disapproval reserved for only the most bizarre and disruptive kinds of actions. Similarly, the standards that are used to judge the behavior of others will depend in part on the degree of participation by community members in the behavior in question. For instance, we would hypothesize that in a community in which most members consume a large amount of alcohol, the quantity of alcohol that would have to be consumed by someone before he or she would be marked as alcoholic is probably much greater than in communities in which moderation or abstinence is the norm.

Group Boundary Maintenance

A second factor hypothesized to affect public sensitivity toward deviant behavior involves the phenomenon of group boundary maintenance. Much has been written about how groups and other social collectivities preserve, maintain, and impart to members the sense of special identity that makes the group a meaningful, stable, and coherent point of reference. Among sociologists, it was Durkheim (1895) who first pointed out that the deviant can have an important role in accomplishing these tasks, and his insights, in turn, provide us with some clues for understanding audience reactions to deviancy.

Durkheim claimed that deviancy could unify a community. He stated that the deviant person is someone who has violated rules of conduct that the rest of the community holds in high respect, and that when its members come together to express their indignation toward the offender, they experience a stronger bond of social solidarity than had previously existed. In other words, in the process of identifying someone as deviant, community members are drawn into more frequent and intense interaction with each other, leading to a condition in which the personal feelings of particular individuals are joined together to form a heightened sense of common morality.

Erikson (1966) has explored the broader implications of this insight for audience reactions toward deviancy. In his analysis of witch trials in the American Puritan colonies, he presents the following argument. To its members, each community or group occupies a unique place in the world, having its own special niche, identity, and way of life. To preserve this uniqueness, Erikson explains, it is essential for group members to be able to control the "fluctuation of its constituent parts so that the whole retains a limited range of activity, a given pattern of constancy and stability, within the larger environment" (p. 10). As the group succeeds in doing this, its members will tend to confine themselves to a particular radius of action and to regard any conduct that drifts outside of that radius as inappropriate or immoral. He writes, "Human behavior can vary over an enormous range, but each community draws a symbolic set of parentheses around a certain segment of that range and limits its own activities within that narrower zone," so that "the group retains a kind of cultural integrity, a voluntary restriction on its own potential for experience, beyond that which is strictly required for accommodation to the environment" (p. 10).

But how does a community manage to do this? Erikson believes that group members cannot acquire a clear sense of their own specialness unless they are able to learn something about what lies beyond the margins of their own groups. Presumably this can be done in a number of ways: by learning about other cultures and groups through travel, reading, or word of mouth; or by joining other groups for a time to learn about them. Another important way in which this knowledge is gained is through the deviant behavior of group members. He explains: "The interactions which do the most effective job of locating and publicizing the group's outer edges seem to be those which take place between deviant persons on the one side and official agents of the community on the other. The deviant is a person whose actions have gone outside of the margins of the group, and when the community calls him to account for that vagrancy it is making a statement about where the nature and placement of its boundaries are" (p. 11). By marking where the outer edges of group life are, deviancy gives the inner structure its special character and, hence, reinforces the framework within which people who belong to the group gain a sense of their own cultural identity.

Between the Rock and the Hard Place at Dear Old Ivy

From Nix, Crystal, "Race Relations at Princeton: Balancing Two Worlds," *The Daily Princetonian*, January 7, 1983.

The phone call I made in desperation last winter is still embedded in my mind. "Mom can you come get me? I can't take it here any longer. I'm getting out."

Amidst jumbled accounts of recent events and half-thought out plans to transfer, I managed to convey the hurt, frustration, and anger I felt at the racial dynamics at Princeton. Earlier in the day, I had had another in a series of run-ins with the type of student who implied my involvement with white-dominated organizations and my friendships with whites strongly suggested that I was "selling out" the black community.

The week before I went home with tears of rage over the three hours I spent trying to explain to a disbelieving white student the real political, economic, and social factors that continue to oppress black people and prevent blacks from rising in society one hundred years after the end of slavery. . . . Those experiences have stayed with me, largely because they are indicative of the rock and the hard place I have found myself between as I thread through both the black and white worlds at Princeton. . . . Getting blacks and whites together is only half the battle. Real interaction comes with a price, and for some, the price may be too high. . . .

A great many white students here are perfectly willing to be friends with blacks, and thus are confused and frustrated about the lack of interaction. The problem is that many of these individuals are only willing to interact on their own terms . . . . A friend of mine

> **never really noticed that whenever we did things together it was always in her predominantly white environment, at mostly white dinner tables or parties, listening to her music. . . .**
>
> **Real interaction, that is, interaction that is mutual rather than one sided, invariably means that certain assumptions will be challenged, experiences will be broadened, and common bonds will be found and strengthened. . . . For both blacks and whites, real interaction means being vulnerable, going to an unfamiliar and perhaps uncomfortable environment, risking being hurt and trying again even if after being slapped in the face. . . . I can understand why blacks and whites sit around, waiting for someone else to take the first step. But I also know how counterproductive sitting around really is. The only way anything is going to change is if we all stop making excuses and take upon ourselves the responsibility to reach out.**

However, group boundary lines, once marked, are seldom immutably fixed. They shift and blur with time and must be redrawn periodically in an ongoing process that never ceases, as long as the group persists. This fact raises a question that brings us to the issue of explaining variations in audience reactions to stigma. The analysis raises the possibility that forces may operate within the social structure of a group by which offenders are recruited and moved to the boundary lines of the group precisely for the purpose of clarifying where these boundary lines are. Erikson's analysis of witch trials leads us to predict that group members will become vigilant about the behavior of miscreants at those moments in a group's history when its boundary lines have become most blurred and indistinct, and at times when the specialness of the group is most threatened. It is at such times that group members are likely to become alert about deviancy, actively seeking it out and sanctioning it publicly. Erikson shows that trials for religious heresy occurred at moments of boundary crisis in the Puritan colonies, and that the issues around which accusations were made and trials conducted entailed moral and value issues that were central to the Puritan identity and that had begun to blur.

In addition to Erikson's analysis, the data of a number of studies provide support for this idea. Lauderdale (1976) conducted an experimental study of the rejection of a deviant by group members. This problem was studied under two conditions, one in which the continuation of the group was threatened, the other when it was not. In both instances the degree of deviation of a confederate from the norms of the group was the same. This procedure enabled Lauderdale to determine the degree and severity of rejection of the same amount of deviation under different conditions of threat to the persistence of the group (i.e., the boundary crises). He demonstrates that the designation of behavior as deviant by group members, as well as the extent of subsequent rejection, is a consequence of shifts that occur in the behavior of group members in response to perceived threats to its existence. He finds that deviants are more severely rejected and stigmatized following an external threat to the persistence of the group than when no such threat exists. Also, his analysis of the process of stigmatization indicates that rejection of the deviant leads to an initial loss of group solidarity, which is then quickly reestablished through the recreation of a clear group boundary line, and with it a movement of this boundary line away from the deviant. While it is not clear why this happens, the fact that it does suggests the need for some revisions of Erikson's original thesis that rejection of the deviant enhances solidarity directly. Lauderdale's findings suggest that this may be true in the long run, but the initial responses of group members leads to an immediate loss of group solidarity.

Inveriarity (1976) has attempted to study the Erikson hypothesis in a different way. He points out that disruptions of solidarity in a group, i.e., boundary crises, lead to increased intolerance for deviancy, and that this is manifested in a heightened repression of deviancy. He attempts to demonstrate this through a study of populism and lynching in Louisiana from 1889 to 1896. Southern whites in the 1890s experienced a boundary crisis analogous to that of the Puritans in Massachusetts during the seventeenth century. Inveriarity's hypothesis is that since the parishes having the highest level of solidarity suffered the most from the Populist movement, they would be the ones that would have the greatest number of lynchings. The data he compiles generally support this prediction.

A study by Davies (1982) examines the relationship between boundary crises and vigilance toward sexual deviancy. He hypothesized that the strong taboos against homosexuality, bestiality, and transvestism that arise periodically in Western societies are explained as a result of attempts to establish and define strong ethnic, religious, or institutional boundaries. Davies argues that when religious, military, or political leaders perceive a decline in the cohesiveness and orderliness of the group, nation, or armies that they lead, they are inclined, in consequence, to impose harsh penalties on forms of sexual behavior that break social or symbolic boundaries. Davies speculates that this may be because they have adopted a code of belief and conduct that emphasizes the need to maintain boundaries of all kinds, including those between humans and animals and between males and females, and because they feel that the restoration of group solidarity is impeded by the formation of sexual relationships that cut across the internal and external boundaries of their group or organization. The pattern he reports is demonstrated to have existed in such diverse groups as Old Testament Jews, the Parsees, ancient Greek states and their armies, early and medieval Christians, the German National Socialist movement, and the modern British armed forces.

In summary, we see that one determinant of an audience's tendency to stigmatize those who possess deviant traits or attributes is the clarity of the boundary lines that set the group off from the remainder of the world and give it its special identity and niche in cultural space. Sociological theory and research on the maintenance of group boundaries lead us to expect that group members will be least tolerant of those possessing such traits and attributes at those moments in a group's history when its particular boundary lines are least clear and distinct. When a group's sense of specialness declines, or when its existence is perceived as threatened, members of the group will become vigilant about deviant attributes and qualities, and will tend to treat the people they single out for marking in a harsh and repressive fashion.

The studies we have just reviewed highlight a facet of the labeling process that deserves emphasis in any analysis of audience reactions to stigmatizing conditions. All of these studies make it clear that in many cases of stigma, especially those involving accusations of witchcraft and heresy, the marking process is political in character. We do not use the term *political* in the narrow sense of rule by government, even though governments may be involved in stigmatizing people. We use it in a broader sense to mean efforts by individuals and groups of people to gain control over others. This idea, that the motivation for labeling someone as deviant may arise from a desire to gain or maintain social position and power over them, is noted and discussed by such people as Schur (1980), Lauderdale (1980), Rock (1977), Quinney (1977), Goffman (1969), and Szasz (1961). There is also a growing body of research that shows how the political process, broadly defined, is involved in the impetus to label and repress.

A particularly revealing example of this facet of the marking process is presented in Bevers' doctoral dissertation (1982) on old age and witchcraft in early modern Europe. His study attempts to explain the affinity between witchcraft and old age in women. He argues that witch denunciations often manifested a serious conflict of interest between poor, older women and better off, younger villagers. The older women were unable to fend for themselves and depended upon young villagers for support. When this support was not forthcoming, the older women resorted to playing upon villagers' beliefs about magic in order to create the illusion that they could exercise power over the younger villagers. The villagers, in turn, interpreted these appeals to magic as an attempt by the women to overturn the traditional patriarchical hierarchy that made middle-age men the heads of households and the final authority within the village. To rid themselves of this problem, the beliefs about magical powers that the women had fostered initially were elaborated by the younger villagers into widespread fears and suspicions about their ability to perform witchcraft. In this way, cantankerous old women were transformed into "the vanguard of Satan's fifth column" some of whom actively embraced the role of witch and acted it out.

This example reveals the political character of the marking process. It also highlights a facet of relationships between the marked and their markers which is not always appreciated. Just as markers may be motivated by political considerations to label someone as deviant, so, too, can marked people use their stigma to gain advantage over others and to define their own identity when it becomes indistinct. This idea is presented by Barth (1969) in his essay on ethnic groups and boundaries, but has not been otherwise explored in the literature on the sociology of deviancy.

Slaughtering the Untouchables

From Auerbach, S., "Killers Stalk India's Untouchables," *The Washington Post*, January 4, 1982.

India ended 1981 with its second massacre of untouchables in six weeks, . . . in the latest attack, four or five armed men at dusk Wednesday entered the village of Adhofur . . . and started shooting at *Harijans*. In fifteen minutes, they killed ten people—including five women and two children—and severely wounded two others. . . .The killings . . . followed by exactly six weeks the November 18 unprovoked daylight slaying of 24 untouchables . . . 18 miles to the north.

It remains unclear what caused the raids on the untouchables, although they are believed to be related to some effort by low-caste Hindus to keep the Harijans in their place. . . .

> **An editorial in the *Times of India* . . . said attacks on untouchables are increasing because the Harijans have become "more assertive and organized than they have ever been in their long and wretched history. That they should have the gall to question their lowly status and even seek to raise it is more than the hidebound upper classes can bear."**

The Economy and Public Tolerance for Deviancy

Sociological research suggests that the ebb and flow of the economy in advanced industrial nations has a major impact on the amount of deviancy that occurs. When there are economic hard times, rates of mental illness tend to go up, as do suicides, homicides and certain other types of violent crimes, and certain types of property crime. There is also an increase in stress-related disorders. Obversely, when economic conditions improve, the rates of many pathological forms of social behavior tend to level off or decrease.

The effect, if any, that the economy may have on vigilance toward and tolerance for deviancy among members of a community is not as well understood, but there are good reasons to believe that the ebb and flow of the economy might affect these things. One reason is related to our previous point that stigmas are perceived as imperiling. The relationship between this fact and cycles of the economy is as follows. Economic hardships are often interpreted by people as indicative of a decline in the social stability of a society. We have already shown that boundary crises, which are occasioned by a real or perceived decline in social stability, tend to heighten public vigilance and intolerance toward deviancy. We would, therefore, expect greater vigilance and harsher reactions toward deviancy during periods of economic decline then during periods of economic prosperity.

Economic cycles may also affect public reactions toward the stigmatized because of their impact on the amount of stress experienced by members of the society. As economic conditions worsen, levels of stress in the community tend to increase. Stress in turn, presumably affects public tolerance for deviancy. Adversely, we would hypothesize that as stress increases, public sensitivity to aberrant and disruptive behavior would heighten, charitable impulses would wane, the capacity of individuals to tolerate dependent behavior would diminish, and tendencies toward scapegoating would increase. As a result, during economic hard times, there should be a heightening of intolerance and a greater hostility toward marginal people, and with it a greater tendency to mark with stigma those who were previously accepted or whose behavior had hitherto been tolerated.

A third reason for supposing that economic cycles might affect public reactions toward the stigmatized is more narrowly materialistic. In some cases, people who possess traits or attributes that can mark them make special economic demands on those from whom they draw economic support. Historically, the severely disabled, the mentally handicapped, and the psychiatrically impaired have been economically marginal and unable to gain employment to support themselves. In addition, some of these conditions entail heavy costs for medical care, special education, therapy, and the like. All of this places a financial strain on "normal" individuals, as well as the community at large. We would, therefore, hypothesize that the ability and willingness of individuals and groups to meet these costs will be adversely affected by worsening economic conditions.

All of these considerations lead to the prediction that the ebb and flow of the economy is likely to have an effect on public sensitivities toward and reactions to people who possess qualities, attributes, and traits that can mark them as stigmatized. As economic conditions worsen, members of society are apt to become more vigilant in seeking out deviancy, more repressive in their treatment of such people, and less able or willing to look after them economically. Conversely, as economic conditions improve and unemployment declines, we would expect the amount of stress in the community to lessen, and with this, a lowering in the stringency of standards used to evaluate the behavior of others. In addition, with increasing financial levels, there should also be a greater willingness by the community and its members to provide economic support for marginal persons. Therefore, we would expect less of a tendency to label behavior as deviant during periods of economic expansion. Moreover, such tolerance is apt to be heightened if a labor shortage accompanies the expansion of the economy. Historically, when the surplus labor force shrinks, or disappears entirely, the search for new sources of labor leads employers to seek out persons who are economically marginal, among them persons who are vulnerable to stigmatization. As such people are drawn into the labor force, their social value increases, and there ought to occur an increase in public acceptance of them.

Although versions of these hypotheses appear in the sociological literature on mental illness, mental retardation, physical disability, and crime, there is a paucity of evidence pertaining to it. Much of the evidence is anecdotal or impressionistic, making it impossible at this time to assess the validity of the hypothesis. Farber (1968) suggests that public attitudes toward the mentally handicapped vary in part as a function of the size of the surplus labor force in relation to the demand for labor. Elsewhere, Scott (1969) has argued that the same is true for the blind. The impression is that mentally handicapped and blind people of working age have been able to make more significant inroads into the community and to become more meaningful actors in it during periods of an acute labor shortage than during periods of labor surplus. For example, during World War II in New York, it is reported that the demand for labor was so great that employers openly advertised for blind and other physically handicapped people to apply for job vacancies, and those who did apply regard this period as a kind of halcyon era for them, not only in terms of employment but general acceptance as well (Chevigny and Braverman 1950).

The most systematic test of this hypothesis appears in the work of Brenner (1973), who studied the relationship between the state of the economy and the rates of admission to psychiatric hospitals. He reports that instabilities in the national economy have been the single most important source of fluctuation in mental hospital admissions for the past one hundred and seventy five years, and that there is evidence to suggest that the impact of the economy has been even greater in the two decades prior to his study. In attempting to account for this relationship, Brenner considers several hypotheses, among them the possibility that the relative intolerance for mental illness by the family and community increases during periods of unemployment. Through careful analysis of the data, he concludes that "neither the need for the financial wherewithal for subsistence, nor intolerance of psychiatric symptoms, nor even actual psychiatric symptoms are *by themselves* [italics added] sufficient to explain the entire relation between economic change and mental hospitalization" (p. 199). He goes on to acknowledge, however, that the evidence indicates that these factors do play "some part in a multicausal sequence whereby an economic downswing serves to increase mental hospital admissions" (p. 199). That is, his data show that although intolerance alone cannot account for the variance associated with hospitalization (his data suggest that social stress is a better explanation for it), they do show that intolerance is a factor in the high correlation he reports between hospitalization and unemployment.

Thus far, we have argued that the main effect of economic downswings on public tolerance for stigmas is to decrease it and of economic upswings to increase it. Although we believe that this is generally true, it is necessary to point out that the ebb and flow of the economy may not affect public attitudes toward all stigmatized groups in the same way. For example, while an upswing in the economy, coupled with a labor shortage, may improve the lot of those whose stigma is based on abominations of the body, it can have an opposite effect on those whose stigma is based on moral perversion. The treatment of criminals supports this assertion. In a study of vagrancy laws, Chambliss (1964) established that, historically, such laws have or have not been enforced, depending upon the state of general labor conditions. The first vagrancy laws were enacted in the context of a labor shortage and were enforced in such a way as to compel serfs to remain with or return to the landowners who owned them. Serfs became vagrants because they wished to flee the landowners who enslaved them. Landowners wanted to keep them because they could exploit this source of cheap labor instead of turning to free laborers, whose wages were rising sharply. Chambliss goes on to show that enforcement of such laws underwent a dormant period when the labor shortage eased and then stiffened again during a new labor shortage.

Research by Scott and Scull (1980) suggests that in another respect public attitudes and reactions toward criminals are akin to those hypothesized to exist for other stigmatized groups. Studying the relationship between penal reform efforts and the surplus labor force, they show that, historically, penal practices have moved back and forth between repression and reform, and that the fluctuations are linked to the ebb and flow of the economy. Specifically, they show that society's treatment of its criminals during any given period of time is a function of the size of the surplus labor force at that time and, related to it, the existing demand for labor. During periods when the surplus labor force is large and the demand for labor small, the methods employed for dealing with criminals tend to be brutal and repressive; conversely, when the labor surplus is small or nonexistent and the demand for labor is large, social reform movements develop that emphasize what are said to be more humane, considerate methods of treatment and care, i.e., rehabilitation through work. Two mechanisms are seen as linking economic conditions to dominant penal practices. The first is direct, by virtue of the fact that criminals comprise a "captive" group that can serve as a source of labor to be exploited during periods of economic growth, and controlled and repressed during periods of social unrest accompanying downswings in the economic cycle. The second is indirect, by virtue of the effect that downswings and labor surpluses have on public attitudes about the value of human life.

A great deal of research remains to be done before we will be in a position to assess adequately the hypotheses set forth about the impact of economic activity on public sensitivities and reactions toward stigmas. The hypothesized relationship seems plausible, and it would be surprising if research were to show that swings in the economy have *no* impact on audience responses to stigma. At the same time we suspect that the impact is neither simple nor straight-forward. It is likely that economic activity has an impact on different audiences in different ways and affects different stigmatized people in different ways. For now, the only conclusion that can be safely drawn is that the economy has a variable but important affect on public sensitivity to, and reactions toward, persons possessing markable traits and attributes.

The Normative Implications of Deviant Behavior

A fourth factor that sociologists hypothesize affects the way audiences of observers evaluate those they have marked involves the implications that the marked person's behavior may have for the normative structure of the society. Gusfield (1967) has pointed out that the behavioral expectancies of a person who is judged to be deviant derive from the normative structure of the group to which he or she belongs. Because the actual behavior of the person who has been stigmatized as deviant will have different implications for sustaining the norms of the group, we can expect public reactions toward such persons to be shaped according to public perceptions of what these implications are thought to be. Gusfield has distinguished between deviants who are "repentant," those who are judged to be "ill," and those who are "the enemy."

The repentant deviant is one who acknowledges a fall from grace, and by that fact confirms the validity of the normative system his behavior has transgressed. The alcoholic who makes a genuine effort to reform, the obese person who diets, the felon who confesses to the error of his or her ways, or the reformed drug addict are all examples.

When Gusfield wrote his essay, he had in mind such deviants as criminals, the mentally ill, substance abusers, and other persons whose behavior violates the behavioral norms of a group. Gusfield's insight about the normative structure can also be applied to the rehabilitation of the physically handicapped. In our society, a part of the content of a rehabilitation program is derived from the dominant normative structure, and success in rehabilitation can be seen as affirming that system of values. For example, one hallmark of successful rehabilitation of the blind is independence in activities of everyday life, such as being able to get about in one's environment without help from other people. The ability to teach people who are blind to navigate independently in their communities is no easy task. Not everyone is able to learn it, and those who do still have difficulty in unfamiliar environments. An alternative would be to provide sighted guides to escort people about, a solution that is accepted as perfectly proper in other countries, including England. In America, this idea has never been accepted. The American value on independence and personal autonomy dictates the content of this facet of rehabilitation and one could make the same point with respect to the stress on employment, good grooming, sociability, independence, and a good public appearance as other features of a successful rehabilitation program. Thus, the norms of the dominant society powerfully affect the way in which we structure our rehabilitation efforts and the specific content we give to them.

The ordinary public reaction to deviants who are repentant and to those who become rehabilitated is approbation. This is true even for the one who convincingly tries but fails to achieve or falls short of a full return to grace. Although the acclaim may be less, the general reaction is one of approval, because the stigmatized person's behavior is perceived as sustaining the norm.

Another category of deviance consists of those whose stigma has been redefined from a sin to a sickness or medical disease. Transforming societal definitions of a disorder from moral transgression to medical disorder can change public reactions to the afflicted persons. It does this by transforming the norm-sustaining implications of the behavior. If a condition like alcoholism is viewed as a sin, the failure of the alcoholic to become reformed undermines the dominant value system of the group. However, by redefining alcoholism as a medical disorder, the norm-sustaining implications of a person's failure to stop drinking are now somewhat defused. The fact that a person with this disease continues to drink will then have less serious implications for the basic normative system. In this regard, it is interesting to note that in recent history, in such domains of deviancy as mental illness, alcoholism, drug abuse, gambling, overeating, and sexual aberrations, efforts have been undertaken to define these disorders as medical illnesses or diseases, rather than due to moral lapses or failures of will power and self-control. A classic example of this is witchcraft. As Szasz (1961) argues and Bever (1983) demonstrates in detail, one way in which authorities managed to control an epidemic of witch trials in Europe during the Middle Ages was by persuading church officials and other prosecutors of witches that many of the people who were being accused of witchcraft were not witches at all, but old people (almost all of them women) who were actually suffering from dementia. By persuading others that so-called witchcraft was actually the result of dementia rather than demonism, they were able to remove the destructive implications of the phenomenon for the normative structure of society at that time.

Finally, the deviant who is an "enemy" is one who, apparently by choice, refuses to be repentant or to uphold and sustain society's norms through his or her behavior. Examples include the mentally ill or alcoholic individual who refuses treatment, the physically handicapped person who refuses rehabilitation programs from which he or she could benefit, the facially disfigured person who refuses plastic surgery to correct the problem, and the repeating criminal. The disapprobation that is reserved for such people stems from the fact that their behavior and actions are viewed as heretical, precisely because they are interpreted as undermining or flaunting societal norms.

Gusfield's theory (1967) provides a useful way of understanding variations in the ways conventional members of society evaluate and respond to people who they have signified as deviant, including people with the same affliction who are accorded different kinds of treatments.

We have looked at some of the factors that sociological theory and research show to be related to public vigilance and reactions to deviancy. We make no claim that our list is exhaustive. Our purpose has not been to develop a formal theory of audience reactions to deviancy, but to sensitize the reader to the ways in which social and cultural contexts impinge upon the face-to-face interactions of marked relationships. We have done this by citing just a few of the variables that are involved and reviewing some of the empirical research pertaining to them.

Social Correlates of the Marking Process

Sociological research indicates that there are notable differences in the tolerance for deviancy among different categories of people comprising audiences of observers. The most systematic and complete research on this subject has been done on mental illness. Horwitz (1982), has cogently summarized this research. He reports that there are significant differences in the tendency of different audiences of observers to label behavior as mental illness. For example, audiences of professional experts are much more likely to label behavior as deviant than are audiences of lay people. Among lay people, research shows that the tendency to label people as mentally ill varies directly with the relational and cultural distance between the observer and the actor. Finally, he reports that the sex, ethnicity, and social class position of markers and of the marked person all have an impact on the amount of deviancy that is labeled and who is labeled. This section of the chapter summarizes Horwitz's main findings.

Labeling of Deviancy among Professional Audiences

Studies of mental illness show that, almost without exception, labeling rather than denial is the response of recognized mental health professionals to signs of unusual or aberrant behavior. Studies show that mental health professionals designate as mental illness virtually all cases that come to their attention. This is true, Horwitz points out, at every stage of the organizational processing of the mentally ill person, from initial contacts with police or social workers, to psychiatric admitting interviews and the screening process, to commitment procedures and in-treatment as well. Studies show that persons who are recognized professionals in mental health routinely presume that individuals who have been referred to them by others or who come to them on their own initiative are mentally ill, and that the intent of initial interviews is not to ascertain if this is true, but to discover the indications, signs, and symptoms that confirm their presuppositions.

Horwitz goes on to point out that not all members of a professional audience are equally disposed to label people as mentally ill. For example, psychiatrists, more than other mental health professionals, seem inclined to diagnose the people they see as mentally ill, and there is evidence to suggest that as the cultural distance (as measured by the acquaintance of the psychiatrist with the culture of the patient) between the mental health professional and the patient increases, the tendency to label mental illness also grows.

An important qualification to this generalization is required. The tendency of professionals to respond to signs of aberrant behavior by facile psychiatric labeling occurs only in contexts in which there is no socially sanctioned reason to deny the existence of mental illness. Horowitz points out that in the military, mental health professionals react entirely differently than they do in civilian settings. Military psychiatrists are more likely to find sanity rather than mental illness, since a label of mental illness can lead to discharge or the avoidance of combat. The important role of context in diagnosis is also evident in the results of Rosenhan's study (1973) of pseudopatients. His work supports Horwitz's basic assertion that professionals routinely assume mental illness, and, in his follow-up study he shows how powerfully a change in context can alter the tendency of professionals to diagnose people presented for commitment whom they would otherwise have diagnosed as mentally ill.

This relative tendency of professionals to label attributes, qualities, and traits as deviant that we see in the case of mental illness is also apparent in certain other types of stigma, such as physical disabilities. To most lay people, being blind or going blind means a complete or nearly complete absence of vision. Professional workers for the blind employ different, less stringent criteria to make a determination of blindness. They use a technical administrative definition that is based upon opthamological measures of visual acuity and/or range of vision loss, derived largely to ensure the creation of a large enough population of "blind" people to justify large public expenditures on their behalf. As a result, lay people who recognize that they have trouble seeing are often surprised and dismayed to be told by medical or social service professionals that they are "blind," because their visual acuity has dropped below the technically defined level for determining eligibility for services. The same is true for the problem of deafness, and it does not seem implausible to argue that it may also apply to such other conditions as mental retardation or learning disabilities.

The Recognition of Deviancy in the Lay Community

Horwitz reports that lay people are much less likely than professionals to recognize and label mental disorders. He contends, "while professionals routinely label individuals as mentally disturbed, the typical lay response is to deny, rather than label, particular cases of mental illness" (p. 52).

Lay people are less likely than professionals to label individuals as mentally ill, but almost all people who are regarded as mentally disordered are initially labeled by a member of the lay community. These facts lead us to consider the conditions under which the labeling of mental disorders occurs.

One variable that predicts whether or not an individual will be viewed as mentally ill is the degree of social distance between him and the audience making the judgment about his behavior. Social distance refers to the degree of familiarity an observer has with the actor; that is, the degree to which life experiences, norms, values, and world views are shared. Horwitz identifies two components of social distance—relational distance and cultural distance. Relational distance means the degree of interpersonal involvement between people, as indicated by such things as the scope, frequency, length, and intensity of their interactions. By this definition, an individual's family and kin are at the closest relational distance, followed by friends, neighbors, acquaintances, and then strangers. By cultural distance he means the extent to which individuals share such characteristics as ethnicity, social class, and religion. He summarizes the research on both of these factors in the following propositions.

With respect to relational distance, he reports that the tendency to label individuals as mentally ill appears to vary directly with the relational distance between the observer and the actor. That is, people at a close relational distance typically deny or normalize signs of mental illness, whereas those at a greater distance are more likely to label someone as mentally disturbed. As the relational distance between people increases, so does the probability that a label of mental illness will be applied. For example, he cites studies of family members of people whose behavior is aberrant and finds that there is a widespread reluctance of family members to recognize and label mental illness and a common tendency to normalize bizarre behavior. He is quick to point out, however, that this generalization applies most clearly to the initial recognition of mental illness. Once a label has been applied, then family members do in fact see it as mental illness.

With respect to cultural distance, Horwitz reports the same pattern: The tendency to label individuals as mentally ill varies directly with the cultural distance between the observer and the actor. He explains:

> The norms used to evaluate the behavior of all people in a collectivity are those of the most conventional groups of the society. This leads to the proposition that the tendency to label individuals mentally ill varies inversely with the degree of the cultural conventionality of the labeled individual. When labelers are members of the conventional culture, individuals who are less conventional in all respects . . . are at a greater risk of being labeled mentally ill than more conventional individuals. As the distance from the conventional culture increases, the probability that an individual will be labeled mentally ill grows (p. 47).

Unfortunately, there is little systematic evidence pertaining to the labeling of persons with other types of stigma, so that we cannot say if the propositions Horwitz has expressed for the mentally ill are generally true for other types of deviancies. Certainly, on the face of it, the propositions regarding relational and cultural distance can plausibly be applied to other stigmatizing conditions, provided that one permits qualifications that are required by the exigencies of particular conditions. For example, one can speculate that the role of relational distance in the labeling of alcoholism may be exactly opposite to that of mental illness, because the alcoholic may be able to hide his or her drinking problem from the view of people in the general public but not from members of his or her immediate family. Perhaps the safest conclusion to be drawn is that relational and cultural distances are likely to be important factors in explaining the tendency of lay persons to label, regardless of what type of stigma we are dealing with, but that the exact role that social distance plays depends upon the kind of condition involved.

Research on the labeling of mental illness shows that the social characteristics of observers affect the chances that they will recognize and label mental illness. In particular, Horwitz reports that the sex and social class background of the person observing the behavior is related to the chances that he or she will label behavior as deviant. With respect to social class, studies indicate that the recognition of mental illness varies directly with the social position of the labeler. Research shows that the higher the class status of the labeler, the more likely he or she is to recognize and label mental illness. The reasons for this are complex, and they appear to be related to the fact that with ascending class position comes a greater correspondence in knowledge about mental illness among lay people and professionals, a greater willingness to seek psychiatric treatment, and an enhanced tendency to label one's self as mentally ill.

With respect to sex, the evidence shows that women are more likely than men to recognize and label mental illness. However, the tolerance for people who have been labeled as mentally ill is greater among women than among men. Studies by Farina and his colleagues, discussed in Chapter 2, confirm this finding.

There are no reliable data on sex and class differences about the tendency to label other types of behavior as deviant. It would be surprising if such differences did not exist, since there is no evident reason why the factors that cause sex and class differences to occur in the case of mental illness would not also operate with respect to most other kinds of stigmatizing conditions.

Research on mental illness also tells us something about the determinants of reactions by audiences to those they have labeled as deviant. Horwitz identifies a continuum along which audiences of observers may respond to mental illness, ranging from exclusion to inclusion. At one end of this continuum is coercion, stigma, and rejection; at the other end is sympathy and care. According to Horwitz, the strength of social resources and social control within informal groups, such as families, neighborhoods, and communities, determines the degree of exclusion of the mentally ill. By and large groups in which social ties are intimate and personal tend to respond inclusively to deviancy, whereas groups in which social bonds are formal and contractual tend to respond exclusively.

Finally, Horwitz points out, audience reactions to the mentally ill are not solely a function of features of the audience and its members' relationships to the person who is labeled. Audience evaluations of the behavior of others, and their responses to it, are also affected by the disordered individuals' social integration, cultures, and social class positions. He reports, for example, that the degree of exclusion of individuals who are labeled mentally ill varies directly with the social marginality of the labeled individual. He writes, "However integration is indexed, people who are more marginal to the community are more likely to be excluded if they are labeled mentally ill" (p. 112). Also, the degree of exclusion of individuals that are labeled mentally ill varies directly with their cultural distance from conventional groups, and inversely with their social power. Lastly, research on mental illness shows that men are more likely than women to suffer exclusion and rejection if labeled.

To summarize, research on deviant behavior, mainly mental illness, supports the following conclusions about audience reactions toward people who possess attributes, traits, and qualities that may stigmatize: (1) With some exceptions, audiences of lay people respond differently to signs and symptoms of deviancy than do audiences of professionals. By and large, professionals tend to label such qualities as indicative of deviancy, whereas lay persons tend to respond to them by denying, ignoring or normalizing the behavior in question. (2) Among lay observers, the social distance between the audience and the person whose behavior and attributes are being observed affects the response of the audience to them. The closer the social distance between the two, the less likely the audience is to label the person as deviant, and, conversely, the greater the social distance, the greater the likelihood that labeling will occur. (3) Certain social characteristics, such as sex and the social class background of the observer affect the chances that they will recognize and label something as deviant. Specifically, the rejection of deviance varies directly with the social class of the labeler; that is, the higher the social class of the observer, the greater is the probability that they will recognize and label behavior as deviant. With respect to sex, the evidence is that women are more likely than men to recognize and label something as deviant. (4) The social cohesiveness of the group to which the audience belongs has a major impact on the responses they show to the deviancy they label. Cohesive social units tend to act inclusively and noncohesive units exclusively to those they label as deviant. (5) Women are more tolerant and accepting of the deviants they label than are men. (6) Audience reactions to the deviant are also a function of the social integration, culture, and social class background of the person who is labeled.

• CHAPTER FOUR •

Stigma and the Self-Concept

THE DEVELOPMENT OF THE SELF-CONCEPT is a distinctly social process. Other people are essential to our efforts to acquire knowledge about the self and to the evaluation and interpretation of our life experiences. A discrediting mark or stigma necessarily modifies this social process and the interpersonal relationships that are so vital for self-knowledge and self-validation. For an individual with a stigmatizing condition, the construction or maintenance of a stable and coherent self-concept may be a particularly difficult and uncertain process.

One of the key differences between the unmarked individual and the markable in the construction of self is in the affective reactions that are received from others. For the stigmatized individual, the reactions, observations, and evaluations elicited from other people may be disproportionately negative. When this occurs, association with others becomes an ordeal, something to be dreaded and curtailed as much as possible. Millman (1980) illustrates this point repeatedly, as she chronicles the plight of women who are stigmatized because of their weight. The influence of the negative responses of others and the difficulties in coming to terms with them are vividly revealed in the stories told by the women Millman studied. Being fat in this culture means that one is fair game for taunts and unsolicited reactions of others. From the kids in the supermarket who cry out, "Hey Mom, look at the fat lady," or "Look at the blimp," or "Get a load of the monster," to the supposedly well-intentioned strangers who stop overweight women on the street and say, "Why don't you try Weight Watchers?" or "I have a fabulous doctor you could go to," it seems that obese women are locked into a social information environment that is almost uniformly negative.

These negative feelings, if not their exact expression, may work themselves deeply into the individual's self-evaluation. Markables may develop concepts of themselves as different from others, as marginal and not connected, and perhaps even as alien. Consequently, each decision to connect with the social world will involve a special effort, a conscious decision of whether the contact is worth the possible humiliation and further negative reaction. Millman writes: "These are hard decisions. They are never made once and for all. Each new social contact, each act committed in public, no matter how trivial or superficial, is dominated by the fat person's concern about how she appears to others. Thus her participation in the world is often tentative, and filled with fear of being discovered, labeled as the freak she fears herself to be" (p. 73).

Millman also quotes from the autobiography of a young woman she has interviewed:

> I always felt, when I went into some boutique, that all the salesgirls were staring at me and snickering, knowing that nothing in the store would fit me. I always had to say, "I'm just looking." . . . I always felt that the first thing anyone would notice is that I was fat. And not only that I was fat, but that they would know why I was fat. They would know that I was neurotic, that I was unsatisfied, that I was a pig, that I had problems. They could tell immediately that I was out of control. I always look around to see if there was anyone as fat as me. I always wondered when I saw a fat woman, "Do I look like that?" (p. 74).

Millman also tells the story of several fat men. The contrast is startling. Fat men are not nearly as self-conscious about their weight as women, and weight is not as important in organizing their lives. Being overweight does not completely engulf the self-concept of men as it seems to with women. In stark opposition to the pain of social contact expressed by many women, Millman quotes men who report the social virtues of being fat. One man in her study expressed it quite directly: "If anything, my weight has helped me in business. People remember me, it breaks the ice—they feel they know me because I stand out" (p. 19). Millman is careful to point out that the differences between men and women with respect to weight stem from a number of sources. She reports, for example, that in the case of most men in her study, they did not become fat until later in life, and thus were spared the "fat child" and the "fat adolescent" experiences.

"Come Out, Come Out Wherever You Are"

(Some comments taken from an article by Margaria Fichtner, entitled "A Proverbial Fat Lady, and Jolly-Well Content," in *Hartford Courant*, date unknown. The article features Carole Shaw, author of *Come Out, Come Out, Wherever You Are*, American R. R. Publishing Company, 1982. The first three comments are taken from that book.)

—"Stand up straight, throw your shoulders back and look the world straight in the eye. Don't be afraid to take up space. You have a perfect right to it."

—"Nobody!—Not your doctor, your lawyer, your spouse, your inlaws—REPEAT, REPEAT—Nobody is entitled to demean you."

—The most familiar type of discrimination large people face is bias during a job hunt. I don't know how you handle the bigot who objects to your weight. Maybe you can humor him into hiring you. 'Did you intend to pay me by the hour or by the pound?' Yet we all know this situation is no laughing matter.

"Don't think [says Carole Shaw in the interview] that the personnel director has any knowledge of what the world is like from a big person's point of view unless she or he is a big person too, or is related to one. They don't know, nor can they be expected to care, that it may be extra difficult for a large size person to find decent clothes. Do not think you are excused if you go to an interview with a stain on your blouse, or a run in your stocking, or so forth. No one can expect preferential treatment in a chic advertising agency . . . if she stumbles in wearing a polyester polonaise."

"You see, it's not just me and 12 other ladies. But even so, you do feel isolated. You never seem to see the other fat ladies on the street. Your eyes aren't tuned to see them. All you see is that everyone seems to look wonderful except you. . . . Maybe there's something wrong with our definition of beauty. You go into the supermarket, and there are 12 different cereals. You go out to buy a car, and there are all types to choose from. Why can't the same be true for people? We got fat; we didn't get stupid."

What is most apparent from these self-descriptions by fat men and women is the dramatic variation in the consequences of a specific stigma for the self-concept. When and how pervasively the self-concept will reflect the negativity produced by a stigma depends on the nature of the stigma and on the reactions of others in the social environment. But it also depends on when and how in the course of self-development the reactions of others are heeded and on how they are interpreted and evaluated. In Millman's book, both the men and women are aware that they are fat and that this condition can produce hostile reactions in others. Yet the women are much more concerned with their weight, as they are likely to be about all aspects of physical appearance. They emphasize the importance of weight to their overall self-evaluation, and, consequently, they are decidedly more stigmatized by their obesity than are the men who do not consider their weight to be a particularly significant attribute in their self-definition.

CONSTRUCTING THE SELF-CONCEPT

The acquisition of knowledge about the self depends on the observation of one's own behavior, on comparison with others, and on seeing ourselves through the eyes of others. Depending on the exact nature of one's theoretical orientation, one of these factors may be given more emphasis and attention than the others in determining how the self-concept develops, but all of these modes of acquiring knowledge are fundamentally altered by stigma.

In this chapter, we will assume that an individual actively constructs a self-concept from the information contained in his or her unfolding experiences, particularly those that involve the self-relevant responses of other people. The self-concept in this culture is assumed to contain representations of our special abilities, achievements, and preferences, the unique aspects of our appearance, and the characteristic expression of our temperament. It is assumed to result from an elaborate interplay of one's own thoughts and feelings about the self with the thoughts and feelings that are elicited or inferred from others' reactions. A crucial feature of the self-concept is the sense of continuity it provides for our life experiences. We experience this continuity because the self-concept typically changes only very gradually over time. Moreover, the self-concept contains representations of the self in the past as well as ideas of the self in the future, both of which contribute to a sense of personal coherence and stability.

The amount of information about the self that is potentially available is vast, since almost all of our actions implicate the self in some way. An individual cannot possibly attend to all of the available information and must, therefore, be highly selective. What information an individual chooses to view as important or diagnostic for the self depends on an array of personal, situational, and historical factors. Of primary importance among these selective factors, however, are one's prevailing generalizations about the self—one's self-schemas (Markus 1977, 1980). These self-schemas allow us to attend to certain features of our behavior while disregarding others.

They can be viewed as summaries and constructions of past behavior that enable individuals to understand their own social experiences. Self-schemas are assumed to develop from the repeated similar categorization and evaluation of behavior by one's self. This process also incorporates the evaluations of others and eventually results in clearly differentiated ideas of the kind of person one is with respect to particular domains of behavior.

Not everyone organizes his or her own experiences in similar ways and not everyone develops the same self-schemas. One person may think about his behavior with respect to how shy he is, how productive he is, what a rotten husband he has been, or how in the future he'll slow down and enjoy things more. Another person may not organize her behavior in these terms at all. Instead she may think about how independent she is, what a good athlete she used to be, or what a creative photographer she is now. We do not all pay attention to the same type of events in our lives and we do not all use the same dimensions, categories, constructs, or metaphors to think about our lives. According to this theoretical orientation, self-schemas define those domains of behavior over which individuals believe they should have control or have claimed for their own responsibility. A self-schema emerges as one begins to experience some feelings of personal responsibility in a particular domain of behavior, and the development of a self-schema consolidates these feelings into a sense of control. Self-schemas are also assumed to contain representations of relevant goals and motives, and thus, in the domains of their self-schemas, people know what to expect for themselves and how to predict and interpret their behavior. In domains for which they do not have such well-established self-schemas for thinking about their behavior, people are likely to be relatively less self-regulated and much more reliant on the reactions and evaluations of others for self-definition. We also seek input from others in our self-schematic domains, but this input is very often tempered and modified by our own strong views about ourselves.

With respect to potentially stigmatizing attributes or qualities of the self, it follows from this reasoning that individuals may attend to a mark, build a self-schema around it, and thus ensure its position as an important element of the self-concept. Alternatively, the individual may choose to deemphasize the mark or even ignore it altogether. For example, some individuals are intensely concerned with their weight, while others who may be equally overweight are not. Some children dwell on the fact that they only have one parent rather than two, whereas others appear not to notice it. Some people continually concentrate on a previous bout with cancer or a prior nervous breakdown, while others appear to ignore these same events, or at least to accord them only minor significance in organizing past experience.

The individual is free to determine the important domains of one's self-schema and to pick and choose what information will be accepted as self-diagnostic or self-validating. Thus, the very heavy drinker who is debilitated by drinking may not think he is an alcoholic and may resist that label. Even more surprisingly, a blind woman may resist being called blind. Depending on their social environments and their patterns of social comparison, these individuals may indeed construct selves that are at variance with others' perceptions of them.

The self/other balance is a delicate one, however. The construct of the self, and the location of its boundaries, is, to a large degree, socially determined. One cannot remain a social being—a member of a society or group—and totally ignore the reality that is generated by it, at least not for long, and not for all aspects of the self. The question of whether a potentially stigmatizing attribute, quality, or experience will become a focal component of the self-concept depends on whether the individual uses the attribute, quality, or experience in organizing, interpreting, and evaluating social experiences. But the antecedents and consequences of this decision cannot be understood without locating the individual in the larger social context and without taking into account the nature of the stigma, the markable's reactions to the stigma, and the reactions of others. When a mark becomes a focal component of the self-concept, the stigmatizing process is engaged. As described in Chapter 1, the stigmatizing process involves linking the mark to a central aspect of the marked person's identity or dispositional makeup.

STIGMA: EMPHASIS AND CONGRUENCE

The self-concept at any one point in time is a construction based on one's own thoughts, feelings, and behavior with respect to the self, and the perception of the thoughts, feelings, and behavior of *other* people with respect to the self. As noted earlier, a marked individual may differ from an unmarked one in that the majority of others' reactions to the self, as well as one's own reactions to the self, may be negative. When, how, or whether a particular mark will be incorporated into the self-concept depends on the configuration of self and other reactions with respect to it. Figure 6 takes the point of view of the markable and locates his or her interactions in social space. It illustrates two factors that are implicated in self-perception of stigmas: (1) the emphasis given the mark by the self; and (2) the emphasis

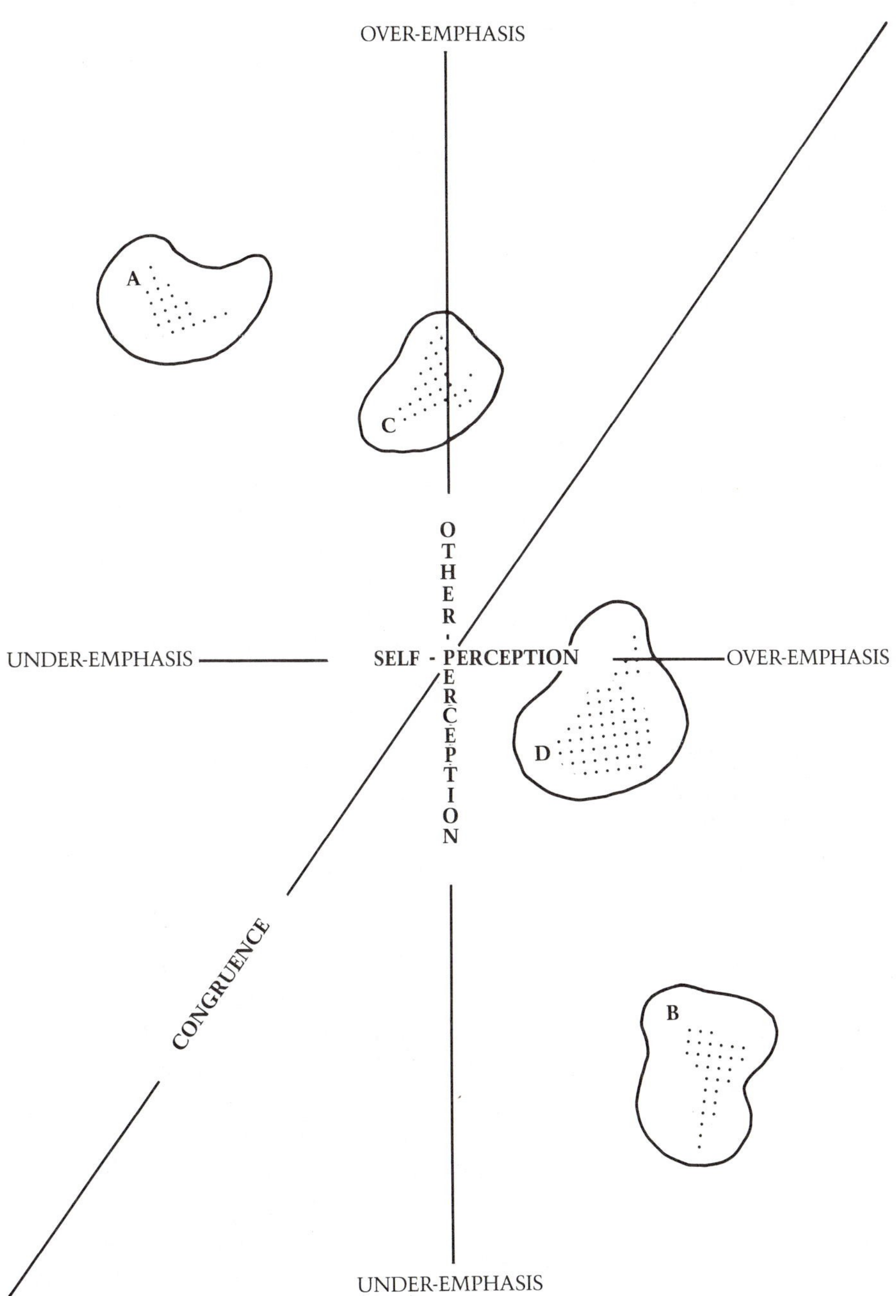

Figure 6. Emphasis given to a mark by self and others.

given the mark by others. Figure 6 can be used to represent both the level of emphasis given the mark by the self and others and the congruence between their perceptions of the mark. The emphasis given a mark refers to how central or focal to the interaction are the evaluations or reactions of the self and the other to the mark. Do thoughts, feelings, and actions relevant to the mark dominate the ongoing interaction? Do reactions to the mark frame or guide the interaction? Is the mark used to interpret or explain the interaction? An affirmative response to any of these questions would indicate that the mark is being emphasized in the interaction rather than being assigned a more peripheral status. For a given mark, a variety of self/other configurations are possible.

Each point in Figure 6 represents an imagined or actual interaction between a markable and another person. For many markables these interactions are likely to be quite heterogeneous. In some, the mark will be heavily emphasized during the course of the interaction; it will engulf the interaction. In other interactions, the mark is quite likely to be downplayed or perhaps ignored altogether. Whether the markable is interacting with different people or one person over time, both ambivalence in reaction and individual variation in responding to a mark result in interactions that differ dramatically with respect to the attention given the potentially stigmatizing attribute. In Chapter 1, for example, we described the case of Joan who must interact with her handicapped roommate, Ruth. In some interactions, Joan feels the need to emphasize Ruth's handicap so as to convey that she is an empathic person who has some understanding of Ruth's problems. At other times, Joan will attempt to downplay Ruth's disability and to put it in the background of their interaction. Ruth, of course, will perceive these differences in Joan's emphasis of her handicap and will exhibit a range of reactions, depending on the nature of Joan's actions and on her own feelings at the time. The self-concept of the markable is a consequence of integrating the cluster of interactions and achieving some understanding and knowledge of the self. To the extent that the self or others repeatedly emphasize the mark in the course of interaction (reactions far from the origin), the mark will become relatively more meaningful and significant and will begin to figure prominently in the construction of the self-concept.

There are those marked individuals who emphasize the importance of their mark (their judgments would lie to the right of the origin), and those who underemphasize the mark and attempt not to attach any importance to it in the evaluation of the self (their judgments would lie to the left of the origin). With respect to the perceptions of others' reactions, the judgments lying above the point of origin represent reactions that emphasize the mark, and judgments below the origin represent reactions that underemphasize the mark. Overemphasis of the mark includes thinking of one's self as more crippled, more deaf, more mentally ill, more fat, etc., than one actually is, and underemphasis of the mark is just the opposite. This framework implies that there is an appropriate emphasis to be given to a mark. In those conditions involving a consensually definable stimulus condition—i.e., the markable cannot see, weighs 300 pounds, or was a state hospital mental patient—it may be possible to make these judgments by using normative standards for weight, vision, sanity, and so on. Not all stigmatizing conditions have such an "objective" status, however. Individuals may be stigmatized or stigmatize themselves even when there is no real basis for the judgments. Moreover, even when the stigma has some objective properties, the appropriate level of emphasis depends on the nature of the social interaction between the markable person and others. The nature of this interaction is dependent on the goals of the interaction, as well as the relationship between the participants. It also depends on what level of emphasis is psychologically comfortable and will allow for the construction of a stable and coherent self-concept. Thus, the appropriate level of emphasis will vary across situations and across individuals.

Congruence in Figure 6 is represented by the self-other judgments that lie on the diagonal. Note that there may be congruence when both self and others emphasize the mark in the evaluation of the individual and when both do not emphasize the mark. The self/other points lying off the diagonal represent a lack of congruence or a discrepancy. The self/other judgments that lie above the diagonal are those where the self emphasizes his or her mark less than others (that is, sees it as less severe, less debilitating, less important). The self/other judgments that lie below the diagonal are those where the self gives more weight to the mark than do others.

We may think of a cluster of self/other points for each target person spreading over some area of the space in Figure 6. These clusters have some regions of highly concentrated points, which represent the modal perceptions. Depending on the diversity and duration of social experience relevant to the stigma, some stigmatized people might have clusters of perceptions that span a large area, whereas others will have clusters spanning relatively small areas. Where the cluster is large, self-perception is likely to be variable or ambiguous. For example, individuals who live in a deaf community but work outside in the hearing world might reasonably be expected to have two distinct and quite disparate regions of highly concentrated points. Constructing a coherent self-concept under these conditions may prove a formidable problem. The difficulty associated with achieving a stable and coherent self-concept is illustrated abstractly by the fact that at least three forms of variation can be identified within this space, as illustrated in Figure 6. Different people making judgments on the same occasion may disagree with each other in their emphasis of the mark, so that there will be variance among the judgments of different others. Also, a particular other person may not make the same judgment on different occasions. Finally, the stigmatized individual may also vary from time to time in judgments of the mark.

Both self/other congruence in the perception of stigma and the level of emphasis given to the stigma are important in self-perception, and especially in determining whether a self-schema will develop in relation to one's stigma. Figure 6 displays four clusters representing different levels of emphasis and agreement. Cluster *A* identifies an individual who sees one's own stigma in less serious terms than others see it. An example might be a person who spent some time in a mental hospital following a brief emotional collapse, but who did not think of himself, either now or then, as mentally ill. In his self-evaluation and in his interactions with others, little weight is given to the mark. Others, however, know that he spent time in a mental hospital, and assume that he was then "crazy" and may suddenly be so again at any moment.

Cluster *B* shows a person who is somewhat overweight by national height-to-weight norms for her age, but who thinks of herself as grossly obese. In contrast, most other people respond to this person as if she had a fairly average physique.

In cluster *C*, the individual attaches some importance to the mark, but not nearly as much as others who attach a great deal of weight to the mark and greatly exaggerate the individual's condition. Person *C* might be a person who has been blind for a substantial period of time and who realizes his limitations, but is also well aware of his abilities. He knows that there are many things he can do quite well. Others, however, regard him as totally helpless. For example, some blind people report stopping on a street corner to make sure of their bearings and suddenly being grabbed by the arm and marched across the street. These others blithely assume that the blind person is lost and would welcome any assistance.

Cluster *D* again represents perceptions of a person who attaches much more importance to her mark than the others in her environment. An example would be a paraplegic who, immediately following her disabling trauma, feels that her life is over and is completely hopeless about the future. In contrast, many of the others in the hospital—doctors, nurses, other disabled patients who have seen many such cases—know that in time this person can learn to get around by herself and to live a life that in many important respects may not be far removed from life before the accident.

The location of the majority of an individual's perceptions in the space represented in Figure 6 can be used to determine the probability that an individual has or is likely to develop a self-schema relative to the stigmatized attribute. For example, the perceptions of person *D* are much more vulnerable to change than the perceptions of *C*. Person *D* is vulnerable because both the objective condition and the perception of others contradict her own perceptions. Under these circumstances, it will be relatively more difficult for her to form an enduring self-schema of herself as crippled and helpless. With respect to Person *C*, his judgments are contradicted by the judgments of others, but they are supported by all sorts of information that derive from his subjectively satisfying accomplishments. It should then be possible for him to maintain a self-schema of himself as a fully functioning, able blind person, even in the face of evaluations from others that suggest he is relatively helpless or dependent.

If an individual gives some substantial emphasis to a mark over a period of time, he or she is likely to develop an integrated network of thoughts, feelings, and expectations with respect to the mark, and the network will function as a self-schema. The mark will become a defining attribute of the self. If self-schemas develop in such a way that individuals define themselves in terms of the mark—as blind people, as fat people, or as alcoholics—they are likely to seek information that is consistent with those views of themselves and act in accordance with those generalizations. As individuals accrue self-knowledge relevant to their mark, they will experience feelings of enhanced personal responsibility and may begin to attach more weight to their own perceptions of the mark when constructing a self-concept. Under these conditions, they may become relatively less reliant on the perceptions of others for information about how to understand or interpret the consequences of the mark.

The least amount of difficulty in incorporating the mark into the self-concept should be experienced by those who have maintained the same level of emphasis of their mark over a period of time and who experience some congruence between self and other perception with respect to the mark. In Figure 6 this would be represented by a cluster of self/other judgments that is not too widespread and that falls near the diagonal. The greatest difficulty and uncertainty about incorporating the stigma into the self-concept will occur when there is an incongruence between self and other perception with respect to the mark. If a discrepancy exists, some type of individual disturbance or change can be expected. Individuals *A* and

C may be unable to reside comfortably in environments where others emphasize their marks more than they do themselves. Consequently, person *A* may attempt to conceal the fact of a previous period of hospitalization, and person *C* may be motivated to persuade others of his essential normality, or, if each fails to do so, may withdraw from all but the most essential of social interactions. Individual *D* may change her own ideas about the mark in the direction of those held by others, while *B* may continue to emphasize her mark privately and publicly behave as if she gives it no more attention than do others. All of these individuals will experience difficulty constructing a stable or coherent self-concept. The changes or patterns of adaptation that occur as a result of the self/other discrepancy depend, of course, on the precise nature of the mark and what impact it has on self-esteem and the overall structure of the self-concept, both factors to be discussed later in the chapter.

The factors that lead to emphasis of a mark and the factors that lead to congruence are critical for understanding how stigma will affect the self-concept. Yet it is often difficult to determine how much emphasis will be given to a particular mark during a particular interaction; it depends on the individuals, the nature of the social environment, the nature of the goals of the social interaction, etc. Thus, in the following sections we will focus primarily on factors that contribute to *congruence* between the perception of self and perception of others, rather than on factors determining the level of emphasis given the mark. It is important to note, however, that the level of congruence or discrepancy, and its stability over time, will often be influenced by how much emphasis has been given the mark. The likelihood of modifying the discrepancy, or the importance of doing so, may also be related to how much importance both self and others have accorded the mark. If, for instance, Ruth, of the earlier example, attends only minimally to her disability and has not allowed it to figure significantly in her view of herself, while Joan insists on focusing on it in the course of their interactions, it will be important for this discrepancy to be modified, if their relationship is to continue.

THE STIGMATIZED SELF: CONGRUENCE AND DISCREPANCY

In the preceding section we suggested that there is no one-to-one correspondence between the evaluations of others and what one thinks of one's self or vice versa, and consequently there are at least three alternative outcomes of the stigmatizing process. When the stigmatizing process is complete, the marker will stigmatize the individual and the markable will simultaneously stigmatize himself or herself in the same way. The stigmatizing by self and others may not be at the same level or to the same degree, but in a first general case both the marker and the markable are implicated in the process. In a second general case, the marker stigmatizes the markable, and the markable disavows or ignores the mark. The markable may be aware of the marker's attempts to stigmatize, but does not accept the mark as a stigma, and does not incorporate it as an aspect of his self-concept. In the third general case, others do not stigmatize the individual, but the individual stigmatizes himself or herself. In this latter case, the individual feels discredited and incorporates the stigma into the self-concept even though there is no corroboration from others.

An Example

Using the "fat" stigma, we can easily find examples of both high levels of congruence and discrepancy between self-stigmatization and stigmatization by others. For the marker, the markable person's obesity most often takes on a master status quality, at least on first encounter. In this case, fat seems to dominate one's impression of another—it becomes the central category, the one from which all others gain their meaning. In many cases, the markable may accept the social reality that is created by others and will stigmatize the self in a similar way.

There are, however, some instances where a major discrepancy exists between marking the self as perhaps slightly overweight and other's stigmatizing the self as "fat." This is likely to be the case if the fat individual has not developed a self-schema with respect to body weight. A study by Markus, Hamill, and Sentis (1980) found that being fat had an impact on how a subject responded to self-relevant information about weight, only if the individual thought she was fat *and* considered this attribute to be very important to her overall self-evaluation. Individuals who varied in weight and in how important they thought weight was to their overall self-evaluation, were compared for the efficiency (speed and confidence) and the consistency of their discriminations with respect to stimuli—trait adjectives, pictures of bodies, pictures of food—that were either relevant or not relevant to weight. The findings indicated that thinking one was fat was the critical factor in explaining differential cognitive performance. For example, two groups of individuals who thought they were fat exhibited similar cognitive performance, despite a 30 percent difference in actual body weight. Moreover, two groups of individuals who were similar with respect to actual body weight, yet differed in the importance assigned to weight as a defining feature of the self, performed very differently from each other in these discrimination tasks. It appears that being fat is not enough to insure that an individual will become sensitive to weight-relevant stimuli. This study also highlighted two types of self/other discrepancy in stigmatization. It identified markable individuals who did not appear to accept the label "fat," even though they were objectively overweight. Second, it identified individuals who described themselves as fat and who showed the appropriate patterns of cognitive discriminations, but who were not objectively overweight. This study suggests that an observable mark will not become an organizing or dominating feature of the behavior unless the individual actively chooses the quality as a defining feature of self.

Congruence

There will never be a perfect correspondence between the evaluations of others and one's own evaluations of self, but if we consider various stigmatizing conditions, with respect to the dimensions outlined in Chapter 2, we can identify a number of situations or circumstances that are likely to foster or encourage such a correspondence. Even though we cannot be sure that a markable person has incorporated the stigma as part of the self-concept, we can speculate that this is likely to be so when the stigma generates extreme and consistent negative reactions on the part of others. This is likely to be the case, for example, when the stigma is non-concealable and aesthetically displeasing. Millman (1980) describes the reaction of one marker to an obese woman:

> Walking through a store, my friend Barbara recently found herself staring at the massive arms (bared by a sleeveless dress) of a woman who weighed over 300 pounds. To Barbara's eyes this flesh was so white, so spongy that she thought, she must spend all of her time at home growing herself like a mushroom. Barbara at first had felt great pity for how hard the woman's life must have been. Thinking about what it must be like to have to make one's own dresses out of bedspreads, or to have such trouble moving about and carrying packages. My friend imagined that being fat must have cost this woman tremendous effort and energy. But her pity had soon turned to anger at what she believed the woman was doing to herself by being so fat. She wanted to shake the woman, to tell her to pull herself together (p. 65).

With some stigmatizing conditions, the markable is likely to find herself confronted with extreme negativity in the direct reactions of others. Should the individual attend to these reactions, she would be likely to stigmatize herself as well. Anything that so adversely affects another when observing the target individual is likely to affect the target individual similarly when observing the self. If a mark is aesthetially displeasing, the markable individual who is a part of the same culture and its network of values, meanings, and understanding, is also likely to react negatively to the mark. Quoting again from Millman, a fat woman describes her own aesthetic reaction to a mark: "There staring me in the face was my thigh. It was enormous, it was gross, it was like a diseased limb, the kind you see in pictures of jungle natives; it spread on forever, like a prairie photographed from a plane, the flesh not green but bluish-white, with veins meandering across it like rivers. It was the size of three ordinary thighs" (p. 180). This negative reaction to an aesthetically displeasing stigma on the part of the markable is likely to be especially strong when the mark has been acquired since birth. Those born with an aesthetically displeasing mark may not have the same extremely negative reaction to the self because they have not had a previous self as a point of comparison

A congruence between self and other stigmatization is also likely when the stigma is so socially disruptive that it interferes with the normal course of social interaction. Social disruptiveness can stem from a multitude of sources, many of which have been outlined in earlier chapters. As an example of how the social disruption produced by a stigma can lead to both self and other stigmatization, we can examine the phenomenon of social responsiveness. There are a variety of stigmas that may cause one to fail to be appropriately responsive socially.

Davis (in press) has documented the importance of responsiveness in interpersonal communication and attraction. When a speaker makes a comment, requests information, or registers an evaluation, the listener is usually expected to give a responsive answer to continue the social interaction. In Davis' research, responsiveness is defined as a reply that is in the same content domain as the speaker's questions or comment, and one that has an appropriate level of detail and elaboration, as well as the proper latency. The stigma of deafness disrupts encounters between the deaf and the hearing in a very real sense, and it is difficult, often impossible, for the deaf participant and the hearing participant to be responsive to each other. Many hearing people report that they are reluctant to repeat their communication to the deaf, although this is often necessary, even if the individual is a skilled lip reader. Higgins (1980) quotes a deaf postal worker who spoke about the very real reluctance of many hearing people to repeat their messages:

> Sometimes hearing people don't want to take the trouble to repeat what they said to me if I didn't understand. The "kids" [young workers] at the post office are pretty good about repeating, but sometimes they don't want to bother either. That bothers me. If a hearing person didn't understand, the other hearing person would repeat what he said. It's the same for a deaf person if they don't understand. But hearing people won't always repeat (p. 141).

This reluctance to repeat one's remarks may not be a consequence of indifference but of a wish to avoid the embarrassment of appearing to patronize another.

Stigmatization by others when the mark is socially disruptive is quite likely to be associated with self-stigmatization. Since the development of the self-concept is a social process and dependent in important ways on social interaction, anything that interferes directly with this social interaction will also interfere with the construction of the self-concept. Even an aesthetically displeasing mark may allow fairly routine social interaction after the initial adjustment on the part of participants to the stigma. Marks such as being deaf or a severe stutterer, however, will interfere with most of the typical forms of social interaction. When social interaction becomes difficult, the mark is relatively more likely to take on exaggerated proportions in the self-concept because the markable person has difficulty in making contact with others and, thus, in using these others as sources and targets for social comparison. Because of the lack of social contact, the individual may selectively dwell on that aspect of the self that causes the social disruption and, consequently, accord it an important role in the self-concept. Of course, if the mark is sufficiently socially disruptive, the individual may feel compelled to withdraw and live in a separate community with others who are similarly stigmatized, thus decreasing the likelihood that the stigma will directly impede social interaction.

In short, those individuals with marks that are nonconcealable, aesthetically displeasing, and socially disruptive are those most likely to experience a congruence between their view of themselves and the view of others with respect to the mark. In those cases, if others assign a central status to the mark in evaluating the individual, converting the mark to a stigma, then the individual is likely to assign a comparably important status to the mark as a defining element of the self. Under these conditions, we can be confident that the mark will feature prominently in the self-concept and that self-stigmatization will occur.

Discrepancy

We can also identify a number of deviant marks and surrounding circumstances that are likely to be associated with an important discrepancy between the marker's view of the mark and the markable's view. The self-concept incorporates a wealth of information that is not immediately available to observers. For example, as noted in Chapter 2, the origin, course, and perceived peril associated with a deviant condition are critical factors in the stigmatization process. Yet, precise knowledge of these aspects of the condition are much more likely to be available to the stigmatized individual than to the observer. Thus, if there is hope that the effects of the condition can be reduced or removed (maybe the operation will work; next month I'll lose weight; soon I'll stop drinking; if I work at it, maybe I'll be able to walk with braces), the markable individual may be able to view the condition as a relatively peripheral aspect of the self. This hesitancy to appraise the self negatively is much less likely in those instances where it is evident that nothing can be done to alter the course or consequence of the stigma. Thoughts about the future course of the condition are the types of thoughts and feelings that will have a decided influence on the individual's stigmatization of himself or herself, but these internal plans and observations are likely to be inaccessible to most observers, at least in short term interactions, and will not affect how observers feel about the markable person.

A difference in knowledge about the mark is also likely to create a discrepancy between self and other stigmatization. Markers may erroneously assume, for example, that they are themselves at peril because of a markable's stigmatizing condition. Terminally ill cancer patients who gather in support groups report the subtly hostile behavior of markers who fear contamination as a result of associating with someone stigmatized with cancer (Dunkel-Schetter and Wortman, in press). One patient, for example, reported the experience of going to dinner at a friend's house and being served on a paper plate while the others received china. Typically, the stigmatized individual has relatively better knowledge of the antecedents, consequences, and relevant characteristics of the stigmatizing condition. In the case of cancer, the markable is probably aware that cancer is not physically contagious and can, perhaps, view the negative reactions of others as uninformed rather than cruel. This may work to mitigate some of the adverse effects of the stigmatizing process.

Somewhat more difficult for the markable to ignore, however, are the reactions of those who assume they are in peril, not because of physical contagion, but because of moral contagion—a feeling that perhaps this dreaded disease has struck the marked person for some set of justifiable reasons. Equally difficult to ignore is the evidence that markers feel they are at peril because of the marked persons' overwhelming feelings of hopelessness, sadness, or depression. Such evidence is not hard to come by, even among more enlightened markers. Several recent studies indicate, for example, that nurses show a significantly longer latency to respond to the calls of terminally ill patients than to the calls of other patients. As potentially difficult as these reactions may be to cope with, it may be possible to do so if the marked person can associate these reactions with fear and ignorance and perhaps maintain some hope of changing them. Under these conditions, the marked person may then stigmatize the self less severely than others would. It is considerably more difficult for the individual to reinterpret or ignore the reactions of others, however, when the condition does indeed imperil others or if it is aesthetically unpleasant or socially disruptive. In these instances there is some social reality that generates the reactions of others.

Some aspects of the origin of the deviant condition (e.g., whether it is by accident or a genetic problem) are also likely to have a greater impact on self-stigmatization than on stigmatization by others, because very often these aspects of the condition will not become known to the potential marker until after some considerable interaction with the markable. The marker is likely to take the mark at face value and not be overly concerned with the markable person's responsibility for it, whereas responsibility for the origin of the stigma may be critically important to the markable person. The marked individual who does not accept personal responsibility for a stigma, as might be the case with either a traumatic accident or a genetic problem, may feel very differently about being stigmatized than the individual who is forced to accept responsibility for the stigma, as might be the case for a person who injures himself in a car accident while drunk. The casual observer, on the other hand, may see two disabled people and assume that they feel or think about themselves in similar ways. There are also variations on this theme. For example, with a behavioral stigma, such as coming from a "broken" home, observers are likely to feel that it is not the child's fault and to assume that the child feels the same way. The child, however, may indeed feel that the stigma *is* his own responsibility because of a feeling that he, or his mere presence, contributed to conflict in the home. Thus, being a product of a broken home may assume substantial importance in the construction of the self-concept.

A discrepancy between self-stigmatization and stigmatization by others is also likely if the mark can be concealed. Obviously, if it can be concealed, others cannot use this information to discredit the individual, and one might assume that the mark might then be relatively unimportant for either the marker or the markable. But a person who exerts tremendous effort to keep some personal information (e.g., time in a mental institution) from public attention, may continually focus on the stigmatizing implications of this secret knowledge and, consequently, maintain its salience in self-definition. A further consequence of a concealable stigma is that the markable person will not receive any direct or reflected information from others about the mark and, thus, will not be able to put this aspect of self into perspective through normal processes of social comparison. There is also some danger with a concealable stigma that the markable will feel "inauthentic," in the sense that there will be a larger than usual discrepancy between the public and private identities. There is relatively little theorizing about how much or how often the self-concept needs to be validated and whether differences exist among people with respect to this need. We do know from studies by Snyder (1974) that some individuals more than others look to the social environment for cues about how to behave, but we are less aware of what impact different strategies for monitoring the self will have on self-concept.

We can conclude, therefore, that if the markable person and others do not share the same understanding of the cause, origin, or peril of stigma, or if the mark is concealable, there is likely to be some discrepancy between the self and other in the degree of stigmatization. Sometimes others will stigmatize the self to a greater degree than will the individual. In those cases, even if the feedback from others is consistently negative, the individual may ignore it or deny it, and construct a view of self that is at variance with that held by others. We have noted, however, that to the extent that the stigma is nonconcealable and socially disruptive, ignoring the social feedback will be relatively more difficult. In other cases, the markable will stigmatize the self to a greater degree than others will. This is likely to be the case if the individual is concealing the stigma or feels responsible for it, or it threatens a particularly salient or important aspect of self.

There has been relatively little attention paid to how much discrepancy between self and other conceptions of self is thought to be appropriate or "healthy" and what the range of individual differences are with respect to this phenomenon. We are, of course, aware of the pathologies associated with extreme divergence between what others think of the self and what the individual thinks. There are, for example, those cases where there is virtually no overlap in the self/other construction of social reality, such as with those individuals who come to believe erroneously that they are Jesus Christ (e.g., Rokeach, 1964), but at the less extreme level, the self/other discrepancy in self-definition has not been a focal concern in social psychology. This discrepancy exists for all individuals, but it varies with the nature of the social context and the nature of the self/other relationship, and, under most circumstances, would be difficult to evaluate. With the presence of a mark, however, there is a referent or anchor for the difference between one's conception of self and other's conception of self. Studies of this divergence in stigmatized individuals might be a useful starting point for an exploration of this general problem.

We have suggested that the self-concept of the markable person was most likely to be affected by consistent, negative feedback from others, and we have outlined some of the conditions that were likely to ensure this type of social information environment, as well as the factors that were likely to moderate its impact. It appears that a stigma will necessarily have some effect on the self-concept because a stigma interrupts and interferes with the social processes that attend the construction and maintenance of a self-concept. Because of the possible divergence between self-stigmatization and other stigmatization, it is not possible to make simple or straightforward predictions about the nature or extent of the influence of a mark on the self-concept. Theorizing about the self-concept of the stigmatized can begin, however, by speculating about the cluster of points representing one's stigma-relevant social interactions. This cluster can be analyzed for its range of emphasis, for the general level of self/other congruence, and for the particular way in which points are distributed within the cluster. This preliminary analysis will provide the basis for determining whether the markable person will indeed incorporate the stigma into his or her view of the self and the importance that will be assigned to this aspect of self.

In the following sections, we will assume a moderate level of agreement between self and other with respect to a marking condition and explore some of the specific ways that such conditions can have an influence on the self. We will consider their influence on self-esteem, on the structure of the self-concept, on the role of others in defining the self, and on past and future selves.

THE INFLUENCE OF STIGMA ON SELF-ESTEEM

The most direct effect of stigma on the self can be seen in the effects of the stigmatizing process on the markable person's self-esteem. This consideration is of primary importance because the nature of self-evaluation is likely to be related in an important way to both the structure and the content of the self, as well as to the coping strategies of the individual.

Self-esteem is usually considered to be a summary evaluation of the attributes of the self or the extent to which individuals are satisfied or pleased with themselves (Rosenberg 1965; Coopersmith 1967). High self-esteem implies that individuals feel positively about themselves, that they respect themselves and feel they are worthy. Low self-esteem suggests negative feelings about the self, a dissatisfaction, and a lack of respect or rejection of the self. Most of the empirical work on self-esteem has considered it to be a relatively stable or enduring quality of the self that refers to the individual's beliefs about himself or herself as a capable, significant, or worthy person. There are some aspects of one's overall evaluation of self, however, that are closer to what is meant by mood or temporary affective feelings about the self (e.g., how do I feel about myself as a person right now under current conditions, compared to how worthy or significant I generally consider myself to be). This affective component of self-esteem may be partially independent of one's set of beliefs or knowledge about the worth of the self, and may indeed be much more contextually dependent. In considering the relationship between stigma and self-esteem, this affective component may be particularly significant. As the element of self-esteem that is potentially the most easily modifiable, it is this aspect that may initially be most responsive to the negative evaluations of others with respect to the mark, perhaps causing individuals to feel depressed or angry when they realize that they have been stigmatized.

Social Support for the Stutterer

("Support Group Puts Stuttering in Its Place," *Hartford Courant*, November 18, 1982, by D. Morales)

Steven Sandler didn't like to talk when he was young. Other children would laugh at him and mimic him when he stuttered. Bullies would beat him up after school. . . .

> **Sandler said he remembers when family and friends reacted negatively to his early stuttering habits. "I became very anxious and nervous about it," he said. Stuttering persisted when he began attending elementary school. . . . "The other kids would laugh at me. I became more and more afraid to talk. . . ."**
>
> **In high school, he would be afraid to ask girls out for dates and didn't socialize much. . . . "I was afraid of rejection," he said. Once, in college, Sandler asked a girl out on a date. "She said no because I stuttered. That devastated me."**
>
> **[Finally, in graduate school, Sandler learned to deal with his speech habit.] "I realize [now] that it was other people's problem if they couldn't deal with my stuttering. Only I can hurt me."**
>
> **[As a result of his own experiences as a stutterer, Sandler holds support group meetings in his apartment for Hartford-area residents who stutter.]**

That a stigma is likely to have a compelling influence on self-esteem is apparent for a number of reasons. Stigmatizing an attribute or feature for an individual is likely to lead to lowered self-esteem because the average evaluation of the attributes comprising the self would change. Moreover, negative feelings about the self, even about aspects of the self that are relatively unimportant, are not easily contained or isolated. They often spread and create an overall negativity toward the self, because the mark is linked to underlying attributions of a more pervasive and general significance. In fact, in Chapter 1 the stigmatizing process was characterized as one in which the marked individual is negatively evaluated and seen as flawed or unworthy. The individual's very identity is at stake. Not surprisingly, then, acceptance of negative evaluations by others and stigmatizing one's self has particularly dire consequences for self-esteem. In stigmatizing one's self, the individual does just what the marker is presumed to do: He goes beyond the particular blemish or deviant attribute to infer underlying negative dispositions or person qualities. It is not just that one is fat or gay or blind or alcoholic, but rather that one is, therefore, fundamentally flawed as a person—sick, weak, immoral, or evil. In Goffman's terms, one has "a spoiled identity."

Sontag (1977), in writing about the metaphorical uses of cancer, quotes from a journal by Katherine Mansfield written as she was dying of cancer. Mansfield writes: "A bad day . . . horrible pains and so on, and weakness. I could do nothing. The weakness was not only physical, I *must heal my Self* before I will be well. . . . This must be done alone and at once. It is at the root of my not getting better. My mind is not controlled." The cancer here is not just a single quality or attribute of the self, it has possessed the self. Mansfield appears from this quote to have linked the cancer with underlying spiritual or mental weakness. Similarly, the fat woman who stigmatizes herself does not do so simply because she weighs too much, but because she is lazy, self-indulgent, secretive, and greedy. These are the kinds of negative thoughts that run deep and take root. They may so alter one's sense of self that even a drastic change in, or a removal of, the stigmatized condition may not shake them.

Whether or not the markable person accepts the negative evaluation of others and, indeed, comes to view the self as unworthy and contemptuous depends on how much emphasis is given to the mark by the self and others, and whether there is congruence between views of the mark held by self and other. Referring again to Figure 6, it is possible to make some predictions about how particular stigmatizing conditions may influence the self-esteem of the markable person. The individual is likely to feel the most devalued when there is a congruence between self and other, and when they both give a great deal of weight to the mark. We noted earlier that congruence between self and other was likely when the stigma was non-concealable or socially disruptive. Giving a great deal of emphasis to the mark on the part of self and other is most likely when the stigmatizing condition is relatively new and knowledge about its full range of effects and the course it will follow is changeable and uncertain. The individual who experiences a severe accident and is left paralyzed or disfigured is an example that fits these criteria. Both the marked individual and the others surrounding him are likely to be horrified by the accident, and these feelings are likely to be fueled by ignorance and fear about the fate of the condition. Similar congruence in emphasizing the mark arises when an individual is diagnosed as having cancer. Not only do such diagnoses trigger the stigmatizing process in friends and relatives, many victims report severe battles with depression and entertain thoughts of suicide as an immediate response to the news that they have a life-threatening illness.

Congruence between self and other stigmatization is likely to be associated with lower self-esteem. It is only when markables can manage to give less weight to the mark than that given by others that they can maintain a relatively high level of self-esteem. Sussman (1973) found, for example, that the deaf have lower levels of self-esteem than those who can hear. To the extent that the mark becomes deemphasized, however, as is the case when a deaf person becomes a member of a deaf community, self-esteem is increased. As part of a deaf community, individuals are able to view themselves as less marginal and to direct their attention away from their deafness to other qualities, thereby giving the mark less weight than it is given in the hearing world. By becoming members of a community of individuals who are similarly stigmatized, individuals, in terms of Figure 6, reduce the spread of their cluster of self/other points. There is less variation and the perceptions of self become more stable and sharply drawn. However, though living with others who are similar may ensure a higher self-esteem and a more stable self-perception, it may also create conditions that make change and growth particularly difficult. Great variation in how others perceive one may create uncertainty, but it also provides the possibility of seeing one's self in alternative ways, should this be desired.

Associating with others who have similar stigmas may serve to enhance or at least protect one's self-esteem, but there are still some differences within communities of stigmatized individuals that suggest that self-esteem continues to be a foundation of how one can relate to the dominant, non-stigmatized world. Thus, Sussman found that the better deaf individuals felt about their speaking and lip-reading capabilities, the higher the self-esteem. Also, Jacobs (1974) found that leaders of a deaf community accord themselves higher prestige and esteem if they have some oral skills. Higgins (1980), however, finds that those who sign have a higher prestige within the deaf community, suggesting that prestige among the deaf and self-esteem may not be automatically highly correlated.

As individuals work to create a discrepancy between self and other stigmatization so that they emphasize the negativity of their mark much less than others, they are likely to improve their levels of self-esteem, and, in some circumstances, they may even be able to achieve a level of esteem higher than the majority, nonstigmatized group. The most striking example of this is found in Rosenberg's study (1979) of self-esteem among blacks in various social environments. He finds that in some college communities where there are vigorous black support groups, the self-esteem of black students is higher than their white counterparts in other college communities. In this example we can speculate about whether these individuals have raised their self-esteem by making their potentially stigmatizable quality less salient, as members of the deaf community have done with deafness, or whether membership in the black community serves to emphasize blackness and strives to turn a potential stigmatizing mark into a virtue or an asset.

To the extent that individuals create a discrepancy between self and other perceptions by attaching a great deal of importance to their mark, they may radically lower their self-esteem, feeling more negatively about themselves than they could feel even if they completely internalized all of the potential negative reactions of others. A good example of this phenomenon can be found among young women who become anorexic. These women usually feel badly about their bodies and themselves, often to the point of self-hatred. Although often painfully thin, they may think of themselves as grossly obese and go to great lengths to arrange their lives so as not to eat.

Typically, most studies of self-esteem have not explored the antecedents, consequences, or correlates of lower self-esteem. It might be argued, as it has been following reports of relatively low levels of self-esteem among women and blacks, that the measures of self-esteem employed in these studies do not tap all aspects of one's self-knowledge about why one is a worthy or capable person. The most commonly used scales, the Rosenberg (1965) and the Coopersmith (1967), are very heavily slanted toward determining the individual's feelings about his or her competence, efficacy, or achievement. They include such yes-or-no questions as, "I am able to do things as well as most other people" and "I feel that my life is not very useful." They do not for the most part include questions about other aspects of one's view of self with respect to the social, emotional, or communal qualities of self. It is true that many stigmatizing qualities do indeed interfere with one's ability to be instrumental in certain ways, but, at the same time, they may not interfere with other aspects of the self-worth. It is even possible that a stigma could enhance one's feeling of self as a noble, long-suffering, or spiritual person, while at the same time rendering one occupationally helpless. Individuals who do manage to overcome some of the difficulties associated with a particularly severe stigmatizing condition and who serve as models and inspirations to others are reasonably likely to feel good about themselves, and perhaps to achieve a level of self-esteem they might not have realized as an unmarked and nondistinctive individual. Further study of the effects of stigma on components of self-esteem other than achievement is necessary here.

A consideration of the influence of stigma on self-esteem is critical because self-esteem is very strongly related to coping. Productive coping and a relatively high level of self-esteem can be viewed as mutually and reciprocally dependent on each other. Yet a positive relationship between these two phenomena may not always be observed, because there may be a divergence between self-judgments of coping and the coping that is apparent to others.

For example, a marked person may convince others that he is coping very well, thereby encouraging them to give less weight to the mark. Privately, however, the marked person may feel very troubled and threatened. Alternatively, over time another individual may perceive a great deal of progress in her own ability to cope with a stigmatizing condition, and finally succeed in attaching less importance to the mark in her view of self. Others, unable to assume this ipsative perspective, may only perceive that the individual is still not meeting normative standards for making the best of things. There also may be among some markers a type of irrational irritation for those marked individuals who appear insufficiently daunted by their conditions and who seem to violate the expected order by coping with or even overcoming them.

The self-esteem of stigmatized individuals will increase to the extent that the individuals come to view themselves as other than helpless, dependent, and worthless. This process is synonymous with removing the stigma associated with a particular mark and is at the heart of controlling the stigmatizing process. The mechanisms by which people come to terms with their stigma or even manage to remove or disassociate themselves from the discrediting aspects of the mark are somewhat curious and not well understood. There are those who come to view themselves as chosen and who see it as their mission to educate the rest of us about what is really important in life. Hunt (1966), who has spent much of his life in an institution for the disabled, writes about what he considers his project: "We have a special insight to offer, because our position gives us an extra experience of life in the passive aspect that is one half of the human reality. Those who lead active lives are perhaps especially inclined to ignore man's need to accept passivity in relation to so many forces beyond his control" (p. 150).

Others may feel that a stigma provides them with an opportunity to change their life course, to alter the flow of events, something that would not be possible without the special circumstances created by a stigma. In the film *Ikiru* by Kurosawa, the protagonist, after learning he has terminal cancer, quits his job and attempts to champion the cause of a slum neighborhood. He is driven by the hope of redeeming an undistinguished life and of doing something worthwhile. Presumably, in so doing, he will be able to accept the stigmatizing condition while simultaneously refuting through his actions the attributions that he is a worthless or spoiled person.

Some people, instead of turning a stigma into a virtue, shield themselves from negative self-evaluation by deciding to spend most of their lives among others who are similarly afflicted. Still others may attempt to educate both themselves and others to the actualities of the mark that has elicited the stigmatizing reactions. In so doing, these individuals may work to disassociate the mark from the particular dispositions that may be erroneously assumed to underlie it. In this sense, cancer would be seen simply as a disease and not as a symbol of weakness, evil, or moral inferiority. How individuals will work to free themselves from negative feelings, or whether they will attempt to do so, depends on the structure and content of the self-concept and the role that is accorded the stigmatizing quality or condition.

THE INFLUENCE OF STIGMA ON THE STRUCTURE OF THE SELF-CONCEPT

Traditionally, the self-concept has been thought to be a complex of physical traits (tall, brown-eyed, blonde), attributes that summarize one's behavior (aggressive, compulsive, or outgoing), demographic characteristics (age, sex, family status), and roles (student, scientist, grandfather). In short, the self may be thought to contain all of the descriptors and attributes that can be elicited by giving an individual the Twenty Statements Test, an inventory that asks simply "Who am I?" twenty times in succession (Kuhn and McPartland 1954).

Investigating the influence of a stigma on the structure of the self-concept is particularly complex. With self-esteem, the primary concern is whether a mark of deviance will lead to a good or bad feeling about the self. With respect to the structure of the self-concept, the parallel concern is with how the mark influences the organization of the self, and the possibilities are infinite. Which aspects of the self are most directly influenced by the stigma? Does the stigma influence a physical characteristic, a pattern of behavior, a role, or all of these? These questions are difficult ones, and it is seldom that a mark will remain confined to just one aspect of the self. Marks are easily elaborated in the stigmatizing process to play a more central role in self-definition. If, for example, a woman has a mastectomy, it may appear that the mark concerns the physical self and that most of her many social roles or patterns of behavior will be relatively unaffected. Following her recovery from successful surgery, this woman should be able to continue in her roles of social worker, wife, mother, and marathon runner, and display her characteristic styles of behavior, thus indicating a self-concept relatively unaffected by the presence of the mark. But if the physical self is very important, perhaps central, in this woman's self-definition, her adjustment to the stigmatizing condition may be decidedly more problematic. In such a case, the stigma is likely to influence how she feels about herself generally and, in turn, will have an impact on all the other features of the self as well.

Thus, it is important to consider how deeply the mark pervades the self. A physically debilitating stigma of relatively small magnitude, like a scalded forearm or a missing finger, is not likely to spread through the entire self-concept if it does not hamper most of the individual's activities. On the other hand, if the mark is mental illness, alcoholism, or indictment for criminal activity, the stigma is likely to permeate all aspects of the self, including both schematic and nonschematic domains. In the case of a very pervasive stigma, a single quality or attribute may come to mark each aspect of the self-concept, as if they were separated only by carbon paper. In dominating the self-concept, the stigma becomes the super category from which all others take their meaning. Under these conditions, the markable may feel that the self is completely changed by the presence of the stigma.

A number of factors converge to give a mark this type of "master status" in the self-concept. With a nonconcealable or socially disruptive stigma, for example, much of the reaction from others is likely to be perceived as negative. This negativity may inhibit social interactions and, as a result, inhibit social comparison by the markable of other nonstigmatized traits or abilities. Thus, the fat person who shies from social contact may fail to discover how bright she really is or how well she can sing. Therefore, withdrawal from social interaction begins a cycle that will become difficult to break. The individual does not receive feedback and evaluation about other nonstigmatized aspects of the self and will continue to focus on the stigmatized quality.

The most likely candidates for pervasive stigmata are those that are linked with attributes that are so prominent and central that virtually everyone will develop a self-schema with respect to them. They include race (if other than that of the majority group), age, sex, and overall physical appearance or attributes. In many cases, it may be almost impossible to deemphasize any stigma associated with these aspects of the self. In understanding the impact of a stigma on the self-concept, it is useful to examine whether the stigma is relevant to an aspect of the self that is central or relevant to one that is relatively more peripheral. If an individual becomes stigmatized in a domain for which a self-schema has been developed, the consequences for the overall self-concept are likely to be relatively dramatic. A trauma that leaves the individual unable to walk will be particularly devastating to the structure of the self-concept for a person who has a well-developed schema about his athletic ability. Self-schemas, as well articulated generalizations about the kind of person one is in particular domains, are assumed to comprise the core of the self-concept, and any stigma that directly threatens or undermines a self-schema is likely to have a pervasive impact on the self-concept. In contrast, if the stigma does not influence one of the individual's self-schemas, it may be deemphasized, and its overall impact on the self-concept may be less grave than an observer might expect.

There are a handful of empirical studies on the self-concept of the stigmatized. In one study (Richardson, Hastorf, and Dornbusch 1964), children aged nine to eleven who were slightly to moderately handicapped were asked to describe themselves. Their impairments included cerebral palsy, post-polio impairments, cardiac disorders, and diabetes. While both girls and boys talked openly about their handicap, the boys seemed more affected by it than the girls, presumably because they were more self-schematic with regard to physical activity. Whereas the girls turned readily to nonphysical activities, the boys had greater difficulty finding compensatory activities. As a consequence, they expressed more difficulties in interpersonal relations and attempted to use humor in their attempts to gain acceptance.

Studies of this type (see also Blos 1978; Barton and Cattell, 1972; Brantley and Clifford 1979; Burns and Zweig 1980; Darling and Darling 1982; Kapp 1979; Kleck and Strenta 1980; Niederland 1965; Richman and Harper 1979) indicate that individuals often experience difficulty incorporating their stigmatizing conditions into their overall view of themselves. They do not provide a clear-cut answer to the question of when the stigma will necessarily engulf the self-concept or take on a master status. For the most part, studies in stigma and the self-concept have not been concerned with the relative importance or centrality of the stigmatizing attribute as compared with remaining attributes of the self. Thus, the results are not very illuminating in the present context. Moreover, these studies have not questioned the nature or the structure of self-concepts organized around the *absence* of roles or abilities. When individuals define themselves in terms of being creative, a good tennis player, or a loving father, they organize their knowledge, feelings, and behavioral experience in terms of what they are or what they have done that supports these self-views. The self-concept then reflects "what I am" and "what I can do." Some of us are not creative, not tennis players, or fathers, however. We may be aware of these aspects of the self, those things we are not, but for the most part we rarely organize our experiences according to them. Most often, we do not form elaborate theories about what we are not. If, however, a negative aspect of self does become important in one's own and other's perceptions, it may be necessary to create some type of structure around it; and the question is, what is the nature of this structure of self-knowledge?

It appears that individuals who are fat or crippled or deaf may think in terms of "what they are not" or "what they cannot do," such as "I am not thin," "I cannot wear nice clothes," "I cannot dance," and "I cannot be accepted as an equal at work." This type of self-knowledge explicitly invokes contrast with other people. Every cognition is tied to knowledge of what others have or can do. It may be that a structure based on such negative self-knowledge is intrinsically less stable than one based on positive self-knowledge, and more directly tied to social comparison with past selves.

It is difficult to construct a concept around a void, and it is cognitively easier to form a concept based on affirmation than on negation (Bruner, Goodnow, and Austin 1956). In this respect, it is noteworthy that the anecdotal evidence seems to suggest that, although the stigma may assume a master status immediately following a trauma, in the sense that the mark organizes all of one's thoughts and feelings about the self, it is not likely to continue to do so. The self-concept then appears to mirror one's actions in the world, and not one's inactions or inabilities. Individuals may feel negatively toward themselves but they are unlikely, except for the times immediately following trauma, to feel incomplete or less than whole. The self-concept, therefore, forms around the qualities, attributes, and abilities that one does have.

Quite surprisingly, many blind people and many deaf people, for example, report coming to experience no sense of handicap at all (Higgins 1980). Hunt (1966), in an essay on the role of stigmatized individuals in society, wrote about his life in an institution with people who had severe and often progressive physical disabilities. He was convinced that individuals who were denied some of the usual self-defining qualities, possessions, or roles find other domains in which to define a self. He writes,

> If the worth of human beings depends on a high social status, on the possession of wealth, on a position as parent, husband, or wife—if such things are all-important—then those of us who have lost or never had them are indeed unfortunate. Our lives must be tragically upset and marred forever, we must be only half alive, only half human. And it is a fact that most of us, whatever our explicit views, tend to act as though such "goods" are essential to a fully human existence. Their possession is seen as the key to entry into a promised land of civilized living. But set over against this common sense attitude is another fact, a strange one. In my

> experience even the most severely disabled people retain an ineradicable conviction that they are still fully human in all that is ultimately necessary (p. 147).

The ability of individuals to achieve personal meaning and understanding, even in the face of severe disability, may attest to the difficulty of constructing a self-concept around a void. Some present and positive qualities must be seized upon as the basis of self-definition.

We suggest then that the self-concepts of stigmatized individuals are also built around the traits, abilities, and qualities they do possess. This point is emphasized here because it is with respect to this issue that actors and observers often differ dramatically. The observer, or the marker, focuses on the potentially stigmatized individual and sees what the individual does *not* have or is *not* capable of doing. This lack is figural, in that it dominates the marker's conception of the markable. For the markable, however, the focus is more likely to be on new or different abilities that represent an adaptation to the mark. This potential asymmetry between the actor and the observer in what each assumes about the markable and what is central to the self-conception is one of the stumbling blocks to relationships between markers and those who are marked. It is difficult for each to grasp the assumptions of the other.

THE INFLUENCE OF STIGMA ON HOW OTHERS ARE USED TO DEFINE THE SELF

Avoidance is at the heart of the stigmatizing process. Very often the most appropriate way for markers to cope with the discomfort, revulsion, or hostility they feel toward various marked individuals is to minimize social contact and interaction. As we have stressed repeatedly, the self is a social product and self-definition is heavily dependent on social consensus. In previous sections, we have discussed how other people are critical for validating one's view of one's self, for eliciting and maintaining various aspects of the individual's social behavior. Other people are also vitally important as standards of comparison for one's attitudes, abilities, and attributes. The avoidance produced by the stigmatizing process directly impedes all of these processes and can radically alter the way in which others are used in defining the self.

In his theory of social comparison, Festinger (1950, 1954) postulated a drive to evaluate one's opinions and abilities, a drive giving rise to social comparison efforts. When there is no objective, nonsocial means of evaluating one's opinions and abilities, it is necessary to do so through comparison with the opinions and abilities of others. Specifically, Festinger stated, "Where the dependence upon physical reality is low, the dependence upon social reality is correspondingly high. An opinion, a belief, an attitude is 'correct,' 'valid,' and 'proper' to the extent that it is shared by a group of people with similar beliefs, opinions, and attitudes" (1950, p. 272). As Kelley (1952) further noted, reference groups can perform "normative" functions or "comparison" functions. The normative function comes into play when individuals attempt to gain acceptance in a reference group and feel pressure to behave as the group desires. The comparison function of reference groups is a more purely informational one in which groups serve as a standard by which to judge the correctness of one's thoughts and feelings.

A stigma establishes a barrier between the marker and the marked, thereby interfering with the natural course of the social comparison process and the dependence on social reality. For both the stigmatized individual and the marker, social contact may become stressful, even painful, and if both seek to avoid it, it will be impossible for the stigmatized person to compare adequately his own opinions and abilities to the others'. As a result, marked persons are likely to feel adrift and uncertain about many of their thoughts and feelings. Of course, with television, popular magazines, and mirrors, some amount of comparison can be accomplished without direct social contact. Individuals can engage in a type of *comparative appraisal,* in which they try to estimate where they stand on some attribute relative to other people (Jones and Gerard 1967). As with imitation and modeling, the referent others need not be aware they are being used as a referent. When social interaction is painful, markables may engage primarily in such comparative appraisal.

Some social comparison needs, however, particularly those concerned with evaluating the subtle nuances of self-referent feelings, beliefs, and abilities, cannot be satisfied through comparative appraisal and can only be fulfilled through fairly extensive social contact that directly engages the referent others in social interaction. In that process of *reflected appraisal,* we infer evaluations about ourselves from the behavior of others toward us (Jones and Gerard 1967). The socially isolated, stigmatized person may not only be denied such reflected appraisal with respect to the particular stigmatized attribute, but also on nonstigmatized qualities and traits. Failure to make the necessary social comparisons will further contribute to the markable person's feelings of alienation and estrangement. The inability to test the social reality of one's attitudes and abilities is likely to lead to the construction of a self-concept that lacks coherence or stability.

Moreover, it is not sufficient for the marked individual to have just any social contact; it must be social contact of a certain nature. Individuals need particular others for their comparison. A major hypothesis of social comparison theory states that "given a range of possible persons for comparison, someone else close to one's ability or opinion will be chosen for comparison" (Festinger 1954, p. 121). "If the only comparison available is a very divergent one, the person will not be able to make a subjectively precise evaluation of his opinion or ability" (p. 121). What constitutes a "similar" other and the ease or difficulty with which one can be selected is related to the type of stigma, to its course and origin, and to its centrality or importance to the self-concept.

The first social comparison impulses of the individual who becomes a paraplegic through an automobile accident may be to compare herself with others who were formerly similar—those who served as useful anchors or standards of comparison for abilities and opinions before the accident. The focus of the comparison is likely to be with respect to mobility and independence, and the stigmatized individual will, inevitably, as a result of the comparison, see herself as "one down" or spoiled, incomplete, or broken (cf., Kelley et al. 1960). This can readily lead to feelings of despair, depression, and withdrawal from everyday activity. As a result of the accident, the formerly similar others have now become very divergent, and the divergence serves to underscore the severity and negative consequences of the trauma. With time, however, the individual may begin to cope with her disabled state and to view herself as a paraplegic. She may now want another type of "similar other" for comparison. This similar other may be another paraplegic who has suffered from a similar paralyzing accident, typically one with a longer history of paraplegia than the individual herself. Social comparison information of this type will be crucial for determining her own rate of adjustment and adaptation, and also in determining levels of aspiration for future development. Within the groups of individuals who share particular types of disabilities, this type of comparison is inevitable and leads to some very clear in-group categories. For example, it leads to in-group terms such as "super crips," which is applied to those who can jump curbs and negotiate stairs while in their wheelchairs. At some point and for some aspects of the self, others who are similarly afflicted will be the most useful comparison others.

Those who work with various stigmatized groups report very positive effects from bringing together people who have similar problems. These types of support groups function to provide the needed similar others and to set the stage for the necessary social comparison. Very often, stigmatized individuals, particularly those who have been afflicted with behavioral stigma, such as wives who are abandoned or battered by their husbands, experience tremendous anguish, emotional turmoil, and loss of self-esteem. Initially, many such women fail to realize that as a result of their stigmatized role, they are no longer precisely the *same* individual, and thus, different others may be needed to validate and anchor this somewhat different self. The rejected women may find others in the group who are not completely divergent from themselves on this key aspect of self-relevant experience. This may enable them to begin to define themselves somewhat differently, to construct a new self-concept in this domain.

When individuals become stigmatized as a result of a trauma, it may be particularly important then for them to have contact with others who are similarly marked, even though their most common reaction may be to withdraw from social contact altogether. Exposure to others with similar problems has a least two important consequences. It allows for comparison with respect to coping with the stigma. Second, comparison with others who are similarly marked or stigmatized should allow individuals to focus on attributes and qualities other than the stigmatized ones, and thereby provide the opportunity for them to view themselves as complex and differentiated individuals with valued attributes and abilities. Moreover, social comparison with others who are similarly afflicted may lead to the discovery of divergence from others with similar stigmatizing conditions. This discovery may in turn lead the stigmatized person back into social interaction with former similar others, in an attempt to find individuals more appropriate for comparison. Thus, a teacher who gives birth to a handicapped child may find after some period of time that she has a much greater need for and use for interaction with a former group of teacher friends than with a support group for parents of children with birth defects. This return to a former reference group may provide the individual with an opportunity to divert some attention away from the stigmatizing condition and focus it on other more positive features of the self. These generalizations about the consequences of social comparison only hold, of course, if the comparison others are models in the sense of coping well.

The role of others in defining the stigmatized self is a problem worthy of further study and may be critical for understanding the impact of a stigma on the self-concept. One of the most dramatic examples of the pernicious consequences of a failure to find similar others comes from individuals who have spent time in hospitals for mental disorders. Very often individuals who are widely different from one another and who suffer from every type of problem, from relatively mild neurosis to severe psychopathology, are treated as one similarly afflicted group. They are, for example, taken en masse on field trips to a museum or to shopping centers. These patients are thereby forced to see themselves as others (i.e., normals in the outside world) see them. The neurotic may then take on some of the stigma of the schizophrenic because the outside visit forces him to take the role of the normal and to realize that in some respects he is indeed similar to these others. It is on these occasions that many patients may feel the most "crazy" and the most uncertain about their progress, precisely because of the lack of appropriately similar others to help achieve a meaningful social reality and to help them diffuse the effects of taking the role of the outside other. Under these circumstances the tendency to cease comparison altogether may increase, and one of the major forces ensuring this individual's link to the larger social community may be removed. Once other people are no longer used as direct-comparison others, interaction with them may cease altogether, and this is particularly so if interaction is likely to lead to further stigmatization (as may be the case with a nonconcealable, aesthetically displeasing, or socially disruptive stigma). The individual may then have little choice except to adjust to less social interaction than is desired or to become part of a social milieu in which the stigma is not salient.

The extent, nature, and variety of social comparison that is necessary for any one aspect of the self is highly dependent on how this aspect of the self has become incorporated into the self-concept. If the stigma relates to an aspect of the self that the individual does not consider central to self-definition, presumably there will be little drive to evaluate this aspect of self. If, however, the stigmatized attribute is considered important to self-definition, other people will be essential, at least until the markable develops a self-schema with respect to this aspect of self. As discussed earlier, self-schemas indicate that an individual has come to terms with a particular quality, trait, or attribute of the self and has established a relatively stable and enduring view of the self in this regard. Self-schemas represent those aspects of the self that are anchored by past experience and, thus, those that are not readily mutable. In the domain of their schemas, individuals are likely to behave consistently in a variety of divergent situations. This does not imply that individuals will be free from a self-serving bias or distortions of social reality in their schematic domains. It means only that they know what to expect for themselves and how to understand and explain their reactions in these domains. In contrast, those aspects of self for which the individual does not have a self-schema are much more the province of the social environment, and in these non-schematic areas of the self other people are necessary to provide structure and meaning.

The person who has been stigmatized since birth with an unalterable condition is likely to have developed a self-schema with respect to the stigma and will not be constantly driven toward social comparison with others on this aspect of self. Achieving a framework of understanding about one's stigmatized quality or attributes is difficult, however, and those marked later in life are much more likely to seek out others to reach a socially confirmed self appraisal. Some of the most critical aspects of successful coping may involve decisions about appropriate comparison others and decisions about shifts in comparison—when and with regard to what shall the markable person compare himself with whom? Timing factors are undoubtedly important, since, as we have noted before, it may be very useful to compare with others who are in the same boat initially, but equally adaptive to shift toward a broader base of social comparison at some later point in time.

The choice of comparison others is not entirely up to the markable person, however. Higgins (1980) reports the difficulties that those deaf people with good speech and some usable hearing have in finding appropriate comparison others. Such hearing-impaired people may first seek to compare themselves with others in the hearing world, only to discover that, despite their ability to speak and to hear somewhat, they are still widely discrepant from most "normal" others, and cannot really evaluate their hearing ability. Those hearing-impaired people may then turn to deaf communities, where their skills of the hearing world will at least provide them some measure of superiority and perhaps some feelings of achievement. Their reception in the deaf community may not be a warm one, however, and they may be viewed as "putting on airs" (Schowe 1979) because of their skills. Higgins quotes a woman experiencing just such difficulties in trying to find appropriate comparison others: "Some of the deaf people feel that I'm hearing and I'm not totally accepted by them. And then again I'm not really accepted by hearing people. So I'm right in the middle. [The deaf] don't really accept me. They say 'You're hearing.' [They say that] because they know I can hear and I can talk" (p. 84). Until this person comes to terms with her disability and develops some fairly stable conception of her hearing ability and its role in her self-definition, she may continue to experience uncertainty over how to evaluate her ability and may be taken to task for her attempts at comparative or reflected appraisal. If a referent other assumes that the individual is too discrepant in ability, and if the discrepancy is such that the referent other appears superior, the individual may well be rejected as deviant.

Thus, the selection of comparison others for the stigmatized individual is a process that challenges one's view of self and that importantly implicates others' view of the self. But the selection process is not left entirely to the individual's discretion. The individual with paralyzed legs who attempts to walk with braces and become a "walker" may be disdained by other wheelchair users who feel that he is using an inappropriate comparison group to define himself. Anybody who is deviant in some respect may have experienced this type of difficulty in finding referent others and may only cease to have conflict when he develops a personal framework or self-schema that is somewhat autonomous and not completely linked to the potentially negative reactions and evaluations of others.

To this point, we have implied that the major obstacle for the stigmatized individual was in locating an appropriate set of comparison others. We must also consider what happens if the individual is not pleased with the results of the comparison. Put in other terms, what happens to the self-concept of an individual who constantly suffers by comparison with others? In any discussion of social comparison, it is important to note that although individuals may indeed be driven to evaluate their abilities and opinions, they also are undeniably concerned with seeing themselves in a good light and feeling good about themselves. Thus, the stigmatized individual may experience a tension between seeking out comforting comparison others (e.g., those who are worse off) and those who are better off and who, therefore, provide some realistic insight into one's degree of disability. In a discussion of this fact, Brickman and Bulman (1977) have noted that hedonic pressures push individuals to avoid social comparison situations in which they might feel insecure, insensitive, guilty, or deviant. Because of these pressures, comparison with inferior others, although in some respects less useful for information about one's relative standing, may have much greater hedonic value than comparison with superior others. Given this, the marked individual, who may already feel unworthy or discredited by the reactions of others, may be understandably reluctant to engage in social comparison that further contributes to these negative feelings. He or she may instead choose comparison with inferior others or cease comparison altogether. This is yet another reason why the marked person may be likely to use other people less than the unmarked person in constructing the self-concept.

Given the difficulties associated with the reactions of others that are likely to be experienced by a markable person, it is hardly surprising that many stigmatized individuals may alter their comparison strategies so that they are no longer comparing themselves with others, but rather with themselves at earlier points in time. To the extent that one is divorced from a great deal of social interaction, this may become an adaptive strategy, and the one most likely to provide accurate information. Unlike comparison with others, even fairly appropriate others, comparison with one's self at an earlier time is likely to generate positively valued information for many stigmatized conditions. A plastic surgeon recounts the story of a small boy with a terribly disfiguring facial tumor who played freely, happily, and unselfconsciously with the other children, stopping only to tell an adult onlooker who was staring, "You think I'm ugly? You should have seen me before my operation" (Chase 1981). Relying on the power of comparison with the former self to make one feel good, the team of plastic surgeons who operate on cleft-palate children at Stanford University Hospital reports that they routinely wait several months before repairing the cleft palate (Chase 1981). The available technology makes this operation feasible almost immediately following birth, but the surgeons choose to postpone this operation because at birth the child is almost universally viewed as an extension or an aspect of the selves of the parents. If the operation is performed immediately, parents appear to spend their time endlessly comparing their children (and implicitly themselves) with other children and are very seldom completely satisfied with the outcome of the cleft-palate operation. Yet, when the operation is performed after the child has been at home with the disfigured face for a few months, the comparison process is fundamentally altered. Following the operation, the parents tend to compare the child primarily with the former self and are universally pleased with the outcome of the operation. It is important to note, however, that comparison with the self at an earlier time may also generate very negative information. The gymnast who dwells on his life before his trampoline accident may simply make his current disability all the more salient.

The Stigma of Being Normal

("Bodybuilder Wins $210,000 for Physique-Ruining Wreck," *New York Times*, March 21, 1983, an AP dispatch)

A jury has awarded $210,000 to a bodybuilder who lost his perfect physique in a motorcycle accident.

Matthew DeCaprio blamed the driver of a school bus for making him look like a normal person. Friday, a Circuit Court jury agreed, ordering King's Academy

> **to compensate the 21-year old for his loss of capacity to enjoy life.**
>
> **His attorney, James Tuthill, showed pictures of his client in bodybuilding poses before the accident. "Look at the size of those muscles," Mr. Tuthill said. "He's 100 percent disabled."**

In sum, the process of successfully coping with a stigma can perhaps be seen as the process of finding appropriate different others. Social comparison with these appropriate others should enable one to construct a positive, coherent, and stable self-concept. In exploring the use of other people in defining the self, it may be important to examine the antecedents and consequences of various comparison strategies and how they may vary across behavioral domains and across people. A clear agenda for future research in social comparison processes would be to identify the condition under which the markable compares himself or herself with (1) normals, (2) other, more miserable markables, (3) markables who are doing well (supercopers), and (4) the previous self. It should also be possible to identify individual differences in social comparison strategies. There are, for example, those individuals who always compare themselves with others who seem better off, or whose fate in life appears more favorable. Others, however, seem riveted to comparison with the relatively downtrodden. Those who face life with a "there but for the grace of God go I" perspective are likely to spend relatively more time feeling good about themselves and their accomplishments and achievements, regardless of their stigma, than are those who feel that everyone else but them has it made. Finally, it should be possible to determine how the social context affects comparison choices for the same person.

INFLUENCE OF STIGMA ON PAST AND FUTURE SELVES

Another very important aspect of the self that must be considered in a discussion of stigma is the role of "other selves"—selves of the future and selves of the past (Markus and Nurius 1982). The role of these other selves is critical to our understanding of the impact of a particular stigma on the self-concept. These selves are not indicated by our usual measures of self-concept, which typically ask the individual to describe his or her present self, but they form the basis for our personal history as well as the essence of our future perspective. The past selves that are incorporated within the self-concept allow the individual to hold onto a self that may have existed before a stigma, and they provide a constant point of comparison. Future selves are essential for growth, development, and motivation. In some cases, the most drastic consequences of a stigma for the self may not be on the present self but on possible selves.

With regard to past selves, some individuals may be able to resist self-stigmatization and the attendant negative self-evaluation by glorifying or romanticizing a particular past self. A person who is victimized by a progressively degenerative physical disease may cling to his past athletic self. Although this aspect of the self is no longer manifest, it was, and in many respects still is, a part of the self, in the sense that the self-concept is an integration of all of our actions in the world. The existence of a past self that is not accessible to most observers is another reason for a lack of congruence between self and other stigmatization, and also a reason why markables may appear to attach relatively less importance to a particular stigma than others in the social environment.

Whether or not past selves have a role in the stigmatizing process depends again on the nature of the mark and on how the individual decides to construct the self. Those who are marked from birth have no past unstigmatized selves. They may, however, have past selves that were relatively more debilitated by the same stigma, and thus, they can use themselves as standards of comparison for present performance. The past self also may be important if the stigma was acquired in an important or consequential earlier phase of one's life. If the stigmatizing condition is an injury from a war, the past self may be particularly important in constructing one's present self. Thus the origin and timing of a traumatic event may dictate how deeply the past self is involved. If the condition arises after the person has married and established his professional identity, the mark may not require radical changes in the self-concept.

Future selves are also important in understanding stigma effects. The young girl who is left paralyzed as the result of an automobile accident is without the use of her legs. But she is also without the use of many possible future selves. Her future selves as a ballerina, a gymnastics coach, a mother running after her children in the park, or a trial lawyer striding forcefully to the bench are all destroyed. Loss of these aspects of the self may contribute to the overwhelming feelings of despair and hopelessness that initially accompany an accident of this sort. They are also examples of other aspects of the self that, as with past selves, are not usually accessible to others, even intimate others, and it is not likely that therapy or rehabilitation training will attend to them. In many cases, these possible selves are not particularly likely outcomes for the individual; they may even be quite remote and far-fetched. But they are symbols that the presently constructed self is not inevitable. They also represent the private self that does not have to be responsive to the demands and requirements of others. When these possible selves are destroyed, it may be necessary that they be replaced, if the individual is to cope effectively with the stigmatizing condition. In fact, an effective therapy for many types of permanently stigmatizing conditions may involve education about potential possible selves through exposure to others who have successfully coped with their own stigmatizing condition. Either the presence or the absence of these possible selves also may be associated with a lack of congruence between self and other perceptions of the stigma. If, for example, the self appears to be overemphasizing the stigmatizing condition relative to others, it may be because of the effects of the stigma on one's possible selves and the consequences this holds for the individual's motivation and future perspective. We should note, however, an intriguing alternative hypothesis about the relationship between stigmatizing conditions and possible selves. It could be that disabling injuries have the potential to release us from the anxieties and obligations of future selves that may have been ordained for us by others (parents, mentors) or by our internalized commitments to success. Thus, various potentially stigmatizing conditions, particularly those that are serious but not completely debilitating (e.g., a bad back or arthritis), can actually have some positive consequences in freeing us from the pressures attendant on trying to realize certain possible selves.

The existence of possible selves is also related to the creation and maintenance of certain stigmas, particularly some behavioral ones. For example, the alcoholic may not be motivated to stop drinking because he possesses a very clear possible self as a nondrinker or a social drinker. The clear image of this possible self may lull the individual into thinking that this self can replace the present self at any time and with very little effort. Present behavior may be discounted as not real and not important. The alcoholic may prefer to believe that real life, the life that counts, will only begin when one stops drinking. Drug abusers and young criminals may entertain the same logic, and the circumstances are similar for overeaters. Many obese people orient their entire lives toward a future when they will be thin. Nothing done in the present is important or significant because this fat self is not the real self. When the possible self becomes this powerful, the individual may actually be able to separate body from mind, or to ignore the body altogether and treat it like a foreign object. This may allow the stigmatizing condition to persist because the actions of the body, such as overeating, are viewed as separate from the self. In these examples the existence of possible selves may then lead the stigmatized individuals to seriously underemphasize the gravity of the current conditions.

CONCLUDING REMARKS

In constructing a self-concept from one's own perceptions and those conveyed by others, there are a number of general concerns that must be confronted by the markable person. The first centers on the question of "Why me?" The answer to this question may well determine the nature and the course of future efforts at self-definition. An attributional approach to this query suggests two general classes of answers—those that involve external, situational factors and those that implicate internal, dispositional causes. The markable person who chooses to find an answer among the first set of reasons is likely to feel victimized and taken advantage of and to decide that life is purposeless or absurd. Those who choose to explore the latter set of causes may conclude that they are being punished for former transgressions by themselves or their ancestors, that they have been chosen to bear the stigma so as to achieve a nobler character through suffering, or that they are experiencing a type of cosmic equity in which they must tolerate pain now in order to receive their rewards in another world.

An intriguing program of research by Coates, Wortman and Abbey (1979), on the way people respond to uncontrollable life events, implies that it is the rare individual who finds comfort in the notion that personal disaster, tragedies, or misfortunes are chance events. Many people seem unable to resist attaching special significance to the fact of being marked. In fact, Coates, et al. find that women who have been raped or assaulted cope more effectively with the trauma if they hold themselves in part responsible for their fate. The same findings have been documented with individual suffering from severe spinal cord injuries. On reflection, these seemingly paradoxical findings are quite reasonable. An answer to the "why me" question that says "No reason, it was chance" implies a chaotic and frightening world in which the individual has little control. Such a view violates many of our prevailing assumptions that the world is a benign or at least a just place (Lerner 1980). Work by Kobasa (1979) on reactions to stressful life events corroborates these suggestions. She finds that executives who are characterized by what she terms "hardiness" cope most effectively with stress. Hardiness is defined as "a strong commitment to self, an attitude of vigorousness toward the environment, a sense of meaningfulness, and an internal locus of control" (p. 1). One of the consequences of such hardiness is that these individuals find a way to view change and unexpected circumstances as a challenge, even when they are extremely incongruous and stress-inducing. These hardy individuals are those who would cope with a stigmatizing condition by viewing it as a personal test.

As stigmatized individuals confront the "why me" problem, they must also decide both if and how they will reflect the stigma in their self-concept. In the previous discussion, we focused primarily on how individuals accept and come to terms with their stigma. We have discussed examples where individuals do not give as much emphasis to their mark as others in the social environment, but we have not considered outright attempts to resist or disavow stigmatization. Such action is likely to occur among those who determine they have been unfairly victimized and feel they do not deserve to be stigmatized. Such resistance to stigmatization may take the form of banding together with fellow targets into "fat is beautiful" or gay-power groups. Such groups have at least two functions. They allow markables to experience social environments in which they are not stigmatized by others, and they provide support for negative evaluation of the stigmatizing majority group. This response to stigmatization is based on resistance to being marked, yet it also involves a change in the self-concept because it requires changing one's set of comparison others, withdrawing from one social environment and embracing another, and redefining an attribute of the self that was previously considered to be negative as positive. Because a resistance to stigmatization involves an incongruence between self-perception and the perception by at least some others, the self-concept of these individuals is likely to be somewhat unstable and vulnerable. Maintenance of some stability and coherence in the self-concept is likely to require considerable energy and activity.

Another way to resist stigmatization, and the one that is most likely among those who accept both the negativity of the mark and some personal responsibility for it, is to reconstitute the self. In so doing, the markable person may decide that the stigmatized attribute is not essential or central to the self-concept. Many individuals seem to have tremendous capacities for such compensation. For example, an individual who is severely injured in an automobile accident may decide that his running ability, a domain of a previous self-schema, is no longer critical for self-definition. He may eventually replace this focus with a concern over his ability as a raconteur, a cartoonist, or an author of short stories. Those individuals with the most diverse or complex self-concepts are likely to be those who cope most effectively with a trauma because they have the option to shift their attention and redefine themselves in alternative domains. Such complexity provides resources for further self-definition and may well be associated with flexible and adaptive responses to a stigmatizing condition (Linville 1982).

Another form of reconstitution of the self-concept rests with some redefinition of what constitutes the "true" self and with what is necessary for one to be "fully human" (Hunt 1966). Those who are severely stigmatized and for whom there is no obvious means of compensation may attempt to expand the internal personal self, effectively reducing the social or relational self. Such individuals may devote their efforts to cultivating the spiritual self and may in fact distance themselves from the physical or material self. Such a reconstitution of self may often involve religious or spiritual figures as the important comparison others. Resisting stigmatization by restructuring the self-concept involves an attempt to gain some congruence between self and other perceptions, and thereby achieving a relatively more stable and coherent self-concept. In so doing, there must be some acknowledgment of the negativity of the stigmatizing condition. But, if the negativity attached to mark is not to engulf the entire self-concept, it will be necessary for the individual to find some other important aspect of self that can be evaluated positively by the self and others so that the weight or importance attached to the mark can be lessened.

In this chapter we have explored the consequences of stigma for the self-concept. Self-concept construction has been viewed as an ongoing process that involves the interweaving of one's own and other's thoughts, feelings, and behavior with respect to the self. A stigma modifies this process by influencing the structure of the self (including past, present, and future selves), self-esteem, and the social comparison. Depending on how the stigma influences these features of the process, the individual will experience relative congruence or discrepancy between self and other perception. When the individual experiences a discrepancy, there is likely to be instability and a change in the self-concept. When some level of congruence is achieved between self and other perception, the individual may be able to construct a stable and coherent self-concept that will mediate effective social functioning, or at least define the problem of social functioning more sharply, so that the individual can begin to cope with it realistically. Further analysis of the effects of stigma on self-concept awaits further conceptual development of the self as an active social process, as well as empirical work documenting how the components of the self-concept reflect and incorporate stigma.

• CHAPTER FIVE •

The Role of Stereotypes in Marked Relationships

EMBARRASSMENT, FRUSTRATION, AND ANGER are just a few of the unpleasant emotions we experience when we find ourselves being stereotyped by others. For stigmatized individuals, the pain of being stereotyped is especially acute. Indeed, stereotyping is at the heart of the stigmatizing process.

Walter Lippman (1922), defined stereotypes more than fifty years ago as the "pictures in our heads" that we hold of others. Although stereotypes have been defined in many different ways since Lippman first introduced the concept (Ashmore and Del Boca 1981; Miller 1982), most definitions state that stereotypes are beliefs about social groups or categories that are (1) overgeneralized, and (2) widely shared. Some authorities also require that the term *stereotype* be confined to "negative" beliefs that have no basis in fact. We will take a more flexible position and define stereotypes as overgeneralized, largely false beliefs about members of social categories that are frequently, but not always, negative. Since the focus of this book is interpersonal relations, our analysis will embrace those overgeneralized beliefs that may be idiosyncratic, as well as those that are widely shared. Obviously, any false belief about a social category, no matter how widely shared, can affect the belief holder's relations with members of that category.

THE RELATIONSHIP BETWEEN STEREOTYPING, CATEGORIZING, AND LABELING

Stereotyping and categorizing are interrelated, even though they are separable cognitive processes. Both processes reflect the tendency of the human mind to organize and simplify the overwhelming complexity of the social and physical world. In Lippmann's words (1922, p. 16), "the real environment is altogether too complex, and too fleeting for direct acquaintance. We are not equipped to deal with so much subtlety, so much variety, so many variations and combinations. And although we have to act in that environment, we have to reconstruct it on a simpler model before we can manage with it."

POORLY CHOSEN LABEL FOR OLDER AMERICANS

Letters to *New York Times*, August 13, 1981.

To the Editor:

I'm surprised that William Safire chose to use the word "geezer" in commenting on proposed changes in Social Security. . . . *The American Heritage Dictionary* calls the word "slang" and defines it as "an eccentric old man." Does Mr. Safire really believe that there is something eccentric about those who currently receive benefits from Social Security and are therefore concerned about the possibility of present or future changes? If he does he very badly misreads this segment of the population. If he doesn't hold such a belief, he is guilty of very sloppy use of the English language, of which he proclaims himself to be an expert. In any event . . . he hinders intelligent discussion of a most important subject. . . .

To the Editor:

We older Americans have power we haven't used yet, and we resent the label "geezer power" attributed to us by William Safire. . . .

Categorization is the process of lumping different social and physical objects into a single category and is often a precursor to the stereotyping process. As Taylor (1981) observes, we do not stereotype individuals, we stereotype individuals as members of categories. A major consequence of thinking of a person as a member of a particular category is that we generate additional information about that person. When we decide that a person is a member of a particular social category, such as the physically disabled, we know, or at least we think we know, everything about that person that we believe to be true of all members of the category. Thus, the set of expectancies that comes to mind when we learn that a person is disabled constitutes the stereotypes that we hold of disabled people. Some of these expectancies undoubtedly will be correct, but not all of them will be, and few if any of them will be true of all disabled people.

Since the categories that locate or identify people so significantly affects both the beliefs others hold of them and the way others relate to them, the process by which a person becomes identified with a particular category is important to understand. Categorization can occur along any dimension on which people vary, such as race, age, gender, personality, social class, religion, and physical health. To describe any one person accurately requires information about that person's membership in these and many other categories. In fact, the uniqueness of any particular individual can be represented by the particular constellation of categories to which he or she is assigned. Categorization per se, therefore, neither deprives individuals of their individuality nor produces erroneous expectancies and beliefs. The problem with our heavy reliance on the categorization process is that people rarely see or relate to one another in terms of all or even more than a few of the categories to which they belong. Often we are seen by others only in terms of a single category, such as age, gender, ethnic group, or nationality. For most of us, the categories in which we are placed vary from context to context. People in a hospital setting, for example, will not view us in terms of the same categories as will people in a university or athletic setting. People will categorize us in terms of those categories that are important to them and that help them differentiate us from the other people within a particular context. The categorization "college student," for example, will be much more informative and useful to a summer employer than to a college administrator or to another college student. Finer categorizations, such as a sophomore or premed student, will be required by those latter individuals.

The process of categorizing marked others has special properties associated with it. People are especially stigmatized when their membership in one category pervades most or all of their social interactions and assumes the character of a "master status" (Goffman 1963). All of us belong to categories that are evaluated negatively in at least some contexts, and within these contexts, we can be described as being stigmatized, but a person only possesses a stigmatized *identity* when membership in one, generally negative, category dominates all his or her interactions. A blind person, for example, can never just be a college student or a lawyer, at best he or she will be "the blind college student" or "the blind lawyer." Most often, he or she will simply be "the blind one."

Misclassification Errors in Categorization

Our general tendency both to view others in terms of only a few categories and to view people within a category as being more similar to one another than they actually are leads us into certain serious errors of judgment. People also can err, however, by placing others in categories to which they do not belong. Misclassification errors are particularly likely to occur when the criteria for category membership are either not directly observable or are vague.

Many categories are defined by criteria that are clear but not easily recognized. For example, the criteria for numerous physical diseases, such as cancer and diabetes, are well-defined, but they are not easily diagnosed during the course of casual interaction. Similarly, while the criteria for being an illegitimate child, a mastectomy patient, a Jew, or an ex-convict are unambiguous, the information pertinent to these criteria is not always readily accessible. In fact, at various points in history, Jews and ex-convicts have been forced to display badges or brands identifying them as such. When the defining characteristic of the stigmatized category is not directly observable, individuals must rely on inference for category assignment.

Interestingly, one of the devices we use to aid us in determining whether or not a person belongs to a category that has concealable criteria is our stereotype of that category. In other words, stereotypic beliefs can guide the categorization process as well as follow from it. This statement is not as puzzling as it may at first seem. A stereotype is, after all, a presumed correlation between one trait (category membership) and other traits (e.g., personality and physical characteristics). Realizing this, it should not be surprising to learn that people often infer category membership from the presence of other characteristics with which they believe the category is correlated. For example, many people think a homosexual can be identified by his or her appearance, and, not too long ago, hair length, particularly on males, was used as a diagnostic cue for political ideology. Some of the cues people use to determine a person's category may actually be empirically correlated with the category (e.g., liberalism and long hair), but the relationship will never be perfect, and many instances of incorrect inclusion will occur.

The stigmatized, of course, are generally aware of the traits commonly associated with their social category and may frequently endeavor to avoid manifesting any of these traits. Homosexuals who wish to conceal their category membership, for example, may studiously avoid dressing or behaving in a manner that conforms to the prevailing stereotypes of homosexuals (Rechy 1963). On the other hand, those stigmatized individuals who wish to be identified with a social category may purposefully conform to the physical stereotype of that category. People's clothing often becomes a uniform that reflects category pride and cohesion (certain gay communities) or more instrumental purposes (prostitutes). Even in these circumstances, however, erroneous judgments of inclusion and exclusion will occur.

Incorrect category inclusion sometimes occurs not because the criteria are nonobservable or concealable, but because the criteria for inclusion are vague or arbitrary. Consider, for example, the criteria that determine whether or not a person is an alcoholic or is mentally ill. There are criteria for these classifications, of course, but the criteria are vague, and in these, as well as many other cases, the difference between members of the category and nonmembers is only one of degree. The sharp distinctions that can be drawn between paraplegics and nonparaplegics, ex-convicts and those who have not been in prison, cannot be drawn between alcoholics and heavy drinkers or between eccentric and neurotic people. There is even arbitrariness involved in the classification of blindness and deafness, as is implied by the designations *legally blind* and *legally deaf.*

"Isn't It Nice that She Knows Her Name and Address?"

Jaekle, Nancy A., "Understanding a Misunderstood Minority," *New York Times,* New Jersey Opinion, December 20, 1981.

[This comment was made by a salesperson] to a woman as she and her daughter waited to be helped. Because of the daughter's slurred speech and awkward gait, it was assumed—automatically—that her mind also did not function very well. When their turn came, the woman asked her daughter, a graduate student who has cerebral palsy, to give the necessary information for the charge account. . . .

The salesperson chose to make a generalization based on hearsay and gut feeling. She made a prejudgment without bothering to verify its merits. Her perception of the handicapped, her beliefs about the minority and the common traits she attributes to its members led her to assume that the young woman was of low intelligence.

Contact with the daughter evoked fear, pity, hate, anger, contempt and sympathy, and, although the salesperson probably felt a combination of all these emotions, she responded from fear and sympathy.

Some physicians [are] guilty of this. They tend to categorize people according to social visibility, grouping individuals into pigeon holes and responding to them in terms of this classification rather than in terms of their uniqueness.

The process of assigning people to categories for which criteria are vague or arbitrary is of special interest to that school of sociologists known as "labeling theorists" (see Chapter 3). Labeling theorists are concerned with the issue of who is and who is not labeled (categorized) in cases that involve vague membership criteria. A common theme in the writings of many labeling theorists is the conviction that the labeling of markable individuals is largely a social-political act that has little to do with the moral or psychological characteristics of the markables (Schur 1980). In the case of mental illness, for example, it has been argued that there is in fact no such category as the mentally ill and that the term *mentally ill* is simply a label that is applied to undesirable people (Szasz 1963). Many of us find it difficult to accept the argument that there is no such condition as mental illness, but the point that we have no clear criteria for mental illness is well taken. The evaluation of test scores and clinical interviews always requires some arbitrariness. Similarly, the term *alcoholic* may conjure up a fairly clear image for most of us, but what exactly is an alcoholic? It is a person who drinks a lot, but how much? When does a person cease being a heavy drinker and become an alcoholic? These are not easy questions to answer.

As we shall see later, one of the most important consequences of having vague criteria for category membership is that it is exceedingly difficult to become uncategorized once categorized. People who are pronounced as alcoholics continue to be viewed as alcoholics until they stop drinking altogether, and even then, at least in the eyes of Alcoholics Anonymous, and likely many others, they remain alcoholics.

WHY DO PARTICULAR STEREOTYPES EXIST?

The processes of stereotyping and categorization may be an unavoidable component of cognitive functioning, but the particular content of categories and stereotypes is not. Individuals and cultures vary greatly in the categories they consider important and in the traits they ascribe to members of different categories. The question of stereotype acquisition is one to which social psychologists have devoted considerable attention. No single theory has emerged from this inquiry (see Ashmore and Del Boca 1981 for a review), but three general orientations have been established: (1) the sociocultural approach; (2) the motivational approach; and (3) the cognitive approach.

The Sociocultural Perspective

According to the sociocultural perspective, we acquire beliefs about others the same way we acquire beliefs about anything—from the information we receive from others and from direct experience. According to this position, beliefs about minorities and other markable groups are transmitted by parents, the media, and other socialization agents. A sociocultural approach is particularly persuasive on the question of how erroneous beliefs are transmitted, but it also offers speculations on how erroneous beliefs emerge in the first place. Selective and unrepresentative experience is one factor pointed to as contributing to the formation of erroneous beliefs. If our interactions with markables are limited to certain contexts or role relationships, we may develop a biased impression of the markable. This is especially likely to occur if we do not recognize the impact that the context or role has on the behavior of the markables. In an insightful discussion of this point, Allport (1954) argued that many of the traits commonly ascribed to minority individuals (e.g., timidity, dependency) are ones that generally characterize people in positions of little power, regardless of ethnicity. Allport referred to those traits that the circumstances of minimal power induce in individuals as "traits of victimization."

Exposure to only a limited and nonrepresentative sample of a social category also can lead to the development of invalid beliefs. For example, the once pervasive belief among psychiatrists that homosexuals suffer from various forms of pathology may have stemmed, at least in part, from the fact that most of the homosexuals that psychiatrists encountered were disturbed ones who were seeking psychiatric help (Rothbart 1981).

Motivational Approaches

Various authorities have contended that stereotypes of social categories are often motivated by social and psychological needs. Those needs that have been proposed to have a functional relationship to social stereotypes are as interesting as they are diverse. The origin of stereotypic beliefs, according to the psychodynamic position, is to be found in the internal conflicts and needs of the belief holder (e.g., Adorno et al. 1950). The process of attributing traits to other groups, the psychodynamic position argues, is often ego-defensive in nature and represents the projection of thoughts or impulses that the attributor wishes to deny in himself. A proponent of the psychodynamic position might contend, for instance, that the reason minorities and outgroups are so often described by markers as dirty, lazy, and sexually promiscuous (Le Vine and Campbell 1972) is because the markers are threatened by the existence of these qualities or impulses within themselves. Projecting these "threatening" traits onto others, presumably enables the markers to direct their hostility and frustration toward the markables and away from themselves. As interesting and provocative as the psychodynamic perspective is, its ability to explain the stereotypes associated with most stigmatized groups would seem limited. How, for example, would it explain why the mentally ill are seen as uncoordinated or why obese people are seen as jolly?

Psychologists not directly associated with Freudian tradition have also proposed motivational accounts of the stereotyping process. Lerner (1980), for example, has argued that people's need to believe in a just world often influences the beliefs they hold concerning certain social categories. According to Lerner, individuals are motivated to believe that the world is stable and orderly, and that there is a general approximation between a person's character or actions and his or her outcomes. This belief is presumed to be important to individuals because it allows them to hold the derivative beliefs that their own actions and character will be rewarded and that they have some control over their lives. Lerner has proposed that the existence of this need predisposes people to hold unjustifiably negative evaluations of victims of misfortune or injustice. Beliefs that members of victim groups are weak, unworthy, foolish, careless, or otherwise different, Lerner argues, distance the markable from the marker and allow the latter to believe that he or she can avoid a similar fate.

In addition to explaining why victims are so often seen to deserve their fates, the concept of a "just world" belief may also help explain why victims of misfortunes are so often seen to be more unhappy, bitter and depressed than they actually are (Cameron et al. 1973; Hunt 1966; Titley 1969). The need to believe that the world is stable and orderly dictates not only that victims of undesirable life events be viewed as possessing qualities that make their fates just, but also that victims of such events be viewed as actually suffering. Witnessing undeserved misfortunes may threaten a person's confidence that he or she will be able to achieve and enjoy a good life, but witnessing a victim of a misfortune who is not devastated by the misfortune threatens a person's conception of what is necessary for personal happiness and a good life. If happiness is so relative and so much a state of mind that even a paraplegic or a blind person can be happy, then most people's recipe for the good life would seem untenable. In short, it may be as psychologically difficult for people to admit that victims of misfortunes can be happy as it is for them to admit that victims do not necessarily have undesirable characteristics. A best selling recent book *When Bad Things Happen to Good People* attempts to argue against "just world" thinking. In this book Kushner (1981) puts forward the central message that afflictions and suffering are for the most part random, the results of natural causes. They are not part of God's retribution for the victim's sin or character flaws. At the same time, the obvious premise of the book (documented by numerous examples) is that a belief in God's equitable interventions is widespread.

A number of writers have argued that, in addition to serving various psychological needs or motives, stereotypes can serve social needs, such as justifying the exploitation and oppression of markable groups. This argument is made most frequently in reference to minority groups (Fishman 1956; Le Vine and Campbell 1972), but it also has been raised in connection with the mentally ill and some other stigmatized groups (Gleidman and Roth 1980; Schur 1980).

The Cognitive Approach

The currently ascendant cognitive approach (Hamilton 1981) argues that just as the process of stereotyping is the result of a basic feature of our cognitive functioning, the content of our stereotypes is also a result of that functioning. Researchers with a cognitive orientation have identified a variety of human information-processing features that they feel bias the content of our stereotypes. Much of this research has stemmed from work done on judgmental heuristics (Kahneman, Slovic, and Tversky 1982; Nisbett and Ross 1980) and illusory correlations (Hamilton 1981). In addition we shall consider the contributions of imaginative role-taking in generating and sustaining stereotypes.

Judgmental Heuristics

One of the aids or heuristics that people use to estimate the prevalence of a particular category, event, or behavior is the ease with which it comes to mind (Tversky and Kahneman 1973). This "availability heuristic," as it is called, generally produces valid judgments, but it can lead to errors, if, for some reason, infrequent events or categories are particularly easily recalled. Consider two apparently very different questions: (1) Are there more words that start with the letter *R* or words that have *R* as a third letter? (2) What percentage of former mental patients are dangerous? These questions have two similarities. First, people will most likely endeavor to answer them both by trying to recall instances of the specific cases. Second, people will most likely err considerably in their answers to both. Most people will estimate incorrectly that there are more words starting with *R* than words that have *R* as the third letter because it is easier to think of words starting with *R*. (In fact, there are three times as many words that have *R* as a third letter.) Similarly, most people will overestimate the percentage of former mental patients who are dangerous because instances of dangerous former mental patients come more readily to mind than instances of nondangerous ones. This bias contributes to the stereotype that mental patients are highly dangerous. Of course, the tendency of the media to give more attention to dangerous mental patients exaggerates this bias even further.

Illusory Correlations

Another factor that contributes to the exaggeration of the perceived relationship between certain social categories and certain traits is the human memory's tendency to associate unusual or distinctive stimuli (Hamilton 1981). The existence of this tendency makes it more likely that we will, among other things, recall negative acts that are associated with a marked individual than ones associated with an unmarked individual. The hostile or disruptive classroom behavior of a minority student, for example, will be more easily recalled than will the identical actions of a majority student. It is not difficult to see how this process of linking markables with distinctive, and often negative, behavior contributes to the formation of stereotypes.

The difficulty that people have in assessing the degree of relationship between social categories and behavioral traits (Crocker 1981) is another factor that contributes to the development of false social beliefs. Statistically speaking, a behavioral trait and a social category can be said to be correlated only when it is possible to predict, with better-than-chance probability, both a person's standing on the trait dimension from knowledge of his or her social category *and* the persons' social category from knowledge of his or her standing on the trait dimension. Predictability in both directions, therefore, is a necessary condition for a statistical relationship to be established, and for a belief in a trait-social category association to be justified. We do not, however, always follow statistical canons in drawing social inferences (Nisbett and Ross 1980). For one thing, we often assume that a trait-category link exists when predictability in only one direction is possible. As an example, consider the following hypothetical situation. Imagine that 99 percent of the intoxicated individuals commonly observed in public places in your city belong to one ethnic group. Would this fact justify the belief that ethnicity and public drunkenness are correlated highly and that members of this particular ethnic group are disposed to drunkenness? Not necessarily. To determine if ethnicity and drunkenness are correlated, one would also need to know what percentage of the ethnic group in question engages in public drunkenness. If a high percentage do, then we would have evidence for a strong relationship. That is, we could predict with reasonable confidence both that a person seen drunk in public most likely belongs to that particular ethnic group *and* that a member of that particular ethnic group was likely to engage in public drunkenness. If, on the other hand, we find that only a very small percentage (say 1 percent) of the members of that ethnic group engage in public drunkenness, then we have a quite different situation. We still can predict with high confidence that a person seen drunk in public will be a member of the target ethnic group, but we cannot be very confident that any particular member of the target ethnic group will be disposed to public drunkenness. Indeed, if we made the latter assumption we would be correct only 1 percent of the time. But, do any of us doubt that if it were the case that 99 percent of the individuals engaging in public drunkenness in a city belonged to one ethnic group that drunkenness would be central to the prevailing stereotype of that group, regardless of how many members of the ethnic group actually displayed this behavior? If the majority of individuals engaging in some activity (drunkenness, crime) belong to a particular social category (the poor, the mentally ill), we are justified in including the social category as part of our image of people who engage in that activity, but we are not justified in including that activity as part of our image of the social category. For this reason, it would be quite wrong to believe that Italians are apt to be involved in organized crime, just because we have learned that most members of the Mafia are Italians.

Imaginative Role-Taking

There is yet another cognitive process that may underlie some stereotypes, which we call imaginative role-taking. Philosophers and psychologists have long recognized the extent to which our knowledge of the thoughts and feelings of others depends upon our ability to imagine ourselves in their situations (Mead 1934; Schutz 1962; Smith 1959). Both the degree and accuracy of social empathy are assumed to increase from infancy through adolescence, and the ability to shift roles appropriately is viewed by many to form the cornerstone of all complex social and moral thought (Flavell 1977; Selman 1981)

The ability to shift roles and perspectives has been identified by some authorities as a process that reduces stereotypic thinking and prejudice (Allport 1954; Campbell 1967). The logic behind this assertion goes something like the following. If people develop stereotypes, at least partially, because they fail to recognize the extent to which the "situation" of the markables determines their behavior, then any efforts on the part of people to try to imagine themselves in the situation of the markables should reduce the number of false beliefs that are held by those people. This seems a sensible analysis and likely has considerable validity in the realm of ethnic stereotypes, or what Goffman (1963) has called tribal stigma. We are not sure, however, that the process of role-taking always functions as positively in the case of physical stigma. In fact, we suspect that imaginative role-taking actually may facilitate rather than undermine stereotype formation in instances of that latter class of markables.

To examine that issue more closely, let us ask a question: Why should imaginative role-taking facilitate rather than inhibit the formation of stereotypes concerning the physically stigmatized? In many ways, it seems that role-taking should yield more valid and extensive insight into the thoughts, feelings, and traits of the physically disabled than many other stigmatized groups. For one thing, it would seem easier to imagine oneself in the role of a person with a physical disability than in the role of a person of a different race or gender. It is a much easier mental exercise to imagine yourself being blind or paralyzed than it is to imagine yourself having a different skin color or genitalia than your own. Also, it would seem that the act of imagining yourself with a tribal stigma, such as black skin, would not provide you with as much insight into the situation of people with that stigma as would the act of imagining yourself blind, deaf, or paralyzed. Even if white Americans could imagine themselves having black skin, this would not in and of itself provide them with much insight into the situation of black Americans. Successful role-taking on the part of white Americans would also require that they imagine themselves in the social-political and historical circumstance of black Americans. It is true that the social and psychological consequences of being physically disabled also will vary from culture to culture, but not nearly as much as will the consequences of a particular tribal mark.

LITERARY STEREOTYPES OF THE HANDICAPPED

Pecile, J., "Handicaps in Literature Usually Are Stereotypes," *Hartford Courant*, June 2, 1982.

You remember them from your reading: club-footed Oedipus, hump-backed Quasimoto, blind and groping Rochester, Quilp the Dwarf, peg-legged Captain Ahab and Captain Hook. . . . Long after we had put down our novels or walked away from such plays and films as "Whose Life is it Anyway?," "The Elephant Man" and the current Broadway hit, "Children of a Lesser God," images of the blind, the lame and the deaf haunt us, remaining in the darker recesses of our mind and continuing to evoke pity and fear.

> **The disabled [according to literary critic Leslie Fiedler] tend to be handled in a heartless way in literature. They often are hopelessly misrepresented and are shown in a negative and stereotyped way in order to play upon our deepest anxieties. . . we, who know that we are only temporarily ablebodied feel guilty about the disability of others because of our wholeness and fear for our own physical disintegration. . . .**
>
> **Literature tells us truths about ourselves, truths which are often disturbing, but we must come to terms with those truths if we want to modify our attitudes toward the handicapped. We see those whose bodies or minds have failed them prematurely as unwelcome reminders of our own vulnerability and mortality: "There, but for the grace of God, go I."**
>
> **Fiedler also commented on current films which seem to be moving in the opposite direction—presenting sympathetic portraits of the handicapped. Examples are films such as "Coming Home," "Ice Castles" and "The Other Side of the Mountain." These films, in fact, tend to elevate handicapped people to heroic status. "I myself find such sagas of maimed jock heroes or heroines false and unconvincing—the product of enlightened good will, which understands both what is salable in the present market and what is considered OK by the righteous and progressive, but has no notion of how the art of fiction really works and why we need the myths it embodies."**
>
> **[These and other remarks were made at a United Nations Conference on Prejudices Faced by the Handicapped.] As one of the participants in the [conference] put it, "Disabled does more for literature than literature has done for disability."**

Because of the relatively greater ease of role-taking in the case of physical disabilities, it might be argued that the process of role-taking offers a richer source of information about the feelings, attitudes, and traits of the disabled than it does for other stigmatized groups. But if that is so, wouldn't this imply that beliefs about the disabled should be more genuine not less? Not necessarily. There is still the question of the accuracy of the information yielded by role-taking. In the case of physical disabilities and other acquired limitations, we are not sure that the information that role-taking provides is always very accurate. Individuals may be able to imagine quite accurately how they would feel or think immediately upon becoming disabled, but they do not do as well in anticipating how they would feel after having been disabled for some period of time. It is exceedingly difficult for people to realize the extent to which people adapt to a disability—especially in the long run. The tendency of people to try to imagine themselves in the situation of a disabled other, coupled with their inability to recognize the adaptation that occurs in a disabled person, may account for many of the misconceptions that exist concerning the disabled. This process may explain, for example, why the disabled so often are seen as being more unhappy, depressed, and bitter than they are actually.

WHY DO FALSE BELIEFS PERSIST?

As we have seen, a number of explanations have been offered for the generation of false beliefs. It is likely that all of them offer at least some insight into the phenomenon, but another, and perhaps more important, question to ask is, "How is it that false beliefs, however they come into existence, are sustained?" With the beliefs being false, one might speculate that as the belief holder encountered disconfirming evidence his or her beliefs would change and gradually be corrected. Unfortunately, this view appears to be unduly optimistic.

The fact that false beliefs can be highly resistant to change has intrigued social psychologists, especially those with a cognitive orientation. The explanations of persistence from the point of view of the sociocultural and motivational approaches are relatively straightforward. According to the sociocultural position, false beliefs persist because the conditions persist that gave rise to them in the first place. Individuals continue to encounter the markables in selective and limited contexts and relationships. Moreover, false beliefs often lead to a further biasing of the holder's relations with the markables (a point we will return to later in the chapter). The consensual nature of social stereotypes can also serve to strengthen and perpetuate them. The more that stereotypes are widely shared, the more difficult they will be to change (Pettigrew 1979). In contrast to the sociocultural perspective, the motivational approach argues that false beliefs persist because of their psychological importance to the holder. The emotional investment of the markers in their false beliefs presumably motivates them to ignore or distort any evidence that might challenge or disconfirm their beliefs.

The cognitive approach also emphasizes biased information-processing in its account of stereotype persistence, but it disputes that it is psychodynamic forces that produce those biases. Instead, the cognitive approach locates the origins of these biases in the basic features of cognitive functioning (Hamilton 1981; Nisbett and Ross 1980). A fundamental tenet of the cognitive approach is that we are forced to be selective in what we attend to by the vastness and complexity of our social world. Our beliefs serve as important guides to this selectivity. We attend to events that our beliefs make salient to us. For example, if we believe that the elderly are prone to senility, we will be especially sensitive to signs of senility in our interactions with the elderly. In addition, we will be less likely to notice evidence that is inconsistent with the diagnosis of senility. Selective perception of this type serves to perpetuate the belief that the elderly are senile, since everyone, the elderly and young alike, exhibits behaviors from time to time that are symptoms of senility. Hamilton (1981, p. 137) states, "I wouldn't have seen it if I didn't believe it," which aptly describes the impact that false beliefs can have on the processing of another's behavior.

But, if we are not fully confident in a false belief and only harbor a suspicion that it is valid, will that still lead to invalid confirmation? Apparently, it often will. It appears that the most common strategy we use to test hypotheses is to look for confirming evidence (Snyder 1981). The more confirming evidence we find, the more confident we are that our hypotheses are correct. The correct way of testing a hypothesis, of course, is to consider both confirming and disconfirming evidence equally. By only considering confirming evidence, we are led to accept the validity of many false beliefs. Consider the hypothesis that blind people tend to be depressed. How would you test this hypothesis? The most appropriate strategy would be to observe large numbers of blind and sighted people to see if depression was more prevalent in the blind group. We rarely go this far, of course. As a substitute strategy, we might simply think of all those blind people we have known and determine what proportion of them were depressed. This strategy has problems, but it still would be much less likely to lead to the invalid acceptance of the hypothesis than the strategy people most commonly use. People generally think only of all the confirming cases (depressed blind people) that they can, and the larger that number, the more confident they are that their belief is valid.

Beliefs not only influence the information we attend to or remember, but also the way that we interpret information. Behavior is frequently ambiguous, and we often rely on our expectancies and preconceptions to help us resolve ambiguity. If our expectancies or preconceptions are false, we may interpret behavior incorrectly. Many studies have shown that the same behavior can be coded or interpreted quite differently, depending on the beliefs or preconceptions of the perceivers (Cohen 1977; Dion 1972; Duncan 1976; Regan, Strauss and Fazio 1974). Imagine if someone were led to believe, erroneously of course, that you had serious psychological problems. How much of your behavior do you think could be interpreted as confirming this belief? Probably a fair amount of it, if you are like most people. In fact, a provocative (if highly controversial) study by Rosenhan (1973) demonstrates just how easily the behaviors of "normal" people can be interpreted as "abnormal," even by trained professionals.

In this study, in order to discover how it feels to be a mental patient, eight well-adjusted individuals attempted to have themselves admitted to a mental hospital. In addition to Rosenhan, the volunteers included two other psychologists, a psychiatrist, a pediatrician, a psychology graduate student, a painter, and a housewife. Each attempted to gain admission to a different hospital in a different part of the country.

At each of the admissions offices, the "pseudopatient" complained that he or she had been hearing voices. The voices seemed to be saying words like "empty," "hollow," and "thud." Aside from giving the symptoms and a false name and occupation, no further deceptions were committed by the pseudopatient. When asked about his or her life history, the pseudopatient reported as accurately as possible his or her relationships with parents and siblings, with spouse and children, and with acquaintances and coworkers. Apparently, hearing voices is enough to get oneself labeled "insane"—all the pseudopatients but one were diagnosed as schizophrenic and admitted to the psychiatric ward.

After being admitted, the pseudopatients immediately ceased to display any evidence of abnormality. Their task was to act perfectly normal, convince the staff that they were "sane," and gain their release. This turned out to be difficult. Despite their outward signs of normality, none of the pseudopatients were detected by the staff. All were eventually discharged, of course, but not as "cured" or "normal"; instead, they were discharged with a diagnosis of "schizophrenia in remission." The average length of hospitalization was 19 days, although it took one unfortunate volunteer 52 days to be discharged.

This study demonstrates the power of labels or beliefs to influence the processing of information. Once the pseudopatient was labeled as schizophrenic, normal behaviors were either ignored or given abnormal interpretations. And normal reactions to the institutional settings were generally attributed by the staff to the pseudopatient's pathology. For example, pacing the long hospital corridor out of boredom was interpreted as chronic tension. Experiencing resentment when mistreated by an attendant—not an uncommon experience—was considered evidence of the pseudopatient's instability. The staff expected pathology, and if obvious pathology was not forthcoming, then more mundane behavior was apparently interpreted to fit the expectation.

One especially important aspect of behavior interpretation involves the explanation of behavior, and this, too, has been found to be affected by expectancies and preconceptions (Deaux 1976; Taylor and Jaggi 1974). Imagine witnessing a heated argument between two coworkers. Imagine further that you know that one of the individuals is an ex-mental patient. How would this latter information affect the way you interpreted or explained the interaction? Wouldn't you be inclined to believe that the ex-mental patient had started the argument or at least was responsible for it?

DETERMINANTS OF THE IMPACT OF FALSE BELIEFS

We have described various cognitive processes and behavioral dynamics that contribute to the generation and perpetuation of erroneous beliefs. Obviously, there is good reason to believe that these factors are actively at work in the stigmatizing process. Even though stereotypes can be insidious and powerful, however, we should not paint too bleak a picture. Reality can, and often does, assert itself in interactions involving the stigmatized. False beliefs can be changed and erroneous expectancies disconfirmed. The question of when false beliefs are likely to be perpetuated and when they are likely to be modified has received little attention to date. Researchers have been concerned primarily with demonstrating how false beliefs are perpetuated.

In the remainder of this chapter, we will attempt to delineate some of the factors that determine when false beliefs about others will be confirmed and when they will be disconfirmed. In confronting the complex issues involved here, it may be useful to review the general characterization of social interaction presented in Chapter 1. Such a review will remind the reader that the beliefs and expectancies of each interaction partner both influence the course of social behavior and are in turn controlled by it. Ultimately, it is important to consider the full range of factors involved when two people interact. First, however, we will concern ourselves with the situation in which the belief holder simply observes the target and does not actually interact with the target person. In considering the question of when false beliefs do and do not survive disconfirming evidence two factors are likely to be particularly important: (1) the basis of the belief; and (2) the content, or nature, of the trait to which the belief pertains.

The Basis of the Belief

Beliefs concerning various individuals or social categories can differ in many respects. One obvious difference concerns the basis of the belief. Beliefs may derive from direct personal experience or from more indirect information, such as hearsay or media portrayal. Also, whether a belief is based on direct or indirect information, it may be focused primarily on the particular target person or on the category to which the target person belongs (Jones and McGillis 1976).

Let us illustrate these distinctions with beliefs about mental illness. Imagine an individual contemplating an encounter with a person who has spent time in a mental institution. Most likely, the individual will hold a number of beliefs or expectations about the former mental patient. It is also likely that some of these beliefs will be valid and others not. These various beliefs may be based on any of the following types of information: (1) direct experience with this individual; (2) direct experience with other mental patients; (3) indirect information about this individual; or (4) indirect information about other mental patients. Of course, more than one type of information may be available.

All types of information may influence the way the marker views the markable, but some types will have a greater impact than others. It seems safe to predict that beliefs based on direct experiences with this particular individual will operate most powerfully in interactions with the person (Fazio and Zanna 1981), and that beliefs based on indirect information about other mental patients will operate most weakly. However, whether beliefs based on direct experience will be more or less powerful than beliefs based on indirect information about this particular individual is difficult to say.

Of course, beliefs based on the same types of information can vary greatly in their strength and resistance to disconfirmation, since the evidential basis of a belief is only one of the factors that will affect its strength. The more central a belief is to the belief holder's image of the target person's social category, the more tenaciously it will be held. An individual's belief that mentally ill individuals are unpredictable, for example, may be more resistant to disconfirmation than his or her belief that blind individuals are interpersonally sensitive, if the person considers unpredictability to be a more central or defining feature of mental illness than sensitivity is of blindness.

An additional, related dimension on which category-based beliefs can differ is the presumed causal relationship between the category and the trait. The stereotypes held by many whites that blacks are poorly educated and have "rhythm" illustrate this difference. Rhythm is more likely to be perceived as a genetically endowed characteristic of blacks, like their skin color, than is poor education. Some whites, of course, believe that a lack of education reflects innately inferior intelligence, but other whites who hold this same expectation interpret this relationship as stemming from society's opportunity structure or from black socialization patterns. Trait-category associations presumed to be genetically mediated will be especially resistant to disconfirmation.

The Content of the Trait

In addition to the evidential basis of a belief, the content of the belief will also affect its potential for disconfirmation. Beliefs about others can pertain to a great range of phenomena: physical characteristics, attitudes, abilities, personality traits, and so forth. False beliefs about some of these phenomena, as we shall see, are more easily disconfirmed than are others.

The Ability and Motivation to Misrepresent One's Traits

What control do we have over the expression of our true selves? After reflection, most of us would probably agree that we have considerable control over how and when we express some aspects of ourselves and very little control over others. False beliefs concerning those aspects of people that we think can be easily concealed or distorted in their expression are especially difficult to disconfirm. False beliefs about another's attitudes, for instance, often persist even when they express contrary views. People are assumed to be able to control the attitudes they express, and, thus, the expression of attitudes that are contrary to those that are attributed to them may have little modifying effect on the beliefs of others. This will be especially true if it is assumed that the person might have some motivation for misrepresenting his or her attitudes. The feelings that a person expresses are also assumed to be very much under a person's control. An unhappy person, for instance, can say he or she is happy and show other signs of happiness without really being happy. Thus, the belief that a person, such as a physically disabled person, is unhappy can be highly resistant to disconfirmation, regardless of how much happiness is expressed by the person.

Such expressions can easily be assimilated to the belief holder's "faking" schema and can be dismissed as attempts at impression management or denial. On the other hand, the false beliefs that another—for example, a former mental patient—is not intelligent or is physically uncoordinated are more easily disconfirmed. People are not perceived to have the ability to appear intelligent or coordinated, if they are not, in fact, intelligent and coordinated (Reeder and Brewer 1979).

The Presumed Variability in the Link between Traits and Behavioral Expressions

Traits differ in more ways than in the extent to which their expression is perceived to be controllable. Traits also differ according to whether they are defined primarily in terms of average or extreme behaviors. Consider first the traits of dishonesty and dangerousness. The level of dishonesty we attribute to another is based primarily on the persons's most extreme acts of dishonesty, rather than on the person's average behavior in this regard. A person believed to be dishonest, such as an ex-convict, is not expected to show evidence of his or her dishonesty in every encounter and need only show this characteristic occasionally to confirm its existence. Similarly, a person's dangerousness is defined more by the person's most extreme behavior in this regard than by his or her average or typical behavior. As a consequence, the false belief that a person, such as a former mental patient, is dangerous may persist for a long period of time without any confirming evidence. It is the person's perceived potential for danger that defines his or her degree of this trait, not the person's average expression of dangerousness. Moreover, since the level of dangerousness and dishonesty a person possesses is diagnosed from the person's most extreme behaviors relevant to these traits, the absence of dangerous or dishonest behavior does not constitute disconfirming evidence.

On the other hand, the degree of warmth, or any other quality pertaining to interpersonal style, attributed to a person tends to be based on the person's average or typical behavior in this domain. A warm person is expected to be warm in most of his encounters, just as a cold person is expected to be cold in most of his encounters. Consequently, it will be difficult to persist in the belief that another is cold (or warm), if he or she does not regularly display coldness (or warmth). As a general statement, it can be said that false beliefs concerning traits that are defined by typical behaviors (e.g., coldness) are more easily disconfirmed than are false beliefs concerning traits defined by extreme behaviors (e.g., dishonesty).

Opportunities for Manifestation of Traits

The opportunities for manifesting some traits are more plentiful than those existing for others. Traits that have to do with interpersonal style, such as warmth, coldness, shyness, and extroversion, are examples of traits that can be manifested in a great many, if not most, of our interactions. The demonstration of moral traits, such as courage and honesty, require more specialized circumstances. One requires a fearful situation to demonstrate one's courage, and a tempting situation to demonstrate one's honesty. The more infrequent such situations are, the more difficult it will be to disconfirm the false belief that another is cowardly or dishonest. Ability traits (e.g., task competence, psychological strength) are other examples of traits that require special, and often infrequently occurring, circumstances for their demonstration. The false belief that a blind person is incompetent at certain tasks, for example, may persist until that individual is observed performing ably in those task situations. This can take a very long time, especially if the individual is consistently protected from opportunities to perform such tasks. As a general principle, it can be stated that the less frequent are the opportunities for manifesting a particular trait, the more difficult it will be to disconfirm a belief pertaining to that trait.

Behavioral Basis versus Latent Basis of Traits

Some traits are seen much more in terms of their surface or behavioral characteristics than are others. Nervousness and jolliness are examples of traits that are associated with fairly distinctive phenotypic expressions. In other words, we diagnose the presence of such traits as nervousness or jolliness from the existence of a certain class of well-defined observable behaviors. Other traits, such as hostility and manipulativeness, are believed to reside as much in the motivating or latent conditions of an action as the action itself. Many different behaviors could be perceived to reflect hostile or manipulative intent. Since motivations, unlike behaviors, must be inferred and cannot be directly observed, the false beliefs that another, say an alcoholic, is hostile or manipulative may be highly resistant to disconfirmation. As a general principle, it can be stated that the more a trait is defined primarily in terms of intention or motivation, the more difficult it will be to disconfirm a false belief concerning that trait.

THE EFFECTS OF FALSE BELIEFS ON INTERACTION

The dimensions of traits that we have discussed up to this point are all relevant to the likelihood that an observer of a person's behavior will confirm or disconfirm a false trait-expectancy concerning that person. Additional aspects of traits become relevant when we consider the contexts in which the belief holder actually interacts with the target.

The Impact of False Beliefs on the Belief Holder's Behavior

We described earlier how a person's false beliefs can influence his or her behavior and, in turn, the behavior of others in such a way as to confirm the initially false belief. Implicit in this position is the assumption that the more impact false beliefs have on the belief holder's behavior, the more impact they will also have on the behavior of the target. Many factors affect the degree of influence that our beliefs concerning others will have on our behavior toward them.

Belief-Behavior Scripts

Imagine the circumstances in which you expect to interact with another whom you believe to be dishonest or, perhaps, alcoholic. How might these expectations affect your behavior toward the individual? They might very well influence your behavior, but probably would not as predictably as the beliefs that the other was hard of hearing, unintelligent, or suffered from a contagious disease. Some interpersonal expectancies simply are more strongly associated with specific actions than are others. When a belief suggests a clear course of action, it can be said that the belief and the associated behavior constitute a script (Abelson 1981). The term script refers to any sequence of events or behaviors that people commonly associate with one another and that they see as forming a coherent pattern. For example, one can speak of the lecture script, which involves a particular set of actions by students and a professor that tend to unfold in a predictable manner, regardless of the individuals occupying the roles of professor and students. An example of the script concept in the present context is what might be termed the "low intelligence" script, which dictates that people speak slowly and simply to a person assumed to be of low intelligence. Not all beliefs have scripted behavior associated with them, however. It is probably inappropriate, for example, to speak of a dishonest or alcoholic script.

Perceived Contingent Costs

A second reason that some expectancies have a greater impact on behavior than others involves the costs that belief holders feel may be incurred, if they do not behave in accordance with their suspicions. Since interactions with people who are malicious, psychologically fragile, or terminally ill can involve many dangers, most people, when they are around individuals whom they believe (correctly or incorrectly) to possess these characteristics, will be inclined to behave in a manner that minimizes the posed. The decision not to modify one's behavior in light of such beliefs would involve considerable risk. As a general principle it can be stated that the greater the perceived risk associated with not modifying one's behavior, the greater will be the influence that the belief has on the belief holder's and, in turn, the target's behavior.

One of the most intriguing implications of this principle is the suggestion that even a tentative belief can have a powerful effect on the holder's behavior, if the behavior anticipated from the target has high costs associated with it. Whether a person thinks that there is a very high or only a moderate probability that a person, such as an ex-convict, is dishonest will likely have very little effect on how the individual responds to the stigmatized person in contexts in which another's dishonesty could be personally costly. The individual will be equally likely to hold on to his wallet and adopt a skeptical attitude to the ex-convict's remarks. Similarly, a person who believes there is only a small chance that he or she could contract cancer from a cancer victim will likely not treat that individual substantially different than a person who believes the possibility of contagion is very high. When the cost of erring is perceived to be high, people will often act as though they have full confidence in their beliefs.

The Impact of False Beliefs on the Target's Behavior

We have already established that false beliefs can influence the behavior of the target through their impact on the belief holder's behavior. At this point, we propose taking a closer look at the various types of influence that false beliefs can engender.

Self-fulfilling Prophecies

The most familiar type of influence initiated by a false belief is that known as the self-fulfilling prophecy effect (Darley and Fazio 1980; Holmes and Miller 1976; Merton 1948; Snyder 1981). In that effect, the false belief of the marker leads him or her to behave in a manner that serves to elicit behavior from the markable that confirms the marker's false belief or prophecy. Perhaps the best-known example of this effect is found in Rosenthal and Jacobson's work (1965) on the effects of teacher expectancies on student performance. In that study, it was found that students who were thought erroneously by their teachers to be "late bloomers" actually came to perform better than other students. Their superior performance resulted presumably because the teachers treated these "superior" students differently.

Self-fulfilling prophecies are common in interactions involving stigmatized individuals and can take a variety of forms. One type of self-fulfilling prophecy occurs when the belief holder's behavior begets similar behavior from the markable. The belief that obese individuals tend to be jolly, for example, may lead people to joke more with obese individuals, thereby eliciting similar jolliness from them. A second type of self-fulfilling prophecy emerges when the belief holder's behavior induces not similar but complementary behavior from the markable. A belief that the physically disabled tend to have dependent dispositions, for example, may induce solicitous behavior from the belief holder, which, in turn, may actually elicit dependent behavior (not reciprocated solicitude) from the disabled person.

Self-fulfilling prophecies also occur when the belief holder's actions fulfill his or her expectations by restricting the behavioral opportunities of the markable. For example, a person's belief that the mentally handicapped cannot perform certain tasks may lead the belief holder to deny mentally handicapped individuals the opportunity to learn to perform these tasks competently.

In general, the greater the impact that beliefs have on the belief holder's behavior, the greater the likelihood that a self-fulfilling prophecy will occur. But the nature of the behavior that derives from the false belief is also important in this regard. The extent to which one person's behavior is constrained by the behavior of another can vary greatly, depending on the behavior in question. The beliefs that a blind person is likely to be dependent and lacks a sense of humor, for example, may produce equally strong effects on the belief holder's behavior, but they may not influence the blind person's behavior to the same extent. A person's ability to demonstrate his or her sense of humor is much less constrained by the behavior of others than is a person's ability to demonstrate his or her independence.

There is another variation of the self-fulfilling prophecy effect that can occur in relationships involving stigmatized individuals. We refer to those situations where an initially accurate belief about a markable person becomes invalid over time. The characteristics of physically or mentally disabled individuals, for example, can and do change over time. People improve. Progress is not always as fast or complete as it might be, however, because initially appropriate reactions from markers may persist long after they cease to be appropriate and, thus, serve to perpetuate the condition. A paraplegic accident victim, for example, may be helpless and in need of assistance after his accident, but he will likely become more independent over time. The persistence of solicitude and unnecessary assistance from others, however, may impede the development of this independence.

Self-defeating Prophecies

False beliefs do not always lead to behavior from the target that is consistent with those beliefs. In fact, the false belief sometimes can induce the belief holder to behave in a manner that produces behavior in others that is just the opposite of the expectancy. For example, the false belief that another is a nervous person may lead the belief holder to behave in a particularly supportive or reassuring manner that, in turn, may produce exceptionally relaxed and calm behavior in the target. Similarly, the false belief that another is incompetent may induce the belief holder (e.g., a teacher) to provide the type of guidance and instruction that would facilitate, rather than impair, the individual's performance. In these instances, the prophecies will have defeated themselves. As we will see, prophecies may also defeat themselves when the markable both infers the marker's false belief from his or her behavior and has the ability and motivation to disconfirm it.

An important point to keep in mind in considering self-defeating prophecies is that the belief holder may be reluctant to revise his or her false belief, even when it appears to have been disconfirmed. Thus, even though the expectation of nervousness may have the effect of inducing behavior from the target that others interpret as calm behavior, the belief holder may interpret the target's behavior as being consistent with his or her initial belief that the target is a nervous person. Rather than attributing the target's calmness to a calm disposition, the belief holder may attribute the target's calm behavior to the nature of the belief holder's own behavior.

Self-altering Prophecies

Another form of expectancy-based interpersonal influence falls somewhere between the self-fulfilling and self-defeating types. In that instance, an expectancy affects the behavior of the belief holder and, in turn, the target, but in neither a fulfilling nor a defeating manner. In what we call the self-altering prophecy, the induced behavior is neither consistent nor inconsistent with the prophecy. For example, the false belief that another's terminal illness is contagious may well affect both the marker's and the target's behaviors, but it will not result in either more or less contamination from the target. Similarly, the expectation that mental patients are dangerous may affect the holder's behavior around former mental patients, but it will not necessarily lead to either greater or lesser danger from the former patients. Such an expectancy may well produce more awkward or unpleasant behavior, but it will not necessarily produce behavior that would be evaluated as more or less dangerous than the behavior occurring independently of such an expectancy.

THE POWER AND MOTIVATION OF THE MARKED TO DISCONFIRM FALSE EXPECTATIONS

In writing about the stigmatizing process, authorities frequently portray the markable as a pawn at the mercy of the marker's beliefs and behaviors. In fact, Ralph Ellison's poignant observation that social scientists tend to view blacks as "nothing more than reactions to oppression" could be said to characterize the approach generally taken to markables by social scientists. It is certainly true, of course, as the previously discussed research by Rosenhan (1973) and Rosenthal and Jacobson (1968) indicates, that the behavior of markables can be greatly influenced by the ways in which others perceive them. But the markable is neither interpersonally powerless nor bereft of beliefs or expectations of his own. And to understand the stigmatizing process fully, it is necessary to analyze closely the factors that affect the nature of the markable's response to the behavior of the marker.

The Extent of the Markable's Awareness of the False Beliefs of Others

Most of us do not like others to hold erroneous beliefs about us, especially if they are negative. But how do we determine what another's beliefs about us are—irrespective of whether they be true or false? Sometimes others communicate their beliefs to us directly, but most of the time we must infer their beliefs from their behavior toward us. Recognizing when others hold erroneous beliefs about us can be more or less difficult, depending on such factors as the degree of influence that another's beliefs has on his or her behavior, as well as our familiarity with the behavioral cues associated with particular beliefs.

Stigmatized individuals are especially likely to be aware when others hold false beliefs about them. Their heightened sensitivity is probably a product of a number of factors. First, since most stigmatized individuals occupy low power positions in relationships (see Chapter 6), they are generally eager to divine the beliefs of others so that they can adopt a course of action that minimizes the chances of exploitation. Second, most individuals are not very experienced in interacting with stigmatized individuals, and thus they do not always conceal their beliefs or feelings as well in these interactions, as they do in their more practiced interactions. Third, stigmatized individuals may have more insight into what others think of them because many of the people with whom they interact will share the same beliefs, a fact that enables the stigmatized to become very familiar with the behavioral cues that reflect those beliefs. All of us engender some thoughts or feelings in the people with whom we interact, but those engendered thoughts and feelings may tend to be highly homogeneous for the stigmatized.

Many stigmatized individuals express confidence that they can recognize the beliefs of others. Physically disabled individuals, for example, frequently report that it is easy to recognize others who expect them to be dependent and helpless. The tendency to speak more loudly, simply, and slowly to blind people will communicate clearly to the blind certain beliefs that others hold about them. Similarly, the terminally ill can readily perceive when others fear contamination from them.

Markable persons may even attribute certain beliefs to others without any behavioral evidence. Markables themselves often hold stereotypes of what others think and feel about them, and these stereotypes guide their relations with nonmarkables (Scott 1969). Many ex-convicts, for instance, assume that everyone, whether he shows it or not, believes that ex-convicts are untrustworthy. The more easily distinguished a particular belief is, the more markables will rely on their stereotypes to determine whether or not a particular potential marker holds the belief in question.

It should be noted that markable persons often receive a considerable amount of information about how they are seen by nonmarkables. Their direct experience provides much of this information, to be sure, but so does the instruction of parents and other markables. Minority and disabled children, for example, often receive extensive instruction from their parents as to the beliefs and attitudes that they will encounter in others. Other markables, such as ex-convicts and former mental patients also become rapidly well-informed about society's prevailing image of them.

To Disavow or Not

What do marked individuals do when they decide that a marker holds a false belief about them? A variety of factors are relevant in this regard. The aversiveness of the false belief for the markable is obviously one important factor. Markables may not find all false beliefs about them to be odious, and may very well find some false beliefs to be flattering, advantageous, or benignly amusing.

The various costs and rewards the markable perceives to be related tc belief confirmation or disconfirmation are another relevant factor. To disabuse another of his or her false beliefs can produce costs as well as rewards for the marked person. Markers will often be displeased when their beliefs are revealed to be invalid. This will be the case especially if they have held and acted upon the invalid beliefs for a long time. At the very least, the discovery of a false belief may produce embarrassment. Interactions between markers and markables, therefore, may continue more smoothly if the markable simply conforms to the expectations of the marker (see Chapter 6). To the extent that continued smooth interaction with the marker is valued by the markable person, he or she may not only avoid contradicting any false beliefs, but may actually endeavor to conform to them. Women, blacks, and blind individuals, among others, commonly report that they are often deterred from violating the false expectancies of others because of the difficulties that can be produced by such attempts.

Determinants of Successful Disavowal

If the perceived rewards to be derived from disconfirming false beliefs outweigh the perceived costs for the marker, the question is how does one disconfirm a false belief. As discussed earlier, the ease with which a false belief can be disconfirmed depends very much on the content of the belief. The false beliefs that an individual is introverted, humorless, and unintelligent can be disconfirmed relatively easily within a short encounter. It is much more difficult to disconfirm the beliefs that one is dishonest or psychologically fragile. A brief interaction does not permit many opportunities for a person to prove his or her honesty, and if people believe that a person (e.g., an ex-convict) is dishonest, it is likely that they will even further restrict such opportunities. A similar problem arises with the imputation of psychological weakness. Without exposure to situations requiring psychological strength, it is difficult for a person, such as a former mental patient, to prove to others that he or she is not "fragile."

The task of contradicting stereotypes about feelings or attitudes has some additional problems, as discussed earlier. On the one hand, a person, even a stigmatized person, has a great many opportunities to express his or her attitudes and feelings. On the other hand, despite the abundance of opportunities, it is not always easy for stigmatized persons to convince others that they truly have the feelings or attitudes they express. A disabled individual, for example, may not be able to communicate successfully to others that he or she isn't bitter or doesn't feel inferior. Others may simply regard such protestations with incredulity, assuming that they reflect repression or attempts at impression management. The strength of the conviction that a disabled person must be depressed and feel inferior, coupled with the belief that it is easy and desirable to create a public facade, makes it enormously difficult for disabled individuals to contradict the stereotypes that others have about their attitudes and feelings.

Since some false beliefs are more easily disconfirmed than others, stigmatized individuals may be selective in the beliefs that they target for disconfirmation. Over time, stigmatized individuals may learn (1) what beliefs are most easily disconfirmed; (2) what beliefs are most centrally related to the stereotypes of markers; (3) what beliefs breed the most discrimination; and (4) how best to disconfirm different beliefs.

One issue that stigmatized individuals must confront when they are considering the process of disconfirmation is their relationship to their social category. Does the stigmatized person attempt to convince the marker of the invalidity of his or her belief as applied to the entire social category, or only as it applies to him or her? Such a decision will depend to a great extent, of course, on the person's sense of similarity or identity with his or her social category. Members of some ethnic categories, such as blacks and Jews, often experience considerable in-group identity and can be as disturbed, or even more disturbed, by those false beliefs held about their social category as by those held about them personally. Members of other categories, however, may show less category identity and may be relatively unconcerned with changing beliefs about their category as a whole. In general, it will be easier to convince people that their stereotype of your category does not apply to you than it will be to convince them that their stereotype of your category is invalid. Markers are generally willing to concede that exceptions exist, especially when the exceptions acknowledge the validity of the marker's general rule.

Disavowals from the Marker

It is not only the stigmatized individual who is a victim of stereotyping. The "normal" may also feel the oppression of false beliefs and expectations. Most people do not like either to think that they are prejudiced or to have others think that they are prejudiced (Dutton 1976; Katz 1981; Rokeach 1968). To the extent that people fear a stigmatized person believes that they are prejudiced, they may well endeavor to convince him or her otherwise. The task of convincing a markable person that you consider him or her "normal" is not an easy one. Verbal pronouncements to this effect may be seen as contrived, but without saying anything, there is the risk of further incrimination. That dilemma—of wanting to communicate your dissimilarities with prejudiced others, but not wanting to seem unnatural or disingenous—is particularly acute in brief encounters. In fact, much of the discomfort experienced by markers in interaction with markables derives from their fear of behaving in a way that will contradict their images of themselves as sympathetic, nonprejudiced people. This fear is so debilitating, and it is so difficult to resolve the dilemma, that many "normals" simply refrain from interacting with the stigmatized.

Although the stigmatized and nonstigmatized may frequently share a desire to contradict the stereotype the other holds of them, their motivation for doing so will rarely be identical. On the one hand, it is likely that the two groups share the goal of wanting others to see them as they see themselves—as they really are—since to feel misunderstood or misperceived is likely to be equally aversive to both the stigmatized and nonstigmatized. On the other hand, the cost of being misperceived or misunderstood is much greater for the stigmatized than the nonstigmatized. It is important for the stigmatized to contradict false stereotypes, so that they can have normal relations with others. The more successful they are in convincing others that they are normal, the more normal will be their relations with others. Since nonstigmatized individuals have many more alternative relationships available to them (see Chapter 6), the goal of facilitating normal relations with the stigmatized is probably much less important to them. The primary goal of their self-presentational efforts will be to validate an image they hold of themselves, or wish others to hold of them, as being unprejudiced and sympathetic.

SUMMARY

The focus of this chapter has been the role that stereotypes play in interactions involving stigmatized individuals. Various social and psychological factors contribute to the formation of stereotypes, and the interpersonal consequences of a particular false belief depend on both the nature and origin of the belief. In considering the role of stereotypes in interactions involving stigmatized individuals, it also is important to consider the role played by the stigmatized individual. Frequently, markable persons know that they are likely to be stereotyped and attempt to disconfirm the stereotypes that are operative. The success of stereotype disavowal depends on the specific belief and its origins, as well as the resources and motivation of the markable.

• CHAPTER SIX •

Power Relations and Self-Presentational Strategies

OUR CENTRAL FOCUS has been on interactions between markers and markables. We are interested not only in the character and course of particular interactions, the affects aroused, and the cognitions generated, but we are also intrigued by the evolution of personal relationships through social interaction. By what sequences of action are relationships transformed and actors' perspectives toward each other changed? In the course of developing relationships between markers and markables, what kinds of things do actors do to increase the gratifications that they derive from each other?

It is useful to keep in mind that interactions involve various outcomes—rewards and costs—for the participants. Potential outcomes serve to define the goals of an interaction. Actors typically have ideas about what may be gained and what may be suffered if they engage in a particular dialogue. These ideas will vary with the duration and the intimacy of the relationship. At the very least, it will be important for us to keep in mind the distinction between (1) casual interactive contacts, such as those involving a brief exchange in public settings (elevators, supermarkets, or buses); (2) structured interactions in which the mark should either be irrelevant or incidental to the roles involved, such as student-teacher relationships or those involving work partners; (3) structured interactions in which the mark is necessarily a central feature, such as doctor-patient, blind person-companion; and (4) long-term personal relationships between spouses, family members, or close friends.

These contexts differ along many dimensions. At one extreme, the casual interaction is likely to be characterized by a joint concern with carrying off the interaction smoothly. Most casual encounters occur in situations in which neither actor has much to gain, but each has something to lose. This orientation to avoid loss typically leads people to behave in a cautious, guarded manner, or to behave in highly standardized ways, thus avoiding the risks attendant on trying to move beyond minimal intimacy. As Goffman (1955) has persuasively argued, many normal interactions—perhaps the majority—are characterized by mutual face protection. Each actor merely wants to leave the interaction with as good a face as he entered it. We suggest that this loss-avoidant orientation may be even more common in marker-markable interactions. This may be the case because of the general discomfort involved in such interactions, and the fact that the tactics of saving face are not well practiced when markable disabilities or deviant behaviors are involved.

Since the markable person is likely to realize (however vaguely) the avoid-loss orientation of the marker, he can facilitate the guarded interchange by providing feedback that indicates everything is in order, and that he intends to respect the intimacy boundaries erected by the marker. He has other expressive options, of course, if the duration of the relationship is not an issue. He may drive up the costs of the casual interaction by making demands or by making the marker feel awkward and embarrassed.

Very different considerations are involved when we turn to the multifaceted long-term personal relationship. Certainly, the strategic options are much more complex, partly because of the partners' higher stake in the relationship, and partly because of the fact that long sequences of interaction may be involved. By definition, the relationship has a history and a future, and the meaning of each interaction will naturally be colored by that history and the prospects involved of long-range losses and benefits.

The distinction between casual interactions and long-term relationships is especially important when the concealability of the mark is considered. If the mark is concealable, and is in fact concealed, it may not intrude on short-run, casual relationships in any direct way. The same may even be true for recurrent relationships occurring within a highly structured role context. There, however, the effects of asymmetrical knowledge may show themselves in the awkward reticence of the markable, as he closes off entire areas of conversational disclosure in an attempt to avoid revealing the nature of his mark. When we turn to intimate multirole relationships (such as those involving husbands and wives), normally concealable marks are typically revealed, so that reactions to the mark are woven into the relationship. There still may be subtle ways to manipulate the momentary salience of the mark, but, in general, the greater the duration and intimacy of the relationship, the less relevant is the concealability dimension.

Most of our scientific knowledge concerning self-presentation comes from laboratory and field experiments in which instrumental relations are highlighted. A typical ingratiation study, for example, might feature a job interview in which the task of a subject is to impress the interviewer with her attractiveness. We know all too little about strategic self-presentation in intimate relationships that have many consummatory as well as instrumental features. In the discussion of power strategies that follows, we shall from time to time ask whether strategies that might be effective in one interaction context (e.g., student-teacher) could be effective in another context (husband-wife). A full discussion of the complexities of long-term relationships will be explored in Chapter 8.

OUTCOMES AND INTERPERSONAL POWER

As we begin to consider the outcomes derived from interactions in a relationship and how they might change over time, the concept of interpersonal power becomes relevant immediately. Although the thought of "reaching for power" carries unpleasant undertones for many of us, no discussion of interpersonal relations can be complete without recognizing the crucial roles of potential and applied power in any given interaction. This is so because, at bottom, power is simply another way of talking about the distribution of potential outcomes in a relationship. If, through my actions, I can both reward (gratify, fulfill) you and punish (frustrate, annoy, diminish) you, by definition I have at least some power over you. As Thibaut and Kelley (1959) put it, the greater the range of outcomes through which I can move you, the more power I have over you. This is a social fact, and not a reference to my ruthlessness or authoritarian bent.

An important set of restrictions on the application of power is imposed by the fact that most relationships are voluntary. Thus, I may have the capacity to injure you in a variety of ways, to impose severe costs on you, but when the goodness of your outcomes falls below the level obtainable in some alternative relationship, you will presumably break off your contacts with me at the first available moment, so that I won't have you to kick around anymore. Because of this very important consideration, each relationship must be seen in the context of other available relationships, and one's power over another is fundamentally affected by the other's social (and, for that matter, nonsocial) options.

An additional constraint on the exercise of my power over you is your counterpower over me. There is no point in my going out of my way to hurt you, if you have just as much capacity and inclination to hurt me. Thus, my effective power—the range of outcomes through which I can realistically move you—is determined partly by the availability to you of others who are willing to provide more favorable outcomes, and partly by your capacity to provide differential outcomes for me.

Although the existence of counterpower is indeed an equalizing force in human relationships, many relationships do involve differential power. In other words, for various reasons, I may be able to drive you through a wider range of outcomes than you can drive me. Maybe I don't "need" you as much, because I have a variety of other attractive relationships to which I can turn—other "fish in the sea." Maybe I'm smarter, or stronger, or wealthier, making it easier for me to generate rewards and impose costs.

A major premise of this chapter is that this kind of power asymmetry is apt to be especially characteristic of relationships between markers and markables. Although we shall consider the possibility of reversals or exceptions to the rule, we propose that it will usually be the case that the markable has less power than the marker, or at least that the marker perceives this differential (cf. Nunnally 1961). We shall go on to show how markables can and do cope with their low power position, as we consider the strategies they may adopt to decrease their power disadvantage.

Before considering the consequences and remedies of power asymmetry, let us first consider the premise itself. How may we deduce from the foregoing reasoning that people with stigmatizing marks will generally have less power than the normal persons with whom they interact? One clue concerns the availability of alternative relationships. Still restricting ourselves for the moment to voluntary relationships, if we assume that stigmatizing marks generally provide a stimulus for avoidance, the markable person probably has fewer social options than the normal marker and, therefore, is more dependent on those available. In addition to this deduction from structural interdependence notions, common sense tells us that at least some markables are behaviorally disabled and cannot effectively navigate or function adequately without the help of others. This adds a dimension of realistic or objective dependence to the dependence derived from the poverty of alternative social relationships. We suggest, further, that a characteristic feature of the stigmatizing process is that realistic capacity deficits are loosely and unfairly generalized to contexts where they are objectively irrelevant. The marker, therefore, tends to exaggerate the extent to which the markable person is incapacitated. We suspect that this tendency is often facilitated by markers who import low-power content from more common instances of power asymmetry. These imported embodiments may amplify the natural power asymmetry that does exist and, thus, create additional problems for the markable person bent on equalizing his social power. We next consider, therefore, some of the substantive guises in which low power may appear in marker-markable relationships.

LOW-POWER SCRIPTS AND INSIDIOUS METAPHORS

It is interesting to speculate (and that is about all we can do at this point) about the hidden metaphors that affect the expectations of normals about markables, and markables about themselves. To the extent that such metaphors are unwittingly and erroneously operative, there may be serious consequences for marker-markable interactions. That is especially true when the markable does not share the metaphor under which the marker structures his behavior toward him. Abelson (1976, 1981) has formally introduced the term *script* to refer to a coherent sequence of events expected by the individual, involving him either as a participant or as an observer. Of particular interest is the "categorical script," which is very similar to the older concept of "stereotype" and where a particular kind of limitation, affliction, or deviant case would, for example, be assimilated into a generic category framing the subsequent interaction. We now speculate about low-power scripts and the scenarios that they may generate.

The Child among Adults

One readily available guiding metaphor, or script, is that of the child among adults. Everyone has been a child, and most adults have interacted with a variety of children. Overlearned behavior patterns that developed in responses to children may be unthinkingly applied to the marked target, including condescension, nodding without listening, talking to other markers as if the markable were not present, and failure to take the markable's wishes seriously. We may hazard the guess that the child-among-adult metaphor is most likely to be applied in the case of mental retardation, certain forms of mental illness (e.g., schizophrenia), and the high dependency variants of alcoholism and addiction. That may be true because those disorders themselves arise from dependency problems during socialization, and the disorders, to some extent, model the features of childish passivity and irresponsibility.

Illness and Disease

The illness-disease script is similar to the child script in its general emphasis on lack of responsibility. It is very different in its implicit prescription for outside intervention. If mental illness or alcoholism is truly a disease, for example, then sympathy is in order, and medical intervention may be the only reasonable remedy. People who are sick must pay for their potential gains in sympathy from others by removing themselves from many normal-functioning roles and by taking time out for repairs. Along with assignment to (and acceptance of) the sick role may come the perception by both markers and markables that the latter's limitations are much more incapacitating than they are in reality.

There are, of course, a variety of sick roles, and each has different implications for interaction. If the sick script incorporates contamination fears, even in cases where fears of contamination are medically groundless, the marker's avoidance tendencies may be fueled by the fear that he will be adversely affected by association with the marked person. This may, for example, contribute to our desire to avoid contact with victims of cancer, of multiple sclerosis, and, especially, those with skin disorders, such as leprosy or psoriasis.

When the sickness is seen as terminal, yet another script is involved. The desire to avoid interacting with the terminally ill may follow from vague fears associated with the recognition of our own mortality, or from realistic desires not to get involved in a relationship destined for separation and grief. Aging itself is a terminal process, but the terminal nature of the process is often exaggerated or accelerated by both the marker and the markable. Many of the problems faced by older people might be more readily solved, if both the elderly and those around them were more aware of the possibility that not all changes in their behavior and in their cognitive functioning are irreversible.

The Moral Deviate

The early labeling theorists wrote in generic terms about social deviance. In their metaphoric view, labels are applied, and the stigmatizing process begins when someone is judged to have broken a societal rule. Much of the early sociological literature on deviance concerned criminal behavior and the attendant problems of rehabilitation. It is hardly surprising that we stigmatize assassins, rapists, child molesters, and muggers. On the face of it, our responses to the physically or mentally limited seem to have nothing to do with the immorality of their deviance. Yet the moral-deviate script may be almost as readily applied to those who commit victimless crimes or are guilty only of stretching the boundaries of propriety, such as prostitutes, addicts, homosexuals, bag ladies, and protesters. These and other departures from majority norms may be cast together so that the markable person is tainted with evil intentions or degenerate origins.

In addition, a century of educational effort to inform us that behavior disorders are a matter of mental illness has not been sufficient to expunge the moral script entirely from our dealings with neurotic and psychotic acquaintances. Little voices in the back of our minds may nag us to tell the depressive to stop moping, the neurotic to stop being afraid of things, and the schizophrenic to get a hold of himself.

Other Scripts and Metaphors

Although the child-among-adults, illness, and moral deviate would seem to be the most well-developed, several other metaphors probably exert subtle influences from time to time. They might include a low socioeconomic class ("poor") metaphor, an unintelligent ("dummy," "stupid") metaphor, a "klutz" or "loser" metaphor, a "blind beggar" metaphor, and a "pathetic freak" metaphor. Obviously, as we have suggested, different metaphors are more appropriate to some conditions than to others. Furthermore, it would be most instructive to chart the movement of marks from one predominant script to another over a period of time, and in response to political action and media coverage. The long-range movement of alcoholism from the moral deviate or child-among-adult script to the illness-disease script is an obvious example of this continuing evolution. The dramatic gains that homosexuals have made in transforming the scripts that apply to them—in this case from moral deviance to psychiatric condition to freely chosen alternative life style—is another example.

Our main point, however, is that the scripts we do have are not applied with precision. There is undoubtedly considerable public confusion about the relationships among mental illness, retardation, epilepsy, and cerebral palsy, but we do not suggest that people are necessarily or genuinely confused about their explicit categorizations of criminals, cancer patients, or the mentally ill. We merely raise the question of whether potential markers may be influenced by the intrusion of misleading metaphors or inappropriately bounded categories in their interactions with markables. Langer's concept of "mindlessness" (1978) may turn out to be relevant in this context. When we are "mindful"; when, for example, someone asks us if we really think cancer is contagious, or if we really think the mentally ill are typically like dangerous criminals, we say, "of course not." But in our more mindless moments—when we are not specifically concerned with rational deductions from the evidence at hand—we may be the victims of more primitive categorization systems, those formed earlier in life and insufficiently challenged in mindful moments. We may be vaguely dissatisfied and uncomfortable in operating with these borrowed scripts, but they spare us the greater discomfort of developing new and complex categories.

Any of those metaphors serve to fill in the content of conditions characterized by relative powerlessness. Other things being equal, children, sick people, poor people, and ex-convicts are low in power for a variety of reasons. To the extent that the act of marking places the marked person in one or more of these categories, he or she must interact with a marker burdened by category-based expectations that are poorly tailored for the particular limitations inherent in his or her condition. Although this state of affairs is hardly unique to interactions between markers and markables, we assume that unfamiliarity with the behavioral consequences of most marks heightens the tendency to apply irrelevant scripts that are borrowed from other interaction classes.

STRATEGIC REACTIONS TO THE MARKABLE CONDITION

We have painted a rather bleak picture of the markable's circumstance in a relationship with normal markers. We have cited various reasons why he or she can only participate in the relationship from a disadvantaged, low-power position. We will now consider the markable person's possible behavioral resources, and how they might be used to improve the outcome potential of the relationship.

It should be emphasized that the markable's strategic options may not be self-consciously reviewed and implemented. To the extent that self-presentational features are involved in an interaction episode, they typically involve overlearned, "mindless" responses to certain cues that define one's power as low or in jeopardy. Thus, if *A's* dependence on *B* is so strong that she has a high stake in *B's* attraction for her and in *B's* constant willingness to exert his power on her behalf, *A* will probably say the kinds of things she thinks *B* would like to hear, agree with his expressed opinions, and convey her own liking and respect through nonverbal gestures, without making a conscious or deliberate decision to do so. It will be a natural outcome of an extensive personal history of myriad social interactions.

To the extent that the markable person is indeed dependent or lacking in interpersonal power, it is hardly surprising that he or she will be motivated to change the situation—somehow to augment his or her capacity to reward and punish within the bonds of stable relationships with normal persons. It is obvious that the person with a visible or revealed mark is in a very different position than the person with a concealed mark. The latter may hope to sustain the concealment or, alternatively, hope to arrange the time and the context in which the impact of revelation will be minimal. Once the mark is apparent, however, the potentially devastating impact of the stigmatizing process becomes a significant hurdle for the markable person. The crucial problem is to bypass or contain the engulfing potential of the stigma. As emphasized in Chapter 5, once a stigmatizing label is applied, there is a tendency to interpret the marked person's past and present actions in terms of the stigma, including his self-presentational actions. An ex-mental patient, for example, may be an inattentive listener because he is worried about being late for an appointment. Nevertheless, the marker who knows about his ex-patient status may interpret that inattentiveness as another indication of the person's being out of touch with reality, of his being preoccupied with inappropriate fantasies. Genuine expressions of indignation may be interpreted as signs of paranoia, taking a second drink may be seen as a frightening sign of an alcoholic once again losing control, and so on. The markable person may respond to these tendencies for others' attributions to be "engulfed" in the mark with efforts to ignore them, or he may become excessively self-conscious about remarks or gestures that might confirm the expectancy or stereotype. This excessive self-consciousness may in and of itself lend confirmation to the expectation that, for example, mental patients are awkward and ineffective. The markable person thus confirms all the difficulties and essentially fails the challenges of "deviance disavowal" (Davis 1961).

Another special problem of the markable person is that the superior power of the marker is constrained by the infusion of inhibitory norms. The normal person in our society typically has more resources to offer and withhold than markable persons, but normative pressures tend to undermine this power differential and inhibit the more negative portions of the outcome range. That fact has two important consequences for the markable who wishes to augment his power.

First, high-power markers who are inhibited from fully exercising their power might find little advantage in relationships with markables. Therefore, normal markers interacting with marked persons are apt to be in the relationship on sufferance. We have already noted the probable avoid-loss orientation, one implication of which is that the marker is tempted to break off the interaction as soon as he can do so gracefully. In the face of such avoidance tendencies, the marked person has the special problem of keeping the marker in the interaction and using his own interaction time to his best advantage. For example, a blind student reports to us that the early phases of interacting with strangers are extremely difficult and awkward. He finds himself under intense pressure to talk and to persuade the sighted person as quickly as possible that he is not particularly saddened by being blind and that he is not morose or bitter.

A second problem that characterizes the early stages of marker-markable interactions that do take place is that the marker is likely to be busily concealing his negative feelings and his desires to be elsewhere. His behavior will typically be bland, constrained, or ritualized, rather than free and open. Thus, the markable person is confronted with the more difficult problem of determining how he is affecting the marker than may be the case in interactions between normals.

It is apparent, therefore, that the strategic problems of the markable person are more complicated than those associated with the sheer absence of power. When faced with markables, normal markers are apt to find themselves in the peculiar position of having high power in the conventional senses (many relationship options, abundant resources for dispensing rewards and punishments), but not being really in a position to use that power. We will explore the dynamics of this "ambivalence" in Chapter 7, but here we merely note that the conflicting power cues may themselves create an aversive situation for the normal marker and prompt him to prefer relationships where the power implications are more straightforward. But, this is by no means preordained. The markable person may easily overestimate the marker's aversion to interaction. This overestimation is part of the markable person's script for markers and creates problems with which the marker, who may have the best intentions in the world, must deal.

PROBLEMS FACING THE MARKER IN INTERACTIONS WITH THE MARKABLE

It is customary in the self-presentation literature to concentrate on the problems of those who lack power and would like to gain more through social interaction. Almost entirely ignored are the more subtle problems of high-power persons who long for credible evidence of respect and affection from those who are dependent on them. Thibaut and Riecken (1955) were the first to single out the informational problems of high-status persons who cannot tell whether the compliance of others is merely a response to superior symbolic force or reflects spontaneous loyalty. The typical marker shares some of the problems of attributional ambiguity that bedevil high-status persons, but there is more to his problems than eliciting believable positive feedback. As discussed in Chapter 5, markers often have to contend with discrediting stereotypes that they suspect are applied to them by many markable groups. Markers are inhibited from overt negative reactions to markables, and their positive reactions are often viewed with suspicion.

Thus, they often must sense that markables attribute negative attitudes to them and will treat solicitous gestures as instances of hypocrisy.

Whites are aware that some blacks look at them only as *ofays* ("foes," in pig latin). The disabled have a variety of denigrating terms for the able-bodied. One broadly-used term is *T.A.B.* ("temporarily able bodied"), a term that conveys a rather cynical warning that "this could happen to you," although the main intent may be to emphasize the circumscribed and fortuitous character of the disability. The concept of *uniplegic* (paralyzed from the neck up) is used when high derision is called for in response to the obtuse remarks or actions by a marker. In any event, just as the markable person faces the challenge of deviance disavowal, the marker faces the delicate task of conveying that he is not an ofay or a uniplegic, that he does not view the markable's social identity as "spoiled," and that he will not convert the sign of deviance into an engulfing master status.

We deal here, once again, with the complex problem of stereotypes. Is it the case, for example, that disabled persons expect normal persons to think that all disabled persons are alike? That all normals have feelings of revulsion, fear, and hostility toward disabled persons? Do the disabled think that all able-bodied people will have an avoid-loss orientation, rather than a something-to-gain orientation, in approaching interactions with them? To the extent that the marker does face markable persons saddled with these assumptions about the marker's orientation to markables, he clearly has delicate self-presentational problems. He must tread the fine line between constrained blandness and disruptive candor. He must reveal much of himself without appearing either boastful or complaining. He must draw out the markable person and individualize his response to him, conveying indirectly that he is able to ignore the mark or take it in stride. This is a very difficult task and one that is fraught with response traps, where it seems that the marker loses when he does one thing, but also loses when he fails to do it. The marker's problems and opportunities will be discussed later in this chapter, but first we return to the markable person and discuss some of the ways in which he can establish the preconditions for effective interactions with normals.

SETTING THE STAGE AND CASTING THE PLAYERS

The Elevated Importance of Setting the Stage

The study of self-presentation has focused on potential behavioral variations in standard settings of differential power, such as the simulated job interview. Some control over one's behavior is obviously crucial for the management of desired impressions. Students of self-presentation have not paid sufficient attention, however, to the importance of situation selection in the interests of strategic self-presentation. It may well be the case that interpersonally adroit persons are effective to a great extent because they choose carefully the social settings that they enter. Whenever possible, they arrange their interactions on their own turf in order to have a home-court advantage. We are not speaking only of the role of familiarity—knowing the situation and its requirements—but also of the role of settings in highlighting one's strengths and concealing one's weaknesses.

We suggest that the role of setting selection, and of the choice and arrangement of props, may have special importance in interactions between markers and markables. This is the case, even if only because mutual discomfort is such a common problem in such interactions and the avoidance of discomfort over how to handle the mark is so dependent on contextual salience and on situational role structures.

Presumably, the markable person will be concerned about the salience of his mark. Usually he will want to reduce that salience, to normalize the interaction, and to bypass the mark and its significance. It is not hard to generate hypothetical examples: (1) Paraplegics may avoid discos because the salience of their handicap in such contexts could make others more uncomfortable than if they were at libraries or concerts. (2) Deaf persons may avoid settings where they are exposed to conversations between two or more hearing people and reading lips is difficult. (3) A blind person who, let us say, is an opera buff may make a special effort to go with friends to the opera where his expertise will become manifest during the evening, permitting him to strike a blow in the direction of deviance disavowal. (4) A former mental patient might try to stay away from settings (e.g., job interviews, hospitals) where questions normally arise about past history. (5) The known epileptic may arrange early in relationships with able-bodied acquaintances to have them meet his beautiful wife, sister, or daughter.

In addition to the choice of situations that will manipulate contextual salience, it would be understandable if markables developed a preference for structured role interactions. To the extent that interaction settings are totally unstructured, the mark is likely to become an unsettling hidden item on the agenda. We have noted that some structured interactions are in effect occasioned by the mark. Doctors, nurses, and physical therapists probably do not experience great discomfort in interacting with the disabled in hospitals or clinical settings because of their well-established interactive roles. These same persons might be considerably more awkward or discomforted trying to converse with a disabled person at the home of a mutual friend. Other interaction settings may be structured along lines that make the mark irrelevant, and these settings may also facilitate relatively smooth interactions. Thus, for example, the teacher who has a conference with a hemophiliac student may concentrate on the term paper idea being discussed, without having to contend with the prospect of the student's premature death or the episodes of painful debilitating bleeding that periodically dominate the student's life.

Casting the Players: Companions, Sponsors, and Benefactors

Just as markables can play a role in the selection of congenial situations, so can they exercise some selective control over interaction partners. If this control is widely exercised, it can create important advantages that otherwise might be lacking. Of particular interest in this respect are normal persons who serve as links between the limited and stigmatized person and the normal world. Such links, or go-betweens, can serve various roles, ranging from sponsorship to physical aid, and they often have the salutory consequence of facilitating a wider circle of interactions in the normal world.

We suspect that such links develop quite naturally in the case of disabilities where the services of another person or persons is routinely required. It is very common for the blind to travel with sighted companions. Gowman (1956) emphasizes the plight of the companion who runs the danger of being thought different or strange and who is constantly being pulled back into the larger orbit of society by group pressures and the preexisting stereotypes that the sighted have of the blind.

Another kind of link is the benefactor. In his study of previously hospitalized adult retardates, Edgerton (1967) emphasizes the crucial importance of normal benefactors who not only help with the practical difficulties of coping with everday life, but also with the retardate's "delicate need for denial" (p. 172). By assuring the retardate that he is as good as anyone, by finding him employment and housing, and by handling financial transactions, the benefactor makes it possible not only for the retardate to survive outside an institution, but in many cases to pass as a normal.

Although the benefactors in Edgerton's study were mainly self-designated informal go-betweens, benefactor systems have since been institutionalized in the programs of the National Association for Mental Retardation and in various state and local programs for rehabilitating former mental patients in the community. Aviram and Segal (1973) discuss such a program in which former patients are each assigned to a neighborhood link who agrees to be available for certain kinds of help. The crucial condition for the success of this program is that the link realize the strict limits to his or her obligations, so that the former patient does not tax the link's patience or expertise.

Although Gowman (1956) stresses the strain inherent in the blind companion's role, there is also a brief mention of the role of the companion as an "interpreter" or a "vital social link" (p. 75), which suggests an interesting sponsorship role that goes beyond physical aid or protective nurturance. Davis (1961) also comments on the opportunities a deviant has of "utilizing the normalization potential inherent in being seen in the company of a highly presentable normal companion" (p. 128). The most likely conditions out of which links or go-betweens develop are those of obvious physical or mental limitations, where it is natural and convenient for a seeing person to help a blind one or a person of normal intelligence to help a retardate. However, we suspect that the concept may be extended to other conditions where physical aid or intervention is not a crucial and obvious need.

The following scenario seems to us quite plausible. A paraplegic graduate student is admitted to a Ph.D. program in political science. He is assigned to share an office with another first-year student who has well-developed interpersonal skills, moderate but genuine compassion for the unfortunate, and a good sense of humor. It seems reasonable to expect that the able-bodied student will of necessity develop a relationship with the paraplegic and that this will become increasingly comfortable as the wheelchair recedes as a focus of concern. As the semester begins, with orientation meetings and get-acquainted parties, the able-bodied student may rather pridefully play the role of sponsor or go-between. By his own easy manner with the paraplegic, he smooths the way for others who may model him or at least capture the spirit of his interactive ease. Perhaps he accelerates the process by complaining that the wheelchair is blocking access to the bar, or that the paraplegic is too lazy to fill his own glass. The paraplegic, of course, takes this in stride with a witty rejoinder that signals to the wider audience that he has things under control and that he is not overwhelmed by self-pity or bitterness.

In reflecting on this scenario, several points bear mentioning. First, the relationship between the markable and the link is initially fortuitous, as are so many relationships determined by propinquity. Second, the fact that the able-bodied officemate is adroit and compassionate may be a crucial factor, although the context of sharing an office and a series of new experiences in graduate school should facilitate comfortable interactions between a wide range of markers and markables. Third, it may be extremely important that the link is one of high status, thus endowing his sponsorship with value. Low-status links may be assigned even lower status as a function of associating with defenseless, dependent markables (cf. Aronson, Willerman, and Floyd, 1966). Finally, we should not underestimate the able-bodied officemate's motivation to serve as a link. Presumably there are rewards, both self-administered and socially derived, attendant on dealing smoothly with difficult interaction situations, especially those involving compassionate service. The other graduate students, initially relieved that they escaped the social ambiguities created by sharing an office with a disabled person, may be genuinely impressed with the link's mastery of a difficult situation (which, in fact, is not at all difficult once it begins to play itself out). Beyond this lies the link's own reasonable interests in sharing the marked officemate with his fellow graduate students. He understandably wishes to diffuse the responsibility for fulfilling the social needs of the markable person. The two officemates, in effect, have formed a symbiotic relationship in which the paraplegic gains sponsored access to a wider circle of acquaintances in a manner that reduces potential embarrassment and behavioral uncertainty, and the able-bodied officemate finds that others increasingly share the burdens of responsibility he has accidentally acquired.

We see no reason why the main features of this scenario could not be applied to job settings in which a new employee is obese, an ethnic minority member, a former mental patient, an ex-convict, or marked in a number of ways. While such developments seem psychologically reasonable to us, the evidence is sparse for social links or go-betweens in the vast majority of stigmatizable conditions. Perhaps the link concept will turn out to be bound in contingencies. The interactional skills and the status of the link are obviously important, as is the desire of the markable to use the link as a bridge to wide acquaintanceships. All things considered, however, we believe that there are several reasons why one might expect links to emerge, and we urge that research be conducted on their frequency and the conditions most favorable for their emergence.

SELECTING SELF-PRESENTATIONAL GOALS

Having commented on setting the stage and selecting the players, we continue to exploit the dramaturgical metaphor by turning to the roles themselves and how they are to be played. The markable person is generally low in power, but not without interpersonal resources. Markers may find it difficult to maneuver within the confines of stereotyping constraints, but they, too, have resources for breaking through and establishing gratifying relationships with those who are disabled and disadvantaged. Although the difficulties facing the marker will receive some attention in the following discussion, we will emphasize the markable person's strategic problems and opportunities. The discussion will be organized around four decisional goals or strategic alternatives: withdrawal, concealment, role acceptance, and confrontation with the hope of "breaking through."

Withdrawal

It is, perhaps, all to common for social psychologists to assume that people constantly hunger for companionship and will do almost anything to avoid being alone. We have followed Thibaut and Kelley (1959) in tying one's interpersonal power to available sources of alternative gratification. These alternative sources, however, need not be cast entirely in terms of alternative social relationships. It may be just as important to know how the available relationships compare with the options of privacy or isolation. At many points in our reflections on interactions between markers and markables, we have referred to strain, conflict, and discomfort on the part of both actors. That would seem to suggest that marker-markable interactions are typically marginal, in the sense that the benefits they may yield are likely to be jeopardized by their costs of discomfort.

The reasonable response to that state of affairs on the part of a marked person might be intense reliance for social contact on a few normals who handle their interactions smoothly and do not inflict high costs on the markable person. That might be coupled with a preference for isolation when these few skilled actors are unavailable. There is evidence that handicapped people prefer to interact with only a few normals at a time, and dislike to do so in large, semipublic social gatherings (Davis 1961; Higgins 1980). In any event, because the task of maintaining a wide range of casual interpersonal relationships may be arduous and costly for the markable person, we would not find it surprising if he often preferred social isolation to the risk of problematic, strainful interactions. It would be interesting to have data on the distribution of time allocated to social and nonsocial options for markable versus normal persons. In the case of the markable, one might find a greater dependence on television, reading, or other hobbies that can be pursued in isolation.

In many cases, it would appear, withdrawal from interaction in the "normal world" is supplemented by "flocking with birds of a feather." One of the obvious options available to markable persons who wish to avoid strainful interactions is to seek out interactions with other markables. Because of the shared handicap or stigma, fellow markables can presumably interact with less awkwardness and strain.

A notable example of banding together with those who are similarly disabled, largely in the interests of avoiding strain, is the deaf community. Higgins (1980) portrays the power and importance of this community, and emphasizes that membership is an achieved status. Membership is based on more than the amount of hearing loss; it is tied to such symbols of commitment as the consistent use of sign language.

Problems of when and how to be dependent or seek help, when and how to refer to the mark, and other problematic concerns need not arise between comparably marked persons. On the other hand, restricting one's interactions in this way is not an altogether satisfying solution to the problem of fulfilling one's social needs and, in fact, carries some distinct drawbacks. First, there is the sheer fact of restriction and the implications that follow from it. If the markable person is forced to choose his friends from only his fellow markables, he is clearly deprived of a full range of social options. Beyond this, the implication may emerge that markables are not good enough to interact with "real people"; thus, interactions among markables may carry an aura of defeat, of choosing comfort over the challenge of remaining engaged in the mainstream of societal life.

Undoubtedly, some of those problems are countered by the supportive agendas of the more formally established groups of markables, deviants, minorities, and so on. Perhaps emboldened by those features of the civil rights movement that emphasized the positive virtues of being "black" (and no longer "Negro" or "colored"), other markable groups, such as homosexuals, have seized upon forms of symbolization that fuse political militancy with explicit emphasis on the commonly held mark. Such drawing attention to the mark may occasionally take the form of idealization ("Black is beautiful," "Gay is the way"), but more often than not, it serves as a rallying cry for self-protection and political action (CRIPS, Little People of America, the Anti-Defamation League). Many other groups serve primarily therapeutic purposes, but attention to the mark is drawn by the acknowledgment implied by membership. Those would include such groups as Alcoholics Anonymous, Weight Watchers, and Gamblers Anonymous.

It is commonly assumed that the members of such self-conscious groups of markables gain support from their membership. It is not at all clear, however, whether joining with fellow markables serves the wide range of affiliative purposes mediated by interactions in the "normal" world. By drawing constant attention to a mark, membership in such a group may exaggerate the centrality of the condition and contribute to the maintenance of role engulfment. Also, such membership is not always entirely voluntary. Some markables who might prefer to conceal or deemphasize their mark are pressured to lend their support to the militant or protectionist causes of the category of markables that by definition includes them. For example, a black college student who is ridiculed or criticized by other blacks for interacting with white students might, somewhat reluctantly, be drawn into campus groups emphasizing black consciousness and black identity.

In the case of the deaf community, the existence and salience of a national network of deaf groups means that personal information, about such issues as divorce, employment experiences, and illness, often spreads rapidly wherever the deaf congregate. As Higgins points out, because of their strong tendency to restrict interactions within the deaf community, the spread of gossip through the deaf network is extensive and rapid. Thus, deaf people become less able "to control what other deaf individuals throughout the country know about them" (p. 74).

Concealment

A natural option for those who can conceal their mark is to do so in as many interactions and relationships as possible. Higgins refers to this strategy in his discussions of the deaf coping as conveying the information that "nothing unusual is happening." Because deafness is not a widespread condition and is one that is not visible, deaf people are often treated as unmarked. Even some normals who are aware of another's hearing disability often unwittingly "leave out" the deaf person as they engage in rapid conversation with each other. Under such circumstances, it is difficult and somewhat costly for the deaf person to intervene with requests for repetition and clarification. Also, it is probably true, in general, that there are many normal-deaf interactions in which the deaf person feigns understanding, either to conceal his deafness or to maintain the interactive flow that could be disrupted awkwardly by requests for repetition.

PASSING INTO A SIGHTED WORLD

Michalko, R., "Passing: Accomplishing a Sighted World," *Reflections: Canadian Journal of Visual Impairment*, 1982.

As a person with partial sight, I found adolescence to be a particularly difficult time. Much of my activity

was animated by a sense of normalcy; that is, much of my interaction was animated by the desire to . . . be "one of the guys." I . . . sought to . . . pass as a normal adolescent, by acting as if I were something other than what I was, namely, by acting as if I were a normally sighted adolescent.

[As a sixteen-year old boy, unable to obtain a drivers license, I felt that I had to invent a reason to lay claim to my normalcy.] The reason I invented—one that was sensible to my friends and acquaintances—was that I had been apprehended by the police for driving a car when I had been underage and under the influence of alcohol. This apprehension had resulted in legal postponement of my taking a drivers test. I explained to my friends and acquaintances that I could not legally take a drivers test until I was 17 years old. This gave me a year's grace, so to speak. I would not have to invent another reason for at least another year. . . .

During my adolescence my claim to normalcy . . . required constant vigilance. It was necessary for me to continuously monitor the behavior of others so that I would be able to recognize the sort of interaction that stood for normal sightedness. . . .

[This and other examples from my adolescence involve deception as a basic feature of passing. But deception is not always a basic feature.] I often attend sports events, such as ice hockey games, with friends who are aware that I am a partially sighted person. More specifically, and in relation to hockey, what my friends are aware of is that I am not able to distinguish one player from another; that I am not able to see the puck during the course of the game; that I am not able to tell whether the puck has been passed from one player to another or shot toward the net in an attempt to score a goal.

However, certain things happen during the course of a hockey game that allow me to know whether or not a goal has been scored. For example, with some goals, there is a loud noise when the frozen rubber puck hits the metal posts or bars of the goal net. . . . If . . . this loud noise is closely followed by a tremendous cheer, I can be quite sure that the home team has scored a goal . . . and, of course, if I happen to miss an

> **important event, my friends will describe to me what has happened. What is important, however, is that I orient to those activities that allow me to interact in an appropriate manner at an ice hockey game. . . .**
>
> **Even though the other spectators are not aware of the fact that I am a partially sighted person, my friends are certainly aware of this fact and they know that, despite my response, neither did I see the puck go into the net nor could I have seen the puck go into the net. Even though they know this, my friends still notice my response and take it as being legitimate. This does not seem to be an instance of living a life that could collapse at any moment. . . .**
>
> **What passing [requires] . . . is that such problematic activities as going downstairs, crossing streets, and so on, be endowed with an unproblematic and taken-for-granted appearance. . . . For example, as I approach a set of stairs, I make sure that I stop a few inches before the stairwell begins. Then by snapping my fingers, or by looking at my wristwatch, I . . . produce the appearance of someone who just reminded himself of something. During this time, I slide my foot along the floor until I find the first stair. Having found the stair, I can then proceed down the staircase. . . .**

Goffman (1963) distinguishes between "passing" and "covering." Passing involves deliberate concealment of the mark, while covering involves subtle staging strategies to keep the stigma from looming large in particular interactions. Passing is no doubt tempting when the stigma attached to the mark is great and the mark is easily concealed. Thus, we would expect passing to be the rule rather than the exception in instances of homosexuality, alcoholism, prostitution, being an ex-convict, or being a former mental patient. In cases of sensory deficiency, physical disability, and stammering, passing is more likely to be converted into covering. The decision to pass can be a deliberate preplanned response to calculated probabilities of detection, or passing may emerge out of a natural cycle. Goffman describes this cycle as starting with instances of unwitting or unintended passing, where the passer, to his surprise, is taken as a completely normal person. Passing may then be attempted at "off-duty" times, such as while traveling. The final stage of the cycle is the "disappearance"—the complete passing over to where the secret is known only to the passer himself.

Goffman suggests at one point that the degree of psychological strain involved in passing may be exaggerated by those who believe in the therapeutic wisdom of candor and disclosure. Nevertheless, he provides numerous anecdotes documenting the difficulties and sources of strain that often are associated with concealment. First, even if the passer is successful, he must face prejudice against persons "of the kind he can be revealed to be" (p. 42)—for example, the Jew who passes may have to listen to anti-Semitic jokes. Second, there are problems of maintaining the cover, and stage setting may be crucial. As noted, the markable person may gravitate to settings where the mark is irrelevant—for example, a partially deaf person may more easily pass for normal in a boiler factory. Similarly, there is the practice of "living on a leash— . . . whereby the discreditable person stays close to the place where he can refurbish his disguise" (p. 90). An obvious example is the elaborate planning required by colostomy patients and secret drinkers or drug addicts to maintain concealment of their marks.

The passer also faces the danger of discovery. It is typically the case that when the duplicity is revealed, those from whom the mark was concealed will feel resentment. This is particularly true if the normal person considers himself a close friend of the passer, since disclosure of such things is usually treated as an obligation of friendship. One implication of this is the crucial importance of when to disclose the mark, or disclosure timing. The longer one waits to disclose, the more difficult it is to reveal the mark. Short-run concealment can be attributed to a lack of opportunity, or not wanting to appear to be looking for sympathy. When the passer is uncovered, however, the discredit of a deceitful lack of trust is added to the discredit of the revealed mark. Jones and Gordon (1972) have shown how disclosure timing may depend crucially on the degree to which the markable is seen as personally responsible for his mark. Subjects listened to an interview with a student who had missed a year of high school and later evaluated him as a person. If the year was missed because the student was suspended for plagiarism, the subjects liked him better if he revealed this early in the interview. If the student lost a year because of a parental divorce and relocation, he was liked better if he revealed this late in the interview. It is not clear how far this finding may be generalized, but it does point up the possibility that premature disclosure may be just as discrediting as delayed disclosure, and that the circumstances surrounding the mark and its origins may be crucial in determining the outcome of the disclosure.

Complete passing (total "disappearance") is probably very rare. Much more typical are the mixed cases, where the mark is concealed from some audiences and revealed to a select circle of friends. The danger in this, of course, is the danger of confrontations between those who know and those who do not. If the markable generates a double biography, the segregation of identities may break down through a number of circumstances. Goffman (1963) provides this example: "Every ex-mental patient must face having found in the hospital some acquaintances who may have to be greeted socially on the outside, leading a third person to ask, 'Who was that?'" (p. 67).

Finally, in some instances where the markable may not be able to conceal the mark, he will work to convert its origin and significance. Edgerton (1967) stresses that mental retardates will explain their prior institutionalization by referring to a "bout of nerves" or a "mental breakdown," rather than to their diagnosed intellectual limitations.

Role Acceptance

Sociologists often use the concept of "role socialization" to refer to the process of learning the role that others have assigned you. Certain advantages accrue to the low-power person who "knows his place" and who rewards others by confirming their expectations of him. The self-fulfilling prophecy notion contains the requirement that *A*'s expectancies about *B* will somehow influence *B* to behave in ways that confirm these expectancies (see Chapter 5). Allport (1954) speaks of "traits of victimization," noting that the victims of ethnic prejudice, for example, cannot help but be affected by the constant exposure to high-consensus stereotypes about their inferiority, their stupidity, and so on. Certainly, there is evidence that, under some conditions, some people cannot help wondering whether the stereotypes that others have about their group might be true. It is a short step from such wondering to varying degrees of acceptance of the stereotype. Such acceptance is obviously not inevitable, but we suspect it is an outcome that is not at all rare. There is a natural resistance to thinking ill of ourselves, but sometimes the consensual weight of the stereotype can overwhelm that resistance and create serious self-doubts.

OUT OF THE CLOSET

Finn, Robin "Coming Out," *The Hartford Courant*, February 27, 1983.

Tony Norris . . . knew from the time he was six that, although he liked girls as friends, his relationships with boys and men were by far the greater source of interest. At adolescence he was involved with two male peers,

and much of their conversation, he recalls, revolved around whether there was something wrong with their feelings for each other. Unable to reach a consensus, and just confused by the information in the library books he perused in dark corners because he was afraid to check them out on his card, he went into what he terms his 'dormant phase' from 16 to 22. Rather than become obsessed with deciphering just where he fit into the sexual scheme of things, "I realized my sexuality was too big an issue to deal with during college, and I chose not to come out until a lot of other things about myself were clear."

What Norris did know was that he wasn't inclined to behave like the half dozen "obvious queens" he encountered at college, that even though he secretly had something in common with them that he didn't share with other men, he wasn't prepared to make their alliance. "For anybody who's gay and over the age of 20 . . . there were no positive role models. You were left with the image of the masculine woman or the man with the lisp and limp wrists . . . and the family chuckling over them as they watched T.V."

Of greater interest for our present purposes is the more likely possibility that it may be easier for the markable person to act as if the stereotype were true, whether or not he privately accepts it. Schur (1971) writes of the difficulties facing the deviant who wants to reduce or resist role engulfment. He does not, however, deal with the social mechanisms that allow the maintenance of such engulfment. One obvious problem is that the process of adapting to an engulfing stereotype is rarely an open one. If a marker believes his blind acquaintance is helpless, dependent, grave, and hypersensitive, he may act on those beliefs without negotiating explicitly with the acquaintance about their validity. Thus, it is difficult for the blind acquaintance to challenge a set of beliefs that are never fully articulated. In addition, the marker's behavior may preclude the possibility of corrective feedback from the marked person. As Scott (1969) remarks, "[If] sighted people continually insist that a blind man is helpless because he is blind, their subsequent treatment of him may preclude his even exercising the kinds of skills that would enable him to be independent" (p. 4). In emphasizing the pressures toward socialization into the role of being blind, Scott notes that resisting the stereotypes of the sighted requires extraordinary commitment and personal resources.

In the face of such stereotyped expectations, one general family of self-presentational strategies involves embracing the disability or stigmatizing condition and finding ways to exploit it. Jones and Pittman (1982) distinguish five types of self-presentation strategies and identify them in terms of the attributional goals they attempt to achieve: ingratiation, self-promotion, intimidation, exemplification, and supplication. The physically or mentally limited person is perhaps a natural candidate for considering the supplication option in an effort to cope with his low-power status. According to Jones and Pittman, the supplicant essentially throws himself at the mercy of those people who are more powerful and have more resources. He tries to convey that he is helpless and unfortunate to elicit protective nurturance from others. Social-responsibility norms, of course, include a generalized sympathy for the unfortunate, and many potentially stigmatizing conditions obviously fall into this category. This generalized sympathy is often institutionalized in the form of charitable donations, tax-supported hospitalization and education for the mentally and physically handicapped, and various welfare measures. Contributions to such support systems may reduce the sense of obligation that might otherwise more strongly influence interpersonal relations, but most normals have a helpful disposition toward the disabled that may be triggered by appropriate supplicational cues.

Such cues may be blatant, as in the case of bedridden quadriplegics, or they may be highly discretionary. A paraplegic with a remarkable capacity for taking care of his own daily needs reports having to make frequent decisions about whether and when to turn to others for help. As he sits on his living room couch reading the evening paper, it may happen that he wants a cup of tea. He must decide whether to go through the laborious process of working his body into the wheelchair and rolling into the kitchen, or to ask his wife to bring him the tea. Such individual decisions may appear trivial, but their resolution is probably of great importance for the relationships involved, as well as for the markable person's self-concept.

Such autonomy versus help-seeking decisions are obviously not restricted to wheelchair victims or other physically disabled markables. The depressed executive may confront similar decisions when colleagues volunteer to take over some of his responsibilities temporarily. He is still able to do his job, but the cost of sustained effort may be so great that the offered assistance is an attractive alternative. Many females (who, in certain respects, remain stigmatized in our society) frequently face similar decisions when males offer to carry their bags or to pay for lunch.

Viewed from the rational perspective of total expenditure of energy, it may be more suitable for the wife to get the tea for her paraplegic spouse, for the depressed executive to reduce his stressful responsibilities for a time, and for the female to let the stronger male carry her suitcase. But equitable energy expenditure is only one factor among many that are tied to aid-seeking or aid-accepting decisions. Coping with dependence may be the single most crucial task confronting the physically or psychologically disabled.

One coping style is to take maximum advantage of the social-responsibility norm and the guilt mechanisms that are derived from it. The markable person may take every opportunity to exaggerate his incapacity and to exploit the disposition toward helping possessed by most citizens. Even ignoring the questionable morality of such exploitation, there are serious practical problems in implementing a full-bodied supplicational strategy. The most serious of these is that supplication confirms one of the fears that underly many markers' desires to avoid interaction with markables—the fear that once embroiled in an interaction with a dependent markable, the marker will not be able to extricate himself gracefully. Most people do not mind extending an occasional helping hand, but they are less likely to enjoy being in a relationship in which they are exploited by someone who continually parades his helplessness. Thus, during a given interaction episode, the high-power member may be obligated by social-responsibility norms to help the supplicating markable. Such experiences may be sufficiently aversive, however, that similar interactions will be studiously avoided by the marker in the future. Thus, the supplication strategy is self-limiting, unless the marker has unusually strong nurturance needs or unless the markable low-power person can find ways to compensate the marker for the effort expended on his behalf.

Another serious problem with the supplication strategy is that it collides with the value of self-sufficiency in our society. If there is a social-responsibility norm (help those less fortunate than you), there is also a norm that rewards those who cope, who overcome, who are autonomous, and who do not ask for favors. Furthermore, this self-sufficiency norm is apt to be so internalized that the supplicator who gains by invoking the social-responsibility norm must pay the price of losing at least some self-esteem by not living up to the norm.

The supplicant exploits his stigmatizing mark by implicit appeals to the norms that frame the behavior of able-bodied markers. Intimidation is a more direct form of exploitation. In fact, although intimidation tactics are available to all of us, they may be especially effective when the actor is disabled, fragile, or unpredictable. Intimidation involves making salient the possibility of dangerous consequences if the actor does not get his way. The intimidator conveys, often in subtle ways, that he has the resources to inflict pain or stress and the inclination to do so when thwarted. Our task here is to consider the special contributions of disabling or stigmatizing conditions to an understanding of how intimidation might work. As Jones and Pittman (1982) note: "An otherwise impotent person can gather considerable power by acquiring the reputation of one who cannot stand stress or disappointment without responding with hysterical weeping, coronary distress, or suicidal depression" (p. 239). This suggests that handicapped persons can exploit their own fragility in order to control the demeanor of others. They can purchase a benign and protective response from normal friends and acquaintances, not by eliciting sympathy for their condition, but by arousing fears that their perception of rejection, avoidance, or indifference might bring them to some form of breaking point.

A study by Gita Wilder (1983) provides an illustration of how this might be an especially effective strategy for those marked with a permanent disability. Normal female college students were recruited for an experiment on jury decision-making. The experiment featured an exchange of opinions between two subjects and an attempt to reach a consensus on the guilt or innocence of a protagonist described in a fictitious legal case. One of the two subjects was actually an accomplice in a wheelchair. The experimenter had previously noted (out of earshot of the accomplice) that the condition requiring the wheelchair was either temporary or permanent. Information was also provided indicating that the accomplice was either argumentative and controlling or fragile and easily upset. Initial compliance was greatest in the condition in which the naive subject confronted the fragile accomplice who was permanently disabled. When the accomplice was only temporarily disabled, on the other hand, she induced more compliance when the background information stressed her tendency to be controlling. Thus, the experiment suggests that weakness can be powerful in the hands of the disabled—markers will comply merely to avoid the embarrassment of upsetting a "deviant" person whom they believe might be easily upset.

Other forms of intimidation are more clearly associated with social-responsibility norms. The intimidating markable may play on the normal's potential for guilt and shame, subtly making it known that unsupportive behavior from the marker will result in lowered self-esteem and, quite possibly, public censure. Of course, in some cases of neglect or mistreatment, the response may actually take the form of legal prosecution. Affirmative action and other similar protective laws may thus serve as sanctions that may be invoked by the markable intimidator who is motivated to maintain or gain power in relationships with potential markers.

Like supplication, intimidation drives people apart and creates pressures toward withdrawal. In general, it should not be a very effective strategy except in relationships that are nonvoluntary—the family, student-teacher relations, employer-employee relations in a depressed job market. However, it may also be the case that many marks of disability inject a nonvoluntary component into the relationship at the outset. That is, it is often difficult for the normal in the relationship to extricate himself without creating the impression of prejudicial abandonment. This is apparent in some employer-employee relationships, where it may be difficult to discharge a disabled worker even when he is incompetent. There may, therefore, be resistance to hiring the handicapped unless employers can be convinced that they can also be fired for cause. In any event, to the extent that marker-markable relations are more difficult to terminate than normal relationships, intimidation and supplication strategies may be relatively common among markables.

Confrontation and Breaking Through

A final cluster of strategic goals features the open acknowledgment of the mark, plus a variety of attempts to place the mark in a constructive or laudatory context. At a minimum, acknowledgment may be part of a containment strategy in which the main self-presentational effort is to keep the mark from flooding attributional space and serving as a "master status." At the other extreme, the mark may even lend itself to romantic glorification. Somewhere along the scale are various other strategies designed to use the mark as a frame for the display of other virtues. Exemplification and self-promotion fit into this latter category.

Jones and Pittman (1982) list self-promotion and exemplification as separate strategies in their self-presentational taxonomy. Within the present context, the two strategies share so many similarities that they can conveniently be discussed together. The self-promoter tries to elicit respect or even awe by convincing others of his unusual competence in some domain. It helps if the domain is of central importance (e.g., creative originality) or governed largely by native endowment (e.g., IQ). The exemplifier attempts to impress others with his moral worthiness, trying to arouse in them guilt and self-judgments of unworthiness. There are certain steps that may be taken by the markable person to implement these strategies in special ways.

The crucial attributional understanding to be traded on is the augmentation principle. As formalized by Kelley (1971): "If for a given effect, both a plausible inhibitory cause and a plausible facilitative cause are present, the role of the facilitative cause in producing the effect will be judged greater than if it alone were present as a plausible cause for the effect" (p. 12). From this principle it should follow that a musician who is blind (inhibitory cause) and who plays at a professional level (the behavioral effect) should be judged to have greater musical talent and/or greater self-discipline than an equally talented, sighted musician. The same should follow for a female versus a male bank president (the female must have been both smarter and tougher than the men with whom she competed), or for an alcoholic versus a teetotaling professor (if they have comparable vitas, the alcoholic must have clearly have been more talented to start with).

Augmentation for the would-be self-promoter trades on the disabling significance of the mark. The self-promoter wants his native ability to be credited for overcoming inherent barriers to performance. His performance need not be spectacular or even up to normal standards. In fact, the self-promoter may be basically interested in conveying how talented and accomplished he might have been, if it were not for the afflicting mark. If this hypothetical attribution can be achieved, the self-promoter may gain at least some of the power accorded to those whose actual achievements certify their high abilities.

Jones and Berglas (1978) introduced the concept of self-handicapping to cover instances in which a person actually generates inhibiting circumstances to exaggerate the significance of his accomplishments (as well as to excuse his failures). There is evidence, for example, that drugs (Berglas and Jones 1978) and alcohol (Tucker, Vuchinich, and Sobell 1981) may appeal to those who wish to protect an illusion of high self-competence. We are not extending the self-handicapping notion to suggest that people seek out stigmatizing conditions, but we do suggest that once afflicted with a disabling handicap, an individual may gain social power by exploiting its inhibitory role and, thereby, certifying his superior native ability. The self-promoter's message is, "Even though I am performing adequately now, I would obviously be doing a much more impressive job if I were not afflicted with this handicap."

Use of the augmentation principle by the would-be exemplifier involves moral character as a facilitative cause of coping behavior with the disabling or marking condition serving as the inhibitory cause. From the logic of the principle, it should follow that, for a given level of adaptation or coping, the more disabling the mark, the greater the inferred moral character. This depends, of course, on the state of other facilitative or inhibitory causes. Less character may be attributed when the markable person has great wealth or a uniquely dedicated and helpful wife, teacher, or coach. The nature of the attribution also depends, presumably, on the particular quality of the disabling condition and the particular performance being considered. The performance of solving complex mathematical problems some time after a disabling automobile accident does not necessarily suggest great character. Solving the same problems while suffering intractable pain does. From this we may infer that the markable exemplifier should try to make his pain salient without ever mentioning it. He wants the disruptive character of his disability emphasized without in any way complaining about it. The exemplifier, after all, has admirable self-discipline and "staying power." He conveys the implicit message, "See how I have suffered, and despite that, I have managed to maintain my optimism, my good humor, and my determination to overcome adversity." This may often take a religious twist in that the disabled person appears convinced that it is God's will working in mysterious but acceptable ways, perhaps to test and confirm the marked person's moral strength. The successful exemplifier gains power as others gain sustenance from observing his moral triumphs over the temptations of dependence.

From the examples we have used, it might seem that exemplification and self-promotion are relevant strategies for markables only when the mark in question is physically limiting. The operations of the augmentation principle are certainly more straightforward in cases of sensory or locomotor deficit, and it is an interesting research question whether they play any role in what Goffman (1963) has called tribal and character stigma. There is some evidence (Feldman 1972; Linville and Jones 1980) that black professionals are seen as more intelligent and more highly motivated than comparable white professionals. The "eligibility" of those with character stigmas for the augmentation principle is less obvious. Examples of former psychotics or convicted murderers and rapists who have managed to turn their stigma to their advantage are not abundant, even on television talk shows. The use of character stigmas in exemplification and self-promotion strategies would be most likely when the defining deviance is not severely threatening to society (as, for example, child abuse would be) and reflects great deprivation or maltreatment in the prior socialization of the deviant. For strategic success, it is important that the deviant behavior be seen as quite understandable, given the circumstances, so that later success is seen in the context of the disabling circumstances, rather than merely the ability to refrain from immoral behavior now and in the future.

Even if we consider only those marks reflecting disability, there are related dangers in exemplification and self-promotion strategies. The self-promoter who is too aggressive in his compensatory efforts or too obvious in relating his performance to his unfortunate limitations may be viewed as pathetically insecure and "not cool." The exemplifier may be somewhat frightening almost to the extent that he succeeds. We may respect those who overcome through great force of character without wanting to become a satellite in their social orbit. That is where the ubiquitous strategy of ingratiation becomes important as a buffering ingredient.

Ingratiation is part of the social atmosphere that all of us breathe. We all want to be liked by others, even though some of us may go further out of our way to seek attraction than others. There is no reason to expect that the markable has less interest than normals in being attractive, although he may be willing to settle for less because of his low-power position. We have already noted the importance attached by some markables to keeping the marker in the interaction long enough to manifest one's attractive or impressive qualities. Clearly, ingratiation tactics can contribute to this all-important maintenance of initial contact.

By and large, we would assume that markables go about making themselves attractive in much the same ways that the rest of us do—smiling warmly when appropriate, using compliments, performing favors, and supporting the expressed opinions of those whose affections they seek. The markable person does face some distinctive difficulties in making these tactics effective. Insofar as he is seen as desperate for friendship and human support, his ingratiating overtures may simply be taken as a matter of course, thus confirming the stereotype that handicapped people are always nice because they cannot afford to be otherwise. The overtures might even be resented because of the ulterior motives they appear to reflect.

Because of this, we feel, the markable person is in a special position to need and to be able effectively to use humor in his relations with markers. We suggest that humorous self-deprecation may be a very useful ingratiating tactic, because it shows that the markable person is comfortable with his disability, that he has come to terms with it and can treat it as an amusing affliction. When markables interact with each other, we might well expect instances of black or gallows humor about their own condition. Also, some markables undoubtedly feel a temptation to moralize about appropriate and inappropriate coping strategies and to form distinctions within the marked ingroup. As Bergson (1911) said, "the humorist is a disguised moralist." One blind musician, upon hearing that another blind musician always has his meat cut for him by his sighted companions, was heard to comment, "He's a poor blink." Although this was said to a sighted person, there is no doubt that markables joke among themselves about the right and wrong ways to respond to their limitations. Perhaps even more common are the forms of humor that emphasize the cohesiveness of the disabled in-group through attacks on the normal out-group or frequently encountered out-group segments, such as the medical service professions. Coser (1959) refers to such humor as "the jocular gripe," and notes its significance in creating cohesiveness.

When markables interact with markers there are special opportunities that might be extremely important in reducing potential discomfort and strain. Forms of self-deprecating humor may be especially effective as the markable person displays his ability to keep the mark in perspective and to inform the marker that it is all right (i.e., not upsetting) to talk openly about his condition. A paraplegic might tell a story about the time he got stuck in a revolving door in his wheelchair. An ex-alcoholic might tell humorous stories about his behavior while under the influence. An ex-criminal might jokingly warn a straight friend not to leave his valuables around. Such self-deprecation partakes liberally of the role of the fool, as identified by Klapp (1949). Although he opens himself to ridicule, the fool nevertheless draws attention to himself in a way that makes others enjoy his company, perhaps because he provides an inoffensive reminder of their own effectiveness. The secret for the markable person who is tempted to play the fool's role is presumably to restrict his self-deprecation to functions closely associated with the mark. The blind person who jokes about getting lost in closets or about taking a wrong turn in a shopping center may naturalize his interactions with markers by reciting these anecdotes.

We have suggested that the dangers that may follow from blatant exemplifications and self-promotion may be leavened or contained by successful ingratiation tactics, including self-deprecating humor and aspects of the role of fool. However, if the markable focuses exclusively on ingratiation at the expense of any concern about others' respect for his ability or character, the fool's role itself may become an engulfing substitute for the master status usually generated by the mark. The disabled or flawed person may become a likable klutz, which is better than a feared and totally discredited deviant, but a klutz nevertheless. It seems to follow, therefore, that self-deprecating humor should be focally tied to the direct implications of the mark. A blind person should probably be especially careful to avoid references to his "tin ear" during a concert intermission, and a deaf person should probably not admit failure to comprehend the point of a *New Yorker* cartoon.

FINDING THE HUMOR IN ONE'S OWN DISABILITY

Seawell, M. A., "Class Clown Overcomes the Odds in Comedy," *Peninsula Times Tribune,* May 21, 1981.

[Geri Jewell is a 24-year-old comedian born with cerebral palsy. She deals with the subject openly in her routines.] "Before I became a comic, I was a waitress, but they didn't like the way I tossed salads," she tells her audience. "Now I'm at Shakey's."

"I've been told I drive better than I walk. I've been pulled over once for speeding and four times for walking."

"I got a T-shirt printed that says 'I don't have cerebral palsy, I'm drunk.' It cost me 35 cents a letter. It would have been a lot cheaper if I had polio. . . ."

She has made the usual club circuit. Most comics have to work to get an audience's attention, she said, but that's no problem for her. "I walk on stage and there's total silence. There's a shock when they see me." Her most painful experience was in a packed New York City club where the audience thought she was imitating and making fun of the handicapped and started mimicking her. She walked off the stage in tears and it was weeks before she could go on again. . . .

Comedy [has] a lot to do with enabling her to accept her disability, "but I don't accept it fully. . . . I wish I walked like Barbara Eden. I don't like cerebral palsy, but I can tolerate it."

In the present context, when we speak of acknowledging the mark, we refer to situations in which the mark is visible and the marked person refers to it in ways that reflect his adjustments to it. While we suspect that humorous acknowledgments are often among the most effective, there are other ways to acknowledge the mark. Presumably, some of these may convey the desired implication that the marked person is comfortable with his condition and some of them may not. The actual evidence that explicit acknowledgment plays an ameliorative role in marker-markable interactions is sparse. Kleck, Ono and Hastorf (1966) show that able-bodied individuals often report discomfort and uncertainty when interacting with the disabled. In a series of experiments, Hastorf, Wildfogel and Cassman (1979) showed that this discomfort can definitely be reduced, if the disabled person acknowledges the disability and shows that he is open to questions about it. That was even the case, somewhat to the authors' surprise, when the disclosure was made along with considerable nonverbal nervousness. Similar results were obtained by Belgrave and Mills (1981). These investigators found, however, that mere mention of a disability was not sufficient. In order to increase the naive subject's desire to interact with a confederate in a wheelchair, the confederate had to mention the disability in connection with an incident revealing his physical ineptitude while attempting to sharpen a pencil.

Undoubtedly, there must be occasions when acknowledgment increases the marker's discomfort and places strain on the interaction. Some marks (e.g., physical disability) may be more effectively acknowledged than others (e.g., homosexuality), even if the marked person is aware that the normal person knows about his condition. This is an area in which experimental research is not only feasible, but likely to yield important insights about the role of the marked person's perceived attitude toward his mark.

Finally, in order to place the acknowledgment problem in relief, we might note the disruptive potential inherent in extreme cases of non-acknowledgment. In a Broadway skit, Dudley Moore, playing a one-legged man, appeared at a casting studio to audition for the part of Tarzan. The skit elicited enormous amusement from the audience. The hilarity of the skit seems to have hinged on the fact that throughout it, Moore never acknowledged his one-leggedness, leaving Peter Cook, who played the auditioner, in a serious quandary about how to act. The quandary was immediately apparent to the audience, but was totally ignored by Moore. As the skit progressed, Cook's discomfort became more and more obvious. He labored to arrange his face and words so as not to give away his astonishment and frustration with what he clearly felt was an impossible situation. As he did so, he became more and more flustered and undone. Moore, on the other hand, became increasingly self-confident and demanding. Why in the world, he kept insisting, was Cook so reluctant to allow him to try out for the part? He even took a few turns around the stage to demonstrate his agility (he was not at all agile, of course). By the end of the skit, Cook had been reduced to a state of blithering helplessness.

Power Transformations: Changing the Affective Sign of the Mark

Although we normally think of marks as discrediting blemishes, they may, under some circumstances, be converted into signs of virtue, heroic nobility, or captivating mystery. For many years the Hathaway Shirt Company used a model with an eyepatch to advertise its products. That was undoubtedly intended to be an appealing afflictional sign, and it was presumably successful, or the campaign would not have continued for as long as it did. We suspect that certain marks or stigmas may lend themselves to romantic idealization and that certain bearers of these marks are more successful than others in facilitating this conversion.

If we consider first the nature of the mark, it seems likely that physically limiting conditions that are not grotesquely disfiguring have the greatest potential for romanticization, especially if these conditions have a tragic or heroic origin. It is hard to imagine people wanting to avoid or stigmatize an empty-sleeved Bengal Lancer at a turn-of-the-century London lawn party. Dueling scars have historically been treated by certain members of European society as marks of honor. Even today, in some German universities, dueling scars on the head and cheek are prized as marks of courage by the bearer because they signify engagement in secret society duels (the *Mensur*). Filmmaker Stanley Kramer did an effective job in romanticizing paraplegia in *The Men*. The success of this romanticization depended more on the circumstances of the loss than on how the loss is handled, although the opposite was depicted in the post-Vietnam movie *Coming Home*.

For reasons that are difficult to disentangle, certain markable conditions lend themselves to romanticization less than others. Differences between the deaf and the blind are notable in this regard. In ancient Greece blindness was considered a mark of distinctive talents. Homer, and, in a later age, Milton, after losing their sight, were treated as visionaries. Today, the blind are often attributed almost mystical powers of philosophical insight, poetic sensitivity, or auditory acuity. This impression may be enhanced by the number of celebrated cases involving prodigious musical performances (Art Tatum) or literary feats (Ved Mehta). In contrast, no doubt in part because of the frequency of severe communication difficulties, the deaf are often viewed as mentally handicapped and considered incapable of important artistic or intellectual contributions.

In addition to the roles of causal origin and the intrinsic character of the stigma, power transformations can also be enhanced by manifestations of effective heroic coping. Franklin D. Roosevelt is a well-known example of the capacity to overcome a debilitating affliction, although it is difficult to measure the boost he received in his political career from his capacity to rise above his physical limitations. The case of FDR also suggests that the conversion of a potentially discrediting mark into a positive or romantic sign may be much easier when the individual has other sources of high power—for example, when the individual is otherwise physically attractive, wealthy, or well-positioned in the society. Marks that are almost uniformly stigmatizing for those otherwise low in status may not be stigmatizing for those high in status. They may, in fact, elevate the status to an even higher degree. Such advantages make it easier for the afflicted markable to control or select the contexts and modes of his appearances. This may have been extremely important in FDR's case. People were undoubtedly aware of his incapacities, but he managed to set the stages of his appearances to reduce markedly their salience.

The concepts of heroic striving and status variations may combine in interesting ways. Again, we cite the relevance of the augmentation principle within attribution theory (Kelley 1971). From this principle it follows that an achievement of a certain level by a physically or mentally limited person will be seen as more impressive than the same level of achievement by someone without such limitations. Impressiveness may either take the form of ability attribution or effort-persistence attribution. However, an interesting possibility is that low-status markables may tend to be given credit for heroic effort more than for ability, whereas high-status markables are more likely to be given credit for unusual (genetically based?) talent. In considering these possibilities of origin, however, it should be noted that the certifiability of the achievement itself is crucial. If the achievement is at all ambiguous, it may be possible to downgrade the level achieved by those who are physically or mentally limited to bring the perceived achievement level closer to the expected achievement level.

Information, Education, and Breaking Through

Perhaps the most mature and adaptive goal of the markable person who adopts a confrontational strategy is to "break through" into normal interaction patterns (Davis 1961, p. 27). That refers to the successful avoidance, disruption, or reversal of the labeling process so that the potentially stigmatizing mark is kept in its place as a manageable physical inconvenience or an interesting, but no longer relevant, bit of personal history. Thus, the interaction process is normalized, and the markable person no longer feels that the marker is preoccupied with his disabling condition and no longer fears that he confuses the specific effects of the conditions with irrelevant deviant or low-power scripts.

In attempting to break through, the marker's knowledge of what the marked person can and cannot do is of great importance. Normalization will be precluded if the marker is constantly wondering about the marked person's capacities and his conversational and recreational preferences. Does the paraplegic friend really want to go to a bowling party? Can the former mental patient handle a party attended by those who know about his psychiatric breakdown? Will a blind friend be upset when you try to include him in a theater party? Somehow, information relevant to such concerns needs to be conveyed with sufficient accuracy that the marker can suggest joint activities without fear of embarrassing the markable person or of patronizing him.

Perhaps the most important aspect of breaking through, both a cause and an effect of the process, is the markable person's success in directing the marker's attention to those of his personal values, interests, talents, and aspirations that have nothing to do with the potential mark. In view of role-engulfment tendencies, this may be more easily said than done, but the selection of appropriate settings within which one can make relevant and interesting disclosures may do much to reduce the pervasion of one's whole identity by the mark and its immediate consequences.

The Marker: Strategic Problems and Opportunities

The marker can play a decisive role in facilitating confrontation and education with the markable person. Presumably, past experience with other markables helps to alert the marker to behavioral cues defining the level of dependence and intimacy desired by the markable person. Experience should also help in the timing and style of questions that inoffensively clarify the nature of the disability without intrusively forcing the markable to say more than he wants to about it. As we have implied by describing the typical marker's situation, it is important to distinguish between three sources of behavioral decision problems facing the marker: those stemming from his own negative affect and ambivalence; those arising from his assumptions about the negative affect attributed to him by the markable person; and those arising from the lack of acceptable response options, particularly in the early stages of a relationship.

The ways in which markers cope with negative affect is discussed in Chapter 7, but here we are primarily concerned with markers who are well-meaning and sympathetic, and who want to find ways to help the markable person in the breaking-through process. One clue that emerges from our previous discussions is the importance assigned to inappropriate metaphors for behavioral scripts dealing with the markable. The normal person who is experienced in interacting with the disabled or the deviant may have had sufficient corrective feedback to avoid such metaphor traps. In any event, it is obviously important for the accommodating marker to be sensitive and accurate in processing information about the markable person. He must feel his way into the interaction neither ignoring the liabilities that might genuinely be involved as a consequence of the mark, nor assuming that they affect every aspect of competence and personal character. He must read cues that suggest how the markable views his own mark and how he wants to be treated by others. Basically, all accommodation strategies require a certain persistence in maintaining contact and an orientation that suggests inclusion, rather than avoidance or sufferance. Perhaps the greatest danger to the evolution or healthy relationships between marker and markables is the assumption by both that the other would rather be elsewhere or with someone else. No strategy of accommodation by the marker can be successful unless the markable person can be credibly relieved of the notion that any marker would find him aversive.

Of course, the marker must not merely convey his willingness to convert interaction into a relationship. He must somehow suggest why that relationship would be worthwhile. If the markable person is initially in a dependent or low-power position solely because of the stigmatizing implications of the mark, the marker has a clear opportunity to redress the implied power asymmetry through his strategic actions. In various ways he may try to demonstrate his own vulnerabilities, his own lack of power. Approachability tactics (Blau 1960) involving openness, conciliation, and self-deprecation, may be especially important in conveying the marker's message that the prospective relationship will be one of equal power and the exchange of equal outcomes. Jones and Wortman (1973) consider the special ingratiation strategies available to high-status persons who seek attraction from low-status persons. Their analysis assumes that the high-status person does not want to lose his status; he merely wants to increase his attractiveness while maintaining his respect-worthy position. When a potentially stigmatizing mark is involved in the relationship, however, the unmarked, possibly high-status, person may be more likely to strengthen the relationship by minimizing the dependence implications of the mark and going out of his way not to exploit the power implications of his own relative normality.

In addition to increasing their own personal attractiveness as interaction partners, normals, as we have already noted, often serve in a marked relationship as benefactors, links, or go-betweens in the world of the able-bodied. It seems obvious that such relations will be cherished and maintained by the markable person, to the extent that such a role is effectively performed. Once again we return to the potential role of humor—this time exemplified by friendly insults rather than self-deprecation.

"SHORT PEOPLE GOT NO REASON TO LIVE"

Fish, S., "Short People Got no Reason to Live: Reading Irony," *Daedalus*, 112, no. 1 (1983): 175.

Not too many years ago, Randy Newman wrote and recorded a popular song that quickly became notorious. It was called "Short People" and began by declaring that "short people got no reason, short people got no reason, short people got no reason to live." The song went on to rehearse in detail the shortcomings of short people, which included small voices, beady little eyes, and the inconvenience of having to pick them up in order to say "hello." It wasn't long before groups of short people were organizing to lobby against the song; it was banned in Boston, and there was a bill to the same effect introduced in Maryland's legislature. . . . In the midst of the hullabaloo occasioned by the song, its author rose . . . to say that he had been misunderstood: it was not part of his intention to ridicule short people; rather, he explained, it was his hope that by choosing an object of prejudice so absurd, he might expose the absurdity of all prejudices, whether his objects were Jews or women or blacks or Catholics, or whatever. He was, in short, or so he claimed, being ironic.

Not surprisingly, Newman's statement did not settle the matter. His critics, it seemed, were unimpressed by what he said, and they had various ways of discounting it. Some simply declared that he had lied. Others invoked the familiar distinction between intention and utterance: he may have intended no slur on short people, but his words say otherwise. Still others turned to psychology and explained that while Newman perhaps *thought* that he was free of prejudices, his song displayed his true feelings, feelings he had hidden even from himself. In short . . . rather than providing a point of clarity and stability, Newman's explanations . . . merely extended the area of interpretive dispute. . . .

We have already noted how socially adroit markers may use insulting humor in their role as links. By incorporating the disability in his attempts to put down the disabled person, the marker may be trying to confirm that he, too, can keep the disability in its place, that he is not overwhelmed by its tragic significance, and that it is not too serious a matter to be joked about. It is intuitively apparent, however, that a marker's use of friendly insults can boomerang. Even if the markable person laughs or jokes along with the insulting remarks—indeed, even if he comes up with an effective insulting rejoinder—he may be pained by the remark. Instead of putting the disability in a humorous perspective, the marker may convey his own preoccupations with the central significance of the disability in his own mind. A black friend may not think it is terribly funny when you refer to his "natural rhythm" as you watch him deal a poker hand. A Jewish friend may be hurt by an exaggerated complaint about his never picking up the check. Paraplegics would probably not find innuendos about their sex life particularly amusing.

The role of the marker in attempting to defuse the interaction through humor is indeed a delicate one, but the positive potential of humor in marker-markable relations is, nevertheless, great. Perhaps that can be best understood if we consider some alternative responses to the disclosure of potentially stigmatizing marks or to comments that draw attention to them. One possibility is to deny or downplay directly the salience of the mark. The unmarked person might say, "You don't really have a bad stammer at all," "I never noticed your hairlip," or "It's hard to believe you are blind, the way you get around." Such remarks may be reassuring, but they can also place the markable as "out of touch" or as belittling the magnitude of his problem.

What may be much worse are instances where the marker seems compelled to come up with matching traumas or disabilities, either his own or others. For reasons not entirely clear to us, people are often competitive and self-indulgent about their own brushes with misfortune. Some cannot suppress the knee-jerk impulse to tell mark-relevant horror stories to marked persons. The implication may be, "You think *you've* got it bad; let me tell you what I (a friend, etc.) went through." Such belittlement cannot be very endearing, but we believe competitive horror stories are commonplace. In order to be convinced of this, the reader may wish to imagine the possibility that he will say (or be strongly tempted to say) something about his own hospitalization experiences when he visits a sick friend in the hospital. In any event, the evidence that misery loves miserable company (cf. Schachter 1959) is at best equivocal.

Of course, the sharing of miseries can be part of an instructive, comforting comparison. The friend who says "I was once a mental patient, too," or "Did you know that I also had a massive coronary?" may comfort those with similar afflictions by emphasizing the likelihood of recovery and survival. When a person is "marked" by a rejection slip or a loss of employment, it may be very comforting to learn that others of equal competence were also rejected or fired. Finally, self-accusations of stupidity for a tragic accident may be somewhat relieved by a friend's recital of his own comparable negligence or blame. Thus, the sharing of miseries or horror stories may help to cement the marked relationship, if it conveys a relevant comparison that emphasizes the lack of permanence of the mark, reduces feelings of unique incompetence, or relieves one's guilt concerning the origin of the misfortune.

SUMMARY

In keeping with our dual interests in applications and in general theory, we may ask what the psychology of power and self-presentation suggests about coping with stigma, and then turn to consider any light that an analysis of stigma might shed on more general psychological processes. Turning first to the applications of social psychological theories for understanding stigma, we have proposed that markable people are almost by definition low in power. To the extent that this is true, the appropriate response to this low power may depend on the particular low-power script or scenario that dominates the marker's orientation. Unthinking applications of scripts for dealing with children, the sick, or the morally deviant may operate to place the marked person at a disadvantage that is not justified by his actual social limitations. But the markable person has numerous strategic resources for coping with his dependent position. Many of these resources are tied to the operation of social norms promoting sympathy, benefaction, and the inhibition of aggression. These norms form the backdrop for several self-presentational strategies. Among the available strategies are withdrawal, including association with other markable persons; concealment, in either the strong form of passing or in the weaker form of reducing the mark's salience; role acceptance, which may spill over into exploitation through either supplication or intimidation or some combination of both; and confrontation, animated by the hope of establishing normally gratifying relationships, at least with those most important to the marked person. Confrontational strategies include self-promotion and exemplification, both of which emphasize the limitations imposed by the mark in order to claim admirable talent or moral strength. Although research in the self-presentation field is still in its infancy, we believe that it is constructive to look at the problems and opportunities of markable persons from the power-strategy point of view within social psychology. Whether the disabled or stigmatized person wants basically to be liked and admired, or seeks more limited advantages in the social exchange market, questions of power and its acquisition are clearly involved.

Furthermore, by focusing on the many examples provided by the stigma family, we may gain important insights into the normal processes of self-presentation and into the strategic uses of social interaction for acquiring, augmenting, or protecting our power. Our analysis raises the suspicion that situation- or setting-selection is of great importance as a contextual ingredient of self-presentation among normals as well as the disabled. By looking at the special circumstances of the different conditions of disability and deviance, we can probably speculate fruitfully about the use of props and sets in the shaping of power-enhancing attributions. We also recognize that the more exploitative forms of self-presentation (such as intimidation) may be avoided, if an effective exchange of information about a disabling condition can occur and facilitate a normalizing breakthrough. Discomfort often stems from response ambiguity in marker-markable interactions, and a study of how such ambiguities are successfully resolved, or how response traps are avoided, should illuminate similar processes within interactions between so-called normals. Thus, as we have tried to demonstrate at a number of points in the preceding chapters, the study of marker-markable interactions helps to throw a number of important general issues into relief and to point toward fruitful research avenues that are not, by any means, restricted to interactions involving the disabled or the limited.

• CHAPTER SEVEN •

Affect, Inhibition, and Response Variation

NO ACCOUNT OF THE STIGMATIZING PROCESS would be complete without some consideration of the emotions that are entangled with the labeling of deviance and generated in marked relationships. It is well understood that attributional reasoning and social definitions can influence one's feelings about markable people. The vast literature on prejudice and stereotyping provides abundant evidence that labeling processes, which are themselves to a large extent arbitrary, can nevertheless liberate the kinds of intense emotions observed in racial terrorists and lynch mobs. Social psychologists characteristically treat such instances as examples of affect determined by cognitive preconditioning, although they acknowledge that the affect can also be fed by frustrations in other spheres.

When one looks at the full range of potentially stigmatizing conditions, however, it is natural to wonder whether some of them elicit affect that is not mediated by labels or causal attributions. That is, are there deviant conditions that automatically elicit "primitive" affective responses in the beholder? Perhaps the candidates that come most readily to mind are various physical anomalies: facial disfigurements, withered arms, mastectomy cases, tumors, and hunchbacks—and most obviously, dead and dismembered bodies. Although adaptations to such conditions can undoubtedly occur (one assumes that they occur almost routinely in the medical or nursing professions), most of us experience something ranging from vague uneasiness to extreme revulsion in the presence of such deviant conditions. This is also true with regard to a few behavioral anomalies like grand mal seizures or unrestrained and violent psychotic behavior. It is hard to believe that the initial emotional responses to these conditions are culturally conditioned, although it is obvious that individual experiences can shape and modify the degree and nature of the affect involved.

It is also obvious that there is no simple way to demonstrate the untutored, primitive quality of the human reaction to physical or behavioral deviance. An indirect approach to the question of unmediated affect is to consider the evolutionary significance of stigmatizing responses, as inferred from the data of animal behavior. In short, what do we know about animal responses to physical and behavior anomalies?

The information about such matters is surprisingly sparse and almost entirely anecdotal. The dominance literature of sociobiology (e.g., Wilson 1975) makes it clear that in many species the weak, scrawny, injured, or disabled members are either attacked or forced to the bottom of the hierarchy in obtaining food or nesting space. There is also some evidence that dolphins respond with altruistic behavior when "school" mates are wounded or injured (Pilleri and Knuckey 1969), and other instances of rescue behavior have been observed in wild dogs, elephants, and baboons (Wilson 1975). Fedigan and Fedigan (1977) describe the helpful reactions of other members of tribe monkeys to an infant monkey severely handicapped by cerebral palsy. Not only was the mother unusually solicitous in her efforts to feed her and keep her in contact with the tribe; other adults and even some of the handicapped monkey's peers performed some of the same protective, prosocial functions.

Hebb and Thompson's (1954) anecdotal accounts of chimpanzees in the Yerkes primate colony are among the few descriptions of response to anomalous physical shapes and "dead" (anesthetized) members of the same species:

> Mars, a young animal who had been anesthetized by Nembutal, in order to make physical measurements, was carried out and shown to four of the adults, Jack, Dick, Don, and Detta. The first three of these were markedly excited . . . and Don attempted to attack. . . . Since the sight of an anesthetized infant being carried by one of the staff was common, the observations of above were later repeated with an anesthetized adult. . . . Don, under Nembutal, was wheeled on a hand cart up to the cages of nine other adults. Ami, Nira, and Vera showed fear, and Dena and Bokar did also but then followed this by a show of aggression at a distance; Kambi showed generalized excitation in screaming only; Frank, with hair erect, spat at the anesthetized Don; Pam first avoided then attacked through the cage wire; and Lelia, with general excitation but not avoidance, also attacked. (The youngsters in the infants' enclosure were afraid, one very much so, and all showed signs of marked excitation.) (p. 549)

Here the apparent emphasis is on the diversity of response, but Hebb and Thompson try to summarize the chimpanzee reaction to anomaly under the rubric *excitement*. It is also exceedingly interesting to note their suggestion that this excitement has many of the features of ambivalence, of a mixture of abasement and aggression, and this inherent conflict or ambiguity may account for the wide variations in the overt responses of individual animals.

A similar picture of aversion is captured by Van Lawick-Goodall (1971) in her account of reactions to "Mr. McGregor," a chimpanzee whose legs were paralyzed from the waist down. He was a large, powerful male, one of a group of chimpanzees that Van Lawick-Goodall's team had been observing in the wild state. Mr. McGregor was able to drag himself painfully across the ground, but this left his bottom raw and bleeding, and his thighs, urine-soaked from incontinence, were covered with flies. Van Lawick-Goodall relates:

> **One of the most tragic things about the whole tragic affair was the reaction of the chimps to the stricken paralyzed male. Initially, almost certainly, they were frightened by the strangeness of his condition. We had noticed the same thing when some of the other polio victims appeared in camp for the first time. When Pepe, for instance, shuffled up the slope to the feeding area, squatting on his haunches with his useless arm trailing behind him, the group of chimps already in camp stared for a moment and then, with wide grins of fear, rushed for reassurance to embrace and pat each other while staring at the unfortunate cripple. Pepe, who obviously had no idea that he himself was the object of their fear, showed an even wider grin of fright as he repeatedly turned to look over his shoulder along the path behind him—trying to find out, presumably, what it was that was making his companions so frightened. Eventually the others calmed down; but, though they continued to stare at him from time to time, none of them went near him, and eventually he shuffled off, once more on his own. Gradually the other chimps**

became accustomed to Pepe, and soon the muscles in his legs were strong enough to enable him to walk about upright, as had Faben from the start.

McGregor's condition was patently far worse. Not only was he forced to move about in an abnormal manner, but there was the smell of urine and the bleeding rump and the swarm of flies buzzing around him. The first morning of his return to camp, as he sat in the long grass below the feeding area, the adult males, one after the other, approached with their hair on end, and after staring began to display around him. Goliath actually attacked the stricken old male, who, powerless to flee or defend himself in any way, could only cower down, his face split by a hideous grin of terror, while Goliath pounded on his back. When another adult male bore down on McGregor, hair bristling, huge branch flailing the ground, Hugo and I went to stand in front of the cripple. To our relief, the displaying male turned aside.

After two or three days the others got used to McGregor's strange appearance and grotesque movements, but they kept well away from him. There was one afternoon that without doubt was from my point of view the most painful of the whole ten days. A group of eight chimps had gathered and were grooming each other in a tree about sixty yards from where McGregor lay in his nest. The sick male stared toward them, occasionally giving slight grunts. Mutual grooming normally takes up a good deal of a chimpanzee's time, and the old male had been drastically starved of this important social contact since his illness.

Finally, he dragged himself from his nest, lowered himself to the ground, and in short stages began the long journey to join the others. When at last he reached the tree he rested briefly in the shade; then, making the final effort, he pulled himself up until he was close to two of the grooming males. With a loud grunt of pleasure he reached a hand toward them in greeting—but even before he made contact they both had swung quickly away and without a backward glance started grooming on the far side of the tree. For a full two minutes old Gregor sat motionless, staring after them.

> **And then he laboriously lowered himself to the ground. As I watched him sitting there alone, my vision blurred, and when I looked up at the groomers in the tree I came nearer to hating a chimpanzee than I have ever been before or since. (Pp. 221-2)**
>
> **[Van Lawick-Goodall, J. *In the shadow of man.* Boston: Houghton-Mufflin, 1971.]**

An alternative way to approach the question of primitive or unlearned reactions is to search for crosscultural commonalities of emotional response to deviant or anomalous conditions. Such response commonalities might be evidence for innate biological arousal, but the preferred interpretation of most anthropologists is to stress cultural imperatives, when and if such common reaction patterns are observed. In her treatment of "purity and danger," for example, Douglas (1966) emphasizes the role of order and good form in establishing culturally valid cognitive meaning: "Any given system of classification must give rise to anomalies, and any given culture must confront events which seem to defy its assumptions. It cannot ignore the anomalies which its scheme produces, except at the risk of forfeiting confidence. This is why, I suggest, we find in any culture worthy of the name various provisions for dealing with ambiguous or anomalous events" (p. 39). Douglas takes an example relevant to stigma from Evans-Pritchard's study (1956) of the Nuer tribe. When physically deformed infants are born to the Nuer, they are instantly treated as baby hippopotami accidentally born to humans, and the adults gently lay them in the river where they belong. This convenient reclassification appears to be one way of avoiding the severe emotional implications of anomaly.

In general, Douglas argues, negative emotional reactions are inherent in the symbolic social dangers posed by deviant persons. "A polluting person is always in the wrong. He has developed some wrong condition or simply crossed some line which should not have been crossed. This displacement unleashes danger for someone" (p. 113). Whereas cultural imperatives can be thus identified as the bases of some types of negative emotional response to anomaly, the most impressive feature of such responses is their variability and plasticity. Although it is generally the case that all cultures develop more or less elaborate ritual responses to death and disfigurement, crime, and illness, it is also obvious that these rituals take almost infinitely diverse forms.

If there is some natural, unlearned tendency to respond affectively to deviant appearance or behavior, it is by no means clear that the response can always be labeled as simply aversion or revulsion, or even as predominantly negative. In his "Totem and Taboo" (1913), Freud makes a strong case for human ambivalence toward tabooed objects and topics. Traditionally, the totem is both sacred and dangerous. Tabooed objects are fascinating and appealing, but they represent danger and arouse disgust at the same time. This ambivalence is perhaps still reflected in contemporary society in our morbid fascination with scatology, sexual deviance, and death. The dirty joke is a wide and cluttered canvas of man's ambivalence toward tabooed subjects. The same may be true of many forms of ethnic jokes that may combine a mixture of knowing affection with an awareness of specific deviant features.

We are also tempted to emphasize the ambivalence theme as underlying the success of graphic portrayals of violence in movies. Patrons seem to be simultaneously horrified and fascinated by the realistic portrayal of bullets entering flesh and axes decapitating heads.

Of more direct relevance to the specific question of stigma is an interesting set of experimental findings by Langer et al. (1976) which is consistent with the notion of anomalous or novel stimuli generating ambivalence. Those investigators showed in one study that their subjects, given an opportunity to gaze unobtrusively at a target person who was either normal, pregnant, or wearing a leg brace, gazed for a longer time at the disabled person. In a second experiment, subjects given a prior opportunity to gaze unobtrusively at a prospective conversational partner in a leg brace, subsequently sat closer to the partner than those subjects who were not given the same opportunity of prior, unobtrusive gazing. The difference between the prior-gaze and the no-gaze conditions was not observed when the target person was normal. The conclusion that one may draw from these experiments is that normal people are not simply repelled by physical deviance. In a way, they are fascinated enough to gaze at the deviant person, if it can be done unobtrusively. Without such an opportunity to gaze, however, the normal person, when instructed to engage in a free discussion, feels awkward and uncomfortable in the presence of the disabled and tends to sit at a greater distance from such a person than from normal subjects. These results do not compel an ambivalence hypothesis, but they are consistent with the idea that we are both intrigued by physical deviance and uncomfortable in its presence.

To summarize, it seems reasonable to propose that there are instances of primitive emotional arousal to certain extremes of physical or behavioral deviance. We know amazingly little about the response of animals and primitive peoples to various kinds of anomalous human conditions. The very notion of "unmediated affect" seems to be almost a contradiction in terms. No matter how widespread and uniform the emotional response to particular deviant marks, the response is nevertheless triggered by a perceptual process. Scholars of perception have learned that factors of meaning and motivational significance can enter the perceptual process at or near the earliest stages of its development. In any event, the affect that seems on occasion to be immediately aroused by exposure to the anomalous is very quickly shaped by cognitive factors deriving from cultural and/or individual experience. Furthermore, it is not at all clear that the allegedly "unmediated" emotional reaction is altogether negative. There seems to be evidence of fascination mixed with aversion in many responses to "matter out of place" (Douglas, 1966). Since the role of affect is so important to the study of the stigmatizing process, we turn to a brief analysis of the nature of emotional experience in general.

THE NATURE OF EMOTIONAL EXPERIENCE

Psychologists have speculated, researched, and written about emotion for many decades, but emotional experience is such a complex and elusive phenomenon that it still is not well understood. Since the early 1960s, the main theoretical controversy has centered around the role of cognitive factors in emotional experience. There are two issues involved, both of which are clearly relevant for understanding the role of affect in the stigmatizing process. The first issue is the extent to which emotional reactions are automatic responses to certain stimulus events—an issue that we have already touched upon in the preceding section. The second issue is the extent to which emotional reactions map, reflect, and are dictated by particular patterns of physiological arousal. In other words, are anger and ecstasy defined by different autonomic events, or is there a common arousal pattern that is experienced differently as a function of context-elicited cognitive factors?

Schachter (1964; Schacter and Singer 1962) has taken the most extreme view on the second issue, arguing that individuals will label physiological arousal states in terms of the cognitions available to them: "precisely the same state of physiological arousal could be called 'joy' or 'fury' or any of the great diversity of emotional labels, depending on the cognitive aspects of the situation" (1964, p. 53). Tomkins (1981) is the most vigorous critic of that position. He champions a theory of innate activators of affect. The primary affective responses of interest, enjoyment, surprise, fear, anger, distress, shame, contempt, and disgust are mediated by specific sensory receptors in the skin of the face. But these responses can be easily shaped by affect-related information. "Affect mechanisms" are independent of cognition, but have "evolved to play a number of parts in continually changing assemblies of mechanism" (p. 320). The affect mechanism amplifies perceptions and cognitions, drawing our attention to important events. Most labeling theorists would quite willingly associate themselves with Tomkins' comment that "without affect amplification nothing else matters, and with its amplification anything can matter" (p. 322). One could reinterpret that statement in the stigma area by describing the labeling process as one that often involves affective amplification of rather arbitrary cognitive distinctions. In any event, Tomkins basically summarizes his view of the causal relationship of affect and cognition by stating that "affect can determine cognition at one time, be determined by cognition at another time, and be independent under other circumstances" (p. 324).

Zajonc (1980) has vigorously pushed the independence possibility, arguing that affect and cognition are under the control of separate and partially independent systems that can influence each other in a variety of ways. He argues that evolution has bequeathed an affective system that is precognitive, rapid, free from effective control, and closely linked to preferences and action decisions. Basically, he portrays cognitive elaborations as justifications or rationalizations of affective responses. Since "not all affective experiences are accompanied by verbal or other cognitive representations, and . . . when they are, such representations are imprecise and ambiguous" (p. 160), it becomes easier to understand how affect can be involved in unmediated responses to physical and behavioral anomalies, even though the precise specification of this affect is elusive.

Leventhal (1980) presents a very scholarly and comprehensive treatment of emotion that essentially incorporates all theoretical positions in a complex framework of interactive independent and dependent variables. Compatibly with Tomkins (1981), Zajonc (1980), and Clark and Isen's (1982) positions, he leaves room for emotions themselves, based on "innate motor scripts" and, in addition, refers to emotional experiences that are intertwined and infused with cognitive elaborations. Thus, Schachter's (1964) extreme attributional version of emotional experience is acknowledged in the recognition by other theorists that emotions tend to seek out and attach themselves to "explanations"; they do not exist for long in an attributional vacuum, even though they may be automatically activated through reaction patterns that are innately scripted in some way. The disagreement with Schachter, and it is rather widespread, is with his extreme assertion that the physiological arousal component is itself uninformative with regard to the nature of the emotion being experienced by the organism.

The Question of Control

When we focus on the stigmatizing process as one that involves affective reactions, it is especially important to consider the various attributional fates of affective arousal. Although we have cautioned the reader that the immediate affective response to deviance is not always negative, we may assume that the most primitive, unmediated feeling state is some degree of discomfort that would "normally" give rise to avoidance or rejection responses. A uniquely fascinating feature of deviance in contemporary society, however, is that avoidance and rejection responses—at least the unalloyed forms of such responses— are typically proscribed by societal norms. Thus, the important questions about affect posed by a study of stigma relate more to the matter of emotional control than to whether and how much emotion is unmediated by cognition. Regardless of the degree of cognitive mediation involved in producing the emotion, the important question is how do markers cope with the discomfort experienced during confrontations with physical and behavioral anomalies in a context where total and abrupt social avoidance is difficult or even not permissible?

Most of us tend to think of emotions as more or less automatically induced by what is going on around us. We "fall" in love, we grieve our lost loved ones, we "get anxious" before an oral exam, we laugh "uncontrollably" at a well-told joke. Emotional experience is a vital ingredient of everyday life, but since the birth of psychoanalysis, it has been assumed that an important criterion of personal adjustment is how we "handle" or control our emotions. While emotions happen to us, to some degree we can shape them or reduce their ramifications and persistence. Psychoanalytically oriented therapies generally operate on the assumption that control is enhanced through insight and emotions are dissipated through appropriate catharsis. Contemporary cognitive-behavior therapies (cf. Kendall and Norton-Ford 1982) generally imply that emotions can be controlled through changes in the interpretation of situations. As Ellis (1962) argues, situations do not cause emotions. Beliefs about situations cause emotions. His rational-emotive therapy is, therefore, addressed to the elimination of irrational beliefs or interpretations of situations.

Presumably, then, the affect of discomfort can be controlled through the recognition that revulsion, hostility, or fear are irrational responses to deviant marks and must be replaced by sympathy and understanding. But if emotions "happen to us;" if, as Zajonc (1980) says, affective reactions "occur whether one wants them to or not" (p. 156), how can aversion and hostility be transmuted into sympathy and affection?

There is increasing evidence that affective reactions are not as inescapable as Zajonc has portrayed them, and that indeed, mediating belief systems play an enormously important role in determining whether one responds to a spastic stranger with horror or compassion. The problem is that changing these emotion-defining beliefs involves altering affective systems (mechanisms, scripts) that are presumably quite unresponsive to cognitive pedagogy. Changing the keys that unlock various emotions is more difficult, apparently, than mere cognitive reeducation. That is why behavior therapists have adopted a variety of reconditioning techniques that often take many repetitive sessions before (and if) they have any effect.

A totally different literature is emerging in sociology to suggest the ubiquitousness of emotion management in everyday life. Hochschild (1979) contends that we often find ourselves experiencing emotions that are inappropriate in the situation. In every society there are "feeling rules," guidelines that specify how we want to try to feel. Our awareness of these feeling rules may be latent (only discovered through extensive probing), but we still may feel the "pinch" of a discrepancy when, in a particular setting, we do not experience the emotion we think we should experience, or we experience an emotion that is out of place. This feeling of discrepancy engenders a tense state of anticipated social disapproval that is reduced by "emotion work"; we try in various ways to produce the appropriate emotional feeling in ourselves.

Thoits (1983) has elaborated Hochschild's notions on how one may accomplish this emotion work. These strategies are basically consistent with the accounts of Schachter (1964) and Bem (1972) and partake of the flavor of dissonance theory (Festinger 1957) in suggesting cognitive maneuevers that reduce the unpleasant tension associated with a discrepancy between cognitions (in this case, a self-cognition and a cognition concerning a social norm). Emotional work may involve cognitive search techniques such as "label search" (finding a label for one's emotions that *is* appropriate to the situation), "situational cue search" (finding cues in the situation that justify the emotion experienced), and "feeling search" (scanning one's internal state to identify those feeling components that *are* appropriate). Emotion work may also involve various feeling-change techniques. The person may engage in "direct action on feelings" through drugs, deep breathing, relaxation, and so on. He may engage in "expression work," trading on the hope that surface acting will be transformed into deep acting, and that genuine feelings will develop that are consistent with the expressed gestures. Finally, there are situation-change techniques, whereby the individual can try to alter or eliminate the cues that give rise to the inappropriate affect.

It seems likely that many of these techniques are, or could be, used to convert the destructive emotions that can be aroused by the perception of deviance into appropriate, sympathetic affect. People are not, in other words, totally at the mercy of some automatic discomfort. They have numerous resources for altering their emotional experience in the short run and for totally changing the arousal cues in the long run. In that context, of course, it is absolutely crucial what the "feeling rules" are. If there is an unequivocal feeling rule that one should feel warmth and sympathy in the presence of paraplegic veterans, the state of emotion work will be much different than if the rule is equivocal or the person is uncertain about the norm. Therefore, in this analysis, the nature and degree of emotion involved in the marking process is highly dependent on the social forces that shape feeling rules. Those forces, as we have noted throughout, include parents, teachers, friends, and the media.

The issue of emotional control is also crucial if we consider emotions that are generated by the ongoing interaction within a marked relationship. Thus far, this chapter's emphasis has been on fairly chronic emotional states aroused more by the perception (or even the idea) of particular anomalies than by the reactions of the relationship partners. We have not explicitly considered the shifting emotions that may accompany interactions between markers and markables. We assume that while some such interactions are smooth, others are strained and discomfiting. In the latter case, special problems arise because emotional rules dictate tolerance and forbearance. The marker who feels frustrated, irritated, or awkward may often fear that candor in identifying his feelings will be misinterpreted as stigma. The marked person may also fear that open expressions of anger will be seen as violating the role prescriptions for deviants, who should, after all, be cognizant of their dependent "place" and refrain from rocking the interaction boat. The consequent failure to communicate on either or both sides may generate additional interactive strain and renewed secondary collisions with the emotion rules that are supposed to govern marked relationships.

It is worth noting that feeling rules may conflict with other rules. In particular, if one believes strongly in the just world hypothesis (Lerner 1970), such a belief may collide with and undermine a particular feeling rule that one should feel warmly toward those who have been maimed by accidents and misfortunes. There are many complexities involved in trying to use the emotion work concept, but it seems to have considerable promise as a framework for considering emotional arousal and adaptation in the stigmatizing process.

AMBIVALENCE AND ITS CONSEQUENCES

We have already hinted that physical and behavioral anomalies often lead to conflicting or ambivalent emotional reactions. To the extent that mixed feelings are especially common in marked relationships, analysis of such relationships may illuminate general processes of emotional conflict management and resolution. Our investigation of this issue breaks into two rather distinct questions: (1) What is the evidence for ambivalence, and what are its most common components in the emotional patterns of the marker? (2) If indeed the marker is especially prone to mixed feelings, what are the consequences of this for his behavior toward the mark, and for the evolution of the marked relationship?

Conflicted Emotions: The Nature of the Ambivalence

A number of social scientists have shared the intuition that normal people are often ambivalent in their feelings about markable others. This has been especially noted in attitudes toward the mentally ill, but the insight can be applied to marked relationships involving the physically disabled, ethnic minorities, and repentent criminals. Gergen and Jones (1963) explicitly commented on the prevalence of ambivalent attitudes toward the mentally ill. On the one hand, aversion is triggered by the belief that mentally ill people are often "obstructive, demanding, sullen, self-centered, and/or irrational." At the same time, however, most mentally ill persons are seen as tragic figures victimized by a cruel environment or inadequate genetic resources. For this reason, they arouse some degree of nurturance, perhaps especially to the extent that the person is truly sick, incapacitated, or irrational. "While we may be disturbed by, and avoidant toward the schizophrenic, at the same time we are sympathetically involved in his tragedy and emotionally committed to his rehabilitation" (p. 95).

In an illuminating and provocative monograph, Katz (1981) has developed the relationship between stigma and ambivalence in greater detail. The concept of ambivalence has a long history of use in the language of motivational description, and the general idea that a person can have both positive and negative feelings toward the same other has been accepted for many centuries. The concept was given great prominence in psychoanalytic writings (cf. Bleuler 1910) and plays a central role in Freud's (1923) treatment of the Oedipus complex, the outcome of which is always ambivalence toward both parents. From the vast psychoanalytic literature, we have inherited the general notion that certain feelings are unacceptable and must be denied or repressed, often with a substitution of the opposite feeling, as in "reaction formation." Out of this collision of unacceptable emotion and inhibition comes a variety of psychological phenomena, such as isolation of feelings, projection, and displacement. A version of this general reasoning was offered by Adorno et al. (1950) to account for the development of the prejudiced or authoritarian personality. Those authors contend that the negative, unacceptable components of ambivalence toward parents are covered over by idealization of them and displaced onto ethnic minorities and other out-groups.

Whereas the imagery of psychoanalysis suggests that people must find ways to put the lid on or divert unacceptable feelings, the kind of behaviorally oriented conflict theory elaborated by Miller (1944) takes a slightly different tack. Miller attempted to extrapolate from an experimental paradigm in which rats were taught in separate sessions to approach and then to avoid the same area of a maze alley. Such a learning history, when followed by the absence of either positive or negative reinforcement, produces a conflict in which the animal approaches part of the way to the locus of conflict in the maze area and then stops. This behavior may be explained by assuming that avoidance tendencies become stronger, relative to approach tendencies, the closer the actor is to the object that arouses ambivalence. Indeed, there is independent evidence that this is the case (cf. Miller 1944).

Miller and others (e.g., Whiting and Child 1953) have attempted to extend the theory by several metaphoric translations. Thus, for certain theoretical purposes, spatial distance serves the same functional role as temporal distance. Similarly, physical approach has many of the same theoretical properties as instigated aggression, and distance then translates as similarity to the original frustrator or "instigator." Whereas approach (now, instigation to aggression) may be inhibited in the presence of the eliciting person, since avoidance tendencies drop off more sharply than approach tendencies, it should follow that aggression will often be displaced from the eliciting person to somebody who is moderately but not extremely similar in the more relevant characteristic. Such theoretical reasoning is potentially relevant to considerations of prejudice and gives a rationale to those portions of "scapegoat theory" that predict hostility toward out-group members when the individual is actually frustrated by (instigated by) in-group members.

One implication of approach-avoidance theory for marked relationships involving ambivalent feelings is that the marker's sympathetic and nurturant feelings may cause initial approach behavior, but the closer the individual comes to interaction, or the longer the interaction lasts, the more aversive the situation becomes. Following this line of reasoning, we can account for the ambivalent person who contributes generously to the handicapped as a substitute for satisfying his nurturant feelings through more problematic face-to-face interactions.

Miller's efforts to construct a behavioral theory of conflict are an attempt, in fact, to express psychoanalytic reasoning in quantitative, parametric terms. Both approaches assume that the inhibition of undesirable responses, or unacceptable emotions, has repercussions elsewhere in the personality, and that the inhibited tendencies are reflected either in displaced (substitute) reactions, or toward displaced targets, or both. Ambivalences are thus resolved by a subterranean change in the allocation of conflicting emotions or response tendencies.

Katz (1981) specifically adapts the notion of ambivalence to intergroup relations: "I use the term *ambivalence* to denote a psychological condition in which a person has both positive (i.e., friendly, sympathetic, accepting) and negative (i.e., hostile, denigrative, rejecting) dispositions towards some group. The stronger the positive and negative dispositions and the more nearly equal their respective strengths, the greater the amount of ambivalence" (p. 23). Katz also endorses the commonsense proposition that the positive components contributing to ambivalence are more likely to be openly expressed and acknowledged than the negative components, because they are more likely to be rewarded by social approval.

The empirical evidence supporting the notion of ambivalent affect toward markable others is actually quite sparse. The assumption gains its power largely through its compelling appeal to our intuitions. At least in the case of those markable conditions for which the marked person cannot easily be held responsible, any negative affect that is generated in the contact situation must inevitably come in conflict with our externalized norms of fairness and, perhaps, even more basic feelings of sympathy. Furthermore, ongoing interactions may generate emotions that are more difficult to express in marked than in normal relationships, giving rise to new emotions like guilt and anger at being trapped.

The most convincing evidence that people do have conflicted feelings toward markable others comes from studies in which various response measures reveal a mixture of positive and negative feelings. Typically, the positive feelings are more openly expressed, whereas the negative feelings are revealed through more subtle measures of behavior that are less clearly under the voluntary or conscious control of the potential marker. In one such study, Kleck, Ono, and Hastorf (1966) arranged interviews between naive subjects and a confederate who was either in a wheelchair or not. After the interview, subjects expressed greater liking for the apparently disabled interviewer than for the normal interviewer. In a similar subsequent experiment, however, subjects interacting with an apparent amputee, as compared to those interacting with a "normal" confederate, showed many signs of behavioral discomfort: they terminated the interview sooner; they expressed opinions that were less representative of their actual beliefs; and they showed greater variability of behavior. In an additional study, Kleck (1968) found that when compared to subjects interacting with normal confederates, those interacting with an amputee demonstrated greater motor inhibition (shifted less in their seats) and more opinion distortions, but they also rated the confederate more positively on a variety of trait adjectives.

Farina and his colleague (Farina, Holland, and Ring 1966; Farina, Thaw, Felner, and Hust 1976) have conducted several studies in which normal college students are given the task of teaching another subject a complex motor performance. If the other subject makes a mistake, the naive subject may shock him at different intensity levels and for a duration of his choice. Some subjects learn that their partner was or had been a mental patient, while others are given neutral background information. The interesting finding in the present context is that the subjects tended to shock their learners for a longer duration when they were mental patients (although, in fact, no shocks were actually delivered). There was, however, no difference in shock-intensity levels. Farina suggested that the difference may reflect the greater conscious control that subjects have over the setting of shock intensity as compared to duration. Indeed, subjects were much more accurate in estimating the intensity of the shocks that they administered than in estimating their duration.

It should be noted that this finding does not hold for female subjects confronting female targets designated as mental patients. They, in fact, shocked the mental patient learner for shorter durations than a "normal" confederate. Furthermore, in another study (Farina et al. 1976), subjects who believed the learner was mentally retarded used both less intense and shorter shocks than those administering shocks either to a normal or mentally ill confederate. Thus, though the Farina studies provide some support for the ambivalence notion by showing different responses as a function of the degree of conscious control, they also suggest strongly that affect-related responses, such as the administration of pain, vary widely as a function of the particular stigma involved, as well as the particular characteristics of the stigmatized person.

It may ultimately be important to distinguish between "true" ambivalence, where an individual has both genuinely negative and positive feelings in collision or in alternation, and the conscious concealment or distortion of basically univalent negative feelings. Both the Kleck and Farina studies may be conceivably interpreted as reflecting the subjects' self-presentational concerns. Thus, the subjects, wishing to appear tolerant and accepting in the experimenter's eyes, respond favorably to the markable person, but their underlying feelings are captured by measures that are not under their conscious control.

To complicate matters further, there may be a conscious suppression of primarily negative feelings in some cases and true ambivalence in others. Carver, Glass, and Katz (1978) attempted to explore the subjects' evaluations of an interviewee after reading a written transcript of an interview. The interviewee was always depicted as a lower-class male, rather friendless, and without apparent interests or future plans. He was presented either as normal, physically disabled, or black. Half the subjects evaluated the interviewee by a procedure that has been christened the "bogus pipeline" by Jones and Sigall (1971). This procedure involves tricking subjects into believing that there is a new device that accurately measures their true feelings, hooking them up to the device, and then asking them to estimate the device's "reading" without being able to see the readout meter. The idea behind the bogus pipeline is that subjects will give more candid, more thoughtful responses when estimating their "true" emotional state than when simply rating that state without being attached to a telltale device. Alternatively, the subjects may attempt to report their affective state in a manner they assume to be less affected by "reasons" or other cognitive factors; that is, they may make a special effort to read their own primary affective states without wondering how they *should* feel and without being concerned with justifying their acknowledged feelings.

Carver et al. found in their study that the physically disabled person created a more favorable impression than the normal person, regardless of whether the measure used was a verbal rating or a bogus pipeline estimate. Responses to the black interviewee, however, depended markably on whether the bogus pipeline measure was used. Bogus pipeline subjects rated the black interviewee lower than the normal white interviewee, whereas the impression of those in the rating condition were higher than the impression of the white interviewee and equal to those of the disabled person. Thus, the data suggest that subjects were to some extent aware of their negative feelings toward blacks and were able to cover up these feelings, except when they assumed that negative feelings would be revealed anyway by the bogus pipeline device.

Students of stigma have barely scratched the surface in identifying the emotional patterns aroused by contact with various kinds of markable or deviant others. Despite the great difficulty in getting a true reading on such feelings, it is possible to explore the behavioral consequences of an *assumed* ambivalence and to generate behavioral predictions based on a theory of how ambivalence should affect social behavior.

The Fate of Ambivalent Feelings

Gergen and Jones (1963), as noted, were early proponents of the suggestion that the feelings aroused by mentally ill persons are often ambivalent. They proposed, furthermore, that when normal persons are exposed to consequential behavior from the mentally ill person, the ambivalence can be resolved through a polarized or amplified reaction that is in line with the implications for the marker conveyed by the new information. Thus, if the consequences of the behavior are positive for the normal marker, he will respond with a highly favorable impression of the marked person. If the consequences are negative, he will respond with derogation and aversion. The magnitude of these responses will be greater than comparable responses to a normal person behaving in precisely the same way. In making this prediction, Gergen and Jones note that "ambivalence is often resolved by the suppression or repression of one affective component and enhancement of the other" (p. 96). Aside from a reference to the psychoanalytic formulations of Oedipal conflict resolution, and the Freudian contention that the stronger the conflict the more decisive the resolution, the underlying mechanisms for this "enhancement" are not specified.

In addition to those rather vague notions from psychoanalysis, some versions of conflict theory also incorporate the idea that conflict itself is motivating, and that this conflict-generated drive ultimately energizes the particular form taken by the conflict resolution. Such an assumption of "conflict-drive" has been used by Whiting and Child (1953) and was earlier proposed by Brown and Farber (1951) in their theory of conflict and emotion.

A strong implication of Festinger's theory of cognitive dissonance (1957) is that once conflict resolution begins, cognitive work should ensure that the chosen option gains in appeal, while the foregone option becomes less and less attractive. This provides yet another explanation for the enhancement of responses in the resolution of ambivalent or conflicted feelings. Thus, if ambivalence is also dissonant, additional information can "tip the scale" and begin a resolution process that enhances the value of all other information that supports the particular direction of the resolution.

Katz's (1981) theory of response amplification is somewhat different than any of these notions. It rests on certain considerations of how people like to conceive of themselves and how they respond to events that threaten their self-esteem. Ambivalence creates "a high vulnerability to emotional tension in situations of contact with the attitudinal object or cues associated with the attitudinal object" (p. 25). Such contact situations generally provide information that supports one side of the ambivalent conflict while contradicting the other. (It is important that the information can come both from the ambivalent actor and his actions, as well as directly from or about the target person.) According to Katz, this information makes the conflict more salient and more intolerable, resulting in "heightened efforts at threat reduction." However, the theory does not merely assume that the ambivalence will be resolved in the direction of the new information conveyed by the contact. The component attitude that is "discredited" by the information may be denied or it may be defended. Either of these alternatives can produce amplified responses; that is, "behavior toward the stigmatized person that [is] more extreme than behavior toward a non-stigmatized or otherwise similar person in the same type of situation" (p. 25). It is not clear where the impetus for amplification comes from, but presumably it stems from the intolerability of the now-salient conflict. Phenomenally, the ambivalent marker may either feel a threat to his concept of himself as humane and unprejudiced (if the information is negative), or a threat to his concept of himself as a judicious, discriminating, fair-minded person (if the information is positive). An interesting feature of Katz's theory is the recognition that we can have emotional reactions to our primary feelings, reactions shaped by various aspects of our self-concept.

Unfortunately, a theory that predicts the increased magnitude of a response without being able to predict the nature and direction of the response, is not very useful for making relevant predictions. Katz does provide some clues. The ambiguity of incoming information is important. If the threatening information is fairly ambiguous, it can be discounted more easily and "the discredited component" reasserted. Also important are the response opportunities most readily available. Katz offers the intriguing suggestion that the direction of ambivalent reduction may depend more on the response context than on the merits or direction of the incoming information. Thus, if person *A* is ambivalent toward stigmatized *B*, and *B* does him a very generous favor, the normal presumption would be that the ambivalence would be resolved in a positive direction, perhaps in a highly amplified form of great admiration or affection for *B*. However, if the setting is one in which degrees of punishment are available but degrees of reward are not, the amplified response may actually be a negative one. It is possible, within the framework of Katz's theory, for positive information to lead to rejection or avoidance of the stigmatized person. It is similarly possible for negative information to lead to increased sympathy and nurturance. One imagines that such reversals would be rare, but they are certainly possible implications of Katz's theory.

The evidence for response amplification is strong enough to suggest that there is indeed something to the idea, but it also suggests that an adequate theory of ambivalence resolution will have to be a very complicated one. Gergen and Jones (1963) were able to show response amplification in the impressions formed of psychiatric patients by subjects allegedly interacting with them in a laboratory experiment. The direction of this amplified response was a function of whether the patients' behavior delivered positive or negative consequences to the judging subjects.

Katz and his colleagues studied the response to blacks and to the physically handicapped in a series of cleverly contrived experiments. These experiments are more fully described in his monograph, and are only briefly outlined here:

1. Subjects were induced to give a confederate a shock or a noxious blast of noise when he made an error in an ESP task. The shock (noise) level was either very low or quite high. The confederate was either a normal white male, a normal black male, or a white male in a wheelchair. In the strong shock (noise) conditions (and only there), the black and the disabled confederate were evaluated more negatively at the end of the experiment. (As in all experiments of this type, no noise or shocks were actually delivered.)
2. In two experiments in which subjects were induced to harm a confederate (unintentionally), they were subsequently much more helpful to a black or disabled victim than to a white victim. There were no differences in the absence of a prior harm-induction.
3. Subjects initially induced to help a handicapped person were more likely to help him on a subsequent task than they were to help a normal person they had previously helped. There was no such tendency toward greater help for the disabled in the absence of prior helping.
4. Black help-seekers were given more help than whites of comparable social status.
5. But, wheelchair-bound confederates were helped less and inspired greater anger when they came across as friendly and competent than when

they came across as abrupt and unfriendly. The reverse was true when the confederate was in no obvious way disabled.

6. Measures were taken of the length of time subjects needed to decide whether or not various positive or negative traits were considered characteristic of, first, handicapped people, then obese people, then tall people. There were larger latencies to make such rating decisions about handicapped people, suggesting greater ambivalence in their case. The same subjects were subsequently asked to give their impression of a handicapped or nonhandicapped person, when the particular person was presented either in a positive or negative way. Those with the highest latency scores in rating the handicapped category (ambivalence?) subsequently showed the most polarized ratings of the handicapped person in the direction of the additional information about him—whether positive or negative. There was no relationship between latency and subsequent polarization when the target person was not handicapped.

The latter finding was, perhaps, the most direct coupling of ambivalence and response polarization in the line of research directed by Katz. All of the Katz studies, including the last one, are certainly open to alternative interpretations. There are, however, several important lessons learned from this body of research on ambivalence and response amplification. First, Katz provides considerable evidence that the reaction of middle-class Americans to markable others (at least to blacks and the physically handicapped) are by no means uniformly negative. Such evidence fits a larger pattern of data apparent in work on polarized responses to out-group members. Linville and Jones (1980) found, for example, that white subjects are more favorable toward positively presented black target persons and less favorable toward negatively presented blacks than toward identically described white target persons. In general, there is substantial evidence that negative stereotypes toward a group or category of persons do not necessarily dictate negative reactions to individual members of the category. Much depends on the affective implications of individuating information about the person being judged. Katz's work, as well as that of Linville and Jones, strongly suggests that something about the category stereotype affects the intensity of the response, whereas the concrete individuating information about the person is a more important determinant of its direction.

In addition, Katz's work makes clear that other contextual factors may determine response direction. Thus, in order to predict behavior in a marked relationship, we need to know something about the setting: What response opportunities are most readily available, and what is the relationship between these opportunities and the prevailing affect?

The empirical contributions of Katz and his colleagues are extremely valuable in showing the complex interrelations between affect, context, and response. However, his attempt to tie response amplifications to self-concept threats seems too narrow and exclusionary to cover even the range of data produced by his own experiments. Other bases of amplification must also be considered, some of which have nothing to do with ambivalence or emotional conflict. Linville and Jones (1980), for example, derive polarization toward an out-group member from purely cognitive considerations. They (and Linville 1982) were able to show that (1) people have simpler cognitive structures about members of an out-group than members of an in-group, and (2) simpler structures lead to greater polarization of affective reactions than do complex structures.

Furthermore, the self-concept threat formulation has difficulty in handling anything but an immediate reaction elicited by an experimenter to the stigmatized person. Katz does not consider the fact that this initial reaction (whether positive or negative) should itself be threatening to the self-concept, especially since it is supposed to be excessive or "amplified." The theory thus leaves the actor in a state of wild vacillation between threats to his integrity as a tolerant person and threats to his self-concept as discerning. Perhaps some combination of self-concept threat and dissonance theory could provide a way to break out of this impasse, but at the present it remains a serious difficulty in applying Katz's theory to marked relations in the real world.

Obviously, we have much to learn about the antecedents of response amplification, and it is important not to close off alternative theoretical possibilities prematurely. On the other hand, there are virtues in formulating propositions in clear, straightforward terms, and it seems fair to say that Katz's formulation captures at least part of the truth and should stimulate additional research, perhaps extending his findings to a greater range of stigmatized conditions.

AFFECTIVE EXPERIENCES OF THE MARKED PERSON

When an individual is marked or labeled as deviant by the members of his social group, he is bound to respond emotionally to his status as a discredited outcast. Much of this book assumes that these emotions will be largely negative, unpleasant, and socially destructive. The stigmatized person will presumably confront the prospect of social interaction with the anticipation of rejection. Unquestionably, this anticipation, along with associated feelings of resentment, depression, and possibly self-hatred, makes it difficult for marked relationships to develop in a healthy way, regardless of the goodwill or the forbearance of the marker. It is important to distinguish, however, between the affect associated with the marked person's recognition of social discredit and the affect associated with the physical or behavioral anomaly giving rise to the marking process in the first place. We have repeatedly noted in the preceding chapters that disabled persons reflecting on their disability are often not as emotionally depressed as normals assume them to be.

Indeed, it may be that the normal marker's assumptions of depression and despair in the disabled target person are motivated by the need to believe that one's own intact body is an essential feature of one's well-being. Thus, it may comfort the normal person to believe that the disabled person is depressed or suffering an appropriate sense of deep loss. If a blind or paraplegic person is happy, our own capacities for sight and mobility are thereby belittled. In the preceding section, a rather curious finding was presented without comment—wheelchair-bound confederates inspired greater anger when they were friendly than when they were abrupt. Katz (1981) suggests that this may have occurred because friendliness is unwanted, out-of-role behavior for paraplegics. The importance of disabled persons paying "proper respect" to their handicap is at least implicit in much of the stigma literature (cf. Scott 1969).

Solid data on the emotional life of stigmatized people are not available, but there is some theorizing and a little evidence concerning the effects of life trauma that are relevant in the present context. Kelley et al. (1960) discuss emotional reactions to disabling physical handicaps, and Seligman (1975) and his colleagues have written about the consequences of "helplessness" or loss of capacity in ways that seem to have implications for understanding the response to traumatic life events. Each of these approaches will be drawn on to outline some of the more important emotional consequences of life-altering events, whether they occur in the form of accidents, disease, or the death of a loved one. Many of these events fall naturally into the category of marks that can give rise to the stigmatizing process.

A major theme stressed by Kelley et al. (1960) is that a person's response to trauma can best be understood against the background of his attitudes toward life prior to the trauma. In particular, those authors make use of Thibaut and Kelley's (1959) concept of comparison level (CL) to illuminate different trauma careers or patterns of response to a disabling event. One's CL is essentially a measure of what he normally expects from life. If events produce outcomes for a person that are at or near his CL, he will experience them as relatively neutral events, that is, without any particular emotional response. If a person's outcomes significantly exceed his CL, he will feel a sense of euphoria or elation; if they drop below his CL, the person will be dissatisfied and depressed. The major point of introducing such a concept is to stress the relativity of pleasure. An event that is neutral to one person may be either positive or negative to another, depending on his CL.

The CL, in turn, is a product of the person's past experiences with different kinds of outcomes and of the causal interpretations he makes of those outcomes. Thibaut and Kelley argue that the CL should be most responsive to outcomes that are seen by the individual as self-caused. Thus, a person who generally perceives himself as competent and in control of his outcomes will have a higher CL than a person who receives the same outcomes but feels less responsible for producing them. Kelley et al. (1960), in fact, attempt to contrast persons who feel generally in control of their own outcomes with those who place themselves at the disposal of the fates. It follows from the logic of CL that the latter type of person is generally more exhilarated than the former by good outcomes, since they are more likely to be significantly above (the generally lower) CL.

But what are the implications of CL analysis for one's emotional response to extremely negative events, such as paralyzing accidents, traumatic blindness, the death of a spouse, or the news that one has terminal cancer? Past experiences are not only weighted by causal attributions to make up the current CL; the CL is presumably very much dependent on social comparisons. How do one's social outcomes compare with the outcomes of others, especially those others who are in the vicinity or who are otherwise salient? Schachter (1959) shows in a series of experiments how responsive people are to the perceived reactions of others in trying to evaluate their own emotional experience in the same situation.

A quadriplegic who had been injured in Vietnam combat and who faces the prospect of lying on his back for the remainder of his life, expressed himself to a *San Francisco Chronicle* reporter as genuinely happy and content with his lot, apparently because the most salient comparison others were those in his platoon who had been killed. Similarly, we would expect the posttrauma CL to vary as a function of the victim's continuing exposure to those with similar misfortunes versus those with undiminished capacities.

In any event, it is possible to imagine a variety of factors influencing both the pretrauma CL and the posttrauma CL. Kelley et al. (1960) consider, for example, the person with a CL that was high before the trauma and continues to be high after the trauma. While his outcomes were formerly at or near his CL, they now fall considerably below it. Kelley et al. view this kind of negative effect as a prerequisite for "mourning" a loss of function and control. As the individual becomes aware of his reduced capacity and is less and less reminded of his life in the past, the CL should drop to accommodate the reduction in outcomes. Kelley et al. suggest that when this occurs, "the loss . . . will not be marked so distinctively by dissatisfaction . . . but by a loss of something like self-esteem or pride and a sharp decline in 'trying' to improve one's outcomes (a giving up with response to outcomes once attained)" (p. 177). The suggestion is that mourning the loss is a necessary prelude to the realistic acceptance of the specific limitations involved.

It is interesting to speculate about the impact of a disabling trauma on one who tends to perceive that his life is in the hands of fate and, therefore, who must come to terms with the trauma from the starting point of a low CL. Unquestionably, people differ in the extent to which they believe their lives are controlled by forces other than their own competence—by luck, God's will, inexorable social or economic forces, and so on. If one believes in the fates and has convinced himself by reviewing his past experiences that the fates are friendly, then the trauma may have a shattering significance by revealing that his assumption was incorrect or that the fates are no longer with him. The emotional response to such shattering disconfirmation may, we suspect, be extremely negative.

We also suspect, however, that people under such circumstances are rather adept at redefining their relationship to the fates in the most benign possible way. It is probably not too difficult to shift to a notion of fatalistic balance, a notion that is not dissimilar from the "gambler's fallacy" or similar cognitive maneuvers: "The fates are generally good to me. This bad thing has happened. This pays off the fates for all the previous good outcomes and should start a new run of more good outcomes."

Helplessness and Depression

Seligman (1975) is firmly associated with the position that learning that one is helpless to control one's outcomes often generates depressive affect. His formulation was designed to account for the state of affairs in which an individual (animal or human being) learns in one situation that he cannot solve a set of problems, and subsequently generalizes inappropriately to a new set of problems that he in fact could solve if he only tried. In a reformulation, Abramson, Seligman, and Teasdale (1978) acknowledge that one's causal explanation for being unable to solve the critical set of problems is all-important. The most devastating attributional pattern is one in which the failure is perceived as global, stable, and internally caused. Examples are attributional assumptions concerning intelligence or physical unattractiveness. As explanations for failure, those are global ones, in that they apply to a broad range of situations. They are stable because they are unlikely to change, and they are internal because they refer to a specific characteristic of the person that most others do not share. Based on this reformulation, Seligman and his associates contend that a person becomes depressed when "highly desired outcomes are believed improbable or highly aversive outcomes are believed probable, and the individual expects that no response in his repertoire will change their likelihood" (p. 60). The intensity and duration of the depression will depend on the globality (generality) of the deficit, its stability (irreversibility), and on its internality (distinctive association with the self).

SUICIDE OF A SEVEN-YEAR OLD

"Seven-year-old Boy Dies after Overdose of Pills for Bed-wetting," Associated Press, *Hartford Courant*, January 1, 1982.

Cliff Rich of Clover, South Carolina, had wet his pants during class at Kinard Elementary School . . . and apparently decided the one pill a day prescribed by a urologist for bed-wetting was not enough, his father, Clyde Rich, said.

"We didn't know it bothered him all that much," Rich said. "He never mentioned it, but it must have."

While his parents were away, Cliff climbed to a high shelf where the Tofranil pills were stored and opened the bottle, which had a child proof cap, Rich said. The boy's doctor said he took 40 of them. . . .

"He wasn't really wetting the bed all that much," Rich said. "At school was what embarrassed him. He wet his pants at school maybe once or twice week. He just wished he could stop."

This formulation would seem to have numerous implications for predicting a markable person's emotional response to trauma. This is true since many of the conditions that give rise to the stigmatizing process feature a loss in some important human capacity. Sometimes, as in a permanently disabled accident victim, the loss of capacity is obvious and the potential for recovery is highly restricted. Capacity losses associated with mental illness, disfigurement, minority group membership, or socially discrediting deviance (homosexuality or criminality) are more variable, perhaps, but can be equally engulfing and can produce equally intense and lasting depressive affect.

It is interesting to speculate about the applicability of Seligman's three attributional dimensions to different kinds of physical and social deficit. Thus, physical disabilities may be highly stable in the sense that they are irrevocable, but the deficit may not be particularly global or internal. Even a paraplegic still retains a wide range of physical and mental capacities, as do blind and deaf persons, Parkinson's disease victims, and those suffering from diabetes or epilepsy. For this reason, Seligman's formulation does not necessarily predict a lasting depressive reaction to a disabling trauma. The initial sense of loss may be overwhelming and the accompanying global generalization extensive. However, after the "mourning" period that Kelley et al. (1960) talk about, the coping individual typically corrects the overdrawn global attribution and gains a more precise conception and appreciation of his remaining capacities. Often, as Hunt's (1966) testimony suggests, coping is enhanced by the realization that the remaining capacities are much more precious than the ones that were lost. We speak, of course, of those who end up as successful copers and who avoid long-term depression. Presumably, there are physical trauma victims who, because of the extensiveness of the capacity deficit, or because of other features of historical or contemporary context in their lives, become gripped by hopelessness and despair and are unresponsive to therapeutic attempts.

Those who are "merely" discredited socially suffer deficits of outcome control that may be even more global and are often more internal, even though they are typically less stable. Thus, the former mental patient may be subtly excluded from many sensitive positions as well as from the normal range of social contacts on which many of us depend for enjoyment and self-esteem. The same is even more likely to be true for the ex-convict. In both cases, the role of internality (with accompanying self-blame) may also be much more salient than in the case of traumatic accident.

Constructive Reinterpretations

It should now be obvious that one's response to a trauma with stable "discrediting" consequences depends greatly on his understanding of why the trauma occurred and why it happened to him rather than someone else. Bulman and Wortman (1977) found that in their sample of spinal cord accident victims, the best copers were those who blamed themselves for the accident *but* who did not feel that the accident could have been avoided. One explanation for this curious pattern of response is that the good copers tended to be injured while involved in freely chosen leisure activities, such as motorcycle racing or hang gliding. Thus, in a general sense, the accident was their fault, but it was basically unavoidable if one pursued the activity often enough or over a long enough period of time. All twenty-nine of the victims interviewed acknowledged asking themselves, "Why me?," and the most common response was some version of the notion that "God has a reason." That reason included helping the individual learn about himself, teaching him to overcome, constituting a test of character, and so on. Only three individuals attributed their accident to "chance," to the exclusion of other causes. Apparently, the search for a silver lining is fairly common as an attempt to avoid the despair of undergoing a totally meaningless life-altering trauma.

This study merely scratches the surface of a "why me" approach to victimization and coping. For our current purposes, it would be important to extend the questions into the domain of true stigmatization and social discredit. Unquestionably, we would find individual differences in coping related to how this question is answered. Bulman and Wortman's results, on the other hand, may prove quite inapplicable in the context of social versus physical trauma. Rather, one might expect to find that those who cope best with the stigmatizing implications of their condition are those who attribute the discrediting reaction to limitations of the stigmatizer, rather than internalizing the reactions by stigmatizing themselves. We are suggesting, therefore, that while the reaction of self-blame may be very adaptive with regard to the occurrence of the trauma itself, it may be very maladaptive in response to any associated social discredit.

SUMMARY

In this chapter we have focused on the role of affect or experienced emotion in the stigmatizing process. For the most part, the focus has been on the normal marker and his response to physical and behavioral anomalies. Some limited evidence was presented to suggest that such anomalies can give rise to various innate or "preprogrammed" forms of anxiety and excitement, but the role of beliefs and attributions as affect mediators is obviously of extreme importance. Our emotional reactions to deviance not only depend on what is culturally defined as deviant; any given society has implicit "emotion rules" that define how its members should feel about deviance, death, and disfigurement. Thus, markers are socialized and pressured to have certain feelings when confronting deviant others. Those emotion rules can amplify a natural feeling of anxiety and revulsion, can convert these feelings into primitive anger, or, very often, can overlay negative feelings with more sympathetic and nurturant ones. Various combinations of negative and positive feelings have been commonly noted in the literature on stigma. Also, there is convincing evidence that such ambivalences tend to be resolved through amplified responses that may either be extremely positive or extremely negative, depending on the subtleties of context and of the available response opportunities.

There has been little systematic study of the emotional experiences of markable persons, although there have been several investigations of theories about responses of individuals to life-altering traumas. The empirical evidence suggests a wide range of individual differences in response to such traumas, and theorists have tried to uncover the antecedents of constructive (coping) versus destructive (depressive and antagonistic) reactions. Most theorizing has focused, once again, on the attributional aftermath of the trauma. That in turn may be understood in terms of the victim's pretrauma orientation to the origin and significance of received outcomes. To a certain extent, one's attitude toward life prior to a trauma can predict the outcome of coping with a traumatic event. As little as we know about one's emotional reactions to traumas that cause significant impairments in his capacities, we know even less about the emotions of those born with diminished capacity and about those whose capacities are jeopardized not by physical limitations, but by social stigmatization. Research into the emotions caused by social victimization would be fruitful, since it might show rather different coping patterns than those we are beginning to see in emotional reactions to the physical trauma itself.

• CHAPTER EIGHT •

The Long-term Relationships of Marked People

Rita de Sales French

"IT WAS A CASUAL FRIEND. We hadn't seen her in months, but I knew she had heard of his illness. Now she stared at him. I turned to see what she saw; a sick man huddled in a black raincoat . . . a man she had seen robust and now saw frail, stoop-shouldered, with an aged gaunt gray face, the eyes—even the eyes!—lustreless. She was an actress and good at her craft. But for a moment, before she could hide it, the horror stood clear in her face. 'Why Hal!' she said. 'Why, don't you look *marvelous!*' " (Lear 1980, p. 54).

The opening quotation contains several important aspects of long-term relationships. It is written by the wife of a man who has been stricken with heart disease. Her reaction to seeing a mutual friend brings forth several complex issues. First, she is trying on an outsider's point of view in seeing her husband through the friend's eyes and realizes that people in general see the characteristics of the mark and often confer upon it a "master status." Second, she realizes that in the presence of such a mark people become extremely uncomfortable and try to cover up their reaction to the mark. Third, the wife, who is obviously committed to the relationship with her markable husband, may, even though she does not herself bear a mark, feel socially stigmatized or marked because of her close relationship with her husband.

In this chapter we concern ourselves with the effects of marking conditions on long-term interpersonal reationships. Marked people often face overt rejection as well as subtle forms of rejection and disdain in their interactions with strangers. One might expect that a mark—although accepted at some level—would have some of the same and some additional negative effects in more intimate and more enduring relationships. One might also expect that the nature of these effects might vary greatly as a function of the particular features of the mark—whether it is concealable, functionally disabling, progressive in its course, and so on.

Marked people, through their own efforts and with the help of new legislative policies and support groups, have been living more independently and openly and, hence, have been coming into contact with general society more than they have in the past—a trend that will doubtless continue. By definition, there are far more "normal" than "deviant" people in the world, and if markable people do develop relationships with others, a large proportion of these others will be normal markers. This chapter discusses the issues and problems inherent in the establishment and maintenance of long-term relationships by marked people. Since very little is known about establishment, most of our focus will be on the maintenance of long-term relationships involving stigma.

In considering the development of long-term relationships between normal markers and deviant markables, several questions immediately come to mind. Are such relationships qualitatively different from relationships between two normal people or between two marked people? Do the marked people place a higher value on relationships with normals outside the family unit than with family members or with other marked individuals? If so, does this mean that they must always be the dependent partner in the relationship? Why and how does a normal person make the commitment to enter into a relationship with a markable person? Is this commitment process different when the mark arises from trauma, where an already ongoing relationship may be called into question, than when the existence of the mark precedes the potential relationship? Suppose that a casual but satisfying relationship that depends primarily on a mutually enjoyed activity (e.g., tennis, sex, travel) is severely altered because the affected person can no longer function in the activity. Will the activity be replaced and the friendship continued? What are the issues that each member of the relationship must face in continuing the relationship on a new basis? When the mark is an obvious basis for stigmatizing reactions in society, how does the normal partner cope with the tendency for society to discredit him or her as well?

Given limited opportunity for meeting people, how does a person who has become paraplegic—and thus possibly less acceptable to others as a potential partner in a relationship—attain close relationships? How do families react when a mentally retarded child is born or when a member is diagnosed as being an alcoholic? How are relationships and roles within the family affected? How does a stroke victim like Hodgins (1964), whose major life work was literary, face his newly acquired inability to pronounce or write the simplest words? How does he face himself, his colleagues, and his employer after such an incident?

For families into which a markable child is born, do relationships take on different characteristics than those found in "normal" families? For example, is sibling rivalry the same, absent, or exacerbated if one of the brothers or sisters is born with a stigmatizing condition? Under what conditions does such an event threaten family harmony, and when does it increase cohesiveness?

It is clearly easier to pose these questions than it is to answer them, and for some there are no answers. Until quite recently, social psychology has not focused much attention on the development and maintenance of long-term relationships. Most studies of interpersonal relationships involve brief encounters between people in a laboratory setting who will not see one another again after the experiment. Subjects are sometimes led to believe that there will be future interactions with a fellow subject, or subjects are asked whether or not they would like to interact with a subject in the future. For the most part, however, interactions in typical research settings are brief and circumscribed. For example, De Jong (1980) found that subjects who believed that obesity in a fellow interactant was due to an external cause, such as a thyroid problem (rather than having no explanation about the cause of the obesity), were more willing to interact with the thyroid-caused obese person in the future. From this study we would predict that a relationship would be more likely to develop between persons in the thyroid-explanation condition, but we do not know whether such a relationship would actually develop, or what form it would take, if the subjects were given the opportunity for extensive further contact. We are, therefore, left with only a hunch about what might happen, given one experimental condition versus another, but we really do not know very much beyond that.

When we move from the study of casual to long-term marked relationships, it becomes especially important to distinguish between the debilitating and disruptive effects of the markable condition itself, and the stigma potentially associated with it. As pointed out in Chapter 1, one can be marked without being stigmatized. Stigma arises out of an interaction between a marker and a markable person, in which the marker disdains, shuns, criticizes, or mocks the markable person primarily because of the possession of the mark. But the marking process itself does not necessarily lead to strained interaction and the disruptive affect associated with stigma. In fact, it is rather difficult to imagine a stable marked relationship in which the marker fully stigmatizes the marked person, as we have been using that term. Marked relationships may even shift over a period of time, back and forth along a continuum from benign marking (acknowledging that a condition has implications for the relationship) to full stigmatization, with all the associated accompaniments of revulsion and negative affect. Even in those cases where stigma is not an issue within the relationship itself, it may be an issue for both members of the relationship in coping with the outside world.

Thus, the existence of a mark may differentially affect three major areas of life. First, in some cases there are direct and practical consequences of the mark for the relationship. They include economic hardship, increased time burdens associated with caretaking, and restriction of activities and opportunities for employment and recreation. Second, in most relationships involving a mark, an alteration of psychological costs and benefits may take place. There may be shifts in dependence, in the perception of the old versus the new circumstances under which the relationship is to operate. The mark also may produce such emotional consequences as guilt, anger, compassion, and so on. Third, problems more specifically related to the classical notion of social stigma may result—feelings of shame, awkwardness in dealing with outsiders, revulsion and ambivalence stemming from the attributional implications of the mark, and what the mark implies about the identity of the marked person.

The emphasis on these three potential problem areas may vary with the short-term or long-term nature of the relationship and may vary significantly with the kind of mark involved. For example, there is likely to be more caretaking involved if one is in an intimate, rather than casual, relationship with a marked person, and there are likely to be more problems of social stigma involved with alcoholism than with paraplegia. Thus, similarities observed in people's reactions to stigma on a short-term basis may lead to very different reactions to stigma when people are involved on a long-term basis with marked individuals.

Before going on to discuss these issues more fully, we must first define the nature of the interpersonal relationships to be considered in this chapter.

Relationships involving normals and markables tend to fall into four basic categories, given here in order of their increasingly voluntary nature. The first consists of individuals with congenital marks interacting with their families of origin. When a disabled or mentally retarded (and, therefore, markable) child is born into a family, all family members are affected. The parents, in addition to parenting their "normal" children, are faced with the task of raising and nurturing the markable child. The second class of marked relationships consists of those between two previously "normal" individuals, one of whom undergoes a potentially stigmatizing trauma or illness. In that category, the principal issue for the affected individuals is whether to persist in the relationship as previously defined, work toward a new definition, or abandon the relationship entirely. The third category consists of freely chosen relationships, wherein one party bears the markable condition before the relationship is established. Many couples marry or choose to develop close ties with one another with full knowledge of the potentially stigmatizing condition borne by one of them.

Finally, there is also the formation of long-term relationships wherein both members have a similar or comparable stigmatizing condition. These relationships may be freely chosen because of the mutual support and understanding that stems from bearing the same mark. Or they may be accepted by default under either the true or the false apprehension that relationships with "normal" people are not available. Some stigmatized people may, however, avoid such relationships because they wish to dissociate themselves from those who remind them of their mark. Simpson (1982), a woman recovering from tubercular meningitis, describes her feelings toward other disabled people who offered her their support: "It was inconceivable that my self should be impaired. I began to hate people with infirmities with an unending dogmatic strength, refusing to be identified with them. . . . I did not want to be admitted to their motley company, to be identified as 'one of them' " (p. 99).

We do not know very much about the development and maintenance of relationships among stigmatized people bearing the same or similar mark. We also do not know very much about the development of intimate relationships between normal and stigmatized people who possess full knowledge of the stigmatizing condition and its attendant problems. There have been biographies and anecdotal accounts of close relationships under such circumstances, but we do not know of systematic studies of these relationships and their course.

There is, however, literature in the field of developmental psychology that addresses the impact of congenital stigmas on the family. Although we are primarily dealing with long-term relationships among normal and marked adults in this chapter, we present a brief summary of some of this literature.

IMPACT OF STIGMA ON FAMILY RELATIONS

In a review of the literature on parental and family reactions to the birth of a disabled child, Howard (1978) reports an array of feelings and responses commonly felt by parents when they learn that their child is abnormal. These reactions and feelings include shock, depression, guilt, denial, anger, sadness, and anxiety (Klaus and Kennell 1976). Some parents experience feelings of shame and anticipate social rejection and ridicule, while others are prone to feelings of guilt over previous sexual conduct (Jamison 1965).

Some parents report ambivalent feelings and even death wishes (Heisler 1972), while many parents blame the physicians for the child's problem.

As time goes by, these parents eventually adjust to their child's condition (Moloney 1971; Klaus and Kennell 1976), but they are subject to many setbacks and disappointments as their child does not reach anticipated developmental stages at the proper times. Busch-Rossnagel (1981) cites a follow-up study by Rose (1961), who found that mothers of Rh-incompatible children experience anxiety at each new maturational period achieved by their children. Busch-Rossnagel concludes that "even when impairment does not still exist, the threat of one in the past is capable of producing a handicap" (p. 293). Parents worry very much about their child's future and must, in a number of cases, face the decision to keep the child at home or to place the child in an institution. Some parents, even experienced ones, are unable to apply their parenting skills in caring for a disabled child. The experience of parenting a "normal" child apparently does not prepare parents psychologically for parenting an "abnormal" child (McAndrew 1976). Unfortunately, it is difficult to disentangle the effects of coping with the disability from the effects of stigma on the parent-child relationship.

There is often great financial and emotional strain in those families. Some parents worry about neglecting the normal children in the family, while others develop overly involved or symbiotic relationships with the disabled child to the exclusion of forming or maintaining other relationships in the family. Even the spousal relationship may, in effect, be abandoned (Bueker et al. 1981; Smith et al. 1981). Many parents may find it difficult to rear the disabled child, especially in handling the difficult balancing act between caring and support on the one hand and the overprotective undermining of autonomous strivings on the other. Many parents may find it difficult to face the realities of the child's developing sexuality in adolescence and the child's eventual need for intimacy with others outside the family unit. Those are potential problems faced by *all* parents, but when a child is disabled or marked, the problems may be intensified.

The siblings of deviant children may evidence more problems than do the siblings of normal children (Grossman, 1972). They may feel guilty for being normal and try to make up for the loss the parents feel from having a child who cannot function fully (Schreiber and Feeley 1965). Siblings may also resent the family's constricted life because of the stigmatized child's condition. They may feel overburdened with caring for their siblings and may feel ashamed of them (Schreiber and Feeley 1965). Featherstone (1981) notes that brothers and sisters of disabled children often complain about feeling responsible for their disabled siblings. She states, "Heavy responsibility can drain the life out of anybody—big or little. Responsibility can weigh heavily on the thin shoulders of a child" (p. 171). Many families of disabled children face endless hours of caring for and comforting them. The chronic nature of this responsibility is often too much for families to bear. Parents typically experience, in addition, the feeling that the condition is irrevocable and the need for adjustment endless. Featherstone (1981), who speaks from her own experience in caring for her handicapped child, writes:

> A disabled child forces parents to think of their old age in ugly dismal terms. I remember, during the early months of Jody's life, the anguish with which I contemplated the distant future. Jody cried constantly, not irritable, hungry cries, but heartrending shrieks of pain. Vain efforts to comfort him filled my nights and days. One evening when nothing seemed to help, I went outside, intending to escape his misery for a moment, hoping that without me he might finally fall asleep. Walking in the summer darkness, I imagined myself at seventy, bent and wrinkled, hobbling up the stairs to minister to Jody, now over forty, but still crying and helpless. Parents' thoughts linger on the costs—human as well as monetary—of raising such a child, and on the probability that they will ultimately fail to provide all he needs (p. 19).

This overworked mother also felt a pressure to keep her child at home and provide for him and the family. When Jody got bigger, she was often overwhelmed by a full schedule of bathing and diapering. With all of her time accounted for, she became furious when it was suggested that she brush the child's teeth four times a day to keep the gums from growing over them (a side effect of Dilantin, a medicine which controls seizures). It was just too much. Other problems secondary to the disabling condition may also pose special difficulties for families.

David (1963), in his study of children hospitalized with polio, notes that families operate differently when a disabled child is hospitalized and have to adjust when the child returns home again. He identified three major sources of conflict in these families: (1) the leniency toward the other children in the family during the child's hospital stay was difficult to abandon once the child returned home; (2) character changes in the hospitalized child (e.g., more selfish demandingness due to hospitalization) were difficult to deal with; and (3) the uncertainty and ambivalence of parents concerning the proper handling of the returned child and his residual impairment-caused problems.

Although the literature on family impact is becoming more substantial, Howard (1978) can still note at the conclusion of her review that there are no longitudinal studies of disabled children and their families that compare them to normally matched control groups. Most of the studies reported above do find negative effects of the child's condition on the family. It is important to point out, however, that there also can be positive effects of potentially stigmatizing conditions on some families (Featherstone 1981). Korn, Chess, and Fernandez (1978), in their study of disabled children born following the 1964 rubella epidemic, report that many families made positive statements about their lives with affected children. The common assumption of distress in such families might in some cases become a self-fulfilling prophecy.

A survey (Breslau 1982) of 835 mothers (370 of whom had physically disabled children) showed that mothers of disabled children did not report more marital stress (although divorced and separated mothers placed more blame on the child's disability for their marital breakups). The study also showed that siblings of disabled children were no more likely to suffer severe psychiatric impairment (although they did show more aggressive behaviors at home and at school) than did control children. Perhaps it is not surprising that the literature on family reactions to diverse conditions of deviance and disability is large, varied, and sometimes conflicting.

So far we have spoken of the effects on the family of a child born with a potentially stigmatizing affliction. Some chronic illnesses affecting parents (e.g., schizophrenia, alcoholism) may be deviant conditions that have always been part of the child's life. In a study by Anthony (1969; 1970) of the effects of severe psychiatric illness (psychosis) and physical illness (tuberculosis) on the family, it was found that several different responses to parental illness were possible. Anthony employed a somewhat novel technique called "unroofing," which consisted of going into the homes and living with families for about a week to observe interactions and to see what sense the family members made of the illness. He found that different families responded to the situation in at least three ways, which Anthony called growth and differentiation, breakdown and rally, and rout and disintegration.

Families in the first category, those that are drawn closer together by the experience of serious illness, generally coped well before the illness, and aspects of the parents' lives were predictive of good general adjustment in an adult. Those aspects were a happy childhood; good school, marital, and work records; and a history of adequate coping with everyday life crises.

Families in the second category, those that temporarily break down under the impact of severe parental illness, deal primarily with issues of change, contagion, and constriction. Children see their afflicted parent change from a caretaker or loving figure to a source of danger. Fear of physical contagion (getting tuberculosis or becoming psychotic) interferes with the parent-child relationship in a profound manner. Families may become constricted, "which manifests itself in a rigidity of operation, a lack of spontaneity of feeling, a narrowness of thinking and a refusal to take chances. The individual members behave as if they were walking on eggs and as if any unusual act on their part might release a holocaust" (Anthony 1969, p. 447). In those families where a parent is psychotic, the members somehow manage to survive. The children learn that their parent is different and illogical, they worry about being and about becoming like him or her, but their family life is not totally disrupted by the tragedy.

In deteriorating families, the third category, the members lose significant contact with one another. They do not seem to care about the household or about one another. Some stay together without experiencing much feeling for each other, while others drift apart.

Sometimes, however, the process may be arrested and reversed, even in families where disintegration seems inevitable. Anthony describes four stages in the regeneration process. The first consists of "massive denial of deviance, non-recognition of the illness, naive rationalization of symptoms, and an appeal to specific family mythology to explain away the illness." The second is a recognition that one member is ill and must be isolated from the rest of the family. In the third, the family reintegrates with society and tries to prepare the ill person for contact outside of the family (e.g., to "normalize" the person). In the fourth stage, the "family group starts to differentiate and to integrate and to work and play together as a group." In families where there is severe psychosis, humor may be used to put the psychosis into perspective and to place the ill person on a continuum vis-à-vis other people—"Everyone is sick but some are sicker than others" (Anthony 1969, p. 450).

This process is usually accompanied by the generation of theories to account for the presence of psychosis or illness in the family. Once a family settles on an explanation for how the illness evolved in the family, it usually has a stabilizing effect on the members. Individual members may develop their own formulations that help the family members to accept the effects produced by the psychotic or ill members' behavior (Anthony 1969).

EFFECTS OF TRAUMATIC MARKS ON LONG-TERM RELATIONSHIPS

When a relationship has already been established and one of the partners incurs a potentially stigmatizing condition, we assume that some adjustment will have to be made by both partners. In the remainder of this chapter we address ourselves to this kind of relationship. We do so because we believe that issues found in this type of situation will also tend to arise in the other kinds of marked relationships, but that the traumatic occurrence brings the issues more sharply into focus.

In order to understand the impact of disabling or stigmatizing trauma on established relationships, it is necessary to characterize some of the general features of such relationships in social psychological terms. In theorizing about the development and maintenance of *close personal relationships*, Kelley (1979) uses the term "to refer to lovers, marriage partners, best friends, and persons who work closely together. An everyday description of this kind of relationship will refer to its long-lasting nature; the fact that the persons spend much time together, do many things together, and (often) share living or working quarters; the intercommunication of personal information and feelings; and the likelihood that the persons see themselves as a unit and are seen that way by others" (p. 1).

Berscheid and Walster (1978) have studied interpersonal attraction and have identified several important variables for explaining why we are attracted to others. We are attracted to others to the extent that they provide us with rewards and/or reduce our costs. The major ways in which others provide rewards and reduce costs are: (1) others are highly rewarding when they evaluate us positively by expressing personal liking for us; (2) others are highly rewarding when they reinforce or validate our attitudes and opinions; and (3) others lower the costs we must face by reducing anxiety and standing by when we are lonely, fearful, or under stress. Kelley (1979) postulates that interdependence, mutual responsiveness to one another's outcomes, and the attribution of behavior to stable dispositions of the actor are important concepts for understanding the structure and functioning of close personal relationships.

The attribution problem in close personal relationships is an interesting one. Kelley believes spouses attribute most behavior to dispositions. The tendency to attribute behavior to stable dispositions of the actor, called the fundamental attribution error (Ross 1977; Nisbett and Ross 1980), has been demonstrated in diverse experimental settings (Jones 1979). We do not know much, however, about the frequency with which people outside laboratory settings spontaneously make attributions (whether situational or dispositional). For marked relationships, the attribution question takes on special importance. We believe there may be an overattribution of behavior (positive and negative) to the mark. Such an attribution seems to defy easy classification as either dispositional or situational, which raises an intriguing set of issues that we shall discuss later in the chapter.

Let us suppose that a husband has been injured in an automobile accident and is left a paraplegic. Let us further imagine the likely effects on his and his wife's feelings and emotional state. We assume that the couple had no major problems in their relationship before the accident.

The previous role relationships characterizing the marriage may be completely upset by the consequences of the disabling trauma. In addition to losing his role as breadwinner (and perhaps lover), the husband may feel many contradictory or conflicting emotions. He may be both grateful to and angry with his wife as she attempts to care for him. He may not be able to express himself clearly because he is uncertain about what he wants or needs. He may need her care but resent her for giving it. He may attribute his wife's caretaking behavior or her interest in him to feelings of pity rather than love. A question that may loom large in his mind is, "Would she have chosen me in my present condition?"

The wife may also feel several conflicting emotions. She may feel deep love and compassion, in addition to feeling trapped, angry, or cheated. She may contemplate desertion, then immediately feel guilty for having such a thought. Such a mixture of feelings exemplifies the ambivalence discussed in Chapter 7.

In such a relationship, it might be difficult to determine if costs and rewards based on the relationship existing before the accident apply to the new set of conditions. We do not mean to imply that the new relationship is one of overwhelming costs alone, since new rewards may in fact come out of the new set of circumstances. With such an array of potentially conflicting and confusing emotions, it would be difficult to determine the partners' "true" feelings about the new status of the relationship. We see that a cost-benefit analysis in some sense does apply here, but we also see that there is a much more complicated and confusing set of emotions and issues for the couple to face than a dispassionate cost-benefit analysis would seem to imply.

In Kelley's terms the couple is faced with the task of reestablishing the terms of their interdependence, given the fact that one party, at least for a time, will be much more in need than the other. Kelley calls this "unilateral dependence," wherein there is the latent threat that the less dependent person may initiate dissolution. As suggested by the discussion of comparison level in Chapter 6, he or she is "more likely to find something better to do with the time and effort required by the interaction" (p. 44). They are also faced with the task of establishing a new attributional system that explains the continuance of the relationship in the face of the stigmatizing condition—for example, what perceived dispositions are possessed by each party that warrant a continuation of the relationship, despite greater perceived costs.

In addition to the emotional responses mentioned, the situation is one in which caretaking becomes a dominant issue. Financial matters may be a large problem for the couple. The time and energy involved in physical caretaking may become overwhelming, if the wife takes on the role of primary caretaker. Practical difficulties may arise when she then attempts to allocate time and energy to activities other than caretaking.

A third problem faced by the couple involves their place in society. Feelings of shame may overwhelm them, and they may be reluctant to chance excursions into public places. Old friends may be dropped because of the awkwardness of interacting with them. The nature of the accident may be very important in this context. If the condition was acquired through some perceived fault of the husband (driving while drinking), others may blame the victim for his condition and thus perceive him as morally weak and unworthy.

All of these issues have been previously mentioned as major areas of life that are potentially upset by the presence of the mark. To recapitulate, they are: (1) the objective consequences of the mark—caretaking, economic hardship, increased time burden, and restriction of activities; (2) the interpersonal consequences—shifts in dependence, emotional reactions, and shifts in the circumstances under which the couple is to function; and (3) the social consequences—feelings of shame, awkwardness in dealing with outsiders, and the attributional implications of the mark.

For this particular example, we stress the objective and interpersonal consequences. For some other marks, such as alcoholism and mental illness, the social consequences may play a more dominant role.

In addition to the issues mentioned, several others deserve a prominent place in a discussion of interpersonal relationships involving potential stigma. The additional issues are pertinent not only to the marital relationship, but to other personal relationships as well. Before speaking of the issues themselves, however, we will first describe the manner in which we derived them. There are many different kinds of interpersonal relationships, and there are many different types of stigmatizing conditions. Our discussion might be fruitful for a certain type of stigma, but it might not be so for another type or for a different kind of relationship.

Therefore, we chose to examine some of the variables discussed in Chapter 2, which described six important dimensions of stigma: concealability, course, disruptiveness, aesthetic qualities, origin, and peril. We selected four of these to draw the reader's attention to issues in long-term relationships: origin, concealability, aesthetic qualities and course. If we consider the two extremes of each dimension, these reflect eight different and important possible properties of stigmatizing conditions: how and when the condition was acquired (at birth or later in life); whether or not the condition could be seen by others; whether it impeded function; whether the condition was aesthetically displeasing; whether the condition was manageable (or arrested), or whether it would follow a downward course or lead to death in the near future. We also chose to examine four major forms of interpersonal relations: intimate/familial; informal/voluntary; occupational/coworker; and professional/therapeutic. We felt it important to examine all of those relationships because they pose different sorts of problems for the marked person.

In order to discipline our thinking about these relationships and types of stigmata, we formed a table with those headings and concentrated on filling in the cells with likely problems and feelings that a stigmatized person and his/her normal partner might face.* The exercise generated 64 cells—eight kinds of potentially stigmatizing marks and four relationships, each from the point of view of the members of the relationship. After this process was completed, we examined all of the cells to see what common problems might be present. If a problem cut across many of the kinds of relationships and was present for many of the different stigmata, we felt that it was useful to consider that problem more fully. In a way, we informally derived the "prototypic" interpersonal problems faced by members of relationships in which one of the parties bears a discrediting mark.

The interpersonal problems we derived that were common to many of the cells in our table are: (1) ambivalence (conflicting reactions to the mark, to the new roles the stigmatizing condition forces upon the participants, and to the long-term relationship itself); (2) difficulties with clarity (ambiguity of care, direct statements of need, intention, and limits, the establishment of new role relationships); (3) overattribution to the mark (both parties in the relationship may wrongly attribute positive and/or negative behavior on the part of the other to the mark; and (4) strain, including both the pressure felt regarding new role relationships and the strain of simply not knowing how to behave in an interaction. We believe that these interpersonal problems are important in the adjustment process after trauma and that they also apply to the development of personal relationships with the congenitally stigmatized.

*We thank Perrin L. French, M.D., a psychiatrist at the Menlo Park Veterans Hospital, for his assistance on this task.

Table 1. Characteristics of Stigmata by Types of Long-term Relationships Used to Derive Interpersonal Problems

	Origin		**Concealability**		**Aesthetic**		**Course**	
	Traumatic	**Long Term**	**Hidden**	**Overt**	**Aesthetic**	**Functional**	**Stable**	**Terminal**
Intimate/ Familial	Self / Other	Self / Other	Self / Other	Self / Other	Self / Other	Self / Other	Self / Other	Self / Other
Informal/ Voluntary	" / "	" / "	" / "	" / "	" / "	" / "	" / "	" / "
Occupational/ Coworker	" / "	" / "	" / "	" / "	" / "	" / "	" / "	" / "
Therapeutic/ Professional	" / "	" / "	" / "	" / "	" / "	" / "	" / "	" / "

EFFECTS OF TRAUMATIC MARKS ON FOUR INTERPERSONAL RELATIONSHIPS

Of necessity, we are not able to present for discussion here all the factors associated with different types of marks for all the kinds of relationships. We will present the effects of a mark acquired later in life (as opposed to a mark present at birth or in early childhood) on four kinds of interpersonal relationships—those with family, friends, coworkers, and "helping" professionals. In terms of our entries in Table 1, we are presenting one important feature of the possible kinds of marks (i.e., traumatic), and looking at the effects on a broad range of relationships likely to be experienced by a traumatically marked person. Although there are many potential problems—some common and some unique to each of the kinds of relationships—we present the four problem areas that cut across all of them: ambivalence, clarity, overattribution, and strain. Even though we discuss only these four problems, we present all of the entries for a given relationship to show the range of practical, emotional, and social ramifications the potentially stigmatizing mark has for long-term interpersonal relationships.

Intimate/Familial Relationships

We begin with the intimate/familial relationship. Table 2 shows some of the problems faced by both members of a marriage partnership after the husband has incurred or developed a traumatic condition.

We note that a number of entries in Table 2 involve physical caretaking. Obviously, not all marks involve this. Alcoholism, recovery from mental hospitalization, and other conditions do not ordinarily involve physical care. We add them here to try to be inclusive. Those other marks are also associated with a greater emphasis on social stigma. For example, the concerns of a couple where the husband has recently returned from mental hospitalization for acute depression will be more oriented toward social stigma than physical caretaking.

Breast Cancer: Stigma and Self-stigma

Bennetts, L., "Relationships: Breast Cancer and Sexuality," *New York Times*, March 1, 1982.

When a victim of breast cancer recovers from a mastectomy [according to Regina Kriss, a behavioral scientist who has spent years counseling and studying

post-mastectomy patients], the message she gets from family and society is "aren't you lucky you are alive!" But some problems may just be beginning . . . many if not most suffer difficulties in adjusting their self images to the bodily loss, and their sexual interaction with men may be profoundly affected. . . .

A woman married for many years, finds after her operation that her husband is remote and cold, unable to communicate his feelings or comfort her. "He hasn't touched me in two years," she says bitterly. A single woman has other problems: terrified of rejection, she shrinks from contact with men, cutting off relationships before they have a chance to develop. "I don't want to be touched," she says. "Even the thought of intimacy scares me to death." Both women feel undesirable, seeing themselves as "mutilated" and thinking no man could ever want them again.

Such reactions are common, according to Mrs Kriss. . . . "Your breasts are a symbol of your femininity, your desirability, your ability to entice. This is a very breast-oriented society, and it's like everything you can offer a man is gone. It isn't a vanity problem. It's an essential part of your core existence as a woman. . . ."

Men's reactions to mastectomy present another dimension to the problem. "Nobody knows how mastectomy affects a man in terms of sexual desire," Mrs. Kriss said. "It's a confrontation with death, with illness and aging. I think it inhibits sexual drive. Men won't admit how affected they are. They feel terrible about it and they are saddened by it, but they may be physically turned off by it."

Mrs. Kriss believes, on the other hand, that when dealt with correctly, with therapy if necessary, the situation that follows a mastectomy may offer the opportunity for personal growth. "You wouldn't choose it, but you can make it work for you," she maintained. "A mastectomy is a terrible test, and it has the potential to destroy a person, but it also has the potential to offer the greatest growth. If a woman feels a man loves her in spite of it, she has a very secure relationship and good communication. A woman feels very secure when she feels someone loves her for her, because she's special, not just because she is attractive."

Table 2. **The Effects of Traumatic Stigma on the Familial Relationship (Spousal)**

Feelings and Concerns Affecting the Marked Relationship

Husband (Traumatic stigma, e.g., paraplegia)	Wife
Fears the loss of wife's love and affection	Wonders what future life together will be like. Will it consist of caretaking primarily?
Fears regarding own health. Will I get worse? Will I be able to function?	Need to fill new role (e.g., caretake, pay bills, go to work)
Guilt regarding cost to wife	May feel overwhelmed with caretaking of husband and other family members.
Gratitude to wife, appreciation for her loyalty	Compassion for husband
Testing limits of wife's love	Blame third party, fate, doctors
Concern regarding role as breadwinner, lover, and parent	Feels trapped
Wonders if wife's attention is derived from pity rather than love	Feels cheated
Concerned about overwhelming wife with needs	Anger at husband
Envy of wife for being normal	Blame husband (Was the accident his fault?)
How stigma was acquired may affect relations. Is she blaming me for the accident?	Recommitment versus desertion
Ambivalence	Embarrassment/shame vis-à-vis third parties and larger society
Denial of the illness or condition. "There's nothing wrong with me, I don't need her help."	Guilt
Anger at fate, situation	Ambivalence
Need to fill new role	Disgust
Resolution of ambiguity about care needed or desired	Ambiguity of care to be given
Overattribution to stigma	Overattention to stigma
Will I be able to work again?	Will I have to spend all of my time caring for him?
May feel isolated and helpless	Worry about financial situation, social situation
Denial may lead to inability to mourn loss of capabilities and of previous relationship with wife	May hope for a cure, speedy recovery
	May feel isolated and helpless if not embedded in a social support system

The common denominator, however, is the psychological response within the couple. We also realize that the couple is embedded within a social system and that their adjustment to the mark has much to do with how society in general perceives it. Certain marks, such as obesity, mental illness, and heroin addiction, are associated with moral weakness, and members of a marked relationship are faced with reconciling that fact with their continued commitment to one another. Any particular mark chosen to demonstrate certain points will fall short on demonstrating others. To the extent that any mark can be perceived as involving a moral taint, the societal reaction must play a part in the affected couple's adjustment and commitment to one another, for they are likely to hold the same convictions regarding the mark as does society at large.

Although there are many reactions of interest to us in this table, we focus on the four interpersonal problems that we feel cut across the many factors associated with the types of marks and types of relationships.

Ambivalence

We use the term ambivalence as in Chapter 7 to mean conflicted or mixed (positive and negative) feelings toward the same person. Ambivalence probably persists to some degree in even the best of close interpersonal relationships. One could always have made other choices, or one is not completely satisfied with all of the characteristics of one's spouse. When it is out of control, ambivalence is a hallmark of obsessive compulsive ritual-making, where commitment to one choice immediately leads to its undoing by the opposing choice. Immobilization and dedication to the ritual results, and the individual has insufficient energy or will to proceed with his or her life.

In order to enter into a long-term relationship such as marriage, ambivalence must have been resolved, at least to the extent that a decision to marry was made and actually carried out. After the marriage, ambivalence may still persist at the emotional level, even though once the choice was made, dissonance-reduction processes may have come into play to maintain and bolster the original decision. However, changes brought about by the trauma heighten residual or unresolved ambivalence and generate new feelings of ambivalence for both parties. This usually means that ambivalence resolution and recommitment to the relationship are part of the work that couples face in a marked relationship. This recommitment may then facilitate the ameliorative effects for the dissonance-reduction process.

As noted in Chapter 7, it is not completely understood what factors lead to the successful reduction of ambivalence. Presumably, ambivalence often exists without the ambivalent person being explicitly aware of its components. Despite vague feelings that all is not well, some marked relationships may survive, since some couples stay together by default, leaving their ambivalences unresolved. They simply go through the motions of living together, perhaps sustained by the feeling that they have a unique cross to bear. Other couples in a marked relationship may feel drawn closer together by the traumatic event and its resulting costs without making a conscious recommitment to the relationship.

We do not know whether acknowledgment of ambivalence within the couple typically has positive or negative effects on the relationship. Honesty and open communication are usually thought to be qualities characterizing successful relationships. We might expect, therefore, that openness about conflicting feelings in a newly marked relationship may be helpful, and perhaps necessary. Couples may also need to mourn the loss of their old life together before they can face a commitment to a new one. They may need first to compare their old lives together to the present one and make adjustments to losses and rewards in each. If they expect that their old life together will be restored, they may be unable to accept the limitations of a new one and, as a consequence, be unable to mourn effectively the loss of the old (Kelley et al. 1960). It is difficult to gather data on these topics. Most researchers have good reason not to trust retrospective reports concerning emotional process and decision-making in a relationship. It seems important to examine the posttraumatic coping process as soon after the trauma as possible. The families of the marked individuals would need to be interviewed, in addition to the marked person. It would be necessary to follow these people over time to see the possible effects of the trauma on the relationship. It should be pointed out, however, that immediate posttrauma assessments can themselves be misleading. If the couple and the surrounding family are busy mobilizing their strengths for a rehabilitation effort, it may be as much as a year or two later that they can really assess their relationship with a clear perspective. Only then may they evaluate their situations more thoughtfully.

Successes and failures of ambivalence reduction and recommitment should be objectively, if crudely, reflected in the divorce rate in marked versus otherwise comparable normal relationships. There is not any good evidence that the divorce rate is higher than in the general population for couples with certain kinds of marked members (Trieschmann 1978). There are, however, some data that show that married couples who have stayed together vary on how happy and satisfied they are with their relationships. One interesting theme seems to have emerged from some of this literature. Put simply, the more well-defined the nature of the stigmatizing condition, the happier and more satisfied are the family members.

Clarity

If our imagined marked husband (Table 2) has conflicting feelings or is trying to play down the impact of the mark, he may not be very clear in communicating his views to his spouse. He may keep her in the dark about his needs because he is confused about them himself. Or he may be experiencing clear emotional or even physical needs, but refrain out of pride from making them known to anyone, especially his wife. The mark may itself leave much leeway in the determination of how and when physical or emotional help is needed. The wife may begin to feel inadequate. She may feel that she can no longer predict what pleases her husband and she may be genuinely confused about the nature or seriousness of the new condition. She may overestimate or underestimate the degree to which her husband is physically or emotionally needy. Therefore, she may be prone to offer insufficient or excessive care. Since she is placed in the unhappy position of trying to second-guess his feelings, the relationship may deteriorate or teeter precariously, burdened by noncommunication and inaccurate feedback.

Zahn (1973) offers some evidence in support of the importance of the clarity issue. She found that people with a clear-cut impairment tended to have better interpersonal relationships within their families. She found less disruption in spousal and family relations for disabled people who were the most sexually impaired as a result of their disability. She also found that the quality of close primary relationships suffered when the disabled member's status was ambiguous, as when a husband is able to work but is not working. In summarizing her findings, Zahn states: "Characteristics of impairment that clearly indicate sickness or impairment tend to be associated with better interpersonal relations. This clarity, as indicated by severity of functional limitations, inability to work, and established sexual impairment legitimizes the sick or disabled role for incumbents . . . and facilitates unimpaired interpersonal functioning" (p. 122).

Many stigmatizing conditions do not carry unambiguous impairment with them, and, in most cases, they do not provide clear cut information about the emotional needs of the disabled person. As Albrecht (1976) states, "The patient and his family do not know whether the person is disabled, the extent and consequences of the disability, how long the disability might last, or what adjustments they will have to make to cope with the disability" (p. 15). In cases of mild mental retardation, family members often suffer embarrassing situations (sometimes for years) because of ambiguity about the diagnosis. When other people notice a handicapped person's difference, family members are at a loss to explain because they were never given a clear label or diagnosis of the condition (Featherstone 1981).

We do not mean to imply that the failure to communicate is purposeful or to hold the marked person especially responsible for neglecting to communicate clearly his needs. We only wish to point out that clarity in a relationship is a very important variable and special pains may be necessary on the part of both parties to achieve it. Beletsis and Brown (1981) have demonstrated that communication breakdowns found in the families of alcoholics have serious and lasting consequences for the children of such families. When the drinking problem is mislabeled or concealed from friends and neighbors, the alcoholic's children grow up in an atmosphere of denial and deception. As adults, they are often unable to trust other people.

Clarity and ambivalence are intimately related. If one is ambivalent about one's situation and relationships, the ambivalence will permeate communication with others. Partners in the marriage may each communicate conflicting messages. A marked husband may communicate, "I need you to tell me you still love me and won't abandon me/I don't need you to worry about my future or self-esteem/I can get along without you." His wife may communicate, "I love you more than before/I resent you for doing this to me." The following excerpt from Lear (1980) eloquently suggests how difficult it must be to sort out and communicate ambivalent feelings in a close relationship:

> My life here, now, is nursemaid to a man gone strangely old from sickness and garrulous from loneliness, clutching at sleeves, wanting to talk to confirm that he still exists, and I ache for him but I resent him as well, this sick, sunken man who is my beautiful Hal whom I adore. The intensity of the anger that hovers here, beneath what I take to be love, is frightening. I understand the wretched banality of such an anger as this, I do not have to be a professor of whatever to understand the how and the why of such an anger, yet it shames and appalls me. And of course, he knows (p. 379).

And from Hal's point of view the situation is described thus:

> I love you I love you I love you, she said all the time. And he would wonder, what is this love she feels? In part it is love. In part it is guilt. In part it is fear. For many months she had been loving him

> too lavishly, with too much display of affection, and always he felt an air of desperation about it, he felt like saying: "I'm still alive. Let me alone."
>
> So the I love you was not simple. When was it? The truth of it was, she was entrapped, and on some level hostility was a natural response. He understood it. He even sympathized with it. He simply did not want to be the butt of it. It was a terrible thing to be so dependent upon someone who in many ways resented him, although of course she loved him. When she cut him short, or answered him in hostile ways, or listened to him with ostentatious impatience—at such times he fiercely resented her; although, of course, he loved her (p. 379).

Attribution

Even if communication is clearly given and ambivalence is resolved or acknowledged, the partners in a marked relationship may still perceive the actions of the marked member as caused predominantly by the mark. The marked person may explain the partner's actions as reactions to his or her stigmatizing condition. The marker may constantly interpret the marked person's actions as influenced by the presence of the mark. One might assume that the tendency to exaggerate the mark's causal significance would eventually disappear in most close personal relationships. The closeness and variety of contacts should tend to illuminate rather than obfuscate patterns of social causation. That might normally be the case, but a complicating factor may lie in the marked person's profound conviction, perhaps irrationally held, that the spouse may abandon him or her. That conviction can lead to a paranoid sensitivity, first affecting attributional influences and, ultimately, leading to a self-fulfilling prophecy: the conviction of abandonment leads to behavior that brings about the reality of abandonment. The marker may also find it difficult not to exaggerate the causal significance of the mark. If it develops that each partner feels the other to be acting out of some response to the stigmatizing condition instead of to freely felt impulses and motives, each party could come to feel as an object, rather than a subject in the marriage. The stigmatized husband might interpret his wife's caretaking efforts as a reflection of her Christian duty, rather than an expression of her love and concern.

Traumatic stigmatizing conditions create a salient, highly available, stimulus for explaining subsequent behavior. By comparison, we might expect that partners in marriages involving congenital conditions may not be as prone to attributing behavior to the mark, since they met and chose one another with full knowledge of the mark's presence. Assuming that communicative clarity has a chance to triumph over potentially disruptive fears of abandonment, we might expect the tendency to search for causal attribution, and the tendency to attribute all behavior to a traumatic stigma to decline over time. But for the period of time right after the trauma, during which the couple usually struggles with ambivalence resolution and recommitment, the tendency to attribute behavior to the stigma may be at its peak. Lear writes:

> I could see him trying, the words trying to get themselves ordered, push themselves past his lips, and the tears, too, falling upon his lips, and finally, with a pain that wrenched my own heart: "I don't know why you should stay with me. I'm a cripple."
>
> "Don't say that. You're *not* a cripple."
>
> "Stop denying." He said it kindly, the rage gone now, a kind of reasoned resignation in its place. "I'm not feeling sorry for myself. It's simply a reality" (p. 277).

It might, however, be useful on many occasions for the "normal" person to attribute negative behaviors of the stigmatized person to the stigma. In that way, the stigmatized person's negative behavior might not be taken "personally." For example, he or she may be irritable or depressed because of the condition and not because of some enduring negative disposition. Such attributions often make caretaking possible in the face of grouchy, unappreciative responses.

The stigmatized person, on the other hand, may not wish to have much of his or her behavior attributed to the stigma. He or she may feel diminished as a person by possessing a condition that "takes over" his or her personality. It might be a frustrating experience to express negative feelings without having others take them seriously, without considering them in their own right and at face value. Married couples in marked relationships might find it difficult to argue as effectively as in the pretrauma days because the normal spouse may be too "understanding."

Nevertheless, it might also be useful at times for the stigmatized person to attribute his own behavior to the stigma. He or she may not wish to think of himself or herself as an unpleasant person and may fall back on the stigma as a ready excuse for negative behavior. This can, of course, shade easily into use of the stigma to manipulate the other person in a close relationship by "getting one's way" in decisions affecting the family or dyad.

Another possible explanation for the attribution of positive and negative behavior to the stigma comes from Taylor and Fiske's (1978) and McArthur's

(1982) work on salience. They put forth that any vivid or outstanding feature is more likely to be attended to and the response to it evaluatively polarized. For example, a person who stands out in a group (a black in a group of whites, a female in a group of males) will be seen by others as more positive or more negative than the other members, depending on the value of the behavior he or she engaged in.

For a relationship such as marriage, the stigma, over time, should recede or become less vivid. It might, however, become salient when a stranger or third party joins with the dyad, as we saw in the quotation that opened this chapter. Husband and wife, therefore, must agree on how the mark is to be handled when third parties are present. For example, should the wife tell the third party about the potentially stigmatizing condition in the husband's absence? Will there be open discussion of the mark? The reactions of outsiders may be just as important to the normal spouse as to the marked spouse. People who are very close to an individual bearing a discrediting mark will often take on a "courtesy stigma" (Goffman 1963). That is, they will act as though they themselves bear the discrediting mark in the presence of a third party, and the third party may reinforce this assumption of discredit (see Chapter 2 for further discussion).

Strain

Disability may produce permanent shifts in roles played by members of the family. Carpenter (1974) found that working and nonworking wives of disabled husbands tended to handle household money. Husbands were consulted, however, on making big decisions (e.g., buying a new car). Clarity of the disability can contribute to adjustment because it reduces ambiguity concerning task responsibilities. However, with such disabilities as mental illness and drug and alcohol abuse, clarity may not lead to adjustment because disordered or disruptive behavior may be intrinsically threatening to the relationship. In a follow-up study of well and poorly functioning mental patients released from a veterans hospital, Spiegel and Wissler (1982) found that poorly functioning husbands and their wives received incongruent scores on the MOOS Family Environment Scale (Moos and Moos 1981). This incongruency score is believed to measure isolation since each partner perceives family functioning differently. The poorly functioning couples were separate while together, shared little, enjoyed little together, and were not very expressive. Well functioning mental patients and their wives received scores in the range of a normal control group (Spiegel and Wissler 1982).

Family members may not always be equipped to take on the roles required of them. Beletsis and Brown (1981) found that children of alcoholics often play parenting roles within the family and develop a precocious but shallow maturity. They took on the role required of them, but it was at a great cost; their own development suffered as a result. Other studies suggest that some people readily take on caretaking roles voluntarily and fill them rather well.

As noted in Chapter 6, Edgerton's (1967) study of previously institutionalized mildly retarded adults describes the role of the benefactor. Benefactors are husbands, family members, employers, neighbors, and professionals who help the disabled individual cope with life outside an institution. Those benefactors help the mentally retarded adult deny the condition and pass for a normal person in society. They also offer love and assurances that the retarded person is worthwhile. Edgerton calls this phenomenon "the benevolent conspiracy." He gives several examples of the most important feature of the benefactor's role in close personal relationships with the mentally retarded people in this study: "(Ex-patient, remonstrating with herself and bursting into tears about burning a shirt she was ironing) 'I'm just so stupid; I can't do anything right.' (Husband, a normal man) 'Cut that out. Anybody can burn a shirt. Don't talk that way. You're good enough to be my wife so don't talk that way'" (p. 200). An employer of the mentally retarded describes his relationships as follows: "I've had half a dozen of these Pacific people work for me over the years, and they've all had a need to be loved—I guess you could say—that it's hard to deal with them. You've got to give them attention and affection every minute or you disappoint them terribly. It's the price you've got to pay if you're going to have them around. You've got to give them love every minute and you've got to mean it. I can do it because I do like them and they know it" (p. 202).

Those benefactors were under no constraint to act as they did. "Each one had a sincere personal interest in the well being of the ex-patient that somehow made the sacrifice of time, effort and money worthwhile" (p. 204).

Informal/Voluntary Relationships (Friends)

We now turn to our next major form of interpersonal relationship, that of the informal and voluntary friend. This type of relationship may be a most important one for stigmatized people to develop and maintain. The mentally retarded adults in Edgerton's study (1967) were motivated to guard a fragile self-esteem. "They seek evidence that normal persons think well of them, regard them with affection, and accept them as worthwhile human beings" (p. 214). The voluntary nature of the relationship may be an indication of true caring on the part of the "normal" friend. Family members, coworkers, and professionals are under some obligation to interact with the stigmatized person, but the voluntary friend is not. An expression often heard in time of trouble is that one "finds out who true friends are" by virtue of their willingness to help or by virtue of their presence through good and bad times. Table 3 shows the likely effects of traumatic conditions on this type of relationship.

Ambivalence

The marked person, it seems, resolves ambivalence about former friends by withdrawing from them and eventually starting anew with different people. It might even be necessary for the marked person to make new friends, rather than clinging exclusively to the old, which may reflect the desire tc see if he or she is still capable of attracting people. Old friends may be suspected of duplicity (or at least inertia), if they continue on in a relationship. New friends chose the marked person despite its stigmatizing potential; they are less likely, therefore, to be suspected of making the choice out of pity.

Marinelli and Dell Orto (1977) report that after trauma, paraplegics experience a reduction in the number of social contacts they have, the number of different community settings they are a part of, and the number of different roles they play. After an initial withdrawal, paraplegics seemed to go through a sequential selection process about their choice of social settings and their choice of friends. They use three criteria for choosing settings—ones that were physically accessible, provided flexible opportunities for leaving the scene, and, for one reason or another, reduced the salience of the stigma. Another tactic might be to choose situations in which others would behave in an accepting manner. McCarthy (1982) reports that previous studies showed that 40 percent of young disabled adults reported church attendance as their only activity.

The sequential process by which paraplegics regained social contacts included avoiding pretrauma friendships, beginning by associating instead with individuals of lower social status, and then associating with new individuals of equal status.

An important opportunity for the development of friendships in which equal status is possible is provided on the job, but McCarthy (1982) reports that disabled individuals are often disappointed by the impersonality of the workplace. Marinelli and Dell Orto (1977) report that rehabilitation programs generally underprepare posttrauma individuals for the social and interpersonal problems that they may face.

Table 3 **The Effects of Traumatic Stigma on the Informal/Voluntary Relationship**

Feeling and Concerns Affecting the Relationship

Stigmatized Person (Traumatic stigma, e.g., paraplegia)	**Long-term Friend**
Overattribution to stigma	Need to redefine relationship (if based on activity like a sport)
Withdrawal	Denial of stigma in hopes of reinstating old relationship
Denial of stigma	Revulsion
Desire to tell friend about stigma, may overemphasize it	Withdrawal out of courtesy to imagined sensitivity of stigmatized person
Bitter, inconsolable	Feels happy the trauma didn't happen to self
Uncomfortable about special needs, unable to ask for or accept help	Feels vulnerable to death and disease
May feel infantalized, patronized if help is given by the friend	Desire to help, not knowing what to do
Fears other is remaining friendly out of pity	Ambivalence
May fear causing revulsion and fear in friend	Project feeling of own despair onto stigmatized person vis-à-vis stigma. I would feel terrible and overwhelmed if this happened to me
New role relationship (if friendship based on activity together, like a sport)	Rationalize way out of relationship
May interpret other's passivity as rejection	Desire to keep reminders of past from stigmatized person
Envious of friend for being normal	Fear of the condition itself (contagion)
Ambiguity about care needed or desired	Overattribution to stigma
Wonders what friend's other friends and acquaintances will think of the stigma.	Blame stigmatized person for burden stigma places on relationship
Wonders if friend would be ashamed that he has the condition	Guilt over negative feelings
	Ambiguity about how to help.
	Will I always have to help if I offer to help now?
	Will I be this person's only friend if I continue in the relationship?

For disabled people, the development of new friends of lower status may not wholly reflect friendships achieved only by default. The step-by-step development of self-efficacy (Bandura 1977) on the interpersonal level may require this sort of beginning, just as there are required beginnings in physical rehabilitation. One's shattered self-esteem produced by the trauma may require a reconstruction that takes time and proceeds in increments. By adopting lower-status friends, the disabled person may provide himself or herself with vital mastery experiences (e.g., being admired by a younger friend for courage, knowledge, or experience) that result in feelings of increased self-worth.

In a sense, the withdrawal from old friends and the establishment of new friends relieves the marked person of the burden of asking for help from a person from whom help was not previously needed. It relieves the stigmatized person and the friend of problems raised by uncertainty about explanatory causal attributions for supportive aid, and it relieves the strain induced by the necessity of establishing new roles.

Attribution

Making new friends does not relieve all of the burdens, but with different people the stigmatized person may avoid feeling as if he or she is constantly being compared to his or her pretrauma self. Other problems, however, may arise for the new relationship. For example, both members of the marked relationship may feel that the marker is probably befriending the marked person by default. That is, the friend may not have been successful with other preferred "normals" and is settling for a less desirable choice. Thus, attribution problems may arise in friendships with new people as well as in continuing relationships. It is also possible that the marked person may feel uncomfortable about the possibility that the new acquaintance is avoiding candid feedback concerning their acts— they are engaging in a form of "forgiveness," as illustrated in the experiment by Hastorf, Northcraft, and Picciotto (1979). Those authors found that subjects refrained from administering negative evaluations for poor performance on the part of an apparently disabled other. A "norm to be kind" prevents normals from giving accurate feedback to disabled people. In fact, the other issues mentioned earlier—clarity, ambivalence, and strain—are still important and need to be addressed in the relationship, but they may be rendered more manageable by virtue of the fact that the relationship develops after a trauma whose social implications can be at least partly understood by both members. New commitments may signal greater understanding and genuine promise of support than the attempted maintenance of old commitments under changed circumstances.

Strain

Long-term friends, in addition to sharing activities and a similar outlook on life, often fulfill various roles in their relationships with one another. Those roles may not be as clear-cut as familial role relationships, but they may be important nonetheless. When one member of the friendship becomes traumatically disabled or stigmatized, strain may be placed on the previous roles played by members. For example, in a relationship where members played adviser/advisee roles for one another, the adviser who became disabled may feel uncomfortable in the previous role.

In addition to the strain produced by an abrupt change in role relationships, there is another form of strain that can be profoundly discomforting to the smooth functioning of informal, voluntary relationships. That is the strain produced by reactions to the mark. Kleck, Ono and Hastorf (1966) and Comer and Piliavin (1972) have found that marked people and normals in short-term relationships feel uncomfortable in one another's presence. Among other things, they end conversations more quickly, avoid eye contact with one another, and feel anxious while interacting with one another. A possible explanation for this discomfort is that the participants are strained by the feeling of not knowing what to do. If one imagines interacting with a friend who has recently contracted cancer, become paraplegic, lost a baby, or gone through a divorce, it is not difficult to imagine feeling discomforted in a situation with that person.

What should be done? Should the unaffected friend mention his or her fears? Is it better to bring up the condition and joke about it or ignore it entirely?

Strain need not be wholly psychological or emotional. It can also be produced by uncertainty about ordinary physical acts. Should one help a disabled friend get around? Perhaps the friend will resent the help or feel infantalized by it. That kind of strain is usually surmounted by members of long-term relationships. It may, however, reappear when a third party interacts with the dyad.

Sex among the Disabled

Cohen, L., "Disabled Rebel at Sex Taboo," *Hartford Courant*, November 15, 1981.

The beautiful woman slinks into the room, gives her man a look that says, "come hither," and slips out

of her clothes. Susan Daniels has always been impressed with movie scenes like that. Her left arm is dead, her right arm can't do much and her right leg is almost as weak as her right arm. "I don't slip out of my clothes," she explains. "I have a war with my clothes—and I usually win."

The physically handicapped don't usually win, when the game is sex. From the moment they are blinded, deformed, paralyzed or afflicted with a spastic palsy, the handicapped are assumed to be asexual. Their genitals are assumed to be as dead as Sue Daniel's left arm, and their sexual desires are ignored or dismissed as something too disgusting to discuss. . . .

"Society has defined a role for the handicapped to play, and sex isn't part of that role," says George Allen, a counselor for the handicapped in Hartford who is blind. "We're sort of large children."

[Sue Daniels, head of rehabilitation counseling at the Louisiana State University Medical Center in New Orleans], tells the story of one institutionalized boy who asked a staff secretary for a date fifteen different times. She always declined, with a polite excuse. "Most guys learn by the time they are 15 years old that if you ask a girl out, and she has to wash her hair instead, unless she's a real knockout, you don't ask her out again. There are parameters of jerkhood. It's important to have appropriate behavior. When you're disabled, you stand out like a sore thumb. . . ."

But a growing number of disabled people do overcome the obstacles, do learn the social ropes and do cope with the awkwardness that will always make them somewhat different. . . .

Families can play an important role in teaching and in providing advice on sexuality, . . . but parents tend to concentrate on physical infirmities.

[According to Lyn Wabrek of Hartford Hospital], "The handicap has precluded the family from putting its energies into teaching social relationships. . . . I wish that sometimes they would put the braces aside—or tell the child to put the brace on himself, even if it takes five hours—and say, 'for the next hour, we're going to talk about something important.' "

The key to the sexuality issue, the experts agree, is

a recognition that sex is as real a concern for the handicapped as it is for anyone else.

Another possible explanation for the strain is that the marked person hopes to downplay the mark while the marker is busy wondering about what might be expected of him or her. A study by Hastorf, Wildfogel, and Cassman (1979) showed that acknowledgment of the mark by the marked person reduces such negative interactions. Therefore, it could be that the best method for downplaying the stigma is to acknowledge it. If the stigmatized person sets the tone for putting the stigma into perspective (it does not overwhelm him or her or constitute his or her entire being) and clarifying what is expected of the other person in the relationship, then anxiety can be reduced and the interaction can progress more smoothly.

After trauma it may be some time, however, before the affected person may learn to put others at ease. Unfortunately, many friendships voluntarily made in pretrauma days may not last through a necessary transitional period for the afflicted person. Discomfort and strain may prove to be too much to bear for many friends during this time.

We must distinguish the strain caused by a mark at a first meeting from the more subtle but still present strains that exist in long-term relationships. There may not be any "shock" in long-term relationships, but there will be the continuing hurdles of when help should be offered, dealing with a third party, or the sharing of the positive rejection by society at large.

Clarity

One would expect open and clear communication on the part of good friends about most issues and feelings, but it is apparently very difficult even for friends to breach the gap in communication where stigma is concerned. The marked person may feel terrible about asking for help from a friend, and the friend may wonder whether to proceed within the framework of the pretrauma relationship or to begin negotiations toward constructing a new framework. Clear messages of physical or emotional need may never pass between members in the relationship. Hodgins (1964) describes this matter very well:

> Help, by which I mean practical, immediate, ingenuous and efficacious help, is not nearly so likely to come from a close, dear and lifelong friend as it is from acquaintances or friends of shorter standing. . . . A close and long-time friend is deeply grooved in his relationship with you as you were. Now something has happened to you, and you are somewhat different in ways both evident and

> subtle. Your old friend stands before you, unhappy and ill-at-ease; anxious to give no outward sign that he notices anything at all and inwardly wondering how best he can readjust himself to the somewhat different you he perceives. The more recent or more casual friend need dig himself out of no such deep trench, and the perspectives by which he views you need comparatively little adjustment (p. 99).

Occupational Relationships (Coworkers)

We have seen that stigmatized people do well in relationships when they share equal status with other people. One such important arena for this kind of relationship to flourish is in the workplace. We do not know the frequency with which people purposefully change places of employment after a disabling or stigmatizing trauma. We do know that many cases of discrimination have been reported by those who are functionally disabled and by those with terminal illnesses such as cancer, but we cannot address these issues here. We will, however, focus on the effects of trauma on long-term relationships for those people who do go back to work at the same job. Table 4 shows the likely effects of traumatic marks on the marked individual and on coworkers or colleagues.

Much of what has been said in the preceding section about informal/voluntary relationships applies in the occupational relationships. One major difference, however, is the fact that coworkers cannot avoid the stigmatized person completely in the workplace. Another major difference is the fact that mastery and competence issues become prominent in the mind of the marked person, and perhaps in the mind of his or her coworkers, especially if the trauma has been functionally disabling in any way. Depending upon the nature of the workplace, competition may also play an important part in the development or maintenance of long-term relationships for the stigmatized person in his or her job.

Our same four interpersonal problems, therefore, also apply to the workplace. Marked persons and their coworkers each have ambivalent feelings toward one another. They face the clarity problems. Can the marked person definitely do his job or not? How much do coworkers need to help? They also face the attribution problem—good or bad performance on the part of the marked person may be attributed to the mark. Strain on the participants may be greater for this kind of relationship because there is no easy escape, and there is some necessity to get along for the sake of the job or company. This type of relationship, although it may not be interpersonally intimate, shares some of the characteristics of the intimate/familial relationship (e.g.,

Table 4 **The Effects of Traumatic Stigma on the Occupational Relationship (Coworker)**

Feelings and Concerns Affecting the Relationship

Stigmatized Person (Traumatic stigma, e.g., paraplegia)	**Coworker**
Ambivalence, ambiguity about care, needs	Uncertain of how to act, what to say, whether to render help
Attribution to stigma	Fear of criticizing stigmatized
Desire to demonstrate competence at job despite stigma	Ambivalence
Denial of stigma impinging on performance	Difficult to escape the relationship with the stigmatized person
Maintenance of place in hierarchy at work	Feels pity
Shame and disgrace attached to demotions, cut in salary, failure to be promoted	Fears contagion
Fear of being dependent on others to do job	Lowered expectations of stigmatized person's performance, suspicious of decreasing quality of work.
Fear of being fired	May resent special needs and treatment of stigmatized person
Feel people are critically assessing competence	Guilt for wanting to get out of the relationship
May feel like a "featherbedder" at work, tolerated out of pity	Attribute negative feelings to stigmatized person's disposition rather than situation
May not be willing or able to participate in social aspects of work	Gossip about stigmatized person
May feel left out of the social aspects of work	Reinterpretation of stigmatized person's past behavior as negative

coworkers may resent the stigmatized person for causing trouble or discomfort or for not pulling his or her own weight).

McCarthy (1982) is less optimistic for the disabled person seeking camaraderie at work. He quotes Neff (1971) as depicting the workplace as "assemblies of relative strangers with whom intimacy is both discouraged and is relatively inappropriate."

The workplace, however, may provide the marked person with an opportunity to develop comfortable relationships with others because they are limited to certain roles and bounded by time. If his or her performance is primary and adequate, the chances of developing satisfying relationships in the workplace will most likely increase.

Therapeutic Relationships ("Helping" Professionals)

The final relationship we consider is the therapeutic/professional one. We include it because we feel it to be a very important relationship for many disabled persons who are potentially or actually stigmatized. It is a relationship from the outset of asymmetrical dependence, and it generates an enormous amount of affect in stigmatized people. It might truly be called a "love/hate" relationship. Table 5 shows the likely effects of traumatic stigma on the therapeutic/professional relationship.

In a sense, the therapeutic/professional relationship is one that both parties would rather not have. The helper is motivated to make the marked person better so that he or she will not need the professional in the future. The disabled person would rather not have to be in the dependent situation of needing help at all.

The marked person and the professional face the same four issues (ambivalence, clarity, attribution, and strain) in their relationship. The marked person needs and may resent needing the professional. The professional may want to be needed, but may also need to maintain distance from the marked person. That distance, in part, may be for the patient's sake—the doctor must retain a professional manner in the face of upsetting and debilitating illness. Sir William Osler taught the medical students of his day to "educate your nerve centres so that not the slightest dilator or contractor influence shall pass to the vessels of your face under any professional trial." (Osler 1951, p. 90). This distance may also be necessary for the professional so that the extremity of the patient's feelings does not become his or her own.

After being told that there was nothing more the doctor could do for her husband, Lear wanted to just talk so that she could make her situation more bearable. The doctors were willing, but asked her to wait two weeks until the next regular appointment. Lear (1980) writes about this incident: "You cannot tell me how to make it bearable. That is not your specialty. In fact, it is precisely because that is what you cannot do, that being what they never trained you to deal with, that you will now begin to avoid me. Us. Not medically . . . but in other, ambiguous ways, none remotely conscious. You will call rather less often . . . you will sigh when they say, 'Mrs. Lear is on the line' " (p. 347).

Table 5 **The Effects of Traumatic Stigma on the Therapeutic Relationship ("Helping" Professional)**

Feelings and Concerns Affecting the Relationship

Stigmatized Person (Traumatic stigma, e.g., paraplegia)	"Helping" Professional
Ambivalence: resentment, gratitude	Trained to treat stigmatized person as an instance of a disease category
Resentment for being needy	Need to distance self, yet maintain empathy
Rage at doctor for inability to "cure"	May doubt own ability for intimacy outside of work
Out of control of own care (react with depression or hostility, clinging dependency)	May feel wanted, appreciated
Difficulty accepting self as a category of people with a particular illness or condition	Need to cure, professional self-esteem may depend on it
Professionals get paid for caretaking, don't really care about the stigmatized person	Disappointed in patients who do not get well
Feels intimate with professional but it is not reciprocated	Resentment
Gratitude and respect for expertise	Ambivalence
Worry about disappointing doctor who wants to "cure"	Attribution problems, person seen as case
Sense of personal failure if not cured or making progress	
Distrust	
Worry about competence of professionals	
Fear of telling truth, worry about appearing weak	
Professional can go home, has an outside life that doesn't include the stigmatized person	
Resented for hardships stigmatized person must bear in treatments (effects of drugs, hair falling out)	
Age, race, sex of professional may affect patient's trust	
Feels professionals to be sadistic or patronizing	
Resents professional enforcing rules	
Desires to "informalize" the relationship	
Sensitive to kind of treatment given by professionals—an indicator of self-worth (if treated badly feels self as blameworthy for stigma)	
Wants to do away with need for the professionals (in a sense doesn't want a relationship with professionals)	

Lear's dying husband, Hal, a doctor himself, told his wife "When nothing more can be done do you know what doctors wish? They wish that the patient would die. Not consciously, of course, but that is what they wish. Because as long as the patient lives, he is a reproach. He is a constant reminder of what doctors do not want to face" (p. 461).

Ambivalence may also be caused by the formal nature of the relationship—the marked patient is giving the professional a fee and the professional is rendering a service. The professional is often criticized for the quality of his or her service and may suspect that the patient not only doubts his or her professional ability, but may someday sue for malpractice.

Parents of disabled children complain that the interviews with the doctors are brief, that the medical jargon interferes with communication, that the lack of definitive diagnosis is upsetting, that the unwillingness of the doctor to discuss the cause of the illness and focus on the cure is frustrating and unsatisfying, that doctors' lack of knowledge and disinterest in self-help groups prevents getting immediate emotional and practical help for the family, and that doctors are not comfortable with feelings (Featherstone 1981).

The isolation a parent feels when a child is born disabled is exacerbated by the lack of a clear diagnosis and a lack of available agency support. McMichael (1971) writes: "It is usually many months, and even may be years, before parents see any specialized agency with experience in the problems of handicapped children" (p. 86).

The clarity problem is of utmost importance in this relationship. In order to help the marked person, the helpers must know the marked person's concerns and symptoms. A therapeutic alliance must be based on open and clear communication (e.g., concern about sexual functioning in a paraplegic or a heart attack patient) for the treatment to be effective. A helper cannot allay fears or help solve problems if he or she does not know what they are or to what extent the patient has concerns about them.

The attribution problem in this kind of relationship may also be of great importance. The marked person may feel objectified or dehumanized by being treated as a case or an instance of a disease entity. Lear (1980) describes one of many instances of being treated as a case: "He had been wakened from a sound sleep so that medical students could listen to his heart—collecting heart sounds, he said, as though they were bird sounds—and he had told them off. 'I'm not just an interesting heart sound,' he had told them. 'I'm a tired *person*' " (p. 448). Since most doctors are now specialists, it is rare to develop a relationship with a general practitioner who often sees patients when they are relatively healthy. Most therapeutic relationships with disabled persons require specialists. The specialist sees many such cases, but the disabled person sees only a few professionals. The disabled person may resent the professional who attributes his behavior to the stigmatized condition. He or she may feel depersonalized like an object or a case.

There is also some evidence that professionals may come to resent their patients. Yukor, Block, and Young (1966) report that negative attitudes develop toward the disabled or infirm over time in hospital and medical workers.

Maslach and Jackson (1981; 1982) and Jackson and Maslach (1982) have studied a similar phenomenon and have referred to it as the "burn out" syndrome. They believe that "burn out" involves three components. Professionals who play a caretaking role experience emotional exhaustion, depersonalization of the people they care for, and a feeling of reduced personal competence. In her surveys, Maslach has found that professionals responsible for the direct care of people who have chronic problems (nurses and nurse's aides who care for patients directly, as opposed to doctors who write orders and leave personal caretaking to others) are those people who experience "burn out." The precipitating set of circumstances, therefore, is caring for people who do not improve over a long period of time.

Strain is perhaps less of an important issue for this type of relationship because the roles are clear-cut. The stigmatized person, however, may wish to become closer to the professional than the professional would like or is able to allow. We assume that most people work out this relationship after a period of negotiation.

Although we do not know how prevalent it is, some professionals do allow such relationships to develop, and it is not unusual for the disabled person to become romantically involved with and marry a professional. These relationships often involve much close physical contact and caretaking (e.g., a physical therapist working with a paraplegic on a rehabilitation unit for some months).

SUMMARY AND CONCLUSIONS

We do not wish to imply that the kinds of relationships we have described necessarily vary in depth or superficiality. We believe that in each realm the relationships can be intense and very important. Some stigmatized persons put most of their energy and value in their family life, while others place more emphasis on their work. We also do not wish to imply that all relationships for stigmatized people have predominantly negative elements; we have focused on potential problems, rather than potential beneficial changes, brought on by the presence of the stigma.

Since we need more knowledge about the development and maintenance of close long-term relationships in "normal" people, we can only infer that they are qualitatively different or more difficult for stigmatized people. We do know that the mark is generally a burden that has to be dealt with by the members of the marked relationship.

The question is how further to study this problem. We feel that longitudinal studies of the interpersonal lives of the stigmatized should be undertaken. Those studies, to be effective, must follow the course of the relationship over an extended period of time. They would offer some hope for gathering the kind of information we deem essential for understanding marked or stigmatized people and their dilemma. Even with a longitudinal approach, however, the study of relationships with marked people becomes further complicated by the many types of potentially stigmatizing conditions and by the numerous problems that are involved in assessing the private thoughts that accompany observable interactions. It would be useful, perhaps, to adopt the approach taken here; that is, to try to find issues that would be common to the many forms of stigmata and that would cut across the many kinds of relationships. For example, is it really adaptive for marked people and their partners to communicate openly *all* of their feelings to one another? We saw that when the effects of the mark were clear (the person was definitely sexually impaired), people were happier with their lot. But how far should this clarity be taken? Would it be functional for the wife of a Vietnam veteran to agree openly with her distraught and suicidal husband that his behavior in war was indeed monstrous and inhumane? We think not. We do think, however, that taking such issues as clarity, attribution, ambivalence, or strain produced by changes in roles and studying them exhaustively may lead to a further understanding of marked relationships and perhaps of normal relationships as well.

Our stance is that increasing clarity appears to be a positive benefit, in the long run, even if it produces a short run increase in personal anguish and interpersonal strain. Open communication appears to be necessary and adaptive up to a point. Ambivalence reduction—especially if it results in generally positive feelings—appears to be functional, because if members of a relationship are chronically avoiding commitment, the relationship may not be very satisfying to either party. Does acknowledgment of the stigma really work to make long-term relationships better, or would a healthy denial play an ameliorative role? We do know that "normal" subjects do not like to listen to depressed people over the telephone. It makes them feel depressed (Coyne 1976). Marked people report that they quickly learn that others do not wish to dwell on negative aspects of the marked conditions. Simpson (1982), after her miraculous recovery from tubercular meningitis, states: "If I whine, I will be avoided. If I attempt what others believe I will fail at doing, I will make them tense and nervous in my presence. But if I make them comfortable because I present myself as relaxed and self-confident, they will allow me to take chances and to manage for myself without dependence on others or without their feeling obliged to offer intrusive help" (p. 156). Simpson did not allow her illness to define her, to assume a "master status."

We also know that people react more favorably to stigmatized people whom they consider as not blameworthy for their condition (De Jong 1980). Do actual friendships form more easily for marked people who are not held blameworthy for their condition? The attribution problem is more complicated. It might be useful at times for the marked person and his or her partner to attribute behavior and feelings to situations rather than to dispositions (Ross 1977, Nisbett and Ross 1980). That is, the stigmatizing condition does cause a lot of suffering and discomfort. It might be important for marked persons and their families to understand that negative feelings and behaviors do often arise from the burden of coping with stigmas. The realistic attribution of causes to the stigma is warranted in those cases. Many self-help groups for the stigmatized person and his or her family, and the "process" meetings among the staff in hospitals, do function to alleviate dispositional attributions of blame or inadequate coping. Self-help groups can play an ameliorative role in the lives of many stigmatized people (Spiegel 1976).

However, this propensity to shift the attribution to the mark can be dysfunctional. If the marked person's behavior is never taken at face value, he or she may feel unable to be a true actor or participant in a relationship. Or, if a marked person's family denies his or her negative dispositional qualities by attributing them to the condition, there may be no room for positive growth for either the person or the family members. As a result the marked person may be allowed special privileges in the family, a development that does not foster maturation and independence. If the mark is allowed to assume the master status of stigma, then the stigmatized person relates not as a person but as an object, a case, or condition.

For some families it is very difficult to reconcile the appropriate status of the disabled member. Featherstone (1981), whose child, Jody, is blind, hydrocephalic, retarded, and has cerebral palsy and seizures, struggles to define Jody's place in the family. When a normal child in the family questioned her parents' conviction that people were more important than animals because they possessed consciousness (understanding and fear of death), Featherstone reacted this way:

> We had not examined our own ideas. What if the family dog understood more than Jody? Would we value the dog more highly than our son? No. Yet surely our answer led that way.
>
> We asked friends and students why people mattered more than animals. My sister-in-law answered: "We value people because we are people. . . . We love Jody because he is like us." This argument raises as many problems as it settles. It brings us back once again to the whole question of deviance and disability. If we value people because they resemble us, where does this leave the people who are different? Yet I think she is right: at bottom we value other people because the conjunction of difference and similarity reinforces a sense of common humanity. We ourselves are like, and yet not like, others. There is very little difference between one man and another, William James says, but what difference there is, is very important" (p. 237).

Featherstone disqualifies Jody's condition as a master status when she says, "He is part of a web of shared experience. He makes us aware of our own fragility and limitations, and of how much we share with people whose interests and circumstances differ dramatically from our own. He 'contributes' in his own quiet way" (p. 236).

In this chapter we have attempted to reduce a large and varied problem—that of long-term marked relationships—to a manageable set of issues that might lend themselves to fruitful investigation. We examined the kinds of relationships that marked persons may experience with spouse, friends, coworkers, and professionals. We also examined the implications that the type of mark may have for a particular relationship.

From an examination of the different types of marks and their implications for the varied types of relationships, we derived four interpersonal problems that may occur in such relationships. They were the problems of ambivalence, clarity, attribution, and strain. We found each of these problems to be potentially present in all the types of relationships and for most kinds of marking conditions, although we presented only traumatic marks in our discussion of the four interpersonal problems.

It is difficult to approach the study of stigma with confidence because it is subject to frequent shifting of ground. There are so many kinds of potential stigmas, and there are so many different lives and relationships that become affected by their presence that as soon as one begins to identify or grasp an issue relevant to one type of stigma, an exception immediately springs to mind. A person with paraplegia, an ex-mental patient, and a person with black skin may have very little in common, yet all may have been objects of derision and disdain in their interactions with others. We believe that the approach taken here might help to unify the study of the interpersonal relationships of stigmatized people.

• CHAPTER NINE •

Some Conclusions and Implications

IN THIS FINAL CHAPTER, we have three objectives: we hope to pull together the major themes of the preceding chapters, summarize the problems posed for individuals and for society by stigma within marked relationships, and consider the possibility of reducing or isolating those stigma commonly found in contemporary society. We will also elucidate some of the values shared by the authors and move tentatively from analysis to application.

MAJOR THEMES

The preceding chapters have attempted to explore the terrain of stigma, with special reference to relationships between people with and people without major stigmatizing attributes. We have labeled these "marked relationships" and referred to markables and markers to distinguish between the member of the relationship who is the potential victim of stigmatization and the potential stigmatizer. We have considered marked relationships from a number of different perspectives, cognizant of the difficulties of saying anything about them that would apply to all of them. Despite the difficulties in generalizing about such diverse conditions, the following general themes, or propositions, have emerged, and their recital serves to summarize our major conclusions.

Common Processes of Stigmatization

The first major theme is, in fact, the basic premise that justifies this volume: Stigmatization is an identifiable, important social phenomenon that reflects several common processes. One process is *categorization*, the tendency to lump people together and to generalize about central personal characteristics from superficial features. Categorization creates expectancies that shape the course of interaction within both casual and long-term relationships. Stigmatization is an extreme form of categorical inference, whereby some clue regarding membership, some physical mark, or some bit of observed or reported deviant behavior gives rise to drastic attributional outcomes. Often, we have stressed, these attributions "engulf" the identity of the individual; they become the filter through which his or her other characteristics are seen. They are also imbued with strong affect, primarily negative in tone.

An important feature of this characterization process is that, in addition to being extreme, it is in several senses *arbitrary*. That is, the affect generated is not appropriate, not justified by the actual consequences of the mark for the marker or the necessary consequences of the mark for the relationship. There is, thus, insufficient cognitive support for those negative feelings aroused in the categorization process. A major consequence of this is the presence of derivative emotional reactions, such as guilt and sympathy. The mixture of positive and negative emotions can be labeled *ambivalence*, a commonly observed feature of the stigmatizing process.

We have also noted in numerous contexts the putative role of the *just world hypothesis* in contributing to stigma. There is substantial experimental and anecdotal evidence to suggest that it is difficult to come to terms with catastrophic accidents or illnesses without blaming the victim or entertaining the assumption that he or she for some reason deserved to be ugly, crippled, or devastated by mental illness. This may even be found in the victim's suspicions about his own unworthiness.

The stigmatizing process is also facilitated in complex ways by the *social functions* served by the labeling and negative treatment of deviants. Although most of the deviant types we have talked about are not a direct threat to our personal security or well-being, they do pose a symbolic threat to group identity and cohesion. The distinctive labeling of deviants can reaffirm in-group values, emphasize in-group superiority, and thereby promote solidarity.

To summarize, the stigmatizing process involves engulfing categorizations accompanied by negative affect that is typically alloyed into ambivalence or rationalized through some version of a just world hypothesis. The process can serve a social function, and the rewards of in-group solidarity feelings may help to sustain the process once the labeling of deviance occurs.

Variations of the Mark

Having first emphasized the common features of the stigmatizing process, we must quickly note that these processes are affected by variations in the particular characteristics of the deviant mark. As we leave the rather high level of abstraction assumed by the preceding discussion, we encounter concrete variations having important consequences. Thus, it makes a difference to marked relationships whether the mark is concealable, whether it is socially disruptive, whether it is aesthetically displeasing, or whether and how it imperils the markers. Various aspects of the mark's origin and projected course are also important. A major proposition is that these variations are less important in casual interactions, interactions governed by concerns of face-saving and potential social discomfort, than they are in long-term intimate relationships.

Self-stigmatization

An important emphasis in the stigma literature has been the conversion of actual or presumed stigmatization by others into self-stigmatization. In general, it has been assumed that at one level or another of personal reactions, the stigmatized person accepts the discredit conveyed by society and discredits himself. Even without such passive acceptance of the in-group consensus, the stigmatized person will at least bear certain unfortunate consequences of being stigmatized or victimized. Such traits of victimization can include denial, aggressive counterattack, glorification of the mark, and so on.

The reaction of markables in the marking and stigmatizing process has been a recurrent focus of our analysis. We have noted the sad outcomes of self-stigmatization along with the traits of victimization, but we have also noted elements of growth and mature understanding in the responses of many victims to the tragedies that befall them. One cannot help but be impressed with the remarkable resiliency of human beings. In addition, an important theme has been the variation in impact, depending on how the self of the markable person is organized. Is he or she "self-schematic" in ways that will amplify or mute the significance of the mark?

Discomfort and Discredit

The distinction between discomfort and discredit has also been a recurrent theme, although not always identified in those terms. We have tried to reserve the concept of stigma for outcomes of a discrediting process, where the target person is viewed as morally flawed and arouses revulsion in the marker. We have noted on many occasions, however, that marked relationships can be awkward and problematical, even when the element of discredit is not involved. We can identify here two kinds of discomfort. The first stems from *communication breakdown*. Such breakdowns can take many forms, but they center on the marker's uncertainty concerning how the markable person prefers to be treated. They include barriers to the validation of credibility. Even when the marker openly attempts to share his or her feelings, or even when the marker, in fact, responds without considering the mark, the markable person may have doubts about the authenticity of the marker's behavior and suspect that he would really prefer to be somewhere, or with someone, else. The markable person may also have difficulty establishing credibility when he claims that the mark is of minimal significance or a genuine source of pride.

The second type of discomfort is largely restricted to long-term relationships. This is the discomfort associated with establishing *mutually acceptable patterns of interdependence.* The marker needs to work through the problems of nurturance and become sensitive to the circumstances under which the markable person does or does not need help, wants or does not want attention drawn to the mark. In addition, in the case of marked relationships featuring disability, one can include the discomfort costs associated with what we might call housekeeping duties—the sheer time- and energy-consuming nuisance of the requirements of nursing interventions.

Avoidance tendencies, and tendencies to limit interactions to minimal role requirements, may reflect those types of anticipated discomfort, discredit, or both. Although stigma phenomena are common, it is also the case that markable persons can erroneously assume that they are discredited in the eyes of others, an assumption that can lead to obvious relationship problems in the absence of actual stigma. That is one point at which stereotypes—and stereotypes about stereotypes—can enter the process to convert perceived awkwardness and other signs of discomfort into perceived rejection and discredit. It may be the case, therefore, that the frequency or ubiquitousness of stigma is considerably less than might be assumed by marked persons themselves. Such a conclusion would, however, be extremely difficult to verify and might be highly contingent on the nature of the mark involved.

The Extent of Stigmatization

Although cases of "full-blown" stigma may tend to be overestimated by marked persons, it is still the case that various components or aspects of the stigmatizing process are extremely widespread in everyday life. In fact, a major purpose of this volume has been to convince the reader that stigma is a problem that we all share, that we all confront in one way or another. Issues of marking and potential discredit are constantly intruding on everyday life. We deal not with oddities in the back wards of social life, but with issues that commonly intertwine with other features of social discourse. Each of us has some understanding of how it feels to be marked—we have all been there. Similarly, we have all from time to time reflected on our own marking behavior, stopping to wonder whether our negative impressions of someone are justified, or whether we are unfairly reacting to superficial features.

If this is the case, then the study of stigma is made more important by its actuarial prominence. In addition, however, we have stressed that the *processes* are no more unique than the outcomes are ubiquitous. Thus, a persistent theme has been the yield of focusing on stigma for a deeper understanding of such crucial social psychological issues as categorization and the development of expectancies, cognition-affect relationships, social comparison processes, changes in the self-concept, dissonance processes, and many others that are not exclusively designed to account for stigma.

Dynamics of Marked Relationships

Finally, we have focused on the dynamics of marked relationships and how they may be transformed by activities of the marked person as well as the marker. Relationships can move in the often unfortunate direction of self-fulfilling prophecies. Initial stereotypes or expectancies lead to marker actions that elicit confirming behavior from the markable person. That characterizes some relationships more than others. The degree of expectancy confirmation depends importantly on the nature of the expectancy, and the inevitability of expectancy-behavior linkages. It also depends on the power context of the interaction and on the strategic resources of the markable person. There are a number of strategies available to marked persons that can enable them to escape the stigmatization process or to reduce its significance for social interaction. By studying various processes of deviance disavowal, one establishes contact with the broader literature of self-presentation and sheds light on the potential for active impression management in both normal and marked relationships.

LEARNING NOT TO LIVE WITH STIGMA

In most of the previous chapters, we have taken the phenomena of stigma as givens and expressed our fascination and sense of challenge. We have attempted to analyze and conceptualize, to stand aside and summarize anecdotal and experimental data in a effort to understand the determinants and dynamics of a complex and consequential process. A paradoxical outcome of such an exposure of determinants and dynamics might be a fatalistic conclusion that a certain level of stigmatization is an inevitable, intractable feature of any social group. After all, if stereotypes are normal by-products of the inevitable selecting and packaging of data from a complex world, if the identification and discrediting of deviants promotes in-group solidarity, and if people have primitive affective responses to others that they cannot control, will stigma not always be with us?

Contemporary cognitive approaches to stereotyping in social psychology, as well as the labeling perspective in sociology, are alike in projecting a rather weary fatalism. The subprocesses involved in stigmatization are seen as either ingrained human proclivities or as social imperatives, essential for the maintenance of social control in heterogeneous societies. The present authors have tried to resist this conclusion. It is obvious that the concrete manifestations of the "tendency to stigmatize" change over time, over settings, and across cultures. It might be tempting to conclude that stigmatization is an intractable problem, but that any given stigma is tractable—i.e., its effects can be minimized. We see no reason to assume that the level of stigmatization is necessarily fixed—either for individuals or for societies. We are optimistic that the frequency and intensity of stigmatization can be reduced in our society through a greater recognition of our avenues of susceptibility and a fuller understanding of the negative social consequences of stigma.

Perhaps the appearance of fatalism arises from the social scientist's tendency to assume that what is must be. Perhaps a deliberate focus on processes of change will help to overcome such assumptions. If our faith that the general tendency to stigmatize can be reduced is justified, is the reduction of stigmatizing tendencies in society on balance necessarily a good thing? Is "destigmatization" an important social objective? Are the conditions for minimizing stigma worthy foci for research and social policy? Our answer to each of these questions is yes, and for the following reasons.

First, our values as scientists must inevitably pit us against irrationality, overgeneralization, and the misplaced rationalization of affect. The same values direct us toward careful, accurate, and appropriate attributional analysis, bringing us as close as possible to an understanding of the actual determinants of our own and others' actions in our relationships. Such analyses are necessary to weigh in against the pernicious "just world hypothesis," a hypothesis that subverts the attribution process by introducing a form of divine equity—there must be a God or a supreme regulator who makes sure that people only get what they deserve. As Kushner (1981) vigorously and convincingly argues, bad things do happen to good people. If the "just world hypothesis" can be held in check, stigma will at least be more confined to instances in which the individual is morally responsible for his own mark.

A case can sometimes be made for the social and individual benefits of "benign" self-deceptions and self-enhancing attributions but there are also bound to be long-range costs of such erroneous human inferences. Most social scientists believe, and we are among them, that accuracy and clarity of attributional understanding is generally beneficial to human welfare and to social adaptation. Such a belief may be most dramatically exemplified in the sphere of international relations, where the knowledge that one nation has concerning the true motives and goals of another may be a critical determinant of war or of peace. We would assert that attributional clarity is also a factor in the health of millions of relationships between individual people, although the consequences of any one of these relationships may be less apocalyptic than planetary survival.

Second, it is also highly debatable whether the vigorous labeling and discrediting of deviants actually facilitates group cohesion and solidarity. It is popularly assumed that in-groups need out-groups in order to define and assert their own values or membership criteria. Those who remember World War II can testify to the boost of patriotic solidarity that appeared to derive from the presence of common enemies. Undoubtedly, too, the holocaust was in part motivated by the assumption that it would consolidate and unify the Aryan in-group. This is an area, therefore, in which analysis can be treacherous and in which apparent gains in solidarity must be balanced against other values and goals. Ethnocentrism would seem to be a vehicle for the achievement of a certain type of in-group solidarity, but ethnocentrism clearly threatens the solidarity of larger, more inclusive in-groups. We have affirmed the symbolic significance of stigmatization as a way of defining what is normal by casting out the abnormal. That contributes to our understanding of stigma as a social process, but more constructive ways might be found to reaffirm those group values that are essential for solidarity—more constructive, that is, than runaway attributions that engulf deviant persons in a pervasive aura of discredit.

In-group cohesion is perhaps served by the humor of stigma—Jewish jokes, Polish jokes, moron jokes, or preppy jokes—but there is a fine and important line between jokes told with supercilious malice and jokes that lighten the entire issue of deviance by casting stereotypes in a ridiculous extreme. The profound if hackneyed point is that group solidarity can actually be strengthened by an acceptance of the values of diversity. In a truly successful democracy, perhaps, the stigmatizer would be the deviant, and we would be writing books about the unfortunate consequences of engulfing the stigmatizer in discredit.

A final reason for doing whatever we can to reduce stigma is perhaps the most important and the most poignant. It can be briefly stated: The psychic pain of feeling rejected and discredited, of surmising that others want to avoid you and can barely suppress their revulsion in your presence, must be of concern to anyone with a capacity for human empathy. If we add to this pain of discredit the untold moments of awkwardness and discomfort in marked relationships, it is obvious that we would all be happier if marking and stigmatizing processes could be minimized and their effects reduced.

PROCESSES OF DESTIGMATIZATION

Having concluded that many of the consequences of stigma are dysfunctional both for the individual and for society, we now consider some of the ways in which those consequences might be minimized. We will focus not on the deviance disavowal strategies of the individual, a topic we have covered at numerous points in the preceding chapters, but on the processes whereby the categories eliciting the reactions of stigma evolve and change over time. That is a topic about which little is known, but understanding the conditions of stigma evolution and control is obviously of extreme importance, so we shall attempt to offer a few tentative speculations.

We begin by noting that destigmatization may involve the reduction of a mark's attributional salience, positive changes in its valence, or both. To the extent that stigma refers to an "engulfing identity" or a "master status," destigmatization could be said to occur only when a social category ceases to be as socially significant or engulfing. On the other hand, if we wish to use the term *stigma* to refer to any discredited or devalued mark, destigmatization could be said to occur whenever the mark becomes more positively evaluated. Change in the valence attached to the mark may be necessary for a reduction of master status quality, but it is not sufficient. Consider the difference between divorce and homosexuality. The valence attached to the mark of divorce certainly has become more positive over the past few decades, and the mark of divorce would seem to be less engulfing than it was previously. The mark of homosexuality, on the other hand, would seem to have undergone a similar decrease in negative valence over the past decade or two, but it is not transparently clear the mark of homosexuality is any less engulfing. It is also the case that ethnic or tribal memberships can rapidly change valence without as rapidly losing or gaining attributional salience. Being Japanese may be somewhat less engulfing to most Americans than it was during World War II; the valence of this ethnic category, however, has undergone even more striking changes. Similar changes in valence have occurred in modern times with regard to other ethnic categories (e.g., the Irish, Jewish people), but it is again less clear that there has been a corresponding reduction in attributional salience or significance.

Perhaps the point can be made more forcefully when we consider changes in the significance of deviance with regard to body weight. Toward the end of World War II in Germany, there was a severe scarcity of food and few people had as much to eat as they would have liked. The typical citizen was undernourished and underweight. Only very important and powerful people had food in abundance, and their enviable position was indicated by their corpulence. Hence, fatness came to signify social power and distinction, obesity itself came to be admired and desired, and, with the increased availability of food, fat Germans eventually became common. Thus, we may arrive at the interesting conclusion that obesity is particularly degrading only in societies where food is abundant and readily accessible. In the German example, the category of "fat" remained equally salient while undergoing radical shifts in valence or favorability. It is more difficult, in general, to think of examples where the valence of a mark remains the same but its significance for interpersonal relations is reduced.

"Accidental" Social Forces and Destigmatization

There are, of course, persistent efforts by educators and ministers, and by stigmatized groups themselves, to bring about increased tolerance and reduced stigmatization. Those efforts may be better understood and evaluated, however, if we first take a broader look at some of the historical forces that affect, as a by-product, attitudes toward different categories of people. We have already touched upon the impact of wars on shifting ethnic attitudes, and the impact of variations in national prosperity on the value attached to obesity. Any dramatic historical event has the capacity to produce altered responses to those involved. To take some examples from recent history: stereotypes toward Iranians were undoubtedly affected by the hostage crisis; Argentinians are no doubt viewed differently as a consequence of the Falklands-Malvinas war; and Polish jokes now seem inappropriate to the new view of heroic Solidarity figures and others who have risked their freedom to express antagonism to governmental control and intervention.

Within a complex, heterogeneous society like America, the linkage of change to social status is extremely important. Potentially stigmatizing marks have a vastly different fate, depending on whether they are associated with high or low social status—with wealth, prestige, and "winners," or with poverty, ignorance, and "losers." Certain "deviant" behaviors are inherently expensive, and may take on cachet because of that. The use of cocaine seems almost restricted to the wealthy, and users are, by and large, less stigmatized than heroin addicts. One reason for this may be the association of heroin use with squalid surroundings and "buys" financed by muggings and larceny. The popular image of cocaine does not include such discordant notes. If the divorce rate climbs, the impact of this on stigma is crucially affected by its association with class. If an increase in divorce were associated primarily with the lower classes, then it would presumably become more stigmatizing to be divorced. It would be an indication of the inability of inadequate persons to manage the problems of getting along with others. On the other hand, if the increase were associated with opportunities provided by at least moderate wealth, divorce might even become positively chic. Climbing divorce rates among the middle and upper classes might generate concern about the dissolution of the American family, a structural interpretation that itself would facilitate destigmatization of divorce.

No doubt there is a contrast relevant to stigma between "being in psychotherapy" and "being in analysis." The former, as we have noted, is viewed by many as a stigmatizing confession of a state of mental illness sufficiently extreme to be beyond self-help. The latter indicates the ability to afford the luxury of leisurely self-examination. It connotes an intellectual journey that liberates creative impulses, rather than a treatment to reduce a stigmatizing illness, which thereby signifies its presence and its severity.

Deviance and social status are linked in various ways that go well beyond the role of money in paying the price of certain forms of deviant behavior. In the realm of mental illness, for example, the social class of patients and their families plays a crucial role as a determinant of diagnosis and treatment, and undoubtedly, therefore, as a determinant of the degree of stigma attached. When England's George III suffered a mental breakdown early in the nineteenth century, there were dramatic repercussions for the care and treatment of the "insane." Fashionable doctors were suddenly motivated to become acquainted with the management of mental illness, and the stigma attached to such conditions was reduced as pressure rose to treat many cases of mental illness in their own homes rather than exclusively in asylums (Hunter and Macalpine 1963, p. 960). That historical example can be easily buttressed by more contemporary findings that show the relationship between social class and mental disorder (cf. Dohrenwend and Dohrenwend 1969).

Social class plays a similarly important role as a determinant of criminal sentencing (Hogarth 1971; Wheeler, Weisburd and Bode 1982). Jurors and physicians are notably selective in their application of potentially stigmatizing labels. Social class has a great deal to do with this selectivity.

"We Shall Overcome": Group Militancy and Self-Help

Against the backdrop of these shifting social forces, themselves a complex product of historical circumstances, the role of activism by stigmatized groups is obviously an important destigmatizing impetus. Perhaps the most radical and far-reaching development in the past thirty years, as far as stigma-in-society is concerned, has been the innovation of organized efforts by various stigmatized groups to change society's image of them. Prior to World War II, the landscape of protolerance activism was dotted by a few organizations that we now view as rather conservative in their tactics. Examples were the Urban League (founded in 1910), the National Association for the Advancement of Colored People (founded in 1909), and the Anti-Defamation League (founded in 1913), each primarily concerned with education and litigation to protect the status of ethnic minorities.

It was not until the 1950s that the black power movement got its start. In many ways that was the prototype of later campaigns by stigmatized groups—not just to protect their rights and their legal status, but actively to transform the valence of category membership. Instead of attempting to reduce the attributional salience of race, the black power movement attempted to *increase* the salience while changing the valence from negative to positive. One black organization after another followed the "black is beautiful" theme with varying degrees of enthusiasm, and the white majority was at least forced to reevaluate their silent assumptions about blacks being content with their (inferior) place. Black power pressures ushered in a new era of public sensitivity. Symbolic of this was the virtual disappearance of the words "colored" and "negro" (to say nothing of "nigger" or "nigra") in the brief period between 1965 and 1970. If the black power movement also aroused resentment and private ridicule in certain quarters of the majority or the "establishment," it nevertheless struck a dramatic blow for black pride and dignity, a blow that undoubtedly had significant enhancing effects on the self-esteem of young black citizens.

The success of the black power movement—for example, in affecting court decisions and executive policies regarding affirmative action—could hardly have been lost on other stigmatized groups. Many of these groups, such as the Disabled Veterans of America, have been primarily concerned with information-sharing and litigation concerning physical access. Others, however, have been more directly involved in destigmatizing their image. That is certainly true of the Little People of America, the National Association for Retarded Citizens, and the Mental Patients Liberation Project.

In recent years, the most dramatic example of attempted destigmatization through group activism is the gay rights movement. That movement has many similarities to the black power movement, with most of the major differences arising from the concealable nature of the stigma. Thus, a prominent goal of the gay rights movement has been to augment its impact by increasing its numbers—by urging homosexuals to "come out of the closet." But other goals have resembled those sought by blacks—legal protection, equal access to housing and employment, and the avoidance of public labels that imply derision. (An excellent recent discussion of changing social conceptions of the homosexual may be found in D'Emilio, 1983.)

It is not easy to evaluate the total impact of group efforts to change the majority's image of them. It is important to consider both immediate and long-range effects, while also considering the distinction between public policy and legal protection on the one hand, and private attitudes of the majority on the other. One feasible model would show immediate effects of group demands on particular kinds of legal changes. Some of these changes undoubtedly bring about changes in underlying attitude, if not in the short run, then in the longer run, as the legal protections are perceived as unexceptional "givens" by new generations. Thus, we do not believe in the blanket statement that you "cannot legislate morals," as so many conservative pundits tried to say after the 1954 Supreme Court decision on desegregation. Social psychological research has taught us a great deal about the conditions under which public compliance leads to private attitude change. Legislation can certainly affect behavior, and if there are elements of choice in the compliance, there should be changes in attitude to "justify" the new behavior.

CAN EVEN PEDOPHILIA BE DESTIGMATIZED?

Nelson, B., "Eton Patz Case Puts New Focus on a Sexual Disorder, Pedophilia," *New York Times*, January 4, 1983.

When disturbing new evidence recently revived the case of Eton Patz, the six-year-old boy who disappeared three years ago near his home in Manhattan, [it was brought out that] the police continue to investigate the possibility that Eton was abducted to be sexually used.

The statements of the North American Man-Boy Love Association focused the attention of an incredulous public on the fact that there are not only people

> **who have sexual relations with children, but who publicly assert that it has benevolent effects. At a news conference last week in New York, a spokesman for the association would not say at what age his group thought that a boy was too young to give informed consent to have sexual relations with an adult. . . .**
>
> **Most homosexual groups have been just as severe as heterosexual ones in condemning sexual relations with children. Lesbian groups have been especially adamant in condemning such practices. . . .**
>
> **The pedophile often tells himself that he is doing the child a favor by providing more care and affection than the child would otherwise receive. . . . Some of the few people who publicly support sexual relations between adult and children point to prior periods when such practices were prevalent, such as in ancient Greece. Sexuality experts, however, note that the unions then were between men and adolescents, not younger children. Moreover, the relationships were institutionalized as a "mentorship," and the boys were supposed to leave this period of their lives to resume heterosexual development.**

On the other hand, there is the potential of such group pressures producing antagonism and "backlash." It could be argued that much of the appeal of the Reagan campaign in 1980 was nostalgia by the white middle class majority for the days before affirmative action and busing made life more complicated. Reagan ushered in an administration whose major figures soon made it apparent that they would ride, if not lead, a backlash countering the federally sponsored racial advances of the 1960s and 1970s. It is hard to discern the intensity or forecast the fate of the current backlash, but a consideration of various possibilities does suggest that minority militancy runs serious risks when it substitutes power and disruption for moral appeal. The majority, once mobilized to confront a threat defined primarily in terms of power, obviously has more power than the minority. Thus, minority militancy can best succeed if it applies its power realistically to redress morally indefensible grievances. It will produce intransigence, and later backlash, to the extent that it summarily reduces the sense of freedom of individual members of the majority, thereby producing a state of psychological reactance (Brehm and Brehm 1981) that motivates attempts to restore the threatened freedom.

By and large, destigmatization has surely been faciliated by groups acting on their own behalf, taking the initiative as aggrieved members of a minority confronting discrimination. The progress may have the character of two steps forward and one step back, however, as each change in the direction of increased tolerance carries with it the seeds of resistance. The key for destigmatization is to control the resistance and to make sure that the backward movement is smaller than the advances.

Society's Efforts to Foster Tolerance

Tolerance of diversity is a publicly prized value in a democratic society. Such societies are, after all, dedicted to the worth of their individual citizens. We have become realists, of course. We know that absolute, deviance-blind tolerance is as unachievable as international harmony and lasting world peace. Depending on one's definition of tolerance, it is not even clear that a totally forgiving society would be a desirable one to live in. Be that as it may, the multifaceted processes of education and socialization to which Americans are exposed are persistently protolerance. What is the nature of these educational efforts and what kinds of outcomes do they produce under what circumstances?

Education for tolerance takes many forms and occurs on many levels. Directed primarily toward the mind, it presumably also affects the heart. Formal education for civic responsibility is generally included within grade- and high-school social studies curricula. There, at the very least, students are exposed to the norms of society with regard to equitable treatment of minorities, as well as the equal protection statutes of our legal heritage. Although it would be easy to overemphasize the impact of such formal instruction, something about exposure to formal education does correlate with reduction of prejudice. Quinley and Glock's (1979) study disclosed that the more years of formal education a person had received, the less likely was he to express negative feelings and attitudes toward Jews. Selznick and Steinberg (1969) found that 52 percent of those people with a grade-school education held unfavorable views of Jews, whereas this was true for only 15 percent of college graduates. Kelman (1973) has argued that the process underlying the impact of education should include individualizing, the adding of dimensions, and the humanizing of out-group members by imparting specific information about them.

As encouraging as the results relating education to prejudice are, it is difficult to assess the role of social desirability in evaluating such research. It may simply be that better educated people are more sensitive to the norms of tolerance and put more importance on the appearance of avoiding prejudice. Moreover, even the available studies indicate that the effect of education is not uniformly favorable. For example, in the Selznick and Steinberg study, it was found that people with a college education were more likely to defend social club discrimination against Jews than were people of lesser education. Nevertheless, it does seem that one's level of formal education is correlated with a reduced tendency toward racial prejudice. This correlation, according to analyses by Bettelheim and Janowitz (1964), is actually based on the "social experience of education specifically and not merely the sociological origins of the educated" (p. 18).

The unacceptability of race prejudice toward major ethnic minorities, such as Jews and blacks, *does* find its way into the formal educational system at various points. Presumably, the further one goes in the system, the more likely he or she is to confront antiprejudice instruction. It is less likely, however, that attitudes toward the mentally ill, alcoholics, stammerers, the obese, paraplegics, and other markable groups are covered in any formal curriculum. Insofar as education affects those attitudes, it is largely the subtle, osmotic education by peer consensus coupled with the effects of the media. Presumably, peer tolerance itself grows with years of education—the more years one stays in school, the more one is likely to be exposed to a tolerant peer culture. This is probably true for a variety of reasons, including the tendency for education to foster understanding of attributional complexity in impression formation and the obvious relevance of selective factors determining which persons stay in school through high school and beyond. To the extent that this is true, peer pressure and formal education should tend to reinforce each other in the direction of tolerance and resistance to the stigmatizing process. That is not to say, of course, that one has to be a highly educated person to be tolerant or that all highly educated persons are necessarily tolerant.

Education about norms of fairness and tolerance, whether it occurs in schools or in churches, presumably forms an important intellectual context for evaluating marked persons. However, such evaluations are probably more influenced by the prototypes we form of particular marks on the basis of our experience with marked people. Some of this experience is direct, some of it is conveyed by peers, and some of it is carried by the media—television in particular. Mark prototypes usually consist of two major subsets of concerns or prominent themes in the depiction of the marked person. One might be called the *adaptation subset*; the potential marker forms an impression of the constraints imposed by the mark and the opportunities remaining of the likelihood that any person with such a mark is bitter, depressed, irritable, heroic, aloof, and so on. The potential marker is concerned in that instance with the impact of the mark on the markable person's adaptive resources, his coping behavior, and his orientation to the world.

The other important cluster of prototype features might be called the *origin subset*. There the potential marker is concerned with the causes or determinants of the mark and what they tell him about the integrity or character of the markable person. Was the mark produced by the markable person's negligence, self-indulgence, or cowardice? Does it reflect a physical illness, a genetic anomaly, or decision errors?

Generally speaking, those mark prototypes are an issue when we consider the impact of consensus and the media. To put it another way, those who wish to promote destigmatization will probably have greater success by manipulating mark prototypes than by preaching tolerance for diversity. The television medium in particular seems to offer unlimited opportunities for prototype manipulation in America. That is true because of its involvement potential and its prominence in almost every home. It is also true because many of us have had limited personal contact with markable persons of particular types. We tend not to have intimate, long-range, personal experiences with people who are blind, retarded, psychotic, homosexual, or alcoholic. We may know a little about some of these types, but very little about the rest. Therefore, we are all the more vulnerable to prototype manipulation when such exotic deviants are portrayed in television dramas or discussed on television talk shows. The vivid prototypes provided by television portrayals can subsequently exert their influence through the availability heuristic (Tversky and Kahneman 1973). We draw on the concrete, vividly remembered case of "Bill" (portrayed by Mickey Rooney in a television drama) or Charley (portrayed by Cliff Robertson in "Flowers for Algernon") when we think of the retarded. It becomes difficult to imagine the true range of life styles associated with alcoholism, once we have seen Ray Milland in *The Lost Weekend*, Burt Lancaster in *Come Back Little Sheba*, or Jack Lemmon and Lee Remick in *Days of Wine and Roses*. The images of dramatic roles are more readily "available" to us than pallid statistics about the incidence of mental retardation or alcoholism, or the information that each label covers a great variety of subtypes. Talk-show guests can also create memorable mark prototypes. Homosexuals, stammerers, ex-alcoholics, and ex-addicts can (and try to) reveal themselves as genuine, multidimensional human beings.

It might also be pointed out, in passing, that the frequency with which marked persons appear on talk shows or are portrayed in dramatic roles is not solely motivated by impulses of moral pedagogy. Television producers obviously sense a widespread interest in the phenomena of deviance, and writers apparently are challenged by the problems of creating markable characters that are credible and appealing without being unrealistically romanticized.

Is there any good evidence that television really makes a difference in the destigmatization process? The existing evidence shows that television clearly has an impact, but it is not always in the direction of increased tolerance. A study by Gerbner (1980) indicates compellingly that mental patients may be more strongly degraded because of television. He reports that television portrays mental patients as unpredictable, dangerous, and evil. For example, he finds that whereas 40 percent of all prime-time "normal" characters are violent, 73 percent of the mentally ill are depicted as violent. For female characters during prime-time, 24 percent of them are violent, while 71 percent of females portrayed as mentally disordered are shown to be violent. Gerber believes that those programs can lead to an unreasonable fear, degradation, and ostracism of those who have been afflicted with a mental disorder. He cites one study that entailed asking respondents in 413 households to name criminally insane people without defining the term. All those named by the subjects were murderers and many were mass murderers. In fact, he asserts, only 14 percent of people diagnosed as criminally insane are ever accused of murder.

On the other hand, Wuthnow (1982) comments on a study conducted by the American Jewish Committee following the television drama "Holocaust," a nine hour miniseries broadcast in 1978 by the NBC network. In judging the findings of the AJC, we should remember that the program was seen more than thirty years after the events, and virtually every viewer must have known about the atrocities in some detail before viewing their dramatization. Nevertheless, about 40 percent of the viewers said that their feelings about Jews had been changed by the program, and virtually all changes were in the positive direction. Those who had watched the program were more in favor of American support for Israel than those who had not. It would be surprising if the very popular miniseries "Roots," which traced the experience of black Africans being transported to America as slaves and trying to survive thereafter in a slave society, did not have a similar impact on attitudes toward black people. We know of no evidence, however, to document this presumption.

Television producers and writers are, of course, constrained in many ways. In general, the evidence suggests that the thrust of television programming is toward greater tolerance of almost every type of deviance, except, perhaps, violent crime. In fact, it is almost inconceivable that we would see a television drama that openly ridiculed the retarded or emphasized the incapacities of the deaf, the blind, or those who are otherwise physically disabled. Even assuming the good intentions of television dramatists and producers, plot requirements dictate credible realism and also a "problem" confronting the players, which is then overcome. The disabling mark must be truly disabling in some sense or there is no drama. The requirements of suspense and credibility create risks in carrying out the protolerance intentions of the dramatist that have implications for destigmatization. Although the major thrust of the drama may be to humanize and destigmatize the disabled heroine, the episode may also make salient aspects of the disability that were heretofore unrecognized or seldom considered. Thus, retarded protagonists may be revealed as confused about sexuality, the mentally ill may have difficulty controlling their tempers, and the physically disabled may confront problems (like brushing their teeth or turning pages) that the normal viewer had not considered. In terms of our earlier distinction, television dramas may increase the attributional salience of certain categories of stigma while attempting to change the valence in a more positive direction. More often than not, such dramas probably facilitate destigmatization, but there are undoubtedly some dramas that raise more spectres than solutions, and there are invariably some audience members who come away with increased negative affect toward the mark portrayed. It is also possible that some portrayals manage to set unrealistic public expectations of ultimate mastery, and, indeed, many disabled persons are resentful of such dramatizations for that reason.

It is interesting to speculate, once again, about the short-range versus long-range effects of such dramatic presentations. As far as we know, this problem has never been addressed empirically, but it is important to discover whether the positive or the negative implications of a stigma-oriented drama will ultimately carry the day. Does the sentimental warmth toward the stigmatized character vanish more rapidly than the sense of consensual discredit that was also dramatized? Or do the negative aspects ultimately get submerged in the positive glow of "overcoming"?

Things Are Changing for the Handicapped

From Johnson, S. "Disabled in professions grow," *The New York Times,* July 18, 1983.

People with serious physical handicaps are beginning to enter professions, such as science, medicine and law, in greater numbers, experts says. . . . Dr. Martha Redden . . . of the American Association for the Advancement of Science, said: "The success stories

> **are everywhere. There are deaf students in dental school and quadriplegics in medical school. Our organization alone has 1,000 disabled scientists."**
>
> **She and other experts cited these reasons for the trend:**
>
> **— More handicapped people have the academic credentials for admission to professional schools. . . .**
>
> **— There are fewer physical barriers. Federal legislation requires that universities, libraries and other public buildings be accessible to the handicapped.**
>
> **— New technology enables the handicapped to practice the professions. A computerized video display screen, for example, allows deaf lawyers to communicate during arguments in court by reading the statements of witnesses and then responding to them.**
>
> **— Disabled youngsters have more role models in the professions. The president of the American Medical Association, for instance, is Dr. Frank J. Jirka, Jr., a . . . neurologist who lost his feet in combat during World War II.**
>
> **— Changes have occurred in the labor market. "Brains, not brawn, are important today," said Rhona C. Hartman, director of the Higher Education and the Handicapped Resource Center, . . . of the American Council on Education. "America has a service economy, and that means more jobs for disabled professionals."**

It would also be of interest to know whether "remedial" journalistic and television treatments of various stigmatizing conditions are primarily focused on matters of adaptation or on matters of origin. Our memories of television dramas suggest that most fictional and biographical treatments emphasize the adaptation subset of the mark prototype. There are real problems, to be sure, both physical and social, but the drama is built around how they are overcome. The focus is on the miracle of coping, the availability of hope, the feasibility of cure. On the other hand, talk shows and panel shows often emphasize the origin subset of the prototype. On such programs as the daytime "Phil Donahue Show," guest members from Alcoholics Anonymous solemnly assure us that alcoholism is a disease, just like cancer or tuberculosis. Physicians speak of mental illness in the same way that they speak of heart disease or gout. Homosexuality may be dealt with as a legal right (freedom of sexual choice) or as a form of pathological deviance. Complex issues of interpretation are involved in each of these cases, and others like them. The point is that the public is recurrently exposed to attempts at redefining the attributional underpinnings of various stigmatizing conditions, and the success or failure of such redefinitions can be quite consequential.

Two examples may suffice to demonstrate this point. It is unquestionably the case that the stigma of alcoholism can be reduced to the extent that people believe it is a disease, that it is exclusively a matter of individual differences in physical tolerance and physiological dependence. Alcoholics Anonymous recognized this early and has consistently championed the notion that alcoholics continue to be alcoholics even when they have abstained for years. Thus, a person unfortunately afflicted by a kind of genetic accident with the disease of alcoholism, can never touch a drink without launching once again the dreaded cycle of compulsive indulgence.

In recent years this fatalistic view has been attacked by a number of psychologists interested in the possibilities of behavior modification in the control of alcoholic abuse. A number of reports have emerged suggesting that controlled drinking is possible in previously diagnosed alcoholics (Sobell and Sobell 1978). Some of these findings (Sobell and Sobell 1976) have been scathingly attacked by spokesmen for the disease tradition (Pendery, Matzman, and West 1982), and the contemporary controversy concerning the etiology and cure of alcoholism is intense. In addition to other things, at stake is the degree and kind of stigma that attaches to those labeled alcoholics. If alcoholism is primarily a behavior disorder, one that can be controlled through training and the application of behavioral therapies, then the stigma of alcoholism is akin to the moral blemish attached to mental and emotional disorders. If, on the other hand, alcoholism is primarily a matter of genetic differences and physiological disposition, the stigma associated is more akin to that of a physical blemish (cf. Goffman 1963).

A second example involves beliefs about the nature of mental disorders. It was undoubtedly a sign of progress, historically, when mental and emotional disorders were treated as forms of illness rather than instances of spirit possession. Nevertheless, the illness view also has consequences for stigma that are not entirely positive. Mental disorders may be viewed as a form of disease at one end of a continuum or as an adjustment problem at the other end. Farina and his colleagues (Farina, Fisher, Getter, and Fischer 1978; Fisher and Farina 1979) attempted to shift the beliefs of students in an abnormal psychology course toward one or the other end of this continuum. They were successful in doing so, with the consequence that students in the more biologically oriented "disease" sections of the course were more fatalistic and pessimistic about the treatment of mental disorders. Other studies (e.g., Langer and Abelson 1974) show that a disease view of mental disorders has unfavorable effects. The disordered person is generally seen as more disturbed by those with a "disease" set. More research is needed on the implication for stigma of biological versus social learning views of mental disorders, but there is already reason to believe that educational programs designed to influence beliefs in the biological disease direction may have unfortunate consequences both for the patients themselves and for the public view of mental disorders and their responsiveness to therapeutic efforts.

The Role of "Deviance Frequency"

One function of obvious relevance to the evolution of stigma is the apparent frequency of marked persons in a particular category. The inclusion of the word "apparent" is deliberate. The number or proportion of homosexuals may be relatively constant over fairly long periods of time, but the number of declared homosexuals may expand as such declarations become more expected within the homosexual community and tolerated within the "straight" community. The apparent proportion of epileptics may dwindle as more effective medication regimens reduce or eliminate seizures. The number of criminals may be relatively constant, but the sense of their numbers may be inflated by media attention. And so on. The question we ask here is what difference does it make? Is there any useful way to relate the likelihood of stigmatization to the relative size of the deviant population?

A straightforward hypothesis might be that as the proportion of deviants to normals increases, they will be seen as less deviant, the frequency of potentially ameliorative contacts will increase, stereotypes will be disrupted by exceptions, and the degree and frequency of stigmatization will decline. Something of this sort does seem to be happening in the gay liberation movement. In communities like San Francisco and New York City, it is hard for straights to remain unaware of the sizable proportion of gays in the community. On the average, it would appear that tolerance toward homosexuals by heterosexuals is greatest in communities where the homosexual population is large and visible. It would be difficult to determine, however, the extent to which this is attributed to an increase in the number of benign interactions with deviant group members, or whether it is more a response to the power inherent in significant numbers—the power to protest, to demand redress, and to influence administrative policies and litigation. At this point in our knowledge of such things, it is probably safest to say that both factors are involved to some unknown extent in the gay liberation movement. It is also undoubtedly the case that some gays were attracted to cities like New York and San Francisco in the first place because they sensed greater community tolerance for their particular form of deviance.

The hypothesis of a negative relationship between the size of a deviant group and the likelihood of stigmatization must undoubtedly be qualified in situations where economic or political threat is involved. Group immigration examples point up the potential complexity of the relationship between stigma and the number of potential targets. Before the Irish came to the eastern United States in great numbers toward the end of the nineteenth century, it was probably the case that Irish persons were treated as casually and benignly as those of other ethnic origins. However, the large influx of Irish immigrants and the economic circumstances in which they arrived proved threatening to the majority and generated considerable negative feeling toward Irish people in general. That evolution of stigma in direct response to numbers has undoubtedly been repeated many times as a function of shifting populations: the Japanese to California in the late 1920s and early 1930s; the Okies during the latter part of the same period; the mass migration of blacks to the northern industrial cities of Chicago, Detroit, and Cleveland; and the influx of Puerto Ricans into New York City.

Thus, the gay liberation and the migration examples seem to suggest different models or functions. Any useful model will probably have to consider both the sheer number of marked persons in the deviant category and the extent to which any one of them represents a threat. If homosexuals mind their own business and are generally concealed markables anyway, it does not make a great deal of difference how many there are in the larger community. To the extent that they are pictured as threatening cherished majority values, however, their numbers can presumably work against them. Anita Bryant was able to have homosexual teachers barred from the Miami school system through arguments that they would recruit schoolchildren into the homosexual ranks. What could be more threatening to heterosexual parents than the thought that their children would be weaned away from their preferred sexual orientation? The entire question is one that probably never would have arisen in a community with a smaller proportion of homosexual members, where such members would be unlikely to bring the issue to a head. It suggests that under certain kinds of circumstances, numbers may have a great deal to do with "backlash."

Unfortunately, the concept of threat cannot be as easily operationalized as the number or proportion of marked persons in a category. How much economic threat is equivalent to how much threat of criminal attack or to how much threat associated with contravaluant beliefs? Such questions are difficult, if not impossible, to answer. Matters are further complicated by the factor of legitimacy. Marked persons can be legitimately threatening—they may have every legal right to take your job or besmirch your values—or illegitimately threatening—they have no legal right to mug you or to appropriate your property. In the latter case, the degree of stigmatization probably rises slowly and monotonically with the number of marked persons in the relevant environment. If red-haired people tend to be philanderers, then the more red-haired people in the community, the more any given red-haired person will be stigmatized as a philanderer. That relationship is depicted in the top line of Figure 7.

The solid line depicts a nonmonotonic function for marked persons who convey threats of various sorts that are not beyond the law. That curve

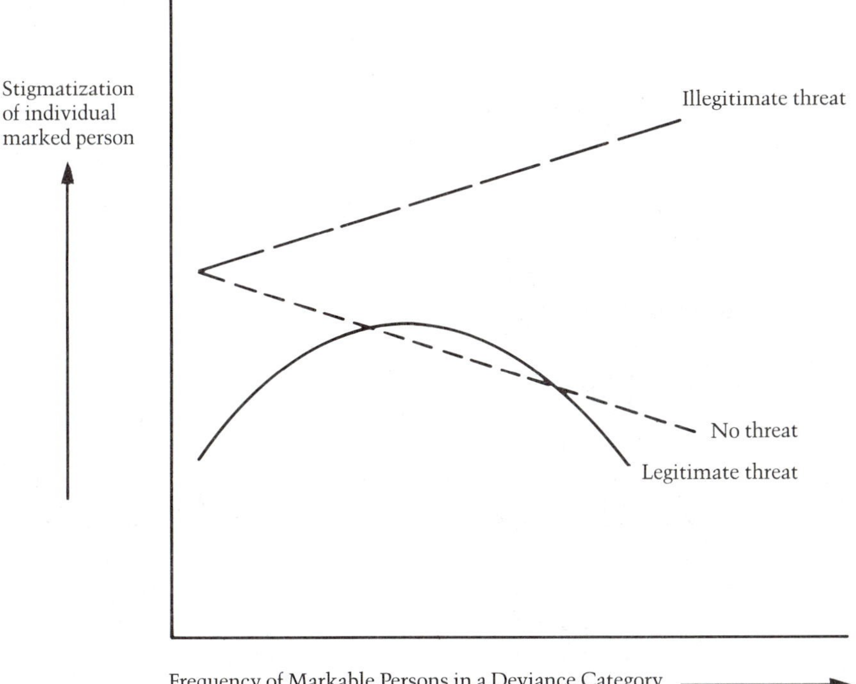

Figure 7. Relationship between frequency of markables and their vulnerability to stigma.

shows the stigmatization toward well-represented groups will be less than that toward moderate-sized groups. We assume that this is true because (1) they are by definition less deviant, and (2) they have more social, political, and legal power. There is some question as to whether this curve should be specifically labeled "public displays of stigmatizing attitude," since private attitudes might not completely correspond with actions constrained by legal redress. We refer the reader to our earlier discussion of the conditions under which behavior that is initially counterattitudinal brings about changes in attitude. If people are legally constrained to put up with the imposition of marked deviants, they may continue to feel privately resentful, but there also may be an important degree of attitudinal accommodation to their behavioral compliance.

Finally, we consider how differences in frequency within a marked category affect attitudes toward category members when they pose a minimal threat. That hypothetical relationship is depicted by the dotted line, indicating a monotonic downward relationship: the greater the frequency, the less stigma attached. There are many examples of such benign categories of deviance—the aged, females in what were formerly male jobs or formerly male schools, the physically disabled, and many if not most ethnic types. We assume that there are some categories of deviance whose members may be stigmatized when they are relatively rare or exotic, but less so as the majority has more opportunities for exposure, contact, and "adaptation" to members of the deviant group.

The discussion of frequency bears some relationship to the issue of degree of association in the literature on prejudice and discrimination. Does increased contact between majority and minority groups tend to break down prejudicial barriers or make them even more impenetrable? The usual answer to this question is that it depends on the context within which contact takes place. Does the contact primarily erode the sense of strangeness and differentness, or does it basically increase the sense of threat? A representative summary of previous research is that of Williams (1947): "Lessened hostility will result from arranging inter-group collaboration, on the basis of personal association of individuals as functional equals, on a common task jointly accepted as worthwhile" (p. 69). The various functions portrayed in Figure 9 bear a clear resemblance to some of those earlier considerations by highlighting the role of competition and threat. They represent, obviously, hypotheses on a very crude quantitative level. It might be even more fruitful to consider the changes in the *quality* of stigmatization that accompany changes in frequency.

A FINAL WORD

This chapter touched on issues that would take volumes to cover with justice. The problems of destigmatization are intertwined with all that we know about persuasion, education, propaganda, and attitude change in general. A comprehensive review of stigma reduction will necessarily involve an acute understanding of social history, institutional structure and dynamics, and cultural anthropology. We have attempted to identify common processes involved in stigmatization and to suggest how these processes might be diverted into more constructive perceptions, attitudes, and behaviors. There may always be residues of "primitive" affect in response to certain forms of deviance, residues that can not be erased or converted by cognitive changes. We believe, however, that the reduction of stigma is not a hopeless enterprise. Any experience or any educational or persuasive effort that increases the complexity of categorical use, any intervention that substitutes valid attributional understanding for "just world" reasoning, should help move society in the direction of tolerance and interpersonal comfort. We hope that this volume will contribute in this direction.

• REFERENCES •

Abelson, R. P. 1976. Script processing in attitude formation and decision making. In *Cognition and social behavior,* eds. J. S. Carroll and J. W. Payne. Hillsdale, NJ: Lawrence Erlbaum Associates.

Abelson, R. P. 1981. Psychological status of the script concept. *American Psychologist* 36: 715–729.

Abramson, L. Y.; Seligman, M. E. P.; and Teasdale, J. D. 1978. Learned helplessness in humans: Critique and reformulation. *Journal of Abnormal Psychology* 87:49–74.

Adorno, T. W.; Frenkel-Brunswik, E.; Levinson, D. J.; and Sanford, R. N. 1950. *The authoritarian personality.* New York: Harper & Row.

Albrecht, G. L., ed. 1976. *The sociology of physical disability and rehabilitation.* Pittsburgh: University of Pittsburgh Press.

Allport, G. W. 1954. *The nature of prejudice.* Cambridge, MA: Addison-Wesley.

Anthony, E. J. 1969. Academic lecture: The mutative impact of family life of serious mental and physical illness in a parent. *Journal of the Canadian Psychiatric Association* 14: 433–453.

———. 1970. The impact of mental and physical illness on family life. *American Journal of Psychiatry* 127:138–146.

Aronson, E.; Willerman, B.; and Floyd, J. 1966. The effect of a pratfall on increasing interpersonal attractiveness. *Psychonomic Science* 4:227–228.

Asch, S. E. 1952. *Social psychology.* New York: Prentice-Hall.

Ashmore, R. D., and Del Boca, F. K. 1981. Conceptual approaches to stereotypes and stereotyping. In *Cognitive processes in stereotyping and intergroup behavior,* ed. D. L. Hamilton. Hillsdale, NJ: Lawrence Erlbaum Associates.

Aviram, U., and Segal, S. 1973. Exclusion of the mentally ill: Reflection on an old problem in a new context. *Archives of General Psychiatry* 29:126–131.

Bandura, A. 1977. Self-efficacy: Toward a unifying theory of behavioral change. *Psychological Review* 84:191–215.

Bar-Levav, R. 1976. The stigma of seeing a psychiatrist. *American Journal of Psychotherapy* 30:473–481.

Barth, F. 1969. *Ethnic groups and boundaries: The social organization of culture differences.* London: Allen and Unwin.

Barton, K., and Cattell, R. B. 1972. Personality before and after a chronic illness. *Journal of Clinical Psychology* 28:464–467.

Becker, E. 1973. *The denial of death.* New York: The Free Press.

Beletsis, S. G., and Brown, S. 1981. A developmental framework for understanding the adult children of alcoholics. *Journal of Addictions and Health* 2:187–203.

Belgrave, F. Z., and Mills, J. 1981. Effect upon desire for social interaction with a physically disabled person of mentioning the disability in different contexts. *Journal of Applied Social Psychology* 11:44–57.

Bem, D. 1972. Self-perception theory. In *Advances in experimental social psychology,* Vol. 6, ed. L. Berkowitz. New York: Academic Press.

Berger, D. L., and Luckmann, T. 1966. *The social construction of reality: A treatise in the sociology of knowledge.* New York: Doubleday.

Berglas, S., and Jones, E. E. 1978. Drug choice as a self-handicapping strategy in response to noncontingent success. *Journal of Personality and Social Psychology* 36:405–417.

Bergson, H. 1911. *Laughter.* London: MacMillan.

Berscheid, E., and Walster, E. H. 1978. *Interpersonal attraction,* 2nd ed. Reading, MA: Addison-Wesley.

Berscheid, E.; Walster, E. H.; and Bohrnstedt, G. 1973. The happy American body: A survey report. *Psychology Today* 6:119–131.

Bettelheim, B., and Janowitz, M. 1964. *Social change and prejudice, including dynamics of prejudice.* New York: Free Press.

Bever, E. W. M. 1983. Witchcraft in early modern Wurttenberg. Unpublished Ph.D. dissertation, Princeton University.

Birenbaum, A. 1970. On managing a courtesy stigma. *Journal of Health and Social Behavior* 11:196–206.

Blau, P. M. 1960. A theory of social integration. *American Journal of Sociology* 65:545–547.

Bleuler, E. 1910. Vortrag über ambivalenz. *Zentralblatt für Psychoanalyse* 1:266.

Blos, P., Jr. 1978. Children think about illness: Their concepts and beliefs. In *Psychosocial aspects of pediatric care,* ed. E. Gellert. New York: Grune and Stratton.

Bobys, R. S., and Laner, M. R. 1979. On the stability of stigmatization: The case of ex-homosexual males. *Archives of Sexual Behavior* 8:247–261.

Brantley, H., and Clifford, E. 1979. Cognitive self-concept and body image measures of normal, cleft palate and obese adolescents. *Cleft Palate Journal* 16 (2):177–182.

Brehm, J. W., and Brehm, S. S. 1981. *Psychological reactance: A theory of freedom and control.* New York: Academic Press.

Brenner, M. H. 1973. *Mental illness and the economy.* Cambridge, MA: Harvard University Press.

Breslau, N. In press. Family care of disabled children: Effects on siblings and mothers. In *Comprehensive management of cerebral palsy,* eds. L. Rubin, G. H. Thompson, and R. M. Bilenker.

Brickman, P., and Bulman, R. J. 1977. Pleasure and pain in social comparison. In *Social comparison processes: Theoretical and empirical perspectives,* ed. J. M. Suls and R. L. Miller. Washington, DC: Hemisphere.

Brickman, P.; Rabinowitz, V. C.; Karuza, J., Jr.; Coates, D.; Cohn, E.; and Kidder, L. 1982. Models of helping and coping. *American Psychologist* 37:368–384.

Brown, J. S., and Farber, I. E. 1951. Emotions conceptualized as intervening variables with suggestions toward a theory of frustration. *Psychological Bulletin* 48:465–480.

Brown, J. S.; Wooldridge, P. J.; and Van Bruggen, Y. 1973. Interpersonal relations among psychiatric patients: The determinants of social attractiveness. *Journal of Health and Social Behavior* 14:51–60.

Bruner, J. S.; Goodnow, J. J.; and Austin, G. A. 1956. *A study of thinking.* New York: John Wiley.

Bueker, J.; Corrales, R. G.; Ro-Trock, L.; and Smith, B. 1981. *Systemic family assessment.* Kansas City, MO: Family Institute of Kansas City.

Bulman, R. J., and Wortman, C. B. 1977. Attributions of blame and coping in the "real world": Severe accident victims react to their lot. *Journal of Personality and Social Psychology* 35:351–363.

Burns, W. J., and Zweig, A. R. 1980. Self-concepts of chronically ill children. *Journal of Genetic Psychology* 137:179–190.

Busch-Rossnagel, N. A. 1981. Where is the handicap in disability?: The contextual impact of physical disability. In *Individuals as producers of their development: A life-span perspective,* eds. R. M. Lerner and N.A. Busch-Rossnagel. New York: Academic Press.

Cameron, P.; Titus, D. G.; Kostin, J.; and Kostin, M. 1973. The life satisfaction of the non-normal persons. *Journal of Consulting and Clinical Psychology* 41:207–214.

Campbell, D. T. 1967. Stereotypes and perception of group differences. *American Psychologist* 22:812–827.

Carpenter, J. O. 1974. Changing roles and disagreement in families with disabled husbands. *Archives of Physical Medical Rehabilitation* 55:272–274.

Carver, C. S.; Glass, D. C.; and Katz, I. 1978. Favorable evaluation of blacks and the handicapped. *Journal of Applied Social Psychology* 8:97–106.

Cash, T. F.; Kehr, J. A.; Polyson, J.; and Freeman, V. 1977. Role of physical attractiveness in peer attribution of psychological disturbance. *Journal of Consulting and Clinical Psychology* 45:987–993.

Cavior, H. E.; Hayes, S. C.; and Cavior, N. 1974. Physical attractiveness of female offenders: Effects on institutional performance. *Criminal Justice and Behavior* 1:321–331.

Centers, L., and Centers, R. 1963. Peer group attitudes toward the amputee child. *Journal of Social Psychology* 61:127–132.

Chambliss, W. S. 1964. A sociological analysis of the law of vagrancy. *Social Problems* 12: 67–77.

Chase, R. 1981. Psychological correlates of plastic surgery. Paper presented at The Center for Advanced Studies in the Behavioral Sciences, April 1981.

Chevigny, H., and Braverman, S. 1950. *The adjustment of the blind.* New Haven: Yale University Press.

Clark, M. S., and Isen, A. M. 1982. Toward understanding the relationship between feeling states and social behavior. In *Cognitive social psychology,* eds. A. H. Hastorf and A. M. Isen. New York: Elsevier North Holland.

Coates, D.; Wortman, C. B.; and Abbey, T. 1979. Reactions to victims. In *New approaches to social problems,* ed. I. H. Frieze, D. Bar-Tel, and J. S. Carroll. San Francisco: Jossey-Bass.

Cohen, C. Cognitive basis of stereotyping. Paper presented meeting of the American Psychological Association, August 1977, San Francisco.

Comer, R. J., and Piliavin, J. A. 1972. The effects of physical deviance upon face-to-face interaction: The other side. *Journal of Personality and Social Psychology* 23:33–39.

Coopersmith, S. 1967. *The antecedents of self-esteem.* San Francisco: Freeman.

Coser, R. L. 1959. Some social functions of laughter. *Human Relations* 12:171–182.

Coyne, J. C. 1976. Depression and the response of others. *Journal of Abnormal Psychology* 85:186–193.

Crocker, J. 1981. Judgment of covariation by social perceivers. *Psychological Bulletin* 90: 272–292.

Cumming E., and Cumming J. 1957. *Closed ranks.* Cambrige, MA: Harvard University Press.

Dailey, W. F.; Allen, G. J.; Chinsky, J. M.; and Veit, S. W. 1974. Attendant behavior and attitudes toward institutionalized retarded children. *American Journal of Mental Deficiency* 78: 586–591.

Darling, R. B., and Darling, S. 1982. *Children who are different: Meeting the challenges of birth defects in society.* St. Louis: C. V. Mosby.

Davies, C. 1982. Sexual taboos and social boundaries. *American Journal of Sociology* 87: 1032–1063.

Davis, D. 1982. Determinants of responsiveness in dyadic interaction. In *Personality, roles, and social behavior,* ed. W. Ickes and E. Knowles. New York: Springer-Verlag.

Davis, F. 1961. Deviance disavowal: The management of strained interaction by the visibly handicapped. *Social Problems* 9:120–132.

Davis, F. 1963. *Passage through crisis: Polio victims and their families.* Indianapolis: Bobbs-Merrill.

Davis, J. M., and Farina, A. 1970. Humor appreciation as social communication. *Journal of Personality and Social Psychology* 15:175–178.

Deaux, K. 1976. Sex: A perspective on the attribution process. In *New directions in attribution research,* Vol. 1, eds. J. H. Harvey, W. J. Ickes, and R. F. Kidd. Hillsdale, NJ: Lawrence Erlbaum Associates.

De Jong, W. 1980. The stigma of obesity: The consequences of naive assumptions concerning the causes of physical deviance. *Journal of Health and Social Behavior* 21:75–87.

Deutsch, A. 1965. *The mentally ill in America.* New York: Columbia University Press.

Dion, K. K. 1972. Physical attractiveness and evaluation of children's transgressions. *Journal of Personality and Social Psychology* 24:207–213.

Dion, K. K.; Berscheid, E.; and Walster, E. 1972. What is beautiful is good. *Journal of Personality and Social Psychology* 24:285–290.

Doherty, E. G. 1971. Social attraction and choice among psychiatric patients and staff: A review. *Journal of Health and Social Behavior* 12:279–290.

Dohrenwend, B. P., and Dohrenwend, B. S. 1969. *Social status and psychological disorder: A causal inquiry.* New York: Wiley Interscience.

Douglas, M. 1966. *Purity and danger: An analysis of concepts of pollution and taboo.* New York: Praeger.

Duncan, B. L. 1976. Differential social perception and the attribution on intergroup violence: Testing the lower limits of stereotyping of blacks. *Journal of Personality and Social Psychology* 34:590–598.

Dunkel-Schetter, C., and Wortman, C. B. In press. The interpersonal dynamics of cancer: Problems in social relationships and their impact on the patient. In *Interpersonal issues in health care,* ed. H. S. Friedman and M. R. DiMatteo. New York: Academic Press.

Durkheim, E. 1895. *The rules of sociological method.* Translated by S. A. Solvay and S. H. Mueller. Glencoe, IL: The Free Press, 1958.

Dutton, D. G. 1976. Tokenism, reverse discrimination, and egalitarianism in interracial behavior. *Journal of Social Issues* 32:93–108.

Edgerton, R. B. 1967. *The cloak of competence: Stigma in the lives of the mentally retarded.* Berkeley, CA: University of California Press.

Ellis, A. 1962. *Reason and growth in psychotherapy.* New York: Lyle Stuart.

Emerick, L. L. 1960. Extensional definition and attitude toward stuttering. *Journal of Speech and Hearing Research* 3:181–186.

English, R. W. 1971. Correlates of stigma towards physically disabled persons. *Rehabilitation Research and Practice Review* 2:1–17.

English, R. W., and Oberle, J. 1971. Towards the development of a new methodology for examining attitudes toward disabled persons. *Rehabilitation Counseling Bulletin* 15:1.

Erikson, K. T. 1966. *Wayward puritans: A study in the sociology of deviance.* New York: John Wiley.

Evans-Pritchard, E. E. 1956. *Nuer religion.* New York: Oxford University Press.

Farber, B. 1968. *Mental retardations: Its social content and social consequences.* Boston: Houghton Mifflin.

Farina, A. 1981. Are women nicer people than men? Sex and the stigma of mental disorders. *Clinical Psychology Review* 1:223–243.

———. 1982. Social attitudes and beliefs and their role in mental disorders. In *In the Eye of the Beholder,* ed. A. G. Miller. New York: Praeger.

Farina, A.; Allen, J. G.; and Saul, B. B. B. 1968. The role of the stigmatized person in affecting social relationships. *Journal of Personality* 36:169–182.

Farina, A., and Burns, G. L. 1982. The impact on social interaction of uncertainty about others' awareness regarding a personal history of mental disorder. Unpublished manuscript, University of Connecticut.

Farina, A.; Felner, R. D.; and Boudreau, L. A. 1973. Reactions of workers to male and female mental patient job applicants. *Journal of Consulting and Clinical Psychology* 41:363–372.

Farina, A.; Fischer, E. H.; Sherman, S.; Smith, W. T.; Groh, T.; and Mermin, P. 1977. Physical attractiveness and mental illness. *Journal of Abnormal Psychology* 86:510–517.

Farina, A., and Fisher, J. D. 1982. Beliefs about mental disorders: Findings and implications. In *Integrations of clinical and social psychology,* ed. G. Weary and H. Mirels, pp. 48–71. New York: Oxford University Press.

Farina, A.; Fisher, J. D.; Getter, H.; and Fischer, E. H. 1978. Some consequences of changing people's views regarding the nature of mental illness. *Journal of Abnormal Psychology* 87:272–279.

Farina, A.; Gliha, D.; Boudreau, L. A.; Allen, J. G.; and Sherman, M. 1971. Mental illness and the impact of believing others know about it. *Journal of Abnormal Psychology* 77:1–5.

Farina, A., and Hagelauer, H. D. Sex and mental illness: The generosity of females. *Journal of Consulting and Clinical Psychology* 43:122.

Farina, A.; Holland, C. H.; and Ring, K. 1966. The role of stigma and set in interpersonal interaction. *Journal of Abnormal Psychology* 71:421–428.

Farina, A.; Murray, P. J.; and Groh, T. 1978. Sex and worker acceptance of a former mental patient. *Journal of Consulting and Clinical Psychology* 46:887–891.

Farina, A., and Ring, K. 1965. The influence of perceived mental illness on interpersonal relations. *Journal of Abnormal Psychology* 70:47–51.

Farina, A.; Thaw, J.; and Boudreau, L. A. 1970. People's reaction to being viewed as blemished and degraded. Unpublished manuscript, University of Connecticut.

Farina, A.; Thaw, J.; Felner, R. D.; and Hust, B. E. 1976. Some interpersonal consequences of being mentally ill or mentally retarded. *American Journal of Mental Deficiency* 80: 414–422.

Featherstone, H. 1981. *A difference in the family: Living with a disabled child.* New York: Penguin Books.

Fedigan, L. M., and Fedigan L. 1977. The social development of a handicapped infant in a free-living troop of Japanese monkeys. In *Primate biosocial development,* eds. S. Chevalier-Skolnikoff and F. E. Poirier. New York: Garland.

Feldman, J. M. 1972. Stimulus characteristics and subject prejudice as determinants of stereotype attribution. *Journal of Personality and Social Psychology* 21:333–340.

Felice, A. 1977. Status of Harijan students in colleges. *Indian Journal of Social Work* 38: 15–25.

Festinger, L. 1950. Informal social communication. *Psychological Review* 57:271–282.

———. 1954. A theory of social comparison processes. *Human Relations* 7:117–140.

———. 1957. *A theory of cognitive dissonance.* Evanston, IL: Row Peterson.

Fisher, J.D., and Farina, A. 1979. Consequences of beliefs about the nature of mental disorders. *Journal of Abnormal Psychology* 88:320–327.

Fishman, J. A. 1956. An examination of the process and function of social stereotyping. *Journal of Social Psychology* 43:26–64.

Flavell, J. H. 1977. *Cognitive development.* Englewood Cliffs, NJ: Prentice-Hall.

Fletcher, C. R. 1969. Measuring community mental health attitudes by means of hypothetical case descriptions. *Social Psychiatry* 4:152–158.

Freeman, H. E. 1961. Attitudes toward mental illness among relatives of former patients. *American Sociological Review* 26:59–66.

Freeman, H. E., and Kassebaum, G. G. 1956. The illiterate in American society: Some general hypotheses. *Social Forces* 34:371–375.

Freidson, E. 1966. Disability as social deviance. In *Sociology and rehabilitation,* ed. M. B. Sussman. Washington, D.C.: American Sociological Association.

Freud, S. 1913, 1953. Totem and taboo. In *The standard edition of the complete psychological works of Sigmund Freud,* Vol. 13, ed. and trans., J. Strachey. London: Hogarth Press.

———. 1923, 1961. The ego and the id. In *The standard edition of the complete psychological works of Sigmund Freud,* Vol. 19, ed. and trans. J. Strachey. London: Hogarth Press.

Gellman, W. 1959. Roots of prejudice against the handicapped. *Journal of Rehabilitation* 25: 4–25.

Gerbner, G. 1980. Stigma: Social functions of the portrayal of mental illness in the mass media. In *Attitudes toward the mentally ill: Research perspectives. Report of an NIMH workshop, January 24–25, 1980,* ed. J. G. Rabkin, L. Gelb, and J. B. Lazar. DHHS Publication No. (ADM) 80-1031. Washington, DC: U.S. Government Printing Office.

Gergen, K. J., and Jones, E. E. 1963. Mental illness, predictability and affective consequences as stimulus factors in person perception. *Journal of Abnormal and Social Psychology* 67: 95–104.

Gliedman, J., and Roth, W. 1980. *The unexpected minority: Handicapped children in America.* New York: Harcourt, Brace, Jovanovich.

Goffman, E. 1955. On face-work: An analysis of ritual elements in social interaction. *Psychiatry* 18:213–231.

———. 1963. *Stigma: Notes on the management of spoiled identity.* Englewood Cliffs, NJ: Prentice-Hall.

———. 1969. The insanity of place. *Psychiatry* 32:357–388.

Goldberg, R. T. 1974a. Adjustment of children with invisible and visible handicaps: Congenital heart disease and facial burns. *Journal of Counseling Psychology* 21:428–432.

———. 1974b. Rehabilitation of the burn patient. *Rehabilitation Literature* 35:73–78.

Gottlieb, J. Public, peer, and professional attitudes toward mentally retarded persons. In *The mentally retarded in society: A social science perspective,* ed. M. J. Bega and S. A. Richardson, pp. 99–125. Baltimore: University Park Press.

Gowman, A. G. 1956. Blindness and the role of the companion. *Social Problems* 4:68–75.

Grossman, F. 1972. *Brothers and sisters of retarded children.* Syracuse, NY: Syracuse University Press.

Gusfield, J. R. 1967. Moral passage: The symbolic process in public designations of deviance. *Social Problems* 15:175–188.

Gussow, Z., and Tracy, G. S. 1968. Status ideology and adaptability to stigmatized illness: A study of leprosy. *Human Organization* 27:316–325.

Hamilton, D. L., ed. 1981. *Cognitive processes in stereotyping and intergroup behavior.* Hillsdale, NJ: Lawrence Erlbaum Associates.

Handlin, O. 1963. *A new history of the people of the USA.* Boston: Little, Brown.

Hastorf, A. H.; Northcraft, G.; and Picciotto, S. 1979. Helping the handicapped: How realistic is the performance feedback received by the physically handicapped? *Personality and Social Psychology Bulletin* 5:373–376.

Hastorf, A. H.; Wildfogel, J.; and Cassman, T. 1979. Acknowledgment of handicap as a tactic in social interaction. *Journal of Personality and Social Psychology* 37:1790–1797.

Hebb, D. O. 1955. The mammal and his environment. *American Journal of Psychiatry* (x): 826–831.

Hebb, D. O., and Thompson, W. R. 1954. The social significance of animal studies. In *Handbook of social psychology,* Vol. 1, ed. G. Lindzey. Cambridge, MA: Addison-Wesley.

Heisler, V. 1972. *A handicapped child in the family.* New York: Grune and Stratton.

Higgins, P. C. 1980. *Outsiders in a hearing world:* A sociology of deafness. Beverly Hills, CA: Sage.

Hobfoll, S. E., and Penner, L. A. 1978. Effects of physical attractiveness on therapist's initial judgments of a person's self-control. *Journal of Consulting and Clinical Psychology* 46: 200–201.

Hochschild, A. R. 1979. Emotion work, feeling rules, and social structure. *American Journal of Sociology* 85:551–575.

Hodgins, E. 1964. *Episode.* New York: Simon and Schuster.

Hogarth, J. 1971. *Sentencing as a human process.* Toronto: University of Toronto Press.

Holmes, J. G., and Miller, D. T. 1981. *Interpersonal Conflict.* Hillsdale, NJ: Lawrence Erlbaum Associates.

Horwitz, A. 1982. *Social control of mental illness.* New York: Academic Press.

Howard, J. 1978. The influence of children's developmental dysfunctions on marital quality and family interaction. In *Child influences on marital and family interaction: A life-span perspective,* eds. R. M. Lerner and G. B. Spanier. New York: Academic Press.

Hunt, P. 1966. A critical condition. In *Stigma: The experience of disability,* ed. P. Hunt. London: Geoffrey Chapman.

Hunter, R., and Macalpine, I. 1963. Three hundred years of psychiatry 1535–1860. Oxford: Oxford University Press.

Inveriarity, J. 1976. Populism and lynchings in Louisiana. *American Sociological Review* 41: 262–279.

Jackson, S. E., and Maslach, C. 1982. After-effects of job-related stress: Families as victims. *Journal of Occupational Behavior* 3:63–77.

Jacobs, L. M. 1974. *A deaf adult speaks out.* Washington, DC: Gallaudet College Press.

Jamison, J. 1964. The impact of mental retardation on the family and some directions of help. *Journal of the National Medical Association 57;* 2:136–138.

Jensema, C. J., and Shears, L. M. 1972. Acceptance of anomalous conditions studied through assessment of stereotype dimensions. *Rehabilitation Counseling Bulletin* 15:242–251.

Jones, E. E. 1979. The rocky road from acts to dispositions. *American Psychologist* 34: 107–117.

Jones, E. E., and Berglas, S. 1978. Control of attributions about the self through self-handicapping strategies: The appeal of alcohol and the role of underachievement. *Personality and Social Psychology Bulletin* 4:200–206.

Jones, E. E., and Gerard, H. B. 1967. *Foundations of social psychology.* New York: John Wiley.

Jones, E. E., and Gordon, E. 1972. The timing of self-disclosure and its effects on personal attraction. *Journal of Personality and Social Psychology* 24:358–365.

Jones, E. E., and McGillis, D. 1976. Correspondent inferences and the attribution cube: A comparative reappraisal. In *New directions in attribution research,* vol. 1, eds. J. H. Harvey, W. J. Ickes, and R. F. Kidd. Hillsdale, NJ: Lawrence Erlbaum Associates.

Jones, E. E., and Pittman, T. 1982. Toward a general theory of strategic self-presentation. In *Psychological perspectives on the self,* ed. J. Suls. Hillsdale, NJ: Lawrence Erlbaum Associates.

Jones, E. E., and Sigall, H. 1971. The bogus pipeline: A new paradigm for measuring affect and attitude. *Psychological Bulletin* 76:349–364.

Jones, E. E., and Wortman, C. 1973. *Ingratiation: An attributional approach.* Morristown, NJ: General Learning Press.

Jones, R. L.; Gottfried, N. W.; and Owens, A. 1966. The social distance of the exceptional: A study at the high school level. *Exceptional Children* 32:551–556.

Kahneman, D.; Slovic, P.; and Tversky, A., eds. 1982. *Judgment under uncertainty: Heuristics and biases.* New York: Cambridge.

Kapp. K. 1979. Self concept of the cleft lip and/or palate child. *Cleft Palate Journal* 16(2): 171–176.

Katz, I. 1981. *Stigma: A social psychological analysis.* Hillsdale, NJ: Lawrence Erlbaum Associates.

Kelley, H. H. 1952. The two functions of reference groups. In *Readings in social psychology,* 2nd ed., ed. G. F. Swanson, T. M. Newcomb, and F. L. Hartley. New York: Holt.

———. 1971. Attribution in social interaction. In *Attribution: Perceiving the causes of behavior,* eds. E. E. Jones, D. E. Kanouse, H. H. Kelley, R. E. Nisbett, S. Valins, and B. Weiner. Morristown: NJ: General Learning Press.

———. 1979. *Personal relationships: Their structures and processes.* Hillsdale, NJ: Lawrence Erlbaum Associates.

Kelley, H. H.; Hastorf, A. H.; Jones, E. E.; Thibaut, J. W.; and Usdane, W. M. 1960. Some implications of social psychological theory for research on the handicapped. In *Psychological research and rehabilitation,* ed. Lloyd H. Lofquist. Washington, D.C.: American Psychological Association.

Kellam, S. G.; Durell, J.; and Shader, R. I. 1966. Nursing staff attitudes and the clinical course of psychotic patients. *Archives of General Psychiatry* 14:190–202.

Kelman, H. C. 1973. Violence without moral restraint: Reflections on the dehumanization of victims and victimizers. *Journal of Social Issues* 29:25–62.

Kendall, P. C., and Norton-Ford, J. D. 1982. *Clinical psychology.* New York: John Wiley.

Kerbo, H. R. 1975. The stigma of welfare and a passive poor. *Sociology and Social Research* 60:173–187.

Kirkpatrick, C., and Cotton, J. 1961. Physical attractiveness, age, and marital adjustment. *American Sociological Review* 16:81–86.

Klapp, O. E. 1949. The fool as a social type. *American Journal of Sociology* 55:157–162.

Klaus, M., and Kennell, J. 1979. *Maternal-infant bonding.* St. Louis, MO: C. V. Mosby.

Kleck, R. E. 1968*a*. Physical stigma and nonverbal cues emitted in face-to-face interaction. *Human Relations* 21:19–28.

———. 1968*b*. Self-disclosure patterns of the nonobviously stigmatized. *Psychological Reports* 23:1239–1248.

Kleck, R. E.; Ono, H.; and Hastorf, A. H. 1966. The effects of physical deviance upon face-to-face interaction. *Human Relations* 19:425–436.

Kleck, R. E., and Rubenstein, C. 1975. Physical attractiveness, perceived attitude similarity, and interpersonal attraction in an opposite sex encounter. *Journal of Personality and Social Psychology* 31:107–114.

Kleck, R. E., and Strenta, A. 1980. Perceptions of the impact of negatively valued physical characteristics on social interaction. *Journal of Personality and Social Psychology* 39(5): 861–873.

Kobasa, S. 1979. Stressful life events, personality and health: An inquiry into hardiness. *Journal of Personality and Social Psychology* 37:1–11.

Korn, S. J.; Chess, S.; and Fernandez, P. 1978. The impact of children's physical handicaps on marital quality and family interaction. In *Child influences on marital and family interaction: A life-span perspective,* eds. R. M. Lerner and G. B. Spanier. New York: Academic Press.

Kuhn, M. H., and McPartland, T. S. 1954. An empirical investigation of self-attitudes. *American Sociological Review* 19:68–76.

Kurtzberg, R. L.; Safar, H.; and Cavior, N. 1968. Surgical and social rehabilitation of adult offenders. *Proceedings of the Seventy-Sixth Annual Convention of the American Psychological Association* 3:649–650.

Kushner, H. S. 1981. *When bad things happen to good people.* New York: Schocken Books, Inc.

Landy, D., and Sigall, H. 1974. Beauty is talent: Task evaluation as a function of performer's physical attractiveness. *Journal of Personality and Social Psychology* 29:299–304.

Langer, E. J. 1978. Rethinking the role of thought in social interaction. In *New directions in attribution research,* Vol. 2, eds. J. H. Harvey, W. J. Ickes, and R. F. Kidd. Hillsdale, NJ: Lawrence Erlbaum Associates.

Langer, E. J., and Abelson, R. P. 1974. A patient by an other name. . . : Clinician group difference in labeling bias. *Journal of Consulting and Clinical Psychology* 42:4–9.

Langer, E. J.; Fiske, S.; Taylor, S. E.; and Chanowitz, B. 1976. Stigma, staring, and discomfort: A novel-stimulus hypothesis. *Journal of Experimental Social Psychology* 12:451–463.

Lauderdale, P. 1976. Deviance and moral boundaries. *American Sociological Review* 41: 660–676.

———, ed. 1980. *A political analysis of deviance.* Minneapolis: University of Minnesota Press.

Lear, M. W. 1980. *Heartsounds.* New York: Pocket Books.

Lehmann, S.; Joy, V.; Kreisman, D.; and Simmens, S. 1976. Responses to viewing symptomatic behaviors and labeling of prior mental illness. *Journal of Community Psychology* 4: 327–334.

Lerner, M. J. 1970. The desire for justice and reactions to victims. In *Altruism and helping behavior,* eds. J. Macauley and L. Berkowitz. New York: Academic Press.

———. 1980. *The belief in a just world: A fundamental delusion.* New York: Plenum.

Lerner, M., and Miller, D. 1978. Just world research and the attribution process: Looking back and ahead. *Psychological Bulletin* 85:1030–1051.

Lerner, R. M., and Lerner, J. V. 1977. Effects of age, sex, and physical attractiveness on child-peer relations, academic performance, and elementary school adjustment. *Developmental Psychology* 13:585–590.

Leventhal, H. 1980. Toward a comprehensive theory of emotion. In *Advances in experimental social psychology,* Vol. 13, ed. L. Berkowitz. New York: Academic Press.

Levine, J. M., and McBurney, D. H. 1977. Causes and consequences of effluvia: Body odor awareness and controllability as determinants of interpersonal evaluation. *Personality and Social Psychology Bulletin* 3:442–445.

LeVine, R. A., and Campbell, D. T. 1972. *Ethnocentrism.* New York: John Wiley.

Levitt, L., and Kornhaber, R. C. 1977. Stigma and compliance: A re-examination. *Journal of Social Psychology* 103:13–18.

Linsky, A. S. 1970. Who shall be excluded: The influence of personal attributes in community reaction to the mentally ill. *Social Psychiatry* 5:166–171.

Linville, P. W. 1982. The complexity-extremity effect and age-based stereotyping. *Journal of Personality and Social Psychology* 42:193–211.

Linville, P. W., and Jones, E. E. 1980. Polarized appraisals of out-group members. *Journal of Personality and Social Psychology* 38:689–703.

Lippmann, W. 1922. *Public opinion.* New York: Harcourt, Brace.

MacDonald, A. P., and Hall, J. 1969. Perception of disability by the nondisabled. *Journal of Consulting and Clinical Psychology* 33:654–660.

Manzoni, A. 1962. *The betrothed.* London: J. M. Dent & Sons.

Marinelli, R. P., and Dell Orto, A. E. 1977. *The psychological and social impact of physical disability.* New York: Springer.

Markus, H. 1977. Self-schemata and processing information about the self. *Journal of Personality and Social Psychology* 35:63–78.

———. 1980. The self in thought and memory. In *The self in social psychology,* ed. D. Wegner and R. Vallacher. New York: Oxford University Press.

Markus, H.; Hamill R.; and Sentis, K. 1980. Thinking fat: Self-schema for body weight and the processing of weight relevant information. Paper presented at American Psychological Association, Montreal.

Markus, H., and Nurius, P. S. 1982. Possible selves. Paper presented at the Society for Experiental Social Psychology, Nashville, Indiana, October 1982.

Maslach, C., and Jackson, S. E. 1981. The measurement of experienced burnout. *Journal of Occupational Behavior* 2:99–113.

———. 1982. Burnout in health professions: A social psychological analysis. In *Social psychology of health and illness,* eds. G. Sanders and J. Suls. Hillsdale, NJ: Lawrence Erlbaum Associates.

Mathes, E. W. 1975. The effects of physical attractiveness and anxiety on heterosexual encounters over a series of five encounters. *Journal of Marriage and the Family* 37:769–773.

McAndrews, I. 1976. Children with a handicap and their families. *Child: Care, health and development* 2, 4:213–238.

McArthur, L. Z. 1982. Judging a book by its cover: A cognitive analysis of the relationship between physical appearance and stereotyping. In *Cognitive social psychology,* eds. A. H. Hastorf and A. M. Isen. New York: Elsevier/North Holland.

McCarthy, H. 1982. Understanding motives of youth in transition to work: A taxonomy for rehabilitation counselors and educators. *Journal of Applied Rehabilitation Counseling.*

McGarry, M. S., and West, S. G. 1975. Stigma among the stigmatized: Resident mobility, communication ability and physical appearance as predictors of staff-resident interaction. *Journal of Abnormal Psychology* 84:399–405.

McMichael, J. K. 1971. *Handicap: A study of physically handicapped children and their families.* Pittsburgh: University of Pittsburgh Press.

Mead, G. H. 1934. *Mind, self and society.* Chicago: University of Chicago Press.

Merton, R. K. 1957. *Social theory and social structure.* New York: Free Press.

Miller, A. G., ed. 1982. *In the eye of the beholder: Contemporary issues in stereotyping.* New York: Praeger.

Miller, A. G.; Gillen, B.; and Schenker, C. 1974. The prediction of perception and obedience to authority. *Journal of Personality* 42:23–42.

Miller, N. E. 1944. Experimental studies in conflict. In *Personality and the behavior disorders,* ed. J. McV. Hunt. New York: Ronald Press.

Millman, M. 1980. *Such a pretty face: Being fat in America.* New York: Berkley Press.

Molony, H. 1971. Parental reactions to mental retardation. *Medical Journal of Australia* April 24:914–917.

Moos, R. H., and Moos, B. S. 1981. *Family Environment Scale Manual.* Palo Alto, CA: Consulting Psychologists Press.

Morrison, J. K. 1980. The public's current beliefs about mental illness: Serious obstacle to effective community psychology. *American Journal of Community Psychology* 8:697–707.

Napoleon, T.; Chassin, L.; and Young, R. D. 1980. A replication and extension of "Physical attractiveness and mental illness." *Journal of Abnormal Psychology* 89:250–253.

Neff, W. 1971. Rehabilitation and work. In *Rehabilitation psychology,* ed. W. Neff. Washington, DC: American Psychological Association.

Niederland, W. G. 1965. Narcissistic ego impairment in patients with early physical malformations. *Psychoanalytic Study of the Child* 20:518–534.

Nisbett, R. E., and Ross, L. D. 1980. *Human inference: Strategies and shortcomings of social judgment.* Englewood Cliffs, NJ: Prentice-Hall.

Northcraft, G. B. 1981. The perception of disability. Unpublished manuscript, Stanford University.

Nunnally, J. C., Jr. 1961. *Popular conceptions of mental health.* New York: Holt, Rinehart & Winston.

O'Grady, K. E. In press. Sex, physical attractiveness, and perceived risk for mental illness. *Journal of Personality and Social Psychology.*

Orcutt, J. D. 1976. Ideological variations in the structure of deviant types: A multivariate comparison of alcoholism and heroin addiction. *Social Forces* 55:419–437.

Osler, Sir W. 1951. *Aphorisms from his bedside teachings and writings*, ed. W. B. Bean, Springfield, IL: Charles C. Thomas.

Pendery, M. L.; Maltzman, I. M.; and West, L. J. 1982. Controlled drinking by alcoholics? New findings and a revaluation of a major affirmative study. *Science* 217:169–175.

Pettigrew, T. F. 1979. The ultimate attribution error: Extending Allport's cognitive analysis of prejudice. *Personality and Social Psychology Bulletin* 5:461–476.

Phillips, D. L. 1964. Rejection of the mentally ill: The influence of behavior and sex. *American Sociological Review* 29:679–687.

Pilleri, G., and Knuckey, J. 1969. Behavior patterns of some Delphinidae observed in the Western Mediterranean. *Seitschrift für Tierpsychologie* 26(1):48–72.

Pollack, S.; Huntley, D.; Allen, J. G.; and Schwartz, S. 1976. The dimensions of stigma: The social situation of the mentally ill person and the male homosexul. *Journal of Abnormal Psychology* 85:105–112.

Posner, J. 1976. Death as a courtesy stigma. *Essence* 1:26–33.

Quinley, H. E., and Glock, C. Y. 1979. *Anti-Semitism in America.* New York: Free Press.

Quinny, R. 1977. *Class state and crime.* New York: David McKay.

Rabiner, E. L.; Reiser, M. F.; Barr, H. L.; and Gralnick, A. 1971. Therapists' attitudes and patients' clinical status. *Archives of General Psychiatry* 25:555–569.

Rabkin, J. G. 1980. Determinants of public attitudes about mental illness: Summary of the research literature. In *Attitudes toward the mentally ill: Research perspectives. Report of an NIMH workshop, January 24–25, 1980*, ed. J. G. Rabkin, L. Gelb, and J. B. Lazar. DHHS Publication No. (ADM) 80-1031. Washington, DC: U.S. Government Printing Office.

Rechy, J. 1963. *City of night.* New York: Grove Press.

Reeder, G. D., and Brewer, M. B. 1979. A schematic model of dispositional attribution in interpersonal perception. *Psychological Review* 86:61–79.

Regan, D. T.; Strauss, E.; and Fazio, R. 1974. Liking and the attribution process. *Journal of Experimental Social Psychology* 10:385–397.

Richardson, S. A. 1969. The effect of physical disability on the socialization of a child. In *Handbook of socialization theory and research*, ed. D. A. Goslin, pp. 1047–1064. Chicago: Rand McNally & Company.

———. 1975. Reactions to mental subnormality. In *The mentally retarded in society: A social science perspective*, ed. M. J. Begab and S. A. Richardson, pp. 77–97. Baltimore: University Park Press.

Richardson, S. A.; Goodman, N.; Hastorf, A. H.; and Dornbusch, S. M. 1961. Cultural uniformity in reaction to physical disabilities. *American Sociological Review* 26:241–247.

Richardson, S. A.; Hastorf, A. H.; and Dornbusch, S. M. 1964. The effects of physical disability on a child's description of himself. *Child Development*, 35, 893–907.

Richman, L., and Harper, D. 1979. Self identified personality patterns of children with facial or orthopedic disfigurement. *Cleft Palate Journal* 16(3):257–261.

Rock, P. E., ed. 1977. *Drugs and politics.* New Brunswick, NJ: Transactions Books.

Rodin, E. A.; Shapiro, H. L.; and Lennox, K. 1977. Epilepsy and life performance. *Rehabilitation Literature* 38:34–39.

Rokeach, M. 1964. *The three Christs of Ypsilanti: A psychological study.* New York: Knopf.

Roosens, E. 1979. *Mental patients in town life: Geel—Europe's first therapeutic community.* Beverly Hills: Sage Publications.

Rose, J. A. 1961. The prevention of mothering breakdown associated with physical abnormalities in the infant. In *Prevention of mental disorders in children,* ed. G. Caplan. New York: Basic Books.

Rosenberg, M. 1965. *Society and the adolescent self-image.* Princeton, NJ: Princeton University Press.

———. 1979. *Conceiving the self.* New York: Basic Books.

Rosenhan, D. 1973a. On being sane in insane places. *Science* 179:250–258.

———. 1973b. On being sane in insane places. *Science* 180:365–369.

Rosenthal, R., and Jacobson, L. 1968. *Pygmalion in the classroom: Teacher expectation and pupils' intellectual development.* New York: Holt, Rinehart & Winston.

Ross, L. 1977. The intuitive psychologist and his shortcomings. In *Advances in experimental social psychology,* Vol. 10, ed. L. Berkowitz, New York: Academic Press.

Rothbart, M. 1981. Memory processes and social beliefs. In *Cognitive processes in stereotyping and intergroup behavior,* ed. D. L. Hamilton. Hillsdale, NJ: Lawrence Erlbaum Associates.

Rothbart, M.; Evans, M.; and Fulero, S. 1979. Recall for confirming events: Memory processes and the maintenance of social stereotypes. *Journal of Experimental Social Psychology* 15: 343–355.

Sack, W. H.; Seidler, J.; and Thomas, S. 1976. The children of imprisoned parents: A psychological exploration. *American Journal of Orthopsychiatry* 46:618–628.

Schachter, S. 1959. *The psychology of affiliation.* Stanford, CA: Stanford University Press.

———. 1964. The interaction of cognitive and physiological determinants of emotional state. In *Advances in experimental social psychology,* Vol. 1, ed. L. Berkowitz. New York: Academic Press.

Schachter, S., and Singer, J. E. 1962. Cognitive, social, and physiological determinants of emotional state. *Psychological Review* 69:379–399.

Scheff, T. J. 1963. Social support for stereotypes of mental disorder. *Mental Hygiene* 47: 461–469.

Schiller, J. C. F. 1882. *Essays, esthetical and philosophical, including the dissertation on the "Connection between the animals and the spiritual in man."* London: G. Bell.

Schowe, B. M. 1979. *Identity crisis in deafness: A humanistic perspective.* Tempe, AZ: Scholars Press.

Schreiber, M., and Feeley, M. 1965. Siblings of the retarded: A guided group experience. *Children* 12, 6:221–229.

Schur, E. M. 1971. *Labeling deviant behavior.* New York: Harper and Row.

———. 1979. *Interpreting deviance: A sociological introduction.* New York: Harper and Row.

———. 1980. *The politics of deviance.* Englewood Cliffs, NJ: Prentice Hall.

Schutz, A. 1962. *The phenomenology of the social world.* Chicago: Northwestern University Press.

———. 1971. *Collected papers, vol. 1: The problem of social reality.* Hague: Martinvs Nijhoff.

Schwartz, C. G. 1957. Perspectives on deviance—wive's definitions of their husband's mental illness. *Psychiatry* 20:275–291.

Schwartz, C. G.; Myers, J. K.; and Astrachan, B. M. 1974. Psychiatric labeling and the rehabilitation of the mental patient. *Archives of General Psychiatry* 31:329–334.

Schwartz, R. D., and Skolnick, J. H. 1962. Two studies of legal stigma. *Social Problems* 10: 133–142.

Scott, R. A. 1967. The factor as a social service organization: Goal displacement in workshops for the blind. *Social Problems* 65:160–175.

———. 1969. *The making of blind men.* New York: Russell Sage Foundation.

———. 1976. A framework for analyzing deviance as a property of social order. In *Theoretical perspectives on deviance,* ed. R. A. Scott and J. D. Douglas, pp. 9–35. New York: Basic Books.

Scott, R. A., and Scull, A. 1980. Penal reform and the surplus army of labor. In *Law and social control,* ed. S. Bricky. Toronto: Prentice-Hall of Canada.

Seligman, M. E. P. 1975. *Helplessness: On depression, development, and death.* San Francisco: Freeman.

Selman, R. L. 1981. *The growth of interpersonal understanding.* New York: Academic Press.

Selznick, G. J., and Steinberg, S. 1969. *The tenacity of prejudice.* New York: Harper and Row.

Shears, L. M., and Jensema, C. J. 1969. Social acceptability of anomalous persons. *Exceptional Children* 36:91–96.

Shuster, M. M., and Lewin, M. L. 1968. Needle tracks in narcotic addicts. *New York State Journal of Medicine* 68:3129–3134.

Sigall, H.; Page, R.; and Brown, A. 1971. Effort expenditure as a function of evaluation and evaluator attractiveness. *Representative Research in Social Psychology* 2:19–25.

Siller, J.; Chipman, A.; Ferguson, L.; and Vann, D. H. 1967. Attitudes of the nondisabled toward the physically disabled. Final Report on Vocational Rehabilitation Administration Project RD-707. New York University School of Education.

Siller, J.; Ferguson, L. T.; Vann D. H.; and Holland, B. 1968. Structure of attitudes toward the physically disabled: The disability factor scales-amputation, blindness, cosmetic conditions. *Proceedings of the 76th Annual Convention of the American Psychological Association* 3:651–652.

Simpson, E. L. 1982. *Notes on an emergency: A journal of recovery.* New York: W. W. Norton.

Smith, B.; Bueker, J.; Corrales, R.; and Ro-Trock, L. 1981. *The structural characteristics of families with handicapped children.* Kansas City, MO: Family Institute of Kansas City.

Snyder, M. 1974. The self-monitoring of expressive behavior. *Journal of Personality Psychology* 30:526–537.

———. 1981. On the self-perpetuating nature of social stereotypes. In *Cognitive processes in stereotyping and intergroup behavior,* ed. D. L. Hamilton. Hillsdale, NJ: Lawrence Erlbaum Associates.

Snyder, M., and Swann, W. B., Jr. 1978. Hypothesis testing processes in social interaction. *Journal of Personality and Social Psychology* 36:1202–1212.

Snyder, M.; Tanke, E. D.; and Berscheid, E. 1977. Social perception and interpersonal behavior: On the self-fulfilling nature of social stereotypes. *Journal of Personality and Social Psychology* 35:656–666.

Sobell, M. B., and Sobell, L. C. 1976. Behavior research therapy. 14:195.

———. 1978. *Behavioral treatment of alcohol problems.* New York: Plenum.

Sontag, S. 1977. *Illness as metaphor.* New York: Farrar, Straus and Giroux.

Spiegel, D. 1976. Going public and self-help. Reprinted from *Support systems and mutual help: Multidisciplinary explorations,* eds. G. Caplan and M. Killilea. New York: Grune and Stratton.

Spiegel, D., and Wissler, T. 1982. Perceptions of family environment among psychiatric patients and their wives. Submitted for publication, *Family Process.* Palo Alto, CA.

Sroufe, R.; Chaikin, A.; Cook, R.; and Freeman, V. 1977. The effects of physical attractiveness on honesty: A socially desirable response. *Personality and Social Psychology Bulletin* 3: 59–62.

Steadman, H. J. 1980. Assessing the sources of perceptions of the dangerousness of the mentally ill. In *Attitudes toward the mentally ill: Research perspectives. Report of an NIMH workshop, January 24–25, 1980,* ed. J. G. Rabkin, L. Gelb, and J. B. Lazar. DHHS Publication No. (ADM) 80-1031. Washington, DC: U.S. Government Printing Office.

Sussman, A. E. 1973. An investigation into the relationship between self-concepts of deaf adults and their perceived attitudes toward deafness. Ph.D. dissertation, New York University.

Szasz, T. S. 1961. *The myth of mental illness: Foundations of a theory of personal conduct.* New York: Harper and Row.

Taylor, D. M., and Jaggi, V. 1974. Ethnocentrism and causal attribution in a South Indian context. *Journal of Cross-Cultural Psychology* 5:162–171.

Taylor, S. E. 1981. A categorization approach to stereotyping. In *Cognitive processes in stereotyping and intergroup behavior.* ed. D. L. Hamilton. Hillsdale, NJ: Lawrence Erlbaum Associates.

Taylor, S. E., and Fiske, S. T. 1978. Salience, attention and attribution: Top of the head phenomena. In *Advances in experimental social psychology,* ed. L. Berkowitz, Vol. 11. New York: Academic Press.

Thaw, J. 1971. The reactions of schizophrenic patients to being patronized and believing they are unfavorably viewed. Unpublished Ph.D. dissertation, University of Connecticut.

Thibaut, J. W., and Kelley, H. H. 1959. *The social psychology of groups.* New York: John Wiley.

Thibaut, J. W., and Riecken, H. W. Some determinants and conequences of the perception of social causality. *Journal of Personality* 24:113–133.

Thoits, P. A. 1983. Transforming emotions: An extension of Hochschild's theory of emotion work, with applications to stress, coping, and social support. Paper presented at the annual meetings of the American Sociological Association, Detroit, August, 1983.

Titley, R. W. 1969. Imaginations about the disabled. *Social Science and Medicine* 3:29–38.

Tomkins, S. S. 1981. The quest for primary motives: Biography and autobiography of an idea. *Journal of Personality and Social Psychology* 41: 306–329.

Trice, H. M., and Roman, P. M. 1970. Delabeling, relabeling, and Alcoholics Anonymous. *Social Problems* 17:538–546.

Trieschmann, R. B. *The psychological, social and vocational adjustment in spinal cord injury: A strategy for future research.* Final report RSA 13-P-59011/9-01, April 30, 1978. Easter Seal Society for Crippled Children and Adults of Los Angeles County.

Tringo, J. L. 1970. The hierarchy of preference toward disability groups. *Journal of Special Education* 4:295–306.

Tucker, J. A.; Vuchinich, R. E.; and Sobell, M. B. 1981. Alcohol consumption as a self-handicapping strategy. *Journal of Abnormal Psychology* 90:220–230.

Tudor, W.; Tudor, J. F.; and Gove, W. R. 1977. The effect of sex role differences in the social control of mental illness. *Journal of Health and Social Behavior* 18:98–112.

Tversky, A., and Kahneman, D. 1973. Availability: A heuristic for judging frequency and probability. *Cognitive Psychology* 5:207–232.

Vann, D. H. 1970. Components of attitudes toward the obese including presumed responsibility for the condition. *Proceedings of the 78th Annual Convention of the American Psychological Association* 5:695–696.

Vann, D. H. 1976. Personal responsibility, authoritarianism and treatment of the obese. Unpublished Ph.D. dissertation. New York University.

Van Lawick-Goodall, J. 1971. *In the shadow of man.* Boston: Houghton Mifflin.

Walster, E.; Aronson, V.; Abrahams, D.; and Rottman, L. 1966. Importance of physical attractiveness in dating behavior. *Journal of Personality and Social Psychology* 4:508–516.

Weyand, C. A. 1983. The associative stigma: Social degradation of a son because of his stigmatized father. Unpublished Ph.D. dissertation, University of Connecticut.

Wheeler, D. S.; Farina, A.; and Stern, J. In press. Dimensions of peril in the stigmatization of the mentally ill. *Academic Psychology Bulletin.*

Wheeler, S.; Weisburd, D.; and Bode, N. 1982. Sentencing the white-collar offender: Rhetoric and reality. *American Sociological Review* 47:641–659.

Whiting, J. W. M., and Child, I. L. 1953. *Child training and personality.* New Haven: Yale University.

Wilder, G. 1983. Ph.D. dissertation, Princeton University.

Wilkins, L. T. 1965. *Social deviance: Social policy, action, and research.* Englewood Cliffs, NJ: Prentice-Hall.

Williams, R. M., Jr. 1947. *The reduction of intergroup tensions: A survey of research on problems of ethnic, racial and religious group relations.* New York: Social Science Research Council, Bulletin 57.

Wilson, E. O. 1975. *Sociobiology: The new synthesis.* Cambridge, MA: Belknap Press.

Wright, B. A. 1960. *Physical disability—a psychological approach.* New York: Harper & Row.

Wright, F. H., and Klein, R. A. 1965. Attitudes of various hospital personnel categories and the community regarding mental illness. Unpublished manuscript, Veterans Administration Center, Biloxi, MS.

Wuthnow, R. 1982. Anti-Semitism and stereotyping. In *In the eye of the beholder,* ed. A. Miller. New York: Praeger.

Yamamoto, K., and Dizney, H. F. 1967. Rejection of the mentally ill: A study of attitudes of student teachers. *Journal of Consulting Psychology* 14:264–268.

Yuker, H. E.; Block, J. R.; and Campbell, W. J. 1960. A scale to measure attitudes toward disabled persons. *Human Resources Study Number 5.* Albertson, NY: Human Resources.

Yuker, H. E.; Block, J. R.; and Younng, J. H. 1966. *The measurement of attitudes toward disabled persons.* Albertson, NY: Human Resources Center.

Zahn, M. A. 1973. Incapacity, impotence and invisible impairment: Their effects upon interpersonal relations. *Journal of Health and Social Behavior* 14:115–123.

Zajonc, R. B. 1980. Feeling and thinking: Preferences need no inferences. *American Psychologist* 35:151–175.

• CREDITS •

page 1
Evan Kemp. © 1981 by The New York Times Company. Used with permission.

page 10
"Dear Abby," Abigail Van Buren, © 1983. CTN.

page 28–29
D. Sobel. © 1981 by The New York Times Company. Used with permission.

page 31–32
M. Pines. © 1982 by The New York Times Company. Used with permission.

page 51–52
C. Simmons. © 1981, *Chicago Tribune.* Used with permission.

page 66–67
M. Moran. © 1983 by The New York Times Company. Used with permission.

page 72
"People in the News," *The Hartford Courant* © 1982.

page 86–87
L. Cohen. *The Hartford Courant* © 1981.

page 90–91
W. E. Geist. © 1982 by The New York Times Company. Used with permission.

page 94–95
C. Nix. *The Daily Princetonian.* © 1983. Used with permission.

page 98–99
S. Auerback. © 1982 by *The Washington Post.*

page 112–113
M. Fichter. *The Hartford Courant* © 1983.

page 131–132
D. Morales. *The Hartford Courant* © 1982.

page 159
N. Jackle. © 1981 by The New York Times Company. Used with permission.

page 166–167
J. Pecile. *The Hartford Courant* © 1982.

page 202–204
R. Michalko. *Can. Jour. Visual Impairment,* 1982, 9–30. Used with permission.

page 206–207
R. Finn. *The Hartford Courant* © 1983.

page 216
M. A. Seawell. © *Peninsula Times Tribune,* Palo Alto, Calif.

page 222
S. Fish. Reprinted by permission of *Dadedalus, Journal of the American Academy of Arts and Sciences,* vol. 112, No. 1, 1983, Cambridge, MA.

page 228
Bloom County © 1983, The Washington Post Company. Used with permission.

page 228–230
J. van Lawick-Goodall. From *In the Shadow of Man* by Jane van Lawick-Goodall. Copyright © 1971 by Hugo and Jane van Lawick-Goodall. Used with permission of Houghton Mifflin Company.

page 268
L. Bennetts. © 1982 by The New York Times Company. Used with permission.

page 282–283
L. Cohen. *The Hartford Courant* © 1981.

page 306–307
B. Nelson. © 1983 by The New York Times Company. Used with permission.

page 312–313
S. Johnson © 1983 by The New York Times Company. Used with permission.

• INDEX •